The Historical Series for Bible Students

EDITED BY

Professor CHARLES F. KENT, Ph.D., *of Yale University,*

AND

Professor FRANK K. SANDERS, Ph.D., *formerly of Yale University*

Volume V

A HISTORY
OF THE
ANCIENT EGYPTIANS

The Historical Series for Bible Students

Edited by Professor CHARLES F. KENT, *Ph.D., of Yale University, and*
Professor FRANK K. SANDERS, *Ph.D., formerly of Yale University*

IN response to a widespread demand for non-technical yet scholarly and reliable guides to the study of the history, literature, and teaching of the Old and New Testaments, and of the contemporary history and literature, this series aims to present in concise and attractive form the results of investigation and exploration in these broad fields. Based upon thoroughly critical scholarship, it will emphasize assured and positive rather than transitional positions. The series as a whole is intended to present a complete and connected picture of the social, political, and religious life of the men and peoples who figure most prominently in the biblical records.

Each volume is complete in itself, treating comprehensively a given subject or period. It also refers freely to the biblical and monumental sources, and to the standard authorities. Convenience of size, clearness of presentation, and helpfulness to the student make the series particularly well adapted for (1) practical text-books for college, seminary, and university classes; (2) handbooks for the use of Bible classes, clubs, and guilds; (3) guides for individual study; and (4) books for general reference.

Vols. **I. HISTORY OF THE HEBREW PEOPLE.**

1. The United Kingdom. Sixth edition.
2. The Divided Kingdom. Sixth edition.

CHARLES F. KENT, Ph.D., Professor of Biblical Literature, Yale University.

II. HISTORY OF THE JEWISH PEOPLE.

3. The Babylonian, Persian, and Greek Periods.
4. The Maccabean and Roman Period (including New Testament Times).

CHARLES F. KENT, Ph.D., Professor of Biblical Literature, Yale University.
JAMES S. RIGGS, D.D., Professor of Biblical Criticism, Auburn Theological Seminary.

III. CONTEMPORARY OLD TESTAMENT HISTORY.

5. History of the Ancient Egyptians.

6. History of the Babylonians and Assyrians.

JAMES H. BREASTED, Ph.D., Professor of Egyptology and Oriental History, The University of Chicago.
GEORGE S. GOODSPEED, Ph.D., Professor of Ancient History, The University of Chicago.

IV. NEW TESTAMENT HISTORIES.

7. The Life of Jesus.
8. The Apostolic Age.

RUSH RHEES, President of the University of Rochester.
GEORGE T. PURVES, Ph.D., D.D., late Professor of New Testament Literature and Exegesis, Princeton Theological Seminary.

V. OUTLINES FOR THE STUDY OF BIBLICAL HISTORY AND LITERATURE.

9. From Earliest Times to 200 A. D.

FRANK K. SANDERS, Ph.D., Professor of Biblical Literature, Yale University, and HENRY T. FOWLER, Ph.D., Professor of Biblical Literature and History, Brown University.

A HISTORY

OF

THE ANCIENT EGYPTIANS

BY

JAMES HENRY BREASTED, PH.D.

PROFESSOR OF EGYPTOLOGY AND ORIENTAL HISTORY IN THE
UNIVERSITY OF CHICAGO; CORRESPONDING MEMBER OF
THE ROYAL ACADEMY OF SCIENCES OF BERLIN

WITH FOUR MAPS AND THREE PLANS

NEW YORK
CHARLES SCRIBNER'S SONS
1908

Copyright 1905, 1908
BY CHARLES SCRIBNER'S SONS

Published May, 1908

TO
The Memory of
MY FATHER
IN REVERENCE AND GRATITUDE

PREFACE

As works on the early Orient multiply, it becomes more and more easy to produce such books at second and third hand, which are thus separated by a long remove from the original monuments forming our primary sources of knowledge. As the use of this volume is in a measure conditioned by the method which produced it, may the author state that it is based directly and immediately upon the monuments, and in most cases upon the *original* monuments, rather than upon any published edition of the same? For this purpose the historical monuments still standing in Egypt, or installed in the museums of Europe (the latter *in toto*), were copied or collated by the author anew *ad hoc* and rendered into English (see *infra*, p. 445, B. Translations, BAR). Upon this complete version the present volume rests. Those students who desire to consult the sources upon which any given fact is based, are referred to this English corpus. A full bibliography of each original monument, if desired, will also be found there, and hence no references to such technical bibliography will be found herein, thus freeing the reader from a mass of workshop debris, to which, however, he can easily refer, if he desires it.

While this volume is largely a condensation and abridgement of the author's longer history, he has endeavoured to conform it to the design of this historical series and to make it as far as possible a history of the Egyptian *people*. At the same time the remarkable recent discoveries and the progress of research made since the appearance of his larger history have been fully incorporated. The discovery of the Hittite capital at Boghaz-Köi in Asia Minor, with numerous cuneiform records of this remarkable people, and elsewhere the evidence that they conquered Babylonia temporarily in the eighteenth century B. C., form the most remarkable of the new facts recently recovered.* The new-found evidence that the first and third dynasties of Babylon were contemporaneous with the second, has also settled the problem, whether the civilization of the Nile or of the Euphrates is older, in favour of Egypt, where the formation of a homogeneous, united state, embracing the whole country under the successive dynasties, is over a thousand years older than in Babylonia. We possess no monument of Babylonia, as Eduard Meyer recently remarked to the author, older than 3000 B. C. The author's journey through Sudanese Nubia during the winter of 1906–07 cleared his mind of a number of misconceptions of that country, especially economically, while it also recovered the lost city of Gem-Aton, and disposed of the impossible though current view that the Egyptian conquest was extended southward immediately after the fall of the Middle Kingdom. Those familiar with the other history will also welcome the improved maps redrawn for this volume.

On the never-settled question of a pronounceable,

* This book was paged in October, 1907, but as the proof was unhappily lost for three months in transport to Europe, the results of the second campaign (summer of 1907) at Boghaz-Köi, which appeared in December, 1907, could not be employed in detail as they might otherwise have been.

that is vocalized, form of Egyptian proper names, which are written in hieroglyphic without vowels, I must refer the reader to the remarks in the preface of my *Ancient Records* (Vol. I., pp. xiv. *ff.*). It is hoped that the index has made them pronounceable. As to the author's indebtedness to others in the preparation of this volume, he may also refer to his acknowledgments in the same preface, as well as in that of his larger history —acknowledgments which are equally true of this briefer work. He would also express his appreciation of the patience shown him by both editor and publisher, who have waited long for the manuscript of this book, delayed as it has been by distant travels and heavy tasks, and the fact that the mass of the material collected proved too large to condense at once into this volume, thus resulting in the production of the larger history first. Even so, the present volume is larger than its fellows in the series, and the author greatly appreciates the indulgence of the publishers in this respect. In conclusion, to the student of the Old Testament, by whom it will be chiefly used, the author would express the hope that the little book may contribute somewhat toward a wider recognition of the fact, that the rise and development, the culture and career, of the Hebrew nation were as vitally conditioned and as deeply influenced by surrounding civilizations, as modern historical science has shown to be the fact with every other people, ancient or modern.

JAMES HENRY BREASTED.

BORDIGHERA, ITALY, *March* 2, 1908.

CONTENTS

PART I

INTRODUCTION

		PAGE
I.	THE LAND OF THE EGYPTIANS	3
II.	PRELIMINARY SURVEY, CHRONOLOGY AND DOCUMENTARY SOURCES	14
III.	EARLIEST EGYPT	29

PART II

THE OLD KINGDOM

IV.	EARLY RELIGION	55
V.	THE OLD KINGDOM: GOVERNMENT AND SOCIETY, INDUSTRY AND ART	74
VI.	THE PYRAMID BUILDERS	103
VII.	THE SIXTH DYNASTY: THE DECLINE OF THE OLD KINGDOM	117

PART III

THE MIDDLE KINGDOM: THE FEUDAL AGE

VIII.	THE DECLINE OF THE NORTH AND THE RISE OF THEBES	133
IX.	THE MIDDLE KINGDOM OR THE FEUDAL AGE STATE, SOCIETY AND RELIGION	139
X.	THE TWELFTH DYNASTY	152

CONTENTS

PART IV

THE HYKSOS: THE RISE OF THE EMPIRE

XI. The Fall of the Middle Kingdom. The Hyksos 173
XII. The Expulsion of the Hyksos and the Triumph of Thebes 185

PART V

THE EMPIRE: FIRST PERIOD

XIII. The New State: Society and Religion . . .
XIV. The Consolidation of the Kingdom; the Rise of the Empire 207
XV. The Feud of the Thutmosids and the Reign of Queen Hatshepsut 214
XVI. The Consolidation of the Empire: the Wars of Thutmose III. 223
XVII. The Empire at Its Height 244
XVIII. The Religious Revolution of Ikhnaton . . 264
XIX. The Fall of Ikhnaton and the Dissolution of the Empire. 280

PART VI

THE EMPIRE: SECOND PERIOD

XX. The Triumph of Amon and the Reorganization of the Empire 293
XXI. The Wars of Ramses II. 303
XXII. The Empire of Ramses II. 314
XXIII. The Final Decline of the Empire: Merneptah and Ramses III. 327

CONTENTS

PART VII

THE DECADENCE OF ANCIENT EGYPT

		PAGE
XXIV.	THE FALL OF THE EMPIRE	347
XXV.	PRIESTS AND MERCENARIES: THE SUPREMACY OF THE LIBYANS	357
XXVI.	THE ETHIOPIAN SUPREMACY AND THE TRIUMPH OF ASSYRIA	367

PART VIII

THE RESTORATION AND THE END

XXVII.	THE RESTORATION	387
XXVIII.	THE FINAL STRUGGLES: BABYLON AND PERSIA	404

CHRONOLOGICAL SUMMARY	419
NOTES ON RECENT DISCOVERIES	439
A SELECTED BIBLIOGRAPHY (INCLUDING ABBREVIATIONS)	444
INDEX OF NAMES AND SUBJECTS	455

MAPS AND PLANS

		FACING PAGE
MAP I.	EGYPT AND THE ANCIENT WORLD	4
MAP II.	THE ASIATIC EMPIRE OF EGYPT	210
MAP III.	THEBES AND ITS ANCIENT BUILDINGS	218
PLAN IV.	THE TEMPLES OF KARNAK	228
THE BATTLE OF KADESH, FIRST STAGE		305
THE BATTLE OF KADESH, SECOND STAGE		307
MAP V.	GENERAL MAP OF EGYPT AND NUBIA.	At the End

PART I

INTRODUCTION

I

THE LAND OF THE EGYPTIANS

1. THE roots of modern civilization are planted deeply in the highly elaborate life of those nations which rose into power over six thousand years ago, in the basin of the eastern Mediterranean, and the adjacent regions on the east of it. Had the Euphrates finally found its way into the Mediterranean, toward which, indeed, it seems to have started, both the early civilizations, to which we refer, might then have been included in the Mediterranean basin. As it is, the scene of early oriental history does not fall entirely within that basin, but must be designated as the eastern Mediterranean region. It lies in the midst of the vast desert plateau, which, beginning at the Atlantic, extends eastward across the entire northern end of Africa, and continuing beyond the depression of the Red Sea, passes northeastward, with some interruptions, far into the heart of Asia. Approaching it, the one from the south and the other from the north, two great river valleys traverse this desert; in Asia, the Tigro-Euphrates valley; in Africa that of the Nile. It is in these two valleys that the career of man may be traced from the rise of European civilization back to a remoter age than anywhere else on earth; and it is from these two cradles of the human race that the influences which emanated from their highly developed

but differing cultures, can now be more and more clearly traced as we discern them converging upon the early civilization of Asia Minor and southern Europe.

2. The Nile, which created the valley home of the early Egyptians, rises three degrees south of the equator, and flowing into the Mediterranean at over thirty-one and a half degrees north latitude, it attains a length of some four thousand miles and vies with the greatest rivers of the world in length, if not in volume. In its upper course the river, emerging from the lakes of equatorial Africa, is known as the White Nile. Just south of north latitude sixteen at Khartum, about thirteen hundred and fifty miles from the sea, it receives from the east an affluent known as the Blue Nile, which is a considerable mountain torrent, rising in the lofty highlands of Abyssinia. One hundred and forty miles below the union of the two Niles the stream is joined by its only other tributary, the Atbara, which is a freshet not unlike the Blue Nile. It is at Khartum, or just below it, that the river enters the tableland of Nubian sandstone, underlying the Great Sahara. Here it winds on its tortuous course between the desert hills, where it returns upon itself, often flowing due south, until after it has finally pushed through to the north, its course describes a vast S.

3. In six different places throughout this region the current has hitherto failed to erode a perfect channel through the stubborn stone, and these extended interruptions, where the rocks are piled in scattered and irregular masses in the stream, are known as the cataracts of the Nile; although there is no great and sudden fall such as that of our cataract at Niagara. These rocks interfere with navigation most seriously in the region of the second and fourth cataracts; otherwise

the river is navigable almost throughout its entire course. At Elephantine it passes the granite barrier which there thrusts up its rough shoulder, forming the first cataract, and thence emerges upon an unobstructed course to the sea.

4. It is the valley below the first cataract which constituted Egypt proper. The reason for the change which here gives the river a free course is the disappearance of the sandstone, sixty-eight miles below the cataract, at Edfu, where the nummulitic limestone which forms the northern desert plateau, offers the stream an easier task in the erosion of its bed. It has thus produced a vast cañon or trench cut across the eastern end of the Sahara to the northern sea. From cliff to cliff, the valley varies in width, from ten or twelve, to some thirty-one miles. The floor of the cañon is covered with black, alluvial deposits, through which the river winds northward. It cuts a deep channel through the alluvium, flowing with a speed of about three miles an hour; in width it only twice attains a maximum of eleven hundred yards. On the west the Bahr Yusuf a second, minor channel some two hundred miles long, leaves the main stream near Siut and flows into the Fayum. In antiquity it flowed thence into a canal known as the "North," which passed northward west of Memphis and reached the sea by the site of later Alexandria (BAR, iv 224, l. 8, note). A little over a hundred miles from the sea the main stream enters the broad triangle, with apex at the south, which the Greeks so graphically called the "Delta." This is of course a bay of prehistoric ages, which has been gradually filled up by the river. The stream once divided at this point and reached the sea through seven mouths, but in modern times there are

but two main branches, straggling through the Delta and piercing the coast-line on either side of the middle. The western branch is called the Rosetta mouth; the eastern that of Damiette.

5. The deposits which have formed the Delta, are very deep, and have slowly risen over the sites of the many ancient cities which once flourished there. The old swamps which once must have rendered the regions of the northern Delta a vast morass, have been gradually filled up, and the fringe of marshes pushed further out. They undoubtedly occupied in antiquity a much larger proportion of the Delta than they do now. In the valley above, the depth of the soil varies from thirty-three to thirty-eight feet, and sometimes reaches a maximum of ten miles in width. The cultivable area thus formed, between the cataract and the sea, is less than ten thousand square miles in extent, being roughly equal to the area of the state of Maryland, or about ten per cent. less than that of Belgium. The cliffs on either hand are usually but a few hundred feet in height, but here and there they rise into almost mountains of a thousand feet. They are of course flanked by the deserts through which the Nile has cut its way. On the west the Libyan Desert or the great Sahara rolls in illimitable, desolate hills of sand, gravel and rock, from six hundred and fifty to a thousand feet above the Nile. Its otherwise waterless expanse is broken only by an irregular line of oases, or watered depressions, roughly parallel with the river and doubtless owing their springs and wells to infiltration of the Nile waters. The largest of these depressions is situated so close to the valley that the rock wall which once separated them has broken down, producing the fertile Fayum, watered by the Bahr Yusuf. Otherwise the

western desert held no economic resources for the use of the early Nile-dwellers. The eastern or Arabian Desert is somewhat less inhospitable, and capable of yielding a scanty subsistence to wandering tribes of Ababdeh. Deposits of alabaster and extensive masses of various fine, hard igneous rocks led to the exploitation of quarries here also, while the Red Sea harbours could of course be reached only by traversing this desert, through which established routes thither were early traced. Further north similar mineral resources led to an acquaintance with the peninsula of Sinai and its desert regions, at a very remote date.

6. The situation afforded by this narrow valley was one of unusual isolation; on either hand vast desert wastes, on the north the harbourless coast-line of the Delta, and on the south the rocky barriers of successive cataracts, preventing fusion with the peoples of inner Africa. It was chiefly at the two northern corners of the Delta, that outside influences and foreign elements which were always sifting into the Nile valley, gained access to the country. Through the eastern corner it was the prehistoric Semitic population of neighbouring Asia, who forced their way in across the dangerous intervening deserts; while the Libyan races, of possibly European origin, found entrance at the western corner. The products of the south also, in spite of the cataracts, filtered in ever increasing volume into the regions of the lower river and the lower end of the first cataract became a trading post, ever after known as "Suan" (Assuan) or "market," where the negro traders of the south met those of Egypt. The upper Nile thus gradually became a regular avenue of commerce with the Sudan. The natural boundaries of Egypt, however, always presented sufficiently effective

barriers to would-be invaders, to enable the natives slowly to assimilate the newcomers, without being displaced.

7. It will be evident that the remarkable shape of the country must powerfully influence its political development. Except in the Delta it was but a narrow line, some seven hundred and fifty miles long. Straggling its slender length along the river, and sprawling out into the Delta, it totally lacked the compactness necessary to stable political organization. A given locality has neighbours on only two sides, north and south, and these their shortest boundaries; local feeling was strong, local differences were persistent, and a man of the Delta could hardly understand the speech of a man of the first cataract region. It was only the ease of communication afforded by the river which in any degree neutralized the effect of the country's remarkable length.

8. The wealth of commerce which the river served to carry, it was equally instrumental in producing. While the climate of the country is not rainless, yet the rare showers of the south, often separated by intervals of years, and even the more frequent rains of the Delta, are totally insufficient to maintain the processes of agriculture. The marvellous productivity of the Egyptian soil is due to the annual inundation of the river, which is caused by the melting of the snows, and by the spring rains at the sources of the Blue Nile. Freighted with the rich loam of the Abyssinian highlands, the rushing waters of the spring freshet hurry down the Nubian valley, and a slight rise is discernible at the first cataract in the early part of June. The flood swells rapidly and steadily, and although the increase is usually interrupted for nearly a month from the end

of September on, it is usually resumed again, and the maximum level continues until the end of October or into November. The waters in the region of the first cataract are then nearly fifty feet higher than at low water; while at Cairo the rise is about half that at the cataract. A vast and elaborate system of irrigation canals and reservoirs first receives the flood, which is then allowed to escape into the fields as needed. Here it rests long enough to deposit its burden of rich, black earth from the upper reaches of the Blue Nile. At such times the appearance of the country is picturesque in the extreme, the glistening surface of the waters being dotted here and there by the vivid green of the waving palm groves, which mark the villages, now accessible only along the dykes belonging to the irrigation system. Thus year by year, the soil which would otherwise become impoverished in the elements necessary to the production of such prodigious harvests, is invariably replenished with fresh resources.

9. As the river sinks below the level of the fields again, it is necessary to raise the water from the canals by artificial means, in order to carry on the constant irrigation of the growing crops in the outlying fields, which are too high to be longer refreshed by absorption from the river. Thus a genial and generous, but exacting soil, demanded for its cultivation the development of a high degree of skill in the manipulation of the life-giving waters, and at a very early day the men of the Nile valley had attained a surprising command of the complicated problems involved in the proper utilization of the river. If Egypt became the mother of the mechanical arts, the river will have been one of the chief natural forces to which this fact was due. With such natural assets as these, an ever replenished

soil, and almost unfailing waters for its refreshment, the wealth of Egypt could not but be chiefly agricultural, a fact to which we shall often recur. Such opulent fertility of course supported a large population—in Roman times some seven million souls (Diodorus I, 31)—while in our own day it maintains over nine million, a density of population far surpassing that to be found anywhere in Europe. The other natural resources of the valley we shall be better able to trace as we follow their exploitation in the course of the historical development.

10. In climate Egypt is a veritable paradise, drawing to its shores at the present day an ever increasing number of winter guests. The air of Egypt is essentially that of the deserts within which it lies, and such is its purity and dryness that even an excessive degree of heat occasions but slight discomfort, owing to the fact that the moisture of the body is dried up almost as fast as it is exhaled. The mean temperature of the Delta in winter is 56° Fahrenheit and in the valley above it is ten degrees higher. In summer the mean in the Delta is 83°; and although the summer temperature in the valley is sometimes as high as 122°, the air is far from the oppressiveness accompanying the same degree of heat in other lands. The nights even in summer are always cool, and the vast expanses of vegetation appreciably reduce the temperature. In winter just before dawn the extreme cold is surprising, as contrasted with the genial warmth of mid-day at the same season. To the absence of rain we have already adverted. The rare showers of upper Egypt occur only when cyclonic disturbances in the southern Mediterranean or northern Sahara force undischarged clouds into the Nile valley from the west; from the

east they cannot reach the valley, owing to the high mountain ridge along the Red Sea, which forces them upward and discharges them. The lower Delta, however, falls within the zone of the northern rainy season. In spite of the wide extent of marshy ground, left stagnating by the inundation, the dry airs of the desert, blowing constantly across the valley, quickly dry the soil, and there is never any malarial infection in upper Egypt. Even in the vast morass of the Delta, malaria is practically unknown. Thus, lying just outside of the tropics, Egypt enjoyed a mild climate of unsurpassed salubrity, devoid of the harshness of a northern winter, but at the same time sufficiently cool to escape those enervating influences inherent in tropical conditions.

11. The prospect of this contracted valley spread out before the Nile dweller, was in antiquity, as it is to-day somewhat monotonous. The level Nile bottoms, the gift of the river, clad in rich green, shut in on either hand by the yellow cliffs, are unrelieved by any elevations or by any forests, save the occasional groves of graceful palms, which fringe the river banks or shade the villages of sombre mud huts, with now and then a sycamore, a tamarisk or an acacia. A network of irrigation canals traverses the country in every direction like a vast arterial system. The sands of the desolate wastes which lie behind the cañon walls, drift in athwart the cliffs, and often invade the green fields so that one may stand with one foot in the verdure of the valley, and the other in the desert sand. Thus sharply defined was the Egyptian's world: a deep and narrow river-valley of unparalleled fertility, winding between lifeless deserts, furnishing a remarkable environment, not to be found elsewhere in all the world.

Such surroundings reacted powerfully upon the mind and thought of the Egyptian, conditioning and determining his idea of the world and his notion of the mysterious powers which ruled it.

12. Such was in brief the scene in which developed the people of the Nile, whose culture dominated the basin of the eastern Mediterranean in the age when Europe was emerging into the secondary stages of civilization, and coming into intimate contact with the culture of the early east. Nowhere on earth have the witnesses of a great, but now extinct civilization, been so plentifully preserved as along the banks of the Nile. Even in the Delta, where the storms of war beat more fiercely than in the valley above, and where the slow accumulations from the yearly flood have gradually entombed them, the splendid cities of the Pharaohs have left great stretches cumbered with enormous blocks of granite, limestone and sandstone, shattered obelisks, and massive pylon bases, to proclaim the wealth and power of forgotten ages; while an ever growing multitude of modern visitors are drawn to the upper valley by the colossal ruins that greet the wondering traveller almost at every bend in the stream. Nowhere else in the ancient world were such massive stone buildings erected, and nowhere else has a dry atmosphere, coupled with an almost complete absence of rain, permitted the survival of such a wealth of the best and highest in the life of an ancient people, in so far as that life found expression in material form. In the plenitude of its splendour, much of it thus survived into the classic age of European civilization, and hence it was, that as Egypt was gradually overpowered and absorbed by the western world, the currents of life from west and east commingled here, as they have

never done elsewhere. Both in the Nile valley and beyond it, the west thus felt the full impact of Egyptian civilization for many centuries, and gained from it all that its manifold culture had to contribute. The career which made Egypt so rich a heritage of alien peoples, and a legacy so valuable to all later ages, we shall endeavour to trace in the ensuing chapters.

II

PRELIMINARY SURVEY, CHRONOLOGY AND DOCUMENTARY SOURCES

13. A RAPID survey of the purely external features which serve to demark the great epochs in the career of the Nile valley people, will enable us the more intelligently to study those epochs in detail, as we meet them in the course of our progress. In such a survey, we sweep our eyes down a period of four thousand years of human history, from a time when the only civilization known in the basin of the Mediterranean is slowly dawning among a primitive people on the shores of the Nile. We can cast but a brief glance at the outward events which characterized each great period, especially noting how foreign peoples are gradually drawn within the circle of Egyptian intercourse from age to age, and reciprocal influences ensue; until in the thirteenth century B. C. the peoples of southern Europe, long discernible in their material civilization, emerge in the written documents of Egypt for the first time in history. It was then that the fortunes of the Pharaohs began to decline, and as the civilization and power, first of the East and then of classic Europe, slowly developed, Egypt was finally submerged in the great world of Mediterranean powers, first dominated by Persia, and then by Greece and Rome.

14. The career of the races which peopled the Nile valley falls into a series of more or less clearly marked

epochs, each of which is rooted deeply in that which preceded it, and itself contains the germs of that which is to follow. A more or less arbitrary and artificial but convenient subdivision of these epochs, beginning with the historic age, is furnished by the so-called dynasties of Manetho. This native historian of Egypt, a priest of Sebennytos, who flourished under Ptolemy I (305–285 B. C.), wrote a history of his country in the Greek language. The work has perished, and we only know it in an epitome by Julius Africanus and Eusebius, and extracts by Josephus. The value of the work was slight, as it was built up on folk-tales and popular traditions of the early kings. Manetho divided the long succession of Pharaohs, as known to him, into thirty royal houses or dynasties, and although we know that many of his divisions are arbitrary, and that there was many a dynastic change where he indicates none, yet his dynasties divide the kings into convenient groups, which have so long been employed in modern study of Egyptian history, that it is now impossible to dispense with them.

15. After an archaic age of primitive civilization, and a period of small and local kingdoms, the various centres of civilization on the Nile gradually coalesced into two kingdoms: one comprising the valley down to the Delta; and the other made up of the Delta itself. In the Delta, civilization rapidly advanced, and the calendar year of 365 days was introduced in 4241 B. C., the earliest fixed date in the history of the world as known to us (MC, 38 ff., BAR, I, 44–45). A long development, as the "Two Lands," which left their imprint forever after on the civilization of later centuries, preceded a united Egypt, which emerged upon our historic horizon at the consolidation of the two kingdoms

into one nation under Menes about 3400 B. C. His accession marks the beginning of the dynasties, and the preceding, earliest period may be conveniently designated as the predynastic age. In the excavations of the last twelve years (since 1895) the predynastic civilization has been gradually revealed in material documents exhibiting the various stages in the slow evolution which at last produced the dynastic culture.

16. A uniform government of the whole country was the secret of over four centuries of prosperity under the descendants of Menes at Thinis, near Abydos, close to the great bend of the Nile below Thebes, and probably also at or near later Memphis. The remarkable development of these four centuries in material civilization led to the splendour and power of the first great epoch of Egyptian history, the Old Kingdom. The seat of government was at Memphis, where four royal houses, the Third, Fourth, Fifth and Sixth Dynasties, ruled in succession for five hundred years (2980–2475 B. C.). Art and mechanics reached a level of unprecedented excellence never later surpassed, while government and administration had never before been so highly developed. Foreign enterprise passed far beyond the limits of the kingdom; the mines of Sinai, already operated in the First Dynasty, were vigourously exploited; trade in Egyptian bottoms reached the coast of Phœnicia and the Islands of the North, while in the South, the Pharaoh's fleets penetrated to the Somali coast (Punt) on the Red Sea; and in Nubia his envoys were strong enough to exercise a loose sovereignty over the lower country, and by tireless expeditions to keep open the trade routes leading to the Sudan. In the Sixth Dynasty (2625–2475 B. C.) the local governors of the central administration, who had already gained

hereditary hold upon their offices in the Fifth Dynasty (2750-2625 B. C.), were able to assert themselves as landed barons and princes, no longer mere functionaries of the crown. They thus prepared the way for an age of feudalism.

17. The growing power of the new landed nobility finally caused the fall of the Pharaonic house, and at the close of the Sixth Dynasty, about 2475 B. C., the supremacy of Memphis waned. In the internal confusion which followed, we can discern nothing of Manetho's ephemeral Seventh and Eighth Dynasties at Memphis, which lasted not more than thirty years; but with the Ninth and Tenth Dynasties the nobles of Heracleopolis gained the throne, which was occupied by eighteen successive kings of the line. It is now that Thebes first appears as the seat of a powerful family of princes, by whom the Heracleopolitans and the power of the north are gradually overcome till the South triumphs. The exact lapse of time from the fall of the Old Kingdom to the triumph of the South is at present indeterminable, but it may be estimated roughly at two hundred and seventy-five to three hundred years, with a margin of uncertainty of possibly a century either way (BAR, I, 53).

18. With the restoration of peace and order under the Theban princes of the Eleventh Dynasty about 2160 B. C., the issue of the tendencies already discernible at the close of the Old Kingdom is clearly visible. Throughout the land the local princes and barons are firmly seated in their domains, and with these hereditary feudatories the Pharaoh must now reckon. The system was not fully developed until the advent of a second Theban family, the Twelfth Dynasty, the founder of which, Amenemhet I, probably

usurped the throne. For over two hundred years (2000–1788 B. C.) this powerful line of kings ruled a feudal state. This feudal age is the classic period of Egyptian history. Literature flourished, the orthography of the language was for the first time regulated, poetry had already reached a highly artistic structure, the earliest known literature of entertainment was produced, sculpture and architecture were rich and prolific, and the industrial arts surpassed all previous attainments. The internal resources of the country were elaborately developed, especially by close attention to the Nile and the inundation. Enormous hydraulic works reclaimed large tracts of cultivable domain in the Fayum, in the vicinity of which the kings of the Twelfth Dynasty, the Amenemhets and the Sesostrises, lived. Abroad the exploitation of the mines in Sinai was now carried on by the constant labour of permanent colonies there, with temples, fortifications and reservoirs for the water supply. A plundering campaign was carried into Syria, trade and intercourse with its Semitic tribes were constant, and an interchange of commodities with the early Mycenæan centres of civilization in the northern Mediterranean is evident. Traffic with Punt and the southern coasts of the Red Sea continued, while in Nubia the country between the first and second cataracts, loosely controlled in the Sixth Dynasty, was now conquered and held tributary by the Pharaoh, so that the gold mines on the east of it were a constant resource of his treasury.

19. The fall of the Twelfth Dynasty in 1788 B. C. was followed by a second period of disorganization and obscurity, as the feudatories struggled for the crown. After possibly a century of such internal conflict, the country was entered and appropriated by a line of

rulers from Asia, who had seemingly already gained a wide dominion there. These foreign usurpers, now known as the Hyksos, after Manetho's designation of them, maintained themselves for perhaps a century. Their residence was at Avaris in the eastern Delta, and at least during the later part of their supremacy, the Egyptian nobles of the South succeeded in gaining more or less independence. Finally the head of a Theban family boldly proclaimed himself king, and in the course of some years these Theban princes succeeded in expelling the Hyksos from the country, and driving them back from the Asiatic frontier into Syria.

20. It was under the Hyksos and in the struggle with them that the conservatism of millennia was broken up in the Nile valley. The Egyptians learned aggressive war for the first time, and introduced a well organized military system, including chariotry, which the importation of the horse by the Hyksos now enabled them to do. Egypt was transformed into a military empire. In the struggle with the Hyksos and with each other, the old feudal families perished, or were absorbed among the partisans of the dominant Theban family, from which the imperial line sprang. The great Pharaohs of the Eighteenth Dynasty thus became emperors, conquering and ruling from northern Syria and the upper Euphrates, to the fourth cataract of the Nile on the south. Amid unprecedented wealth and splendour, they ruled their vast dominions, which they gradually welded together into a fairly stable empire, the first known in the early world. Thebes grew into a great metropolis, the earliest monumental city. Extensive trade relations with the East and the Mediterranean world developed; Mycenæan products were common in Egypt, and Egyptian influences are

clearly discernible in Mycenæan art. For two hundred and thirty years (1580–1350 B. C.) the Empire flourished, but was wrecked at last by a combination of adverse influences both within and without. A religious revolution by the young and gifted king Ikhnaton, caused an internal convulsion such as the country had never before experienced; while the empire in the north gradually disintegrated under the aggressions of the Hittites, who pushed in from Asia Minor. At the same time in both the northern and southern Asiatic dominions of the Pharaoh, an overflow of Beduin immigration, among which were undoubtedly some of the tribes who later coalesced with the Israelites, aggravated the danger, and together with the persistent advance of the Hittites, finally resulted in the complete dissolution of the Asiatic empire of Egypt, down to the very frontier of the northeastern Delta. Meanwhile the internal disorders had caused the fall of the Eighteenth Dynasty, an event which terminated the first Period of the Empire (1350 B. C.).

21. Harmhab, one of the able commanders under the fallen dynasty, survived the crisis and finally seized the throne. Under his vigorous rule the disorganized nation was gradually restored to order, and his successors of the Nineteenth Dynasty (1350–1205 B. C.) were able to begin the recovery of the lost empire in Asia. But the Hittites were too firmly entrenched in Syria to yield to the Egyptian onset. The assaults of Seti I, and half a generation of persistent campaigning under Ramses II, failed to push the northern frontier of the Empire far beyond the limits of Palestine. Here it remained and Syria was never permanently recovered. Semitic influences now powerfully affected Egypt. At this juncture the peoples of southern Europe emerge

for the first time upon the arena of oriental history and together with Libyan hordes, threaten to overwhelm the Delta from the west. They were nevertheless beaten back by Merneptah. After another period of internal confusion and usurpation, during which the Nineteenth Dynasty fell (1205 B. C.), Ramses III, whose father, Setnakht founded the Twentieth Dynasty (1200–1090 B. C.), was able to maintain the Empire at the same limits, against the invasions of restless northern tribes, who crushed the Hittite power; and also against repeated immigrations of the Libyans. With his death (1167 B. C.) the Empire, with the exception of Nubia, which was still held, rapidly fell to pieces. Thus, about the middle of the twelfth century B. C. the Second Period of the imperial age closed with the total dissolution of the Asiatic dominions.

22. Under a series of weak Ramessids, the country rapidly declined and fell a prey first to the powerful high priests of Amon, who were obliged almost immediately to yield to stronger Ramessid rivals in the Delta at Tanis, forming the Twenty-First Dynasty (1090–945 B. C.). By the middle of the tenth century B. C. the mercenary chiefs, whose followers had formed the armies of the second imperial period, had founded powerful families in the Delta cities, and among these the Libyans were now supreme. Sheshonk I, a Libyan mercenary commander, gained the throne as the founder of the Twenty-second Dynasty in 945 B. C. and the country enjoyed transient prosperity, while Sheshonk even attempted the recovery of Palestine. But the family was unable to control the turbulent mercenary lords, now established as dynasts in the larger Delta towns, and the country gradually relapsed into a series of military principalities in constant war-

fare with each other. Through the entire Libyan period of the Twenty-second, Twenty-third and Twenty-fourth Dynasties (945–712 B. C.) the unhappy nation groaned under such misrule, constantly suffering economic deterioration.

23. Nubia had now detached itself and a dynasty of kings, probably of Theban origin had arisen at Napata, below the Fourth Cataract. These Egyptian rulers of the new Nubian kingdom now invaded Egypt, and although residing at Napata, maintained their sovereignty in Egypt with varying fortune for two generations (722–663 B. C.). But they were unable to suppress and exterminate the local dynasts, who ruled on, while acknowledging the suzerainty of the Nubian overlord. It was in the midst of these conflicts between the Nubian dynasty and the mercenary lords of Lower Egypt, that the Assyrians finally entered the Delta, subdued the country and placed it under tribute (670–660 B. C.). At this juncture Psamtik I, an able dynast of Sais, in the western Delta, finally succeeded in overthrowing his rivals, expelled the Ninevite garrisons, and as the Nubians had already been forced out of the country by the Assyrians, he was able to found a powerful dynasty, and usher in the Restoration. His accession fell in 663 B. C., and the entire period of nearly five hundred years from the final dissolution of the Empire about 1150 to the dawn of the Restoration in 663 B. C., may be conveniently designated the Decadence. After 1100 B. C. the Decadence may be conveniently divided into the Tanite-Amonite Period (1090–945 B. C.). the Libyan Period (945–712 B. C.), the Ethiopian Period (722–663 B. C.), and the Assyrian Period, which is contemporary with the last years of the Ethiopian Period.

PRELIMINARY SURVEY

24. Of the Restoration, like all those epochs in which the seat of power was in the Delta, where almost all monuments have perished, we learn very little from native sources; and all too little also from Herodotus and later Greek visitors in the Nile valley. It was outwardly an age of power and splendour, in which the native party endeavoured to restore the old glories of the classic age before the Empire; while the kings depending upon Greek mercenaries, were modern politicians, employing the methods of the new Greek world, mingling in the world-politics of their age and showing little sympathy with the archaizing tendency. But their combinations failed to save Egypt from the ambition of Persia, and its history under native dynasties, with unimportant exceptions, was concluded with the conquest of the country by Cambyses in 525 B. C.

25. Such, in mechanical review, were the purely external events which marked the successive epochs of Egypt's history as an independent nation. With their dates, these epochs may be summarized thus:

Introduction of the Calendar, 4241 B. C.

Predynastic Age, before 3400 B. C.

The Accession of Menes, 3400 B. C.

The first Two Dynasties, 3400–2980 B. C.

The Old Kingdom: Dynasties Three to Six, 2980–2475 B. C.

Dynasties Seven and Eight, 2475–2445 B. C.

Eighteen Heracleopolitans, Dynasties Nine and Ten, 2445–2160 B. C.

The Middle Kingdom: Dynasties Eleven and Twelve 2160–1788 B. C.

Internal Conflicts of the Feudatories, } 1788–1580
The Hyksos, } B. C.

The Empire: First Period, the Eighteenth Dynasty, 1580–1350 B. C.

The Empire: Second Period, the Nineteenth and part of the Twentieth Dynasty, 1350–1150 B. C.

The Decadence
- Last Two Generations of Twentieth Dynasty, about 1150 to 1090 B. C.
- Tanite-Amonite Period, Twenty-first Dynasty, 1090–945 B. C.
- Libyan Period, Dynasties Twenty-two to Twenty-four, 945–712 B. C.
- Ethiopian Period, 722–663 B. C. (Twenty-fifth Dynasty, 712–661 B. C.)
- Assyrian Supremacy, 670–660 B. C.

The Restoration, 660–525 B. C. (Saite Period, Twenty-sixth Dynasty, 663–525 .B. C).

Persian Conquest, 525 B. C.

26. The reader will find at the end of the volume a fuller table of reigns. The chronology of the above table is obtained by two independent processes: first by "dead reckoning," and second by astronomical calculations based on the Egyptian calendar. By "dead reckoning" we mean simply the addition of the known minimum length of all the kings' reigns, and from the total thus obtained, the simple computation (backward from a fixed starting point) of the date of the beginning of the series of reigns so added. Employing all the latest dates from recent discoveries, it is mathematically certain that from the accession of the Eighteenth Dynasty to the conquest of the Persians in 525 B. C. the successive Pharaohs reigned at least 1052 years in all (BAR, I, 47–51). The Eighteenth Dynasty therefore began not later than 1577 B. C. Astronomical calculations (independent of the above dead reckoning), based

on the date of the rising of Sirius, and of the occurrence of new moons both in terms of the shifting Egyptian calendar, place the date of the accession of the Eighteenth Dynasty with fair precision in 1580 B. C. (BAR, I, 38–46). For the periods earlier than the Eighteenth Dynasty, we can no longer employ the method of dead reckoning alone, because of the scantiness of the contemporary documents. Fortunately another calendar date of the rising of Sirius, fixes the advent of the Twelfth Dynasty at 2000 B. C., with a margin of uncertainty of not more than a year or two either way. From this date the beginning of the Eleventh Dynasty is again only a matter of "dead reckoning." The uncertainty as to the duration of the Heracleopolitan supremacy makes the length of the period between the Old and Middle Kingdoms very uncertain. If we give the eighteen Heracleopolitans sixteen years each, which, under orderly conditions, is a fair average in the Orient, they will have ruled 288 years (BAR, I, 53). In estimating their duration at 285 years, we may err possibly as much as a century either way. The computation of the length of the Old Kingdom is based on contemporary monuments and early lists, in which the margin of error is probably not more than a generation or two either way, but the uncertain length of the Heracleopolitan rule affects all dates back of that age, and a shift of a century either way in the years B. C. is not impossible. The ancient annals of the Palermo Stone establish the length of the first two dynasties at roughly 420 years (MC, 201 *f*., BAR, I, 84–85), and the date of the accession of Menes and the union of Egypt as 3400 B. C.; but we carry back with us, from the Heracleopolitan age, the same wide margin of uncertainty as in the Old Kingdom.

The reader will have observed that this system of chronology is based upon the contemporary monuments and lists dating not later than 1200 B. C. The extremely high dates for the beginning of the dynasties current in some histories are inherited from an older generation of Egyptologists; and are based upon the chronology of Manetho, a late, careless, and uncritical compilation, the dynastic totals of which can be proven wrong from the *contemporary monuments* in the vast majority of cases, where such monuments have survived. Its dynastic totals are so absurdly high throughout, that they are not worthy of a moment's credence, being often nearly or quite double the maximum drawn from *contemporary monuments*, and they will not stand the slightest careful criticism. Their accuracy is now maintained only by a small and constantly decreasing number of modern scholars.

27. Like our chronology our knowledge of the early history of Egypt must be gleaned from the contemporary native monuments (BAR, I, 1–37). Monumental records, even when full and complete are at best but insufficient sources, affording data for only the meagrest outlines of great achievements and important epochs. While the material civilization of the country found adequate expression in magnificent works of the artist, craftsman and engineer, the inner life of the nation, or even the purely external events of moment could find record only incidentally. Such documents are sharply differentiated from the materials with which the historian of European nations deals, except of course in his study of the earliest ages. Extensive correspondence between statesmen, journals and diaries, state documents and reports—such materials as these are almost wholly wanting in monumental records.

Imagine writing a history of Greece from the few Greek inscriptions surviving. Moreover, we possess no history of Egypt of sufficiently early date by a native Egyptian; the compilation of puerile folk-tales by Manetho, in the third century B. C. is hardly worthy of the name history. But an annalist of the remote ages with which we are to deal, could have had little conception of what would be important for future ages to know, even if he had undertaken a full chronicle of historical events. Scanty annals were indeed kept from the earliest times, but these have entirely perished with the exception of two fragments, the now famous Palermo Stone (BAR, I, 76–167; BH, 24), which once bore the annals of the earliest dynasties from the beginning down into the Fifth Dynasty; and some extracts from the records of Thutmose III's campaigns in Syria. Of the other monuments of incidental character but the merest fraction has survived. Under these circumstances we shall probably never be able to offer more than a sketch of the civilization of the Old and Middle Kingdoms, with a hazy outline of the general drift of events. Under the Empire the available documents, both in quality and quantity, for the first time approach the minimum, which in European history would be regarded as adequate to a moderately full presentation of the career of the nation. Scores of important questions, however, still remain unanswered, in whatever direction we turn. Nevertheless a rough frame-work of the governmental organization, the constitution of society, the most important achievements of the emperors, and to a limited extent the spirit of the age, may be discerned and sketched in the main outlines, even though it is only here and there that the sources enable us to fill in the detail. In the Decadence and the Restoration, however, the same paucity of documents, so painfully apparent in the older periods, again leaves the historian with a long series of hypotheses and probabilities. For the reserve with which the author has constantly treated such periods, he begs the reader to hold the scanty sources responsible (BAR, I, 1–26).

III

EARLIEST EGYPT

28. THE forefathers of the people with whom we shall have to deal were related to the Libyans or north Africans on the one hand, and on the other to the peoples of eastern Africa, now known as the Galla, Somali, Bega, and other tribes. An invasion of the Nile valley by Semitic nomads of Asia, stamped its essential character unmistakably upon the language of the African people there. The earliest strata of the Egyptian language accessible to us, betray clearly this composite origin. While still coloured by its African antecedents, the language is in structure Semitic. It is moreover a completed product as observable in our earliest preserved examples of it; but the fusion of the Libyans and east Africans with the Nile valley peoples continued far into historic times, and in the case of the Libyans may be traced in ancient historical documents for three thousand years or more. The Semitic immigration from Asia, examples of which are also observable in the historic age, occurred in an epoch that lies far below our remotest historical horizon. We shall never be able to determine when, nor with certainty through what channels it took place, although the most probable route is that along which we may observe a similar influx from the deserts of Arabia in historic times, the isthmus of Suez, by which

the Mohammedan invasion entered the country. While the Semitic language which they brought with them left its indelible impress upon the old Nile valley people, the nomadic life of the desert which the invaders left behind them evidently was not so persistent, and the religion of Egypt, that element of life which always receives the stamp of its environment, shows no trace of desert life. The affinities observable in the language are confirmed in case of the Libyans by the surviving products of archaic civilization in the Nile valley, such as some of the early pottery, which closely resembles that still made by the Libyan Kabyles. Again the representations of the early Puntites, or Somali people, on the Egyptian monuments, show striking resemblances to the Egyptians themselves. The examination of the bodies exhumed from archaic burials in the Nile valley, which we had hoped might bring further evidence for the settlement of the ethnic problem, has, however, produced such diversity of opinion among the physical anthropologists, as to render it impossible for the historian to obtain decisive results from their researches. It has, however, been shown that the prehistoric and the historic Egyptians as now found in the ancient cemeteries are identical in race.

29. As found in the earliest burials to-day, the predynastic Egyptians were a dark-haired people, already possessed of the rudiments of civilization. The men wore a skin over the shoulders, sometimes skin drawers, and again only a short white linen kilt; while the women were clothed in long garments of some textile, probably linen, reaching from the shoulders to the ankles. Statuettes of both sexes without clothing whatever are, however, very common. Sandals were not unknown. They occasionally tattooed their bodies,

and they also wrought ornaments such as rings, bracelets and pendants of stone, ivory and bone; with beads of flint, quartz, carnelian, agate and the like. The women dressed their hair with ornamented ivory combs and pins. For the eye- and face-paint necessary for the toilet they had palettes of carved slate on which the green colour was ground. They were able to build dwellings of wattle, sometimes smeared with mud, and probably later of sun-dried brick. In the furnishing of these houses they displayed considerable mechanical skill, and a rudimentary artistic taste. They ate with ivory spoons, sometimes even richly carved with figures of animals in the round, marching along the handle. Although the wheel was at first unknown to them, they produced fine pottery of the most varied forms in vast quantities. The museums of Europe and America are now filled with their polished red and black ware, or a variety with incised geometrical designs, sometimes in basket patterns, while another style of great importance to us is painted with rude representations of boats, men, animals, birds, fish or trees. While they made no objects of glass, they understood the art of glazing beads, plaques and the like. Crude statuettes in wood, ivory, or stone, represent the beginnings of that plastic art which was to achieve such triumphs in the early dynastic age; and three large stone statues of Min, found by Petrie at Coptos, display the rude strength of the predynastic civilization of which we are now speaking. The art of the prolific potter was obliged to give way slowly to the artificer in stone, who finally produced excellent stone vessels, which, on gaining the use of copper tools, he rapidly improved toward the end of the predynastic period, when his bowls and jars in the hardest stones, like the diorites and porphyries, display magnificent work. The most cunningly wrought flints that have ever been found among any people belong to this age. The makers were ultimately able to affix carved ivory hafts, and with equal skill they put together stone and flint axes, flint-headed fish-spears and the iike. The war mace with pear-shaped head, as found also in Babylonia, is characteristic of the age. Side by side with such weapons and implements they also produced and used weapons and implements of copper. It is indeed the age of the slow transition from stone to copper. Gold, silver and lead, while rare, were in use.

30. In the fruitful Nile valley we cannot think of such a people as other than chiefly agricultural; and the fact that they emerge into historical times as agriculturalists, with an ancient religion of vastly remote prehistoric origin, whose symbols and outward manifestations clearly betray the primitive fancies of an agricultural and pastoral people—all this would lead to the same conclusion. In the unsubdued jungles of the Nile, animal life was of course much more plentiful at that time than now; the elephant, giraffe, hippopotamus and the strange okapi, which was deified as the god Set, wandered through the jungles, though all these animals were later extinct. These early men were therefore great hunters, as well as skilful fishermen. They pursued the most formidable game of the desert, like the lion or the wild ox, with bows and arrows; and in light boats they attacked the hippopotamus and the crocodile with harpoons and lances. They commemorated these and like deeds in rude pictures incised on the rocks, where they are still found in the Nile valley, covered with a heavy brown patina of weathering, such as historic sculptures never display; thus showing their vast age.

31. Their industries may have resulted in rudimentary commerce for, besides their small hunting-boats, they built vessels of considerable size on the Nile, apparently propelled by many oars and guided by a large rudder. Sailing ships were rare, but they were not unknown. Their vessels bore standards, probably indicating the place from which each hailed, for among them appear what may be the crossed arrows of the goddess Neit of Sais, while an elephant immediately suggests the later Elephantine. These ensigns are, in some cases, strikingly similar to those later employed in hieroglyphic as the standards of the local communities, and their presence on the early ships suggests the existence of such communities in those prehistoric days. The later administrative or feudal divisions of the country in historic times, the nomes, as the Greeks called them, to which we shall often have occasion to refer, are likely to have been survivals of such prehistoric petty states as these standards suggest. If this be true, there were probably some twenty such states distributed along the river in Upper Egypt. However this may be, these people were already at a stage of civilization where considerable towns appear and city-states, as in Babylonia, must have developed, each with its chief or dynast, its local god, worshipped in a crude sanctuary; and its market to which the tributary, outlying country was attracted. The long process by which such communities grew up can be only surmised from the analogy of similar developments elsewhere, for the small kingdoms and city-states, out of which the nation was ultimately consolidated, do not fall within the historic age, as in Babylonia.

32. The gradual fusion which finally merged these petty states into two kingdoms: one in the Delta, and

the other comprising the states of the valley above, is likewise a process of which we shall never know the course. Of its heroes and its conquerors, its wars and conquests, not an echo will ever reach us; nor is there the slightest indication of the length of time consumed by this process. It will hardly have been concluded, however, before 4000 B. C. Our knowledge of the two kingdoms which emerged at the end of this long prehistoric age is but slightly more satisfactory. The Delta was, through the historic age, open to inroads of the Libyans who dwelt upon the west of it; and the constant influx of people from this source gave the western Delta a distinctly Libyan character which it preserved even down to the time of Herodotus. At the earliest moment, when the monuments reveal the conditions in the Delta, the Pharaoh is contending with the Libyan invaders, and the earlier kingdom of the North will therefore have been strongly Libyan, if indeed it did not owe its origin to this source. Reliefs recently discovered at Abusir show four Libyan chieftains wearing on their brows the royal uræus serpent of the Pharaohs, to whom it therefore descended from some early Libyan king of the Delta. The temple at Sais, in the western Delta, the chief centre of Libyan influence in Egypt, bore the name "House of the King of Lower Egypt" (the Delta), and the emblem of Neit, its chief goddess was tattooed by the Libyans upon their arms. It may therefore have been an early residence of a Libyan king of the Delta, although the capital of the North was traditionally Buto. As its coat of arms or symbol the Northern Kingdom employed a tuft of papyrus plant, which grew so plentifully in its marshes as to be distinctive of it. The king himself was designated by a bee, and wore upon his head a red crown, both in colour and shape peculiar to his kingdom. All of these symbols are very common in later hieroglyphic. Red was the distinctive colour of the northern kingdom and its treasury was called the "Red House."

33. Unfortunately the Delta is so deeply overlaid with deposits of Nile mud that the material remains of its earliest civilization are buried forever from our reach. That civilization was probably earlier and more advanced than that of the valley above. Already in the forty-third century B.C. the men of the Delta had discovered the year of three hundred and sixty-five days and they introduced a calendar year of this length, beginning on the day when Sirius rose at sunrise, as determined in the latitude of the southern Delta, where these earliest astronomers lived, in 4241 B.C. (MC, 38 ff.). It is the civilization of the Delta, therefore, which furnishes us with the earliest fixed date in the history of the world. It was thus also these men of the Delta who furnished the modern civilized world with its calendar, which, as they devised it, with twelve thirty-day months and five intercalary feast days, was the only practical calendar known in antiquity. The year began on that day when Sirius first appeared on the eastern horizon at sunrise (the heliacal rising), which in our calendar was on the nineteenth of July (Julian). But as this calendar year was in reality about a quarter of a day shorter than the solar year, it therefore gained a full day every four years, thus slowly revolving on the astronomical year, passing entirely around it once in fourteen hundred and sixty years, only to begin the revolution again. An astronomical event like the heliacal rising of Sirius, when dated in terms of the Egyptian calendar, may therefore be computed and

dated within four years in terms of our reckoning, that is, in years B.C.

34. The kingdom of Upper Egypt was more distinctively Egyptian than that of the Delta. It had its capital at Nekheb, modern El Kab, and its standard or symbol was a lily plant, while another southern plant served as the ensign of the king, who was further distinguished by a tall white crown, white being the colour of the Southern Kingdom. Its treasury was therefore known as the "White House." There was a royal residence across the river from Nekheb, called Nekhen, the later Hieraconpolis, while corresponding to it in the Northern Kingdom was a suburb of Buto, called Pe. Each capital had its patroness or protecting goddess: Buto, the serpent-goddess, in the North; and in the South the vulture-goddess, Nekhbet. But at both capitals the hawk-god Horus was worshipped as the distinctive patron deity of both kings. The people of the time believed in a life hereafter, subject to wants of the same nature as those of the present life. Their cemeteries are widely distributed along the margin of the desert in Upper Egypt, and of late years thousands of interments have been excavated. The tomb is usually a flat-bottomed oval or rectangular pit, in which the body, doubled into the "contracted" or "embryonic" posture, lies on its side. In the earliest burials it is wrapped in a skin, but later also in woven fabric; there is no trace of embalmment. Beneath the body is frequently a mat of plaited rushes; it often has in the hand or at the breast a slate palette for grinding face-paint, the green malachite for which lies near in a small bag. The body is besides accompanied by other articles of toilet or of adornment and is surrounded by jars of pottery or stone containing ash or organic

matter, the remains of food, drink and ointment for the deceased in the hereafter. Not only were the toilet and other bodily wants of the deceased thus provided for, but he was also given his flint weapons or bone-tipped harpoons that he might replenish his larder from the chase. Clay models of objects which he might need were also given him, especially boats. The pits are sometimes roughly roofed over with branches, covered with a heap of desert sand and gravel, forming rudimentary tombs, and later they came to be lined with crude, sun-dried brick. Sometimes a huge, roughly hemispherical bowl of pottery was inverted over the body as it lay in the pit. These burials furnish the sole contemporary material for our study of the predynastic age. The gods of the hereafter were appealed to in prayers and magical formulæ, which eventually took conventional and traditional form in writing. A thousand years later in the dynastic age fragments of these mortuary texts are found in use in the pyramids of the Fifth and Sixth Dynasties (see pp. 65–8). Pepi I, a king of the Sixth Dynasty, in his rebuilding of the Dendereh temple, claimed to be reproducing a plan of a sanctuary of the predynastic kings on that spot. Temples of some sort they therefore evidently had.

35. While they thus early possessed all the rudiments of material culture, the people of this age developed a system of writing also. The computations necessary for the discovery and use of the calendar show a use of writing in the last centuries of the fifth millennium B.C. It is shown also by the fact that nearly a thousand years later the scribes of the Fifth Dynasty were able to copy a long list of the kings of the North, and perhaps those of the South also (BAR, I, 76–167); while the mortuary texts to which we have referred will not have survived

a thousand years without having been committed to writing in the same way. The hieroglyphs for the Northern Kingdom, for its king, and for its treasury cannot have arisen at one stroke with the first king of the dynastic age; but must have been in use long before the rise of the First Dynasty; while the presence of a cursive linear hand at the beginning of the dynasties is conclusive evidence that the system was not then a recent innovation.

36. Of the deeds of these remote kings of the North and South, who passed away before three thousand four hundred B.C., we know nothing. Their tombs have never been discovered, a fact which accounts for the lack of any written monuments among the contemporary documents, all of which come from tombs of the poorer classes, such as contain no writing even in the dynastic age. Seven names of the kings of the Delta, like Seka, Khayu, or Thesh, alone of all the line have survived; but of the Southern Kingdom not even a royal name has descended to us, unless it be that of the Scorpion, which, occurring on some few remains of this early age, was probably that of one of the powerful chieftains of the South (BAR, I, 166). The scribes of the Fifth Dynasty who drew up this list of kings, some eight hundred years after the line had passed away, seem to have known only the royal names, and were unable to, or at least did not record, any of their achievements (BAR, I, 90). As a class these kings of the North and South were known to their posterity as the "worshippers of Horus"; and as ages passed they became half-mythic figures, gradually to be endowed with semi-divine attributes, until they were regarded as the demi-gods who succeeded the divine dynasties, the great gods who had ruled Egypt in the beginning

(SU, III). Their original character as deceased kings, as known to the earlier dynasties, led to their being considered especially as a line of the divine dead who had ruled over the land before the accession of human kings; and in the historical work of Manetho they appear simply as "the dead." Thus their real historical character was finally completely sublimated, then to merge into unsubstantial myth, and the ancient kings of the North and the South were worshipped in the capitals where they had once ruled.

37. The next step in the long and slow evolution of national unity was the union of the North and the South. The tradition which was still current in the days of the Greeks in Egypt, to the effect that the two kingdoms were united by a king named Menes, is fully confirmed by the evidence of the early monuments. The figure of Menes, but a few years since as vague and elusive as those of the "worshippers of Horus," who preceded him, has now been clothed with unmistakable reality, and he at last steps forth into history to head the long line of Pharaohs who have yet to pass us in review. It must have been a skilful warrior and a vigorous administrator, who thus gathered the resources of the Southern Kingdom so well in hand that he was able to invade and conquer the Delta, and thus merge the two kingdoms into one nation, completing the long process of centralization which had been going on for many centuries. His native city was Thinis, an obscure place in the vicinity of Abydos, which was not near enough to the centre of his new kingdom to serve as his residence, and we can easily credit the narrative of Herodotus that he built a great dam, diverting the course of the Nile above the site of Memphis that he might gain room there for a city. This stronghold,

perhaps not yet called Memphis, was probably known as the "White Wall," in reference of course to the White Kingdom, whose power it represented. If we may believe the tradition of Herodotus' time, it was from this place, situated so favourably on the border between the two kingdoms, that Menes probably governed the new nation which he had created. He carried his arms also southward against northern Nubia (NGH, 20), which then extended below the first cataract as far northward as the nome of Edfu. According to the tradition of Manetho, he was blessed with a long reign, and the memory of his great achievement was imperishable, as we have seen. He was buried in Upper Egypt, either at Abydos near his native Thinis, or some distance above it near the modern village of Negadeh, where a large brick tomb, probably his, still survives. In it and similar tombs of his successors at Abydos written monuments of his reign have been found, and even a golden fragment of his royal adornments, bearing his name, which this ancient founder of the Egyptian state wore upon his person.

38. The kings of this remote protodynastic age are no longer merely a series of names as but a few years since they still were. As a *group* at least, we know much of their life and its surroundings; although we shall never be able to discern them as possessed of distinguishable personality. They blend together without distinction as children of their age. The outward insignia which all alike employed were now accommodated to the united kingdom. The king's favourite title was "Horus," by which he identified himself as the successor of the great god who had once ruled over the kingdom. Everywhere, on royal documents, seals and the like, appeared the Horus-hawk as the symbol of

royalty. He was mounted upon a rectangle representing the façade of a building, probably the king's palace, within which was written the king's official name. The other or personal name of the ruler was preceded by the bee of the North and the plant of the Southern King, to indicate that he had now absorbed both titles; while with these two symbols there often appeared also Nekhbet, the vulture-goddess of El Kab, the southern capital, side by side with Buto, the serpent-goddess of the northern capital. On the sculptures of the time, the protecting vulture hovers with outspread wings over the head of the king, but as he felt himself still as primarily king of Upper Egypt, it was not until later that he wore the serpent of the North, the sacred uræus upon his forehead. Similarly Set sometimes appears with Horus, preceding the king's personal name, the two gods thus representing the North and the South, dividing the land between them in accordance with the myth which we shall later have occasion to discuss. The monarch wore the crown of either kingdom, and he is often spoken of as the "double lord." Thus his dominion over a united Egypt was constantly proclaimed.

39. We see the king on ceremonious occasions appearing in some state, preceded by four standard-bearers and accompanied by his chancellor, personal attendants, or a scribe, and two fan-bearers. He wore the white crown of Upper or the red crown of Lower Egypt, or even a curious combination of the crowns of both kingdoms, and a simple garment suspended by a strap over one shoulder, to which a lion's tail was appended behind. So dressed and so attended he conducted triumphant celebrations of his victories or led the ceremonies at the opening of canals or the inaugura-

tion of public works. On the thirtieth anniversary of his appointment by his father as crown prince to the heirship of the kingdom, the king celebrated a great jubilee called the "Feast of Sed," a word meaning "tail," and perhaps commemorating his assumption of the royal lion's tail at his appointment thirty years before. He was a mighty hunter, and recorded with pride an achievement like the slaying of a hippopotamus. His weapons were costly and elaborate, as we shall see. His several palaces each bore a name, and the royal estate possessed gardens and vineyards, the latter being also named and carefully administered by officials who were responsible for the income therefrom.

40. The furniture of such a palace, even in this remote age, was magnificent and of fine artistic quality. Among it were vessels exquisitely wrought in some eighteen or twenty different varieties of stone, especially alabaster; even in such refractory material as diorite, superb bowls were ground to translucent thinness, and jars of rock crystal were carved with matchless precision to represent natural objects. The pottery, on the other hand, perhaps because of the perfection of the stone vessels, is inferior to that of the predynastic age. The less substantial furniture has for the most part perished, but chests of ebony inlaid with ivory and stools with legs of ivory magnificently carved to represent bull's legs, have survived in fragments. Glaze was now more thoroughly mastered than before, and incrustation with glazed plaques and ivory tablets was practiced. The coppersmith furnished the palace with finely wrought bowls, ewers, and other vessels of copper; while he materially aided in the perfection of stone vase-making by the production of excellent copper tools. The goldsmith combined with a high degree of

technical skill also exquisite taste, and produced for the king's person and for the ladies of the royal household magnificent regalia in gold and precious stones, involving the most delicate soldering of the metal, a process accomplished with a skill of which even a modern workman would not be ashamed. While the products of the industrial craftsman had thus risen to a point of excellence such that they claim a place as works of art, we find that the rude carvings and drawings of the predynastic people have now developed into reliefs and statues which clearly betray the professional artist. The kings dedicated in the temples, especially in that of Horus at Hieraconpolis, ceremonial slate palettes, maces and vessels, bearing reliefs which display a sure and practiced hand. The human and animal figures are done with surprising freedom and vigour, proclaiming an art long since conscious of itself and centuries removed from the naïve efforts of a primitive people. By the time of the Third Dynasty the conventions of civilized life had laid a heavy hand upon this art; and although finish and power of faithful delineation had reached a level far surpassing that of the Hieraconpolis slates, the old freedom had disappeared. In the astonishing statues of King Khasekhem at Hieraconpolis, the rigid canons which ruled the art of the Old Kingdom are already clearly discernible.

41. The wreck of all this splendour, amid which these antique kings lived, has been rescued by Petrie from their tombs at Abydos. These tombs are the result of a natural evolution from the pits in which the predynastic people buried their dead. The pit, now rectangular and brick-lined, has been enlarged; while the surrounding jars of food and drink have developed into a series of small chambers surrounding the central

room or pit, in which, doubtless, the body lay. The whole was roofed with heavy timbers and planking, probably surmounted by a heap of sand, and on the east front were set up two tall narrow stelæ bearing the king's name. Access to the central chamber was had by a brick stairway descending through one side. The king's toilet furniture, a rich equipment of bowls, jars and vessels, metal vases and ewers, his personal ornaments, and all that was necessary for the maintenance of royal state in the hereafter were deposited with his body in this tomb; while the smaller surrounding chambers were filled with a liberal supply of food and wine in enormous pottery jars, sealed with huge cones of Nile mud mixed with straw, and impressed while soft with the name of the king, or of the estate or vineyard from which they came. The revenue in food and wine from certain of the king's estates was diverted and established as permanent income of the tomb to maintain for all time the table supply of the deceased king and of his household and adherents, whose tombs, to the number of one or two hundred, were grouped about his own. Thus he was surrounded in death by those who had been his companions in life; his women, his body-guard, and even the dwarf, whose dances had diverted his idle hours, all sleep beside their lord that he may continue in the hereafter the state with which he had been environed on earth. Thus early began the elaborate arrangements of the Egyptian upper classes for the proper maintenance of the deceased in the life hereafter.

42. This desire to create a permanent abiding-place for the royal dead exerted a powerful influence in the development of the art of building. Already in the First Dynasty we find a granite floor in one of the royal

tombs, that of Usephais, and toward the end of the Second Dynasty the surrounding brick chambers of King Khasekhemui's tomb enclose a chamber built of hewn limestone, the earliest stone masonry structure known in the history of man. His predecessor, probably his father, had already built a stone temple which he recorded as a matter of note (BAR, I, 134), and Khasekhemui himself built a temple at Hieraconpolis, of which a granite door-post has survived.

43. Such works of the skilled artificer and builder (for a number of royal architects were already attached to the court) indicate a well-ordered and highly organized state; but of its character little can be discerned from the scanty materials at our command. The king's chief assistant and minister in government seems to have been a chancellor, whom we have seen attending him on state occasions. The officials whom we later find as nobles with judicial functions, attached to the two royal residences of the North and South, Pe and Nekhen, already existed under these earliest dynasties, indicating an organized administration of judicial and juridical affairs. There was a body of fiscal officials, whose seals we find upon payments of *naturalia* to the royal tombs, impressed upon the clay jar-sealings; while a fragment of a scribe's accounts evidently belonging to such an administration, was found in the Abydos royal tombs. The endowment of these tombs with a regularly paid income clearly indicates a fiscal organization, of which several offices, like the "provision office," are mentioned on the seals. In all probability all the land belonged to the estate of the king, by whom it was entrusted to a noble class. There were large estates conducted by these nobles, as in the period which immediately followed; but on

what terms they were held we cannot now determine. The people, with the possible exception of a free class of artificers and tradesmen, will have been slaves on these estates. They lived also in cities protected by heavy walls of sun-dried brick, and under the command of a local governor. The chief cities of the time were the two capitals, El Kab and Buto, with their royal suburbs of Nekhen or Hieraconpolis, and Pe; the "White Wall," the predecessor of Memphis; Thinis, the native city of the first two dynasties; the neighbouring Abydos; Heliopolis, Heracleopolis and Sais; while a number of less importance appear in the Third Dynasty.

44. Every two years a "numbering" of the royal possessions was made throughout the land by the officials of the treasury, and these "numberings" served as a partial basis for the chronological reckoning. The years of a king's reign were called, "Year of the First Numbering," "Year *after* the First Numbering," "Year of the Second Numbering," and so on. An earlier method was to name the year after some important event which occurred in it, thus: "Year of Smiting the Troglodytes," a method found also in early Babylonia. But as the "numberings" finally became annual, they formed a more convenient basis for designating the year, as habit seemed to have deterred the scribes from numbering the years themselves. Such a system of government and administration as this of course could not operate without a method of writing, which we find in use both in elaborate hieroglyphics and in the rapid cursive hand of the accounting scribe. It already possessed not only phonetic signs representing a whole syllable or group of consonants but also the *alphabetic* signs, each of which

stood for one consonant; true alphabetic *letters* having thus been discovered in Egypt two thousand five hundred years before their use by any other people. Had the Egyptian been less a creature of habit, he might have discarded his syllabic signs 3,500 years before Christ, and have written with an alphabet of twenty-four letters. In the documents of these early dynasties the writing is in such an archaic form that many of the scanty fragments which we possess from this age are as yet unintelligible to us. Yet it was the medium of recording medical and religious texts, to which in later times a peculiar sanctity and effectiveness were attributed. The chief events of each year were also recorded in a few lines under its name, and a series of annals covering every year of a king's reign and showing to a day how long he reigned was thus produced. A small fragment only of these annals has escaped destruction, the now famous Palermo Stone, so called because it is at present in the museum of Palermo (BAR, I, 76–167; BH, Fig. 29).

45. Already a state form of religion was developing, and it is this form alone of which we know anything; the religion of the people having left little or no trace. Even in the later dynasties we shall find little to say of the folk-religion, which was rarely a matter of permanent record. The royal temple of Menes's time was still a simple structure, being little more than a shrine or chapel of wood, with walls of plaited wattle. There was an enclosed court before it, containing a symbol or emblem of the god mounted on a standard; and in front of the enclosure was a pair of poles, perhaps the forerunners of the pair of stone obelisks which in historic times were erected at the entrance of a temple. By the second half of the Second Dynasty, how-

ever, stone temples were built, as we have seen (BAR, I, 134). The kings frequently record in their annals the draughting of a temple plan, or their superintendence of the ceremonious inauguration of the work when the ground was measured and broken (BAR, I, 91–167). The great gods were those familiar in later times, whom we shall yet have occasion briefly to discuss; we notice particularly Osiris and Set, Horus and Anubis, Thoth, Sokar, Min, and Apis a form of Ptah; while among the goddesses, Hathor and Neit are very prominent. Several of these, like Horus, were evidently the patron gods of prehistoric kingdoms, preceding the kingdoms of the North and South, and thus going back to a very distant age. Horus, as under the predynastic kings, was the greatest god of the united kingdom, and occupied the position later held by Re. His temple at Hieraconpolis was especially favoured, and an old feast in his honour, called the "Worship of Horus," celebrated every two years, is regularly recorded in the royal annals. The kings therefore continued without interruption the traditions of the "Worshippers of Horus," as the successors of whom they regarded themselves. As long as the royal succession continued in the Thinite family, the worship of Horus was carefully observed; but with the ascendancy of the Third Dynasty, a Memphite family, it gradually gave way and was neglected. The priestly office was maintained of course as in the Old Kingdom by laymen, who were divided, as later, into four orders or phyles.

46. The more than four hundred years during which the first two dynasties ruled must have been a period of constant and vigorous growth. Of the seven kings of Menes's line, who followed him during the first two centuries of that development, we can identify only two

with certainty: Miebis and Usephais; but we have contemporary monuments from twelve of the eighteen kings who ruled during this period. The first difficulty which confronted them was the reconciliation of the Northern Kingdom and its complete fusion with the larger nation. We have seen how, in administration, the two kingdoms remained distinct, and hinted that the union was a merely personal bond. The kings on ascending the throne celebrated a feast called "Union of the Two Lands (BAR, I, 140), by which the first year of each king's reign was characterized and named. This union, thus shown to be so fresh in their minds, could not at first be made effectual. The North rebelled again and again, causing bloody wars, in which the kings of the South, Narmer, Neterimu, and Khasekhem deported myriads of captives and cattle. We find the splendid memorials of their victories in the Horus temple at Hieraconpolis (QH, I, pl. 36–41; BAR, I, 124). The later mythology attributed a lasting reconciliation of the two kingdoms to Osiris (Louvre Stela, C. 2).

47. While the severe methods employed against the North must have seriously crippled its economic prosperity, that of the nation as a whole probably continued to increase. The kings were constantly laying out new estates and building new palaces, temples and strongholds. Public works, like the opening of irrigation canals or the wall of Menes above Memphis, show their solicitude for the economic resources of the kingdom, as well as a skill in engineering and a high conception of government such as we cannot but greatly admire in an age so remote. They were able also to undertake the earliest enterprises of which we know in foreign lands. King Semerkhet, early in the dynastic age, and

probably during the First Dynasty, carried on mining operations in the copper regions of the Sinaitic peninsula, in the Wady Maghâra. His expedition was exposed to the depredations of the wild tribes of Beduin, who, already in this remote age, peopled those districts; and he recorded his punishment of them in a relief upon the rocks of the wadi (WRS, p. 96). It is the oldest historical relief known to us. An ivory tablet of King Usephais, and a reference under the reign of Miebis on the Palermo Stone commemorates other victories over the same people (BAR, I, 104). Indeed there are indications that the kings of this time maintained foreign relations with far remoter peoples. In their tombs have been found fragments of a peculiar, non-Egyptian pottery, closely resembling the ornamented Ægean ware produced by the island peoples of the northern Mediterranean in pre-Mycenæan times. If this pottery was placed in these tombs at the time of the original burials, there were commercial relations between Egypt and the northern Mediterranean peoples in the fourth millennium before Christ. We find another foreign connection in the north, in the occasional campaign now necessary to restrain the Libyans on the west (QH, I, pl. 15, No. 7). In the south at the first cataract, where, as late as the Sixth Dynasty, the Troglodyte tribes of the neighbouring eastern desert made it dangerous to operate the quarries there, King Usephais of the First Dynasty was able to maintain an expedition for the purpose of securing granite to pave one of the chambers of his tomb at Abydos.

48. Scanty as are its surviving monuments, we see now gradually taking form the great state which is soon to emerge as the Old Kingdom. These earliest Pharaohs were buried, as we have seen, at Abydos or

in the vicinity, where nine of their tombs are known. A thousand years after they had passed away these tombs of the founders of the kingdom were neglected and forgotten, and as early as the twentieth century before Christ that of King Zer was mistaken for the tomb of Osiris (BAR, I, 662). When found in modern times it was buried under a mountain of potsherds, the remains of votive offerings left there by centuries of Osiris-worshippers. Its rightful occupants had long been torn from their resting-places, and their limbs, heavy with gold and precious stones, had been wrenched from the sockets to be carried away by greedy violators of the dead. It was on some such occasion that one of these thieves secreted in a hole in the wall of the tomb the desiccated arm of Zer's queen, still bearing under the close wrappings its splendid royal bracelets. Perhaps slain in some brawl, the robber, fortunately for us, never returned to recover his plunder, and it was found there and brought to Petrie intact by his well-trained workmen in 1902.

PART II

THE OLD KINGDOM

IV

EARLY RELIGION

49. THERE is no force in the life of ancient man the influence of which so pervades all his activities as does that of the religious faculty. Its fancies explain for him the world about him, its fears are his hourly master, its hopes his constant Mentor, its feasts are his calendar, and its outward usages are to a large extent the education and the motive toward the gradual evolution of art, literature and science. As among all other early peoples, it was in his surroundings that the Egyptian saw his gods. The trees and springs, the stones and hill-tops, the birds and beasts were creatures like himself, or possessed of strange and uncanny powers of which he was not master. Among this host of spirits animating everything around him some were his friends, ready to be propitiated and to lend him their aid and protection; while others with craft and cunning lowered about his pathway, awaiting an opportunity to strike him with disease and pestilence, and there was no misfortune in the course of nature but found explanation in his mind as coming from one of these evil beings about him. Such spirits as these were local, each known only to the dwellers in a given locality, and the efforts to serve and propitiate them were of the humblest and most primitive character. Of such worship we know little or nothing in the Old Kingdom, but

during the Empire we shall be able to gain fleeting glimpses into this naïve and long-forgotten world. But the Egyptian peopled not merely the local circle about him with such spirits; the sky above him and earth beneath his feet were equally before him for explanation. Long ages of confinement to his elongated valley, with its monotonous, even if sometimes grand scenery, had imposed a limited range upon his imagination; neither had he the qualities of mind which could be stirred by the world of nature to such exquisite fancies as those with which the natural beauties of Hellas inspired the imagination of the Greeks. In the remote ages of that earliest civilization, which we have briefly surveyed in the preceding chapter, the shepherds and plowmen of the Nile valley saw in the heavens a vast cow, which stood athwart the vault, with head in the west, the earth lying between fore and hind feet, while the belly of the animal, studded with stars, was the arch of heaven. The people of another locality, however, fancied they could discern a colossal female figure standing with feet in the east and bending over the earth, till she supported herself upon her arms in the far west. To others the sky was a sea, supported high above the earth with a pillar at each of its four corners. As these fancies gained more than local credence and came into contact with each other, they mingled in inextricable confusion. The sun was born every morning as a calf or as a child, according to the explanation of the heavens, as a cow or a woman, and he sailed across the sky in a celestial barque, to arrive in the west and descend as an old man tottering into the grave. Again the lofty flight of the hawk, which seemed a very comrade of the sun, led them to believe that the sun himself must be such a hawk taking his daily flight across the

EARLY RELIGION

heavens, and the sun-disk, wearing the outspread wings of the hawk, became the commonest symbol of their religion.

50. The earth, or as they knew it, their elongated valley was, to their primitive fancy, a man lying prone, upon whose back the vegetation grew, the beasts moved and man lived. If the sky was a sea upon which the sun and the heavenly lights sailed westward every day, there must then be a waterway by which they could return; so there was beneath the earth another Nile, flowing through a long dark passage with successive caverns, through which the celestial barque took its way at night, to appear again in the east at early morning. This subterranean stream was connected with the Nile at the first cataract, and thence issued from two caverns, the waters of their life-giving river. It will be seen that for the people among whom this myth arose the world ended at the first cataract; all that they knew beyond was a vast sea. This was also connected with the Nile in the south, and the river returned to it in the north, for this sea, which they called the "Great Circle" (BAR II, 661), surrounded their earth. It is the idea inherited by the Greeks, who called the sea Okeanos, or Ocean. In the beginning only this ocean existed, upon which there had then appeared an egg, or as some said a flower, out of which issued the sun-god. From himself he begat four children, Shu and Tefnut, Keb and Nut. All these, with their father, lay upon the primeval ocean, when Shu and Tefnut, who represent the atmosphere, thrust themselves between Keb and Nut. They planted their feet upon Keb and raised Nut on high, so that Keb became the earth and Nut the heavens. Keb and Nut were the father and mother of the four divinities, Osiris and

Isis, Set and Nephthys; together they formed with their primeval father the sun-god, Re or Atum, a circle of nine deities, the "ennead" of which each temple later possessed a local form. This correlation of the primitive divinities as father, mother and son, strongly influenced the theology of later times until each temple possessed an artificially created triad, of purely secondary origin, upon which an "ennead" was then built up. Other local versions of this story of the world's origin also circulated. One of them represents Re as ruling the earth for a time as king over men (*cf.*, p. 112) who plotted against him, so that he sent a goddess, Hathor, to slay them, but finally repented and by a ruse succeeded in diverting the goddess from the total extermination of the human race, after she had destroyed them in part. The cow of the sky then raised Re upon her back that he might forsake the ungrateful earth and dwell in heaven.

51. Besides these gods of the earth, the air and the heavens, there were also those who had as their domain the nether world, the gloomy passage, along which the subterranean stream carried the sun from west to east. Here, according to a very early belief, dwelt the dead, whose king was Osiris. He had succeeded the sun-god, Re, as king on earth, aided in his government by his faithful sister-wife, Isis. A benefactor of men, and beloved as a righteous ruler, he was nevertheless craftily misled and slain by his brother Set. When, after great tribulation, Isis had gained possession of her lord's body, she was assisted in preparing it for burial by one of the old gods of the nether world, Anubis, the jackal-god, who thereafter became the god of embalmment. So powerful were the charms now uttered by Isis over the body of her dead husband that

it was reanimated, and regained the use of its limbs; and although it was impossible for the departed god to resume his earthly life, he passed down in triumph as a living king, to become lord of the nether world. Isis later gave birth to a son, Horus, whom she secretly reared among the marshy fastnesses of the Delta as the avenger of his father. Grown to manhood, the youth pursued Set, and in the ensuing awful battle, which raged from end to end of the land, both were fearfully mutilated. But Set was defeated, and Horus triumphantly assumed the earthly throne of his father. Thereupon Set entered the tribunal of the gods, and charged that the birth of Horus was not without stain, and that his claim to the throne was not valid. Defended by Thoth, the god of letters, Horus was vindicated and declared "true in speech," or "triumphant." According to another version it was Osiris himself who was thus vindicated.

52. Not all the gods who appear in these tales and fancies became more than mythological figures. Many of them continued merely in this rôle, without temple or form of worship; they had but a folk-lore or finally a theological existence. Others became the great gods of Egypt. In a land where a clear sky prevailed and rain was rarely seen the incessant splendour of the sun was an insistent fact, which gave him the highest place in the thought and daily life of the people. His worship was almost universal, but the chief centre of his cult was at On, the Delta city, which the Greeks called Heliopolis. Here he was known as Re, which was the solar orb itself; or as Atum, the name of the decrepit sun, as an old man tottering down the west; again his name Khepri, written with a beetle in hieroglyphics, designated him in the youthful vigour of his

rising. He had two barques with which he sailed across the heavens, one for the morning and the other for the afternoon, and when in this barque he entered the nether world at evening to return to the east he brought light and joy to its disembodied denizens. The symbol of his presence in the temple at Heliopolis was an obelisk, while at Edfu, on the upper river, which was also an old centre of his worship, he appeared as a hawk, under the name Horus.

53. The Moon, the measurer of time, furnished the god of reckoning, letters, and wisdom, Thoth, whose chief centre was Shmûn, or Hermopolis, as the Greeks who identified him with Hermes, called the place. He was identified with the Ibis. The Sky, whom we have seen as Nut, was worshipped throughout the land, although Nut herself continued to play only a mythological rôle. The sky-goddess became the type of woman and of woman's love and joy. At the ancient shrine of Dendereh she was the cow-goddess, Hathor; at Sais she was the joyous Neit; at Bubastis, in the form of a cat, she appeared as Bast; while at Memphis her genial aspects disappeared and she became a lioness, the goddess of storm and terror. The myth of Osiris, so human in its incidents and all its characteristics, rapidly induced the wide propagation of his worship, and although Isis still remained chiefly a figure in the myth, she became the type of wife and mother upon which the people loved to dwell. Horus also, although he really belonged originally to the sun-myth and had nothing to do with Osiris, was for the people the embodiment of the qualities of a good son, and in him they constantly saw the ulitmate triumph of the just cause. The immense influence of the Osiris-worship on the life of Egypt we shall have occasion to notice

further in discussing mortuary beliefs. The original home of Osiris was at Dedu, called by the Greeks Busiris, in the Delta; but Abydos, in Upper Egypt, early gained a reputation of peculiar sanctity, because the head of Osiris was buried there. He always appeared as a closely swathed figure, enthroned as a Pharaoh or merely a curious pillar, a fetish surviving from his prehistoric worship. Into the circle of nature divinities it is impossible to bring Ptah of Memphis, who was one of the early and great gods of Egypt. He was the patron of the artisan, the artificer and artist, and his High Priest was always the chief artist of the court. Such were the chief gods of Egypt, although many another important deity presided in this or that temple, whom it would be impossible for us to notice here, even with a word.

54. The external manifestations and the symbols with which the Egyptian clothed these gods are of the simplest character and they show the primitive simplicity of the age in which these deities arose. They bear a staff like a Beduin native of to-day, or the goddesses wield a reed-stem; their diadems are of woven reeds or a pair of ostrich feathers, or the horns of a sheep. In such an age the people frequently saw the manifestations of their gods in the numerous animals with which they were surrounded, and the veneration of these sacred beasts survived into an age of high civilization, when we should have expected it to disappear. But the animal-worship, which we usually associate with ancient Egypt, as a cult is a late product, brought forward in the decline of the nation at the close of its history. In the periods with which we shall have to deal, it was unknown; the hawk, for example, was the sacred animal of the sun-god, and as such a

living hawk might have a place in the temple, where he was fed and kindly treated, as any such pet might be; but he was not worshipped, nor was he the object of an elaborate ritual as later (EHR, 25).

55. In their elongated valley the local beliefs of the earliest Egyptians could not but differ greatly among themselves, and although, for example, there were many centres of sun-worship, each city possessing a sun-temple regarded the sun as its particular god, to the exclusion of all the rest; just as many a town of Italy at the present day would not for a moment identify its particular Madonna with the virgin of any other town. As commercial and administrative intercourse was increased by political union, these mutually contradictory and incompatible beliefs could not longer remain local. They fused into a complex of tangled myth, of which we have already offered some examples and shall yet see more. Neither did the theologizing priesthoods ever reduce this mass of belief into a coherent system; it remained as accident and circumstance brought it together, a chaos of contradictions. Another result of national life was that, as soon as a city gained political supremacy, its gods rose with it to the dominant place among the innumerable gods of the land.

56. The temples in which the earliest Egyptian worshipped we have already had occasion to notice. He conceived the place as the dwelling of his god, and hence its arrangement probably conformed with that of a private house of the predynastic Egyptian. While wattle walls have given place to stone masonry, it was still the house of the god. Behind a forecourt open to the sky rose a colonnaded hall, beyond which was a series of small chambers containing the furniture and implements for the temple services. Of the architect-

ure and decoration of the building we shall later have occasion to speak further. The centre of the chambers in the rear was occupied by a small room, the holy of holies, in which stood a shrine hewn from one block of granite. It contained the image of the god, a small figure of wood from one and a half to six feet high, elaborately adorned and splendid with gold, silver and costly stones. The service of the divinity who dwelt here consisted simply in furnishing him with those things which formed the necessities and luxuries of an Egyptian of wealth and rank at that time: plentiful food and drink, fine clothing, music and the dance. The source of these offerings was the income from the endowment of lands established by the throne, as well as various contributions from the royal revenues in grain, wine, oil, honey and the like (BAR, I, 153–167, 213). These contributions to the comfort and happiness of the lord of the temple, while probably originally offered without ceremony, gradually became the occasion of an elaborate ritual which was essentially alike in all temples. Outside in the forecourt was the great altar, where the people gathered on feast days, when they were permitted to share the generous food offerings, which ordinarily were eaten by the priests and servants of the temple, after they had been presented to the god. These feasts, besides those marking times and seasons, were frequently commemorations of some important event in the story or myth of the god, and on such occasions the priests in procession brought forth the image in a portable shrine, having the form of a small Nile boat.

57. The earliest priesthood was but an incident in the duties of the local noble, who was the head of the priests in the community; but the exalted position of

the Pharaoh, as the nation developed, made him the sole official servant of the gods, and there arose at the beginning of the nation's history a state form of religion in which the Pharaoh played the supreme rôle. In theory, therefore, it was he alone who worshipped the gods; in fact, however, he was of necessity represented in each of the many temples of the land by a high priest, by whom all offerings were presented "for the sake of the life, prosperity and health" of the Pharaoh. Some of these high priesthoods were of very ancient origin: particularly that of Heliopolis, whose incumbent was called "Great Seer"; while he of Ptah at Memphis was called "Great Chief of Artificers." Both positions demanded two incumbents at once, and were usually held by men of high rank. The incumbents of the other high priesthoods of later origin all bore the simple title of "overseer or chief of priests." It was the duty of this man not merely to conduct the service and ritual of the sanctuary, but also to administer its endowment of lands, from the income of which it lived, while in time of war he might even command the temple contingent. He was assisted by a body of priests, whose sacerdotal service was, with few exceptions, merely incidental to their worldly occupations. They were laymen, who from time to time served for a stated period in the temple; thus in spite of the fiction of the Pharaoh as the sole worshipper of the god, the laymen were represented in its service. In the same way the women of the time were commonly priestesses of Neit or Hathor; their service consisted in nothing more than dancing and jingling a sistrum before the god on festive occasions. The state fiction had therefore not quite suppressed the participation of the individual in the service of the temple. In harmony with the conception of the temple as the god's dwelling the most frequent title of the priest was "servant of the god."

58. Parallel with this development of a state religion with its elaborate equipment, the evolution of the provision for the dead had kept even pace. In no other land, ancient or modern, has there ever been such attention to the equipment of the dead for their eternal sojourn in the hereafter. The beliefs which finally led the Egyptian to the devotion of so much of his wealth and time, his skill and energy to the erection and equipment of the "eternal house" are the oldest conceptions of a real life hereafter of which we know. He believed that the body was animated by a vital force, which he pictured as a counterpart of the body, which came into the world with it, passed through life in its company, and accompanied it into the next world. This he called a "ka," and it is often spoken of in modern treatises as a "double," though this designation describes the form of the ka as represented on the monuments rather than its real nature. Besides the ka every person possessed also a soul, which he conceived in the form of a bird flitting about among the trees; though it might assume the outward semblance of a flower, the lotus, a serpent, a crocodile sojourning in the river, or of many other things. Even further elements of personality seemed to them present, like the shadow possessed by every one, but the relations of all these to each other were very vague and confused in the mind of the Egyptian; just as the average Christian of a generation ago, who accepted the doctrine of body, soul and spirit, would have been unable to give any lucid explanation of their interrelations.

59. Like the varying explanations of the heavens and

the world there were many once probably local notions of the place to which the dead journeyed; but these beliefs, although mutually irreconcilable, continued to enjoy general acceptance, and no one was troubled by their incompatibility, even if it ever occurred to them. There was a world of the dead in the west, where the sun-god descended into his grave every night, so that "westerners" was for the Egyptian a term for the departed; and wherever possible the cemetery was located on the margin of the western desert. There was also the nether world where the departed lived awaiting the return of the solar barque every evening, that they might bathe in the radiance of the sun-god, and, seizing the bow-rope of his craft, draw him with rejoicing through the long caverns of their dark abode. In the splendour of the nightly heavens the Nile-dweller also saw the host of those who had preceded him; thither they had flown as birds, rising above all foes of the air, and received by Re as the companions of his celestial barque, they now swept across the sky as eternal stars. Still more commonly the Egyptian told of a field in the northeast of the heavens, which he called the "field of food," or the "field of Yaru," the lentil field, where the grain grew taller than any ever seen on the banks of the Nile, and the departed dwelt in security and plenty. Besides the bounty of the soil he received, too, from the earthly offerings presented in the temple of his god: bread and beer and fine linen. It was not every one who succeeded in reaching this field of the blessed; for it was surrounded by water. Sometimes the departed might induce the hawk or the ibis to bear him across on their pinions; again friendly spirits, the four sons of Horus, brought him a craft upon which he might float over; sometimes the sun-god bore him across in his barque; but by far the majority depended upon the services of a ferryman called "Turnface" or "Lookbehind," because his face was ever turned to the rear in poling his craft. He will not receive all into his boat, but only him of whom it is said, "there is no evil which he has done," or "the just who hath no boat," or him who is "righteous before heaven and earth and before the isle" (Pyramid of Pepi I, 400; Mernere 570, AZ, XXXI, 76–77), where lies the happy field to which they go. These are the earliest traces in the history of man of an ethical test at the close of life, making the life hereafter dependent upon the character of the life lived on earth. It was at this time, however, prevailingly ceremonial rather than moral purity which secured the waiting soul passage across the waters. (But see BAR, I, 252, 279.)

60. Into these early beliefs, with which Osiris originally had nothing to do, the myth which told of his death and departure into the nether world, now entered to become the dominating element in Egyptian mortuary belief. He had become the "first of those in the west" and "king of the glorified"; every soul that suffered the fate of Osiris might also experience his restoration to life; might indeed become an Osiris. Believing thus that all might share the goodly destiny of Osiris, they contemplated death without dismay, for they said of the dead, "They depart not as those who are dead, but they depart as those who are living" (EHR, 96–99). Here there entered, as a salutary influence, also the incident of the triumphant vindication of Osiris when accused; for there is a hint of a similar moral justification for *all*, which, as an ethical influence, we shall yet see, was the most fruitful germ in Egyptian religion (BAR, I, 331, 253, 330, 338, 357).

61. These views are chiefly found in the oldest mortuary literature of Egypt which we possess, a series of texts supposed to be effective in securing for the deceased the enjoyment of a happy life, and especially the blessed future enjoyed by Osiris. They were engraved upon the passages of the Fifth and Sixth Dynasty pyramids, where they have been preserved in large numbers, and it is largely from them that the above sketch of the early Egyptian's notions of the hereafter has been taken (see EHR). From the place in which they are found they are usually called the "Pyramid Texts." Many of these texts grew up in the predynastic age and some have therefore been altered to accommodate them to the Osiris faith, with which they originally had no connection—a process which has of course resulted in inextricable confusion of originally differing mortuary beliefs.

62. So insistent a belief or set of beliefs in a life beyond the grave necessarily brought with it a mass of mortuary usages with which in the earliest period of Egypt's career we have already gained some acquaintance. It is evident that however persistently the Egyptian transferred the life of the departed to some distant region, far from the tomb where the body lay, he was never able to detach the future life entirely from the body. It is evident that he could conceive of no survival of the dead without it. Gradually he had developed a more and more pretentious and a safer repository for his dead, until, as we have seen, it had become a vast and massive structure of stone. In all the world no such colossal tombs as the pyramids are to be found; while the tombs of the nobles grouped about have in the Old Kingdom become immense masonry structures, which, but a few centuries before,

a king would have been proud to own. Such a tomb as that of Pepi I's vizier in the Sixth Dynasty contained no less than thirty-one rooms. The superstructure of such a tomb was a massive, flat-topped, rectangular oblong of masonry, the sides of which slanted inward at an angle of, roughly, seventy-five degrees. It was, with the exception of its room or rooms, solid throughout, reminding the modern natives of the "mastaba," the terrace, area or bench on which they squat before their houses and shops. Such a tomb is therefore commonly termed a "mastaba." The simplest of such mastabas has no rooms within, and only a false door in the east side, by which the dead, dwelling in the west, that is, behind this door, might enter again the world of the living. This false door was finally elaborated into a kind of chapel-chamber in the mass of the masonry, the false door now being placed in the west wall of the chamber. The inner walls of this chapel bore scenes carved in relief, depicting the servants and slaves of the deceased at their daily tasks on his estate, in field and workshop, producing all those things which were necessary for their lord's welfare in the hereafter, while here and there his towering figure appeared superintending and inspecting their labours as he had done before he "departed into the West." It is these scenes which are the source of our knowledge of the life and customs of the time. Far below the massive mastaba was a burial chamber in the native rock reached by a shaft which passed down through the superstructure of masonry. On the day of burial the body, now duly embalmed, was subjected to elaborate ceremonies re-enacting occurrences in the resurrection of Osiris. It was especially necessary by potent charms to open the mouth and ears of the deceased that he might speak and hear in the hereafter. The mummy was then lowered down the shaft and laid upon its left side in a fine rectangular cedar coffin, which again was deposited in a massive sarcophagus of granite or limestone. Food and drink were left with it, besides some few toilet articles, a magic wand and a number of amulets for protection against the enemies of the dead, especially serpents. The number of serpent-charms in the Pyramid Texts, intended to render these foes harmless, is very large. The deep shaft leading to the burial chamber was then filled to the top with sand and gravel, and the friends of the dead now left him to the life in the hereafter, which we have pictured.

63. Yet their duty toward their departed friend had not yet lapsed. In a tiny chamber beside the chapel they masoned up a portrait statue of the deceased, sometimes cutting small channels, which connected the two rooms, the chapel and the statue-chamber, or "serdâb," as the modern natives call it. As the statue was an exact reproduction of the deceased's body, his ka might therefore attach itself to this counterfeit, and through the connecting channels enjoy the food and drink placed for it in the chapel. The offerings to the dead, originally only a small loaf in a bowl, placed by a son, or wife, or brother on a reed mat at the grave, have now become as elaborate as the daily cuisine once enjoyed by the lord of the tomb before he forsook his earthly house. But this labour of love, or sometimes of fear, has now devolved upon a large *personnel*, attached to the tomb, some of whom, as its priests, constantly maintained its ritual. Very specific contracts were made with these persons, requiting them for their services with a fixed income drawn from endowments legally established and recorded for this purpose by

EARLY RELIGION

the noble himself, in anticipation of his death. The tomb of Prince Nekure, son of King Khafre of the Fourth Dynasty, was endowed with the revenues from twelve towns, and as many as eight priests of such a tomb were required for its service (BAR, I, 200–209, 231–235, 191, 226–227, 379; EHR, 123).

Such endowments and the service thus maintained were intended to be permanent, but in the course of a few generations the accumulated burden was intolerable, and ancestors of a century before, with rare exceptions, were necessarily neglected or transferred in order to maintain those whose claims were stronger and more recent (BAR, I, 173, l. 5; 241). It had now become so customary for the king to assist his favourite lords and nobles in this way that we find a frequent mortuary prayer beginning "An offering which the king gives," and as long as the number of those whose tombs were thus maintained was limited to the noble and official circle around the king, such royal largesses to the dead were quite possible. But in later times, when the mortuary practices of the noble class had spread to the masses, they also employed the same prayer, although it is impossible that the royal bounty could have been so extended. Thus this prayer is to-day the most frequent formula to be found on the Egyptian monuments, occurring thousands of times on the tombs or tombstones of people who had no prospect of enjoying such royal distinction; and in the same tomb it is always repeated over and over again. In the same way the king also assisted his favourites in the *erection* of their tombs, and the noble often records the fact with pride (BAR, I, 204, 207, 213–227, 242–249, 370, 210–212, 237–240, 274–277, 308).

64. If the tomb of the noble had now become an

endowed institution, we have seen that that of the king was already such in the First Dynasty. In the Third Dynasty, at least, the Pharaoh was not satisfied with *one* tomb, but in his double capacity as king of the Two Lands he erected *two*, just as the palace was double for the same reason. We find the monarch's tomb now far surpassing that of the noble in its extent and magnificence. The mortuary service of the Pharaoh's lords might be conducted in the chapel in the east side of the mastaba; but that of the Pharaoh himself now required a separate building, a splendid mortuary temple on the east side of the pyramid. A richly endowed priesthood was here employed to maintain its ritual and to furnish the food, drink and clothing of the departed king. Its large *personnel* demanded many outbuildings, and the whole group of pyramid, temple and accessories was surrounded by a wall. All this was on the edge of the plateau overlooking the valley, in which, below the pyramid, there now grew up a walled town. Leading up from the town to the pyramid enclosure was a massive causeway of stone which terminated at the lower or townward end in a large and stately structure of granite or limestone, sometimes with floors of alabaster, the whole forming a superb portal, a worthy entrance to so impressive a tomb. Through this portal passed the white-robed procession on feast days, moving from the town up the long white causeway to the temple, above which rose the mighty mass of the pyramid. The populace in the city below probably never gained access to the pyramid enclosure. Over the town wall, through the waving green of the palms, they saw the gleaming white pyramid, where lay the god who had once ruled over them; while beside it rose slowly year by year another mountain of stone, gradually assuming pyramid form, and there would some time rest his divine son, of whose splendour they had now and then on feast days caught a fleeting glimpse. While the proper burial of the Pharaoh and his nobles had now become a matter seriously affecting the economic conditions of the state, such elaborate mortuary equipment was still confined to a small class, and the common people continued to lay away their dead without any attempt at embalmment in the pit of their prehistoric ancestors on the margin of the western desert.

V

THE OLD KINGDOM: GOVERNMENT AND SOCIETY, INDUSTRY AND ART

65. AT the dawn of the Old Kingdom the kingship had attained a prestige and an exalted power, demanding the deepest reverence of the subject whether high or low. Indeed the king was now officially a god, and one of the most frequent titles was the "Good God"; such was the respect due him that there was reluctance to refer to him by name. The courtier might designate him impersonally as "one," and "to let one know" becomes the official phrase for "report to the king." His government and ultimately the monarch personally were called the "Great House," in Egyptian Per-o, a term which has descended to us through the Hebrews as "Pharaoh." When he died he was received into the circle of the gods, to be worshipped like them ever after in the temple before the vast pyramid in which he slept.

66. Court customs had gradually developed into an elaborate official etiquette, for the punctilious observance of which, already in this distant age, a host of gorgeous marshals and court chamberlains were in constant attendance at the palace. There had thus grown up a palace life, not unlike that of modern times in the East, a life into which we gain obscure glimpses in the numerous titles which the court lords of the time,

with ostentatious pride, have displayed on the walls of their tombs. Every need of the royal person was represented by some palace lord, whose duty it was to supply it. There were many ranks, and the privileges of each, with all possible niceties of precedence, were strictly observed and enforced by the court marshals at all state levees and royal audiences. The king's favourite wife became the official queen, whose eldest son usually received the appointment as crown prince to succeed his father. But as at all Oriental courts, there was also a royal harem with numerous inmates. Many sons usually surrounded the monarch, and the vast revenues of the palace were liberally distributed among them. A son of King Khafre in the Fourth Dynasty left an estate of fourteen towns, besides a town house and two estates at the royal residence, the pyramid city. Besides these, the endowment of his tomb comprised twelve towns more (BAR, I, 190–199). But these princes assisted in their father's government, and did not live a life of indolence and luxury. We shall find them occupying some of the most arduous posts in the service of the state.

67. However exalted may have been the official position of the Pharaoh as the sublime god at the head of the state, he nevertheless maintained close personal relations with the more prominent nobles of the realm. As a prince he had been educated with a group of youths from the families of these nobles, and together they had been instructed in such manly art as swimming. The friendships and the intimacies thus formed in youth must have been a powerful influence in the later life of the monarch. We see the Pharaoh giving his daughter in marriage to one of these youths with whom he had been educated, and the severe decorum

of the court was violated in behalf of this favourite, who was not permitted on formal occasions to kiss the dust before the Pharaoh, but enjoyed the unprecedented privilege of kissing the royal foot. On the part of his intimates such ceremonial was purely a matter of official etiquette; in private the monarch did not hesitate to recline familiarly in complete relaxation beside one of his favourites, while the attending slaves anointed them both. The daughter of such a noble might become the official queen and mother of the next king. We see the king displaying the greatest solicitude and sorrow at the sudden sickness and death of his vizier. It is evident that the most powerful lords of the kingdom were thus bound to the person of the Pharaoh by close personal ties of blood and friendship. These relations were carefully fostered by the monarch, and in the Fourth and early Fifth Dynasty there are aspects of this ancient state in which its inner circle at least reminds one of a great family, so that, as we have observed, the king assisted all its members in the building and equipment of their tombs, and showed the greatest solicitude for their welfare, both here and in the hereafter (BAR, I, 256; 254 *ff.*; 260, 270, 344, 242-249).

68. At the head of government there was theoretically none to question the Pharaoh's power. In actual fact he was as subject to the demands of policy toward this or that class, powerful family, clique or individual, or toward the harem, as are his successors in the Oriental despotisms of the present day. These forces, which more or less modified his daily acts, we can follow at this distant day only as we see the state slowly moulded in its larger outlines by the impact of generation after generation of such influences from the Pharaoh's environment. In spite of the luxury evident in the organ-

ization of his court, the Pharaoh did not live the life of a luxurious despot, such as we frequently find among the Mamelukes of Moslem Egypt. In the Fourth Dynasty, at least, he had as prince already seen arduous service in the superintendence of quarrying and mining operations, or he had served his father as vizier or prime minister, gaining invaluable experience in government before his succession to the throne. He was thus an educated and enlightened monarch, able to read and write, and not infrequently taking his pen in hand personally to indite a letter of thanks and appreciation to some deserving officer in his government (BAR, I, 268–270, 271). He constantly received his ministers and engineers to discuss the needs of the country, especially in the conservation of the water supply and the development of the system of irrigation. He read many a weary roll of state papers, or turned from these to dictate dispatches to his commanders in Sinai, Nubia and Punt, along the southern Red Sea. The briefs of litigating heirs reached his hands and were probably not always a matter of mere routine to be read by secretaries. When such business of the royal offices had been settled the monarch rode out in his palanquin, accompanied by his vizier and attendants, to inspect his buildings and public works, and his hand was everywhere felt in all the important affairs of the nation.

69. The situation of the royal residence was largely determined by the pyramid which the king was building. As we have remarked, the palace and the town formed by the court and all that was attached to it probably lay in the valley below the margin of the western desert plateau on which the pyramid rose. From dynasty to dynasty, or sometimes from reign to

reign, it followed the pyramid, the light construction of the palaces and villas not interfering seriously with such mobility. After the Third Dynasty the residence was always in the vicinity of later Memphis. The palace itself was double, or at least it possessed two gates in its front, named after, and corresponding to the two ancient kingdoms, of which it was now the seat of government (BAR, I, 148). Throughout Egyptian history the façade of the palace was therefore called the "double front," and in writing the word "palace" the scribe frequently placed the sign of *two* houses after it. The royal office and the sub-departments of government were also termed "double;" but these titles doubtless no longer corresponded to existing double organizations; they have become a persistent fiction surviving from the first two dynasties. Adjoining the palace was a huge court, connected with which were the "halls" or offices of the central government. The entire complex of palace and adjoining offices was known as the "Great House," which was thus the centre of administration as well as the dwelling of the royal household. Here was focussed the entire system of government, which ramified throughout the country.

70. For purposes of local government Upper Egypt was divided into some twenty administrative districts, and later we find as many more in the Delta. These "nomes" were presumably the early principalities from which the local princes who ruled them in prehistoric days had long disappeared. At the head of such a district or nome there was in the Fourth and Fifth Dynasties an official appointed by the crown, and known as "First under the King." Besides his administrative function as "local governor" of the nome, he also served in a judicial capacity, and therefore bore also the title

of "judge." In Upper Egypt these "local governors" were also sometimes styled "Magnates of the Southern Ten," as if there were a group among them enjoying higher rank and forming a college or council of ten. While we are not so well informed regarding the government of the North, the system there was evidently very similar, although there were perhaps fewer local governors. Within the nome which he administered the "local governor" had under his control a miniature state, an administrative unit with all the organs of government: a treasury, a court of justice, a land-office, a service for the conservation of the dykes and canals, a body of militia, a magazine for their equipment; and in these offices a host of scribes and recorders, with an ever growing mass of archives and local records. The chief administrative bond which coordinated and centralized these nomes was the organization of the treasury, by the operation of which there annually converged upon the magazines of the central government the grain, cattle, poultry and industrial products, which in an age without coinage, were collected as taxes by the local governors. The local registration of land, or the land-office, the irrigation serivce, the judicial administration, and other administrative functions were also centralized at the Great House; but it was the treasury which formed the most tangible bond between the palace and the nomes. Over the entire fiscal administration there was a "Chief Treasurer," residing of course at the court, assisted by two "treasurers of the god" (*i. e.*, of the king), having charge of resources from mines and quarries for the great public works.

71. As the reader may have already inferred, the judicial functions of the local governors were merely

incidental to their administrative labours. There was therefore no clearly defined class of professional judges, but the administrative officials were learned in the law and assumed judicial duties. Like the treasury, the judicial administration also converged in one person, for the local judges were organized into six courts and these in turn were under a chief justice of the whole realm. Many of the judges bore the additional predicate "attached to Nekhen" (Hieraconpolis), an ancient title descended from the days when Nekhen was the royal residence of the Southern Kingdom. There was a body of highly elaborated law, which has unfortunately perished entirely. The local governors boast of their fairness and justice in deciding cases, often stating in their tombs: "Never did I judge two brothers in such a way that a son was deprived of his paternal possession" (BAR, I, 331, 357). Even a royal *intrigante* conspiring in the harem is not summarily put to death, but is given legal trial (BAR, I, 307, 310). The system of submitting all cases to the court in the form of written briefs, a method so praised by Diodorus (I, 75 *f.*), seems to have existed already in this remote age, and the Berlin Museum possesses such a legal document pertaining to litigation between an heir and an executor. It is the oldest legal document in existence and contains an appeal to the king, which, under circumstances not yet clear to us, was possible (PKM, 82 *ff.*).

72. The immediate head of the entire organization of government was the Pharaoh's prime minister, or as he is more commonly called in the East, the vizier. At the same time he also regularly served as chief justice; he was thus the most powerful man in the kingdom, next to the monarch himself, and for that reason the

office was held by the crown prince in the Fourth Dynasty. His "hall" or office served as the archives of the government, and he was the chief archivist of the state. The state records were called "king's writings." Here all lands were registered, and all local archives centralized and coördinated; here wills were recorded, and when executed the resulting new titles were issued. Over the vast army of scribes and officials who transacted the business of the Great House the vizier was supreme. When we add, that besides some minor offices, he was also often the Pharaoh's chief architect, or as the Egyptian said, "Chief of all Works of the King," we shall understand that this great minister was the busiest man in the kingdom. All powerful as he was, whose name might be followed by the royal salutation, "Life, Prosperity, Health," the people appealed to him in his judicial capacity as to one who could right every wrong, and the office was traditionally the most popular in the long list of the Pharaoh's servants. The greatest sages and authors of proverbial wisdom famous in later days, like Imhotep, Kegemne and Ptah-hotep, had been viziers in the Old Kingdom (BAR, I, 268 *ff.*; 273; 175 ll. 14–16; 190–199; 213–217, 231 *ff.*; 173).

73. Such was the organization of this remarkable state, as we are able to discern it during the first two or three centuries of the Old Kingdom. In the thirtieth century before Christ it had reached an elaborate development of state functions under local officials, such as was not found in Europe until far down in the history of the Roman Empire. It was, to sum up briefly, a closely centralized organization of local official bodies, each a centre for all the organs of the local government, which in each nome were focussed in the local governor

before converging upon the palace. It was the maintenance of the nomes each as a separate unit of government, and the interposition of the governor at its head between the Pharaoh and the nome, which rendered the system dangerous. These little states within the state might too easily become independent centres of political power. How this process actually took place we shall be able to observe as we follow the career of the Old Kingdom in the next chapter.

74. Such a process was rendered the more easy because the government did not maintain any uniform or compact military organization. Each nome possessed its militia, commanded by the civil officials, who were not necessarily trained soldiers; there was thus no class of exclusively military officers. The temple estates likewise maintained a body of such troops. They were for the most part employed in mining and quarrying expeditions, supplying the hosts necessary for the transportation of the enormous blocks often demanded by the architects. In such work they were under the command of the "treasurer of the god." In case of serious war, as there was no standing army, this militia from all the nomes and temple estates, besides auxiliaries levied among the Nubian tribes, were brought together as quickly as possible, and the command of the motley host, without any permanent organization, was entrusted by the monarch to some able official. As the local governors commanded the militia of the nomes, they held the sources of the Pharaoh's dubious military strength in their own hands.

75. The land which was thus administered must to a large extent have belonged to the crown. Under the oversight of the local governors' subordinates it was worked and made profitable by slaves or serfs, who

formed the bulk of the population. They belonged to
the ground and were bequeathed with it (BAR, I, 171).
We have no means of determining how large this population
was, although, as we have before stated, it had
reached the sum of seven million by Roman times.
The descendants of the numerous progeny of older
kings, with possible remnants of the prehistoric landed
nobility, had created also a class of land-holding nobles,
whose great estates must have formed a not inconsiderable
fraction of the available lands of the kingdom.
Such lords did not necessarily enter upon an official
career or participate in the administration. But the
nobles and the peasant serfs, as the highest and the
lowest, were not the only classes of society. There was
a free middle class, in whose hands the arts and industries
had reached such a high degree of excellence; but
of these people we know almost nothing. They did
not build imperishable tombs, such as have furnished
us with all that we know of the nobles of the time; and
their business documents, written on papyrus, have all
perished, in spite of the enormous mass of such materials
which must have once existed. Later conditions
would indicate that there undoubtedly was a class
of industrial merchants in the Old Kingdom who produced
and sold their own wares. That there were free
landholders not belonging to the ranks of the nobles is
also highly probable.

76. The social unit was as in later human history,
the family. A man possessed but one legal wife, who
was the mother of his heirs. As constantly depicted
on the monuments, she was in every respect his equal,
was always treated with the greatest consideration, and
participated in the pleasures of her husband and her
children. Such relations had often existed from the

earliest childhood of the pair; for it was customary in all ranks of society for a youth to marry his sister. Besides the legitimate wife, the head of his household, the man of wealth possessed also a harem, the inmates of which maintained no legal claim upon their lord. The children of the time show the greatest respect for their parents, and it was the duty of every son to maintain the tomb of his father. The respect and affection of one's parents and family were highly valued, and we often find in the tombs the statement, "I was one beloved of his father, praised of his mother, whom his brothers and sisters loved" (BAR, I, 357). As among many other peoples, the natural line of inheritance was through the eldest daughter, though a will might disregard this. The closest ties of blood were through the mother, and a man's natural protector, even in preference to his own father, was the father of his mother. The debt of a son to the mother who bore and nourished him, cherished and cared for him while he was being educated, is dwelt upon with emphasis by the wise men of the time. While there was probably a loose form of marriage which might be easily dissolved, a form presumably due to the instability of fortune among the slaves and the poorer class, yet immorality was strongly condemned by the best sentiment. The wise man warns the youth, "Beware of a woman from abroad, who is not known in her city. Look not upon her when she comes, and know her not. She is like the vortex of deep waters, whose whirling is unfathomable. The woman, whose husband is far away, she writes to thee every day. If there is no witness with her she arises and spreads her net. O deadly crime, if one hearkens!" (PB, I, 16, 13 *ff.*; EA, 223). To all youths marriage and the foundation of a household are recommended as the only wise course. Yet there is no doubt that side by side with these wholesome ideals of the wise and virtuous, there also existed widespread and gross immorality.

77. The outward conditions of the lower class were not such as would incline toward moral living. In the towns their low mud-brick, thatch-roofed houses were crowded into groups and masses, so huddled together that the walls were usually contiguous. A rough stool, a rude box or two, and a few crude pottery jars constituted the furniture of such a hovel. The barracks of the workmen were an immense succession of small mud-brick chambers under one roof, with open passages between long lines of such rooms. Whole quarters for the royal levies of workmen were erected on this plan in the pryamid-towns, and near the pyramids. On the great estates the life of the poor was freer, less congested and promiscuous, and undoubtedly more stable and wholesome.

78. The houses of the rich, the noble and official class were large and commodious. Methen, a great noble of the Third Dynasty, built a house over three hundred and thirty feet square (BAR, I, 173). The materials were wood and sun-dried brick, and the construction was light and airy as suited the climate. There were many latticed windows, on all sides the walls of the living rooms were largely a mere skeleton, like those of many Japanese houses. Against winds and sandstorms they could be closed by dropping gaily coloured hangings. Even the palace of the king, though of course fortified, was of this light construction; hence the cities of ancient Egypt have disappeared entirely or left but mounds containing a few scanty fragments of ruined walls. Beds, chairs, stools and

chests of ebony, inlaid with ivory in the finest workmanship, formed the chief articles of furniture. Little or no use was made of tables, but the rich vessels of alabaster and other costly stones, of copper, or sometimes of gold and silver, were placed upon bases and standards which raised them from the floor. The floors were covered with heavy rugs, upon which guests, especially ladies, frequently sat, in preference to the chairs and stools. The food was rich and varied; we find that even the dead desired in the hereafter "ten different kinds of meat, five kinds of poultry, sixteen kinds of bread and cakes, six kinds of wine, four kinds of beer, eleven kinds of fruit, besides all sorts of sweets and many other things" (DG, 18–26; EA, 265).

79. The costume of these ancient lords was simple in the extreme; it consisted merely of a white linen kilt, secured above the hips with a girdle or band, and hanging often hardly to the knees, or again in another style, to the calf of the leg. The head was commonly shaven, and two styles of wig, one short and curly, the other with long straight locks parted in the middle, were worn on all state occasions. A broad collar, often inlaid with costly stones, generally hung from the neck, but otherwise the body was bare from the waist up. With long staff in hand, the gentleman of the day was ready to receive his visitors, or to make a tour of inspection about his estate. His lady and her daughters all appeared in costumes even more simple. They were clothed in a thin, close-fitting, sleeveless, white linen garment hanging from the breast to the ankles, and supported by two bands passing over the shoulders. The skirt, as a modern *modiste* would say, "lacked fulness," and there was barely freedom to walk. A long wig, a collar and necklace, and a pair of bracelets com-

pleted the lady's costume. Neither she nor her lord was fond of sandals, although they now and then wore them. While the adults thus dispensed with all unnecessary clothing, as we should expect in such a climate, the children were allowed to run about without any clothing whatever. The peasant wore merely a breech-clout, which he frequently cast off when at work in the fields; his wife was clad in the same long close-fitting garment worn by the wife of the noble; but she, too, when engaged in heavy work, such as winnowing grain, cast aside all clothing.

80. The Egyptian was passionately fond of nature and of outdoor life. The house of the noble was always surrounded by a garden, in which he loved to plant figs and palms and sycamores, laying out vineyards and arbours, and excavating before the house a pool, lined with masonry coping and filled with fish. A large body of servants and slaves were in attendance, both in house and garden; a chief steward had charge of the entire house and estate, while an upper gardener directed the slaves in the care and culture of the garden. This was the noble's paradise; here he spent his leisure hours with his family and friends, playing at draughts, listening to the music of harp, pipe and lute, watching his women in the slow and stately dance of the time, while his children sported about among the trees, splashed in the pool, or played with ball, doll or jumping-jack. The hunt in the cool shade of the papyrus marshes, or out in the blazing heat of the desert equally attracted him in his leisure hours. In this lighter side of the Egyptian's life, his love of nature, his wholesome and sunny view of life, his never failing cheerfulness in spite of his constant and elaborate preparation for death, and especially his noticeable humour, we find

pervading characteristics of his nature, which are so evident in his art, as to raise it far above the sombre, heaviness that pervades the contemporary art of Asia.

81. Some five centuries of uniform government, with centralized control of the innundation, in the vast system of dykes and irrigation canals, had brought the productivity of the nation to the highest level; for the economic foundation of this civilization in the Old Kingdom, as in all other periods of Egyptian history, was agriculture. It was the enormous harvests of wheat and barley gathered by the Egyptian from the inexhaustible soil of his valley which made possible the social and political structure which we have been sketching. Besides grain, the extensive vineyards and wide fields of succulent vegetables, which formed a part of every estate, greatly augmented the agricultural resources of the land. Large herds of cattle, sheep, goats, droves of donkeys (for the horse was unknown), and vast quantities of poultry, wild fowl, the large game of the desert and innumerable Nile fish, added not inconsiderably to the wealth and prosperity which the land was now enjoying. It was thus in field and pasture that the millions of the kingdom toiled to produce the annual wealth by which its economic processes continued.

82. Other sources of wealth also occupied large numbers of workmen. There were granite quarries at the first cataract, sandstone was quarried at Silsileh, the finer and harder stones chiefly at Hammamat between Coptos and the Red Sea, alabaster at Hatnub behind Amarna, and limestone at many places, particularly at Ayan or Troia opposite Memphis. They brought from the first cataract granite blocks twenty or thirty feet long and fifty or sixty tons in weight.

They drilled the toughest of stone, like diorite, with tubular drills of copper, and the massive lids of granite sarcophagi were sawn with long copper saws which, like the drills, were reënforced by sand or emery. Miners and quarrymen were employed in large numbers during the expeditions to Sinai, for the purpose of procuring copper, the green and blue malachite used in fine inlays, the turquoise and lapis-lazuli. The source of iron, which was already used for tools to a limited extent, is uncertain. Bronze was not yet in use. The smiths furnished tools of copper and iron; bolts, nails, hinges and mountings of all sorts for artisans of all classes; they also wrought fine copper vessels for the tables of the rich, besides splendid copper weapons. They achieved marvels also in the realm of plastic art, as we have yet to see. Silver came from abroad, probably from Cilicia in Asia Minor; it was therefore even more rare and valuable than gold. The quartz-veins of the granite mountains along the Red Sea were rich in gold, and it was taken out in the Wady Foakhir, on the Coptos road. It was likewise mined largely by southern tribes and obtained in trade from Nubia, in the eastern deserts of which it was also found. Of the jewelry worn by the Pharaoh and his nobles, in the Old Kingdom, almost nothing has survived, but the reliefs in the tomb-chapels often depict the goldsmith at his work, and his descendants in the Middle Kingdom have left works which show that the taste and cunning of the First Dynasty had developed without cessation in the Old Kingdom.

83. For the other important industries the Nile valley furnished nearly all materials indispensable to their development. In spite of the ease with which good building stone was procured, enormous quantities of

sun-dried bricks were turned out by the brick-yards, as they still are at the present day, and, as we have seen, the masons erected whole quarters for the poor, villas for the rich, magazines, storehouses, forts and city walls of these cheap and convenient materials. In the forestless valley the chief trees were the date palm, the sycamore, tamarisk and acacia, none of which furnished good timber. Wood was therefore scarce and expensive, but the carpenters, joiners and cabinet-makers flourished nevertheless, and those in the employ of the palace or on the estates of the nobles wrought wonders in the cedar, imported from Syria, and the ebony and ivory which came in from the south. In every town and on every large estate ship-building was constant. There were many different styles of craft from the heavy cargo-boat for grain and cattle, to the gorgeous many-oared "dahabiyeh," of the noble, with its huge sail. We shall find these shipwrights building the earliest known sea-going vessels, on the shores of the Red Sea and the Mediterranean.

84. While the artistic craftsman in stone still produced magnificent vessels, vases, jars, bowls and platters in alabaster, diorite, porphyry and other costly stones, yet his work was gradually giving way to the potter, whose rich blue- and green-glazed fayence vessels could not but win their way. He produced also vast quantities of large coarse jars for the storage of oils, wines, meats and other foods in the magazines of the nobles and the government; while the use of smaller vessels among the millions of the lower classes made the manufacture of pottery one of the chief industries of the country. The pottery of the time is without decoration, and is hardly a work of art. Glass was still chiefly employed as glaze and had not yet been

developed as an independent material. In a land of pastures and herds the production of leather was of course understood. The tanners had thoroughly mastered the art of curing the hides, and produced fine soft skins, which they dyed in all colours, covering stools and chairs, beds and cushions, and furnishing gay canopies and baldachins. Flax was plentifully cultivated, and the Pharaoh's harvest of flax was under the control of a noble of rank (BAR I, 172, 1. 5). The women of the serfs on the great estates were the spinners and weavers. Even the coarser varieties for general use show good quality, but surviving specimens of the *royal* linens are of such exquisite fineness that the ordinary eye requires a glass to distinguish them from silk, and the limbs of the wearer could be discerned through the fabric. Other vegetable fibres furnished by the marshes supported a large industry in coarser textiles. Among these the papyrus was the most beautiful. Broad, light skiffs were made of it by binding together long bundles of these reeds; rope was twisted from them, as also from palm-fibre; sandals were plaited, and mats woven of them; but above all, when split into thin strips, it was possible to join them into sheets of tough paper, the well-known papyrus. That the writing of Egypt spread to Phœnicia and furnished the classic world with an alphabet, is in a measure due to this convenient writing material, as well as to the method of writing upon it with ink (BAR, IV, 562, 582).

85. The Nile was alive with boats, barges, and craft of all descriptions, bearing the products of these industries, and of field and pasture, to the treasury of the Pharaoh, or to the markets where they were disposed of. Here barter was the common means of exchange:

a crude pot for a fish, a bundle of onions for a fan; a wooden box for a jar of ointment. In some transactions, however, presumably those involving larger values, gold and copper in rings of a fixed weight, circulated as money, and stone weights were already marked with their equivalence in such rings. This ring-money is the oldest currency known. Silver was rare and more valuable than gold. Business had already reached a high degree of development; books and accounts were kept; orders and receipts were given; wills and deeds were made; and written contracts covering long periods of time were entered upon. Every noble had his corps of clerks and secretaries, and the exchange of letters and official documents with his colleagues was incessant. Save at Elephantine, these have all perished (PKM, 82 *f.*).

86. Under such circumstances an education in the learning of the time was indispensable to an official career. Connected with the treasury, for whose multifold records so many skilled scribes were necessary, there were schools where lads received the education and the training which fitted them for the scribal offices, and lifted a youth above all other classes in the opinion of the scribe. The content of the instruction, besides innumerable moral precepts, many of them most wholesome and rational, was chiefly the method of writing. The elaborate hieroglyphic with its numerous animal and human figures, such as the reader has often seen on the monuments in our museums, or in works on Egypt, was too slow and laborious a method of writing for the needs of every-day business. The attempt to write these figures rapidly with ink upon papyrus had gradually resulted in reducing each sign to a mere outline, much rounded off and abbreviated. This cursive

business hand, which we call "hieratic," had already begun under the earliest dynasties, and by the rise of the Old Kingdom it had developed into a graceful and rapid system of writing, which showed no nearer resemblance to the hieroglyphic than does our own handwriting to our print. Thus was created for all time the class distinction between the illiterate and the learned, still a problem of modern society. It was the acquirement of this method of writing which enabled the lad to enter upon the coveted official career as a scribe, to become at last overseer of a magazine, or steward of an estate.

87. Education thus consisted solely of the practically useful equipment for an official career. Knowledge of nature and of the external world as a whole was sought only as practical necessity prompted such search. It never occurred to the Egyptian to enter upon the search for truth for its own sake. Under these circumstances the science of the time, if we may speak of it as such at all, was such a knowledge of natural conditions as enabled the active men of this age to accomplish those practical tasks with which they were daily confronted. They had much practical acquaintance with astronomy, developed out of that knowledge which had enabled their ancestors to introduce a rational calendar nearly thirteen centuries before the rise of the Old Kingdom. They had already roughly mapped the heavens, identified the more prominent fixed stars, and developed a system of observation with instruments sufficiently accurate to determine the positions of stars for practical purposes; but they had produced no theory of the heavenly bodies as a whole, nor would it ever have occurred to the Egyptian that such an attempt was useful or worth the trouble. In mathematics all the ordi-

nary arithmetical processes were demanded in the daily transactions of business and government, and had long since come into common use among the scribes. Fractions, however, caused difficulty. The scribes could operate only with those having *one* as the numerator, and all other fractions were of necessity resolved into a series of several, each with *one* as the numerator. The only exception was two-thirds. Elementary algebraic problems were also solved without difficulty. In geometry they were able to master the simpler propositions; while the area of a trapezoid caused difficulty and error, that of the circle had been determined with close accuracy. The necessity of determining the content of a pile of grain had led to a roughly approximate result in the computation of the content of the hemisphere, and a circular granary to that of the cylinder. But no theoretical or abstract propositions were discussed, and the whole science attempted only those practical problems which were continually met in daily life. The laying out of a ground-plan like the square base of the Great Pyramid could be accomplished with amazing accuracy, and the orientation displays a nicety that almost rivals the results of modern instruments. A highly developed knowledge of mechanics was at the command of the architect and craftsman. The arch was employed in masonry, and can be dated as far back as the thirtieth century B. C., the oldest dated arches known. In the application of power to the movement of great monuments only the simplest devices were employed; the pulley was unknown, and probably the roller also. Medicine was already in possession of much empirical wisdom, displaying close and accurate observation; the calling of the physician already existed, and the court physician of the Pharaoh was a man of rank and influence. His recipes were many of them rational and useful; but more were naïvely fanciful, like the prescription of a decoction of the hair of a black calf to prevent gray hair. Most depended upon magic for their efficacy, because disease was due to hostile spirits. They had already been collected and recorded in papyrus rolls (BAR, I, 246), and the recipes of this age were famous for their virtue in later times. Some of them finally crossed with the Greeks to Europe, where they are still in use among the peasantry of the present day.

88. Art flourished as nowhere else in the ancient world. Here again the Egyptian's attitude of mind was not wholly that which characterized the art of the later Greek world. Art as the pursuit and the production exclusively of the ideally beautiful was unknown to him. He loved beauty as found in nature, his spirit demanded such beauty in his home and surroundings. The lotus blossomed on the handle of his spoon, and his wine sparkled in the deep blue calyx of the same flower; the muscular limb of the ox in carved ivory upheld the couch upon which he slept, the ceiling over his head was a starry heaven resting upon palm trunk columns, each crowned with its graceful tuft of drooping foliage; or papyrus stalks rose from the floor to support the azure roof upon their swaying blossoms; doves and butterflies flitted across his in-door sky; his floors were frescoed with the opulent green of rich marsh-grasses, with fish gliding among their roots, where the wild ox tossed his head at the birds twittering on the swaying grass-tops, as they strove in vain to drive away the stealthy weasel creeping up to plunder their nests. Everywhere the objects of every-day life in the homes of the rich showed unconscious beauty of

line and fine balance of proportion, while the beauty of nature and of out-of-door life which spoke to the beholder in the decoration on every hand, lent a certain distinction even to the most commonplace objects. The Egyptian thus sought to beautify and to make beautiful all objects of utility, but all such objects served some practical use. He was not inclined to make a beautiful thing solely for its beauty. In sculpture, therefore, the practical dominated. The splendid statues of the Old Kingdom were not made to be erected in the market-place, but solely to be masoned up in the mastaba tomb, that they might be of practical advantage to the deceased in the hereafter (Sect. 63). It was this motive chiefly to which the marvellous development of portrait sculpture in the Old Kingdom was due.

89. The sculptor might either put his model into stone by a process of exactly imitating his every feature, or again depict him in accordance with a conventional ideal. Both styles, representing the same man, though strikingly different, may appear in the same tomb. Every device was adopted to increase the resemblance to life. The whole statue was coloured in the natural hues, the eyes were inlaid in rock-crystal, and the life likeness with which these Memphite sculptures were instinct has never been surpassed. The finest of the sitting statues is the well-known portrait of Khafre, the builder of the second pyramid of Gizeh. In the most difficult stone, like diorite, the sculptor skilfully met the limitations imposed upon him by the intensely hard and refractory material, and while obliged, therefore, to treat the subject summarily, he slightly emphasized salient features, lest the work should lack pronounced character. These unknown

masters, who must take their place among the world's great sculptors, while contending with technical difficulties which no modern sculptor attempts, were even more successful in softer material, like limestone, where they gained a freer hand, although the number of postures was strictly limited by convention. In copper the sculptors of Pepi I even produced a life-size statue of the king, the head of which is one of the strongest portraits surviving from antiquity (BH, 104, Figs. 53–54). Superb animal forms, like the granite lion's head from the sun-temple of Nuserre were also wrought in the hardest stone.

The goldsmith also invaded the realm of plastic art. In the "gold-house," as his workshop was called, he turned sculptor, and produced for the temples such cultus statues of the gods as the magnificent figure of the sacred hawk of Hieraconpolis, of which Quibell found the head in the temple at that place.

90. In relief, now greatly in demand for temple decoration, and the chapel of the mastaba tomb, the Egyptian was confronted by the problem of foreshortening and perspective. He must put objects having thickness and roundness upon a flat surface. How this should be done had been determined for him before the beginning of the Old Kingdom. A conventional style had already been established before the Third Dynasty, and that style was now sacred and inviolable tradition. While a certain freedom of development survived, that style in its fundamentals persisted throughout the history of Egyptian art, even after the artist had learned to perceive its shortcomings. The age which produced it had not learned to maintain one stand-point in the drawing of any given scene or object; two different points of view were combined in the same

figure: in drawing a man a front view of the eyes and shoulders was regularly placed upon a profile of the trunk and head. This unconscious incongruity was afterward also extended to temporal relations, and successive instants of time were combined in the same scene. Accepting these limitations, the reliefs of the Old Kingdom, which are really slightly modelled drawings, are often sculptures of great beauty, especially in their exquisite modelling. It is from the scenes which the Memphite sculptor placed on the walls of the mastaba chapels that we learn all that we know of the life and customs of the Old Kingdom. All such reliefs were coloured, so that when completed we may call them raised and modelled paintings; at least they do not fall within the domain of plastic art, as do Greek reliefs. Painting was also practiced independently, and the familiar line of ducks from a tomb at Medum (BH, Fig. 55) well illustrates the strength and freedom with which the Memphite of the time could depict the animal forms with which he was familiar.

91. The sculpture of the Old Kingdom may be characterized as a natural and unconscious realism, exercised with a technical ability of the highest order. In the practice of this art the sculptor of the Old Kingdom in some respects compares favourably even with modern artists. He was the only artist in the early Orient who could put the human body into stone, and living in a society such that he was daily familiarized with the nude form, he treated it with sincerity and frankness. I cannot forbear quoting the words of an unprejudiced classical archæologist, M. Georges Perrot, who says of the Memphite sculptors of the Old Kingdom, "It must be acknowledged that they produced works which are not to be surpassed in their way by the great-

est portraits of modern Europe" (PCHA, II, 194). The sculpture of the Old Kingdom, however, was superficial; it was not interpretative, did not embody ideas in stone and shows little contemplation of the emotions and forces of life. It is characteristic of the age that we must speak of this Memphite art as a whole. We know none of its greatest masters, and only the names of an artist or two during the whole period of Egyptian history.

92. It is only very recently that we have been able to discern the fundamentals of Old Kingdom architecture. Too little has been preserved of the house and palace of the time to permit of safe generalizations upon the light and airy style of architecture which they represent. It is only the massive stone structures of this age which have been preserved. Besides the mastabas and pyramids, which we have already briefly noticed, the temple is the great architectural achievement of the Old Kingdom. Its arrangement has been touched upon in the preceding chapter. The architect employed only straight lines, these being perpendiculars and horizontals, very boldly and felicitously combined. The arch, although known, was not employed as a member in architecture. In order to carry the roof across the void, either the simplest of stone piers, a square pillar of a single block of granite was employed, or an already elaborate and beautiful monolithic column of granite supported the architrave. These columns, the earliest known in the history of architecture, may have been employed before the Old Kingdom, for they are fully developed in the Fifth Dynasty. They represent a palm-tree, the capital being the crown of foliage; or they are conceived as a bundle of papyrus stalks, bearing the architrave upon the cluster of buds at the

top, which form the capital. The proportions are graceful and elegant, and surrounded with such exquisite colonnades as these, flanked by brightly coloured reliefs, the courts of the Old Kingdom temples belong to the noblest architectural conceptions bequeathed to us by antiquity. Egypt thus became the source of columned architecture. While the Babylonian builders displayed notable skill in giving varied architectural effect to great masses, they were limited to this, and the colonnade was unknown to them; whereas the Egyptian already at the close of the fourth millennium before Christ had solved the fundamental problem of great architecture, developing with the most refined artistic sense and the greatest mechanical skill the treatment of *voids* (as opposed to the *masses* of the Babylonian), and thus originating the colonnade.

93. The age was dealing with material things and developing material resources, and in such an age literature has little opportunity; it was indeed hardly born as yet. The sages of the court, the wise old viziers, Kegemne, Imhotep, and Ptahhotep, had put into proverbs the wholesome wisdom of life, which a long career had taught them, and these were probably already circulating in written form, although the oldest manuscript of such lore which we possess dates from the Middle Kingdom. The Palermo Stone (see p. 47) was but a bald catalogue of events, achievements and temple donations, without literary form. It is the oldest surviving fragment of royal annals. As the desire to perpetuate the story of a distinguished life increased, the nobles began to record in their tombs simple narratives characterized by a primitive directness, in long successions of simple sentences, each showing the same construction, but lacking expressed

connectives (BAR, I, 292–294; 306–315; 319–324). Events and honours common to the lives of the leading nobles were related by them all in identical words, so that conventional phrases had already gained a place in literature not unlike the inviolable canons of their graphic art. There is no individuality. The mortuary texts in the pyramids display sometimes a rude force, and an almost savage fire. They contain scattered fragments of the old myths, but whether these had then enjoyed more than an oral existence we do not know. Mutilated religious poems, exhibiting in form the beginnings of parallelism, are imbedded in this literature, and are doubtless examples of the oldest poetry of earliest Egypt. All this literature, both in form and content, betrays its origin among men of the early world. Folk songs, the offspring of the toiling peasant's flitting fancy, or of the personal devotion of the household servant, were common then as now, and in two of them which have survived we hear the shepherd talking with the sheep, or the bearers of the sedan-chair assuring their lord in song that to *them* the vehicle is lighter when he occupies it than when it is empty (BH, p. 92, Fig. 39; DDG, II, pl. viii). Music also was cultivated; and there was a director of the royal music at the court. The instruments were a small harp, on which the performer played sitting, and two kinds of flute, a large and a smaller. Instrumental music was always accompanied by the voice, reversing modern custom, and the full orchestra consisted of two harps and two flutes, a large and a small one. Of the character and nature of the music played or to what extent the scale was understood, we can say nothing.

Such, in so far as we have been able to condense our

present knowledge, was the active and aggressive age which unfolds before us, as the kings of the Thinite dynasties give way to those of Memphis. It now remains for us to trace the career of this, the most ancient state, whose constitution is still discernible.

VI

THE PYRAMID BUILDERS

94. At the close of the so-called Second Dynasty, early in the thirtieth century B. C., the Thinites, according to Manetho, were finally dislodged from the position of power which they had maintained so well for over four centuries, and a Memphite family, whose home was the "White Wall," gained the ascendancy. But there is evidence that the sharp dynastic division recorded by Manetho never took place, and this final supremacy of Memphis may have been nothing more than a gradual transition thither by the Thinites themselves. In any case the great queen, Nemathap, the wife of King Khasekhemui, who was probably the last king of the Second Dynasty, was evidently the mother of Zoser, with whose accession the predominance of Memphis becomes apparent. During this Memphite supremacy, the development which the Thinites had pushed so vigorously, was skilfully and ably fostered. For over five hundred years the kingdom continued to flourish, but of these five centuries only the last two have left us even scanty literary remains, and we are obliged to draw our meagre knowledge of its first three centuries almost entirely from material documents, the monuments which it has left us. In some degree such a task is like attempting to reconstruct a history of Athens in the age of Pericles, based entirely upon the

temples, sculptures, vases, and other material remains surviving from his time. While the multifold life which was then unfolding in Athens involved a mental endowment and a condition of state and society which Egypt, even at her best, never knew, yet it must not be forgotten that, tremendous as is the impression which we receive from the monuments of the Old Kingdom, they are but the skeleton, upon which we might put flesh, and endue the whole with life, if but the chief literary monuments of the time had survived. It is a difficult task to discern behind these Titanic achievements the busy world of commerce, industry, administration, society, art, and literature out of which they grew. Of half a millennium of political change, of overthrow and usurpation, of growth and decay of institutions, of local governors, helpless under the strong grasp of the Pharaoh, or shaking off the restraint of a weak monarch, and developing into independent barons, so powerful at last as to bring in the final dissolution of the state —of all this we gain but fleeting and occasional glimpses, where more must be guessed than can be known.

95. The first prominent figure in the Old Kingdom is that of Zoser, with whom, as we have said, the Third Dynasty arose. It was evidently his strong hand which firmly established Memphite supremacy. He continued the exploitation of the copper mines in Sinai, while in the south he extended his power in some form of control over the turbulent Nubian tribes, just beyond the first cataract, if we may credit a late tradition of the priests (SU, II, 22–26). The success of Zoser's efforts was perhaps in part due to the counsel of the great wise man, Imhotep, who was one of his chief advisers. In priestly wisdom, in magic, in the formulation of wise proverbs, in medicine and architecture, this

remarkable figure of Zoser's reign left so notable a reputation that his name was never forgotten, and two thousand five hundred years after his death he had become a god of medicine, in whom the Greeks, who called him Imouthes, recognized their own Asklepios (SU, II). Manetho records the tradition that stone building was first introduced by Zoser, whom he calls Tosorthros, and although, as we have seen, stone structures of earlier date are now known, yet the great reputation as a builder ascribed to Zoser's counsellor, Imhotep, is no accident, and it is evident that Zoser's reign marked the beginning of extensive building in stone. Until his reign the royal tombs were built of sun-dried bricks, only containing in one instance a granite floor and in another a chamber of limestone. This brick tomb was greatly improved by Zoser, who built at Bet Khallâf, near Abydos, an elaborate brick mastaba, the first of the two tombs now customarily erected by the Pharaoh (infra, p. 72; GMBK). Doubtless assisted by Imhotep, he undertook the construction of a royal mausoleum on a more ambitious plan than any of his ancestors had ever attempted. In the desert behind Memphis he laid out a large mastaba of stone, which he enlarged into a tall terraced monument one hundred and ninety feet high, by superimposing five successively smaller mastabas upon it. It is often called the "terraced pyramid," and does indeed constitute the transitional form between the mastaba, first built in Zoser's time at Bet Khallâf, and the pyramid of his successors, which immediately followed. It is the first large structure of stone known in history.

96. The wealth and power evident in Zoser's costly and imposing tomb were continued by the other kings of the dynasty, whose order and history it is as yet im-

possible to reconstruct. It is probable that we should attribute to one of them the great blunted stone pryamid of Dahshur, and if this conclusion be correct, such a monument is a striking testimony to the wealth and power of this Third Dynasty. At the close of the dynasty the nation was enjoying wide prosperity under the vigorous and far-seeing Snefru. He built vessels nearly one hundred and seventy feet long, for traffic and administration upon the river; he continued the development of the copper mines in Sinai, where he defeated the native tribes and left a record of his triumph (BAR, I, 146–147, 168–169). He placed Egyptian interests in the peninsula upon such a permanent basis that he was later looked upon as the founder and establisher of Egyptian supremacy there, and he became a patron god of the district (LD, II, 137g; BAR, I, 722, 731). He regulated the eastern frontier, and it is not unlikely that we should attribute to him the erection of the fortresses at the Bitter Lakes in the Isthmus of Suez, which existed already in the Fifth Dynasty. Roads and stations in the eastern Delta still bore his name fifteen hundred years after his death. In the west it is not improbable that he already controlled one of the northern oases. More than all this, he opened up commerce with the north and sent a fleet of forty vessels to the Phœnician coast to procure cedar logs from the slopes of Lebanon. This is the earliest known naval expedition on the open sea. He was equally aggressive in the south, where he conducted a campaign against northern Nubia, bringing back seven thousand prisoners, and two hundred thousand large and small cattle (BAR, I, 165, 5; 312, l. 21; 174, l. 9; 146).

97. The first of the two tombs built by Snefru is

situated at Medûm, between Memphis and the Fayum. Erected as a terraced monument, like that of Zoser, its terraces were finally filled out in one smooth slope from top to bottom at a different angle, thus producing the first pyramid. Like Zoser, Snefru's first tomb was much less pretentious than his second, the great stone pyramid which he built at Dahshûr, nearer Memphis. Three hundred years later we still find its town and priesthood exempt by royal decree from all state dues and levies (AZ, 42, 1 *ff.*).

98. With Snefru the rising tide of prosperity and power has reached the high level which made the subsequent splendour of the Old Kingdom possible. With him there had also grown up the rich and powerful noble and official class, whose life we have already sketched—a class who are no longer content with the simple brick tombs of their ancestors at Abydos and vicinity. Their splendid mastabas of hewn limestone are still grouped as formerly about the tomb of the king whom they served. It is the surviving remains in these imposing cities of the dead, dominated by the towering mass of the pyramid, which has enabled us to gain a picture of the life of the great kingdom, the threshold of which we have now crossed. Behind us lies the long slow development which contained the promise of all that is before us; but that development also we were obliged to trace in the tomb of the early Egyptian, as we have followed him from the sand-heap that covered his primitive ancestor to the colossal pyramid of the Pharaoh.

99. The passing of the great family of which Snefru was the most prominent representative did not, as far as we can now see, effect any serious change in the history of the nation. Indeed Khufu, the founder of

the so-called Fourth Dynasty, may possibly have been a scion of the Third. There was in his harem at least a lady who had also been a favourite of Snefru. Khufu, however, was not a Memphite. He came from a town of middle Egypt near modern Benihasan, which was afterward, for this reason, called "Menat-Khufu," "Nurse of Khufu." We have no means of knowing how the noble of a provincial town succeeded in supplanting the line of the powerful Snefru and becoming the founder of a new line. We only see him looming grandly from the obscure array of Pharaohs of his time, his greatness proclaimed by the noble tomb which he erected at Gizeh, opposite modern Cairo. How strong and effective must have been the organization of Khufu's government we appreciate in some measure when we learn that his pyramid contains some two million three hundred thousand blocks, each weighing on the average two and a half tons (PG). Herodotus relates a tradition current in his time that the pyramid had demanded the labour of a hundred thousand men during twenty years, and Petrie has shown that these numbers are quite credible. The maintenance of this city of a hundred thousand labourers, who were non-producing and a constant burden on the state, the adjustment of the labour in the quarries, so as to ensure an uninterrupted accession of material around the base of the pyramid, will have entailed the development of a small state in itself. Not merely was this work quantitatively so formidable, but in quality also it is the most remarkable material enterprise known to us anywhere in this early world, for the most ponderous masonry in the pyramid amazes the modern beholder by its fineness. The pyramid is, or was, about four hundred and eighty-one feet high, and its square base, covering some thirteen acres, measured seven hundred and fifty-five feet on a side, but the average error is "less than a ten-thousandth of the side in equality, in squareness and in level" (PHE, I, 40); although a rise of ground on the site of the monument prevented direct measurements from corner to corner. Some of the masonry finish is so fine that blocks weighing many tons are set together with seams of considerable length, showing a joint of one ten-thousandth of an inch, and involving edges and surfaces "equal to optician's work of the present day, but on a scale of acres instead of feet or yards of material" (*ibid.*). The entire monument is of limestone, except the main sepulchral chamber, which is of granite. The passages were skilfully closed at successive places by plug-blocks and portcullisses of granite; while the exterior, clothed with an exquisitely fitted casing of limestone, which has since been quarried away, nowhere betrayed the place of entrance, located in the eighteenth course of masonry above the base near the centre of the north face. Three small pyramids, built for members of Khufu's family stand in a line close by on the south. The pyramid was surrounded by a wide pavement of limestone, and on the east front was the temple for the mortuary service of Khufu, of which all but portions of a splendid basalt pavement has disappeared. The remains of the causeway leading up from the plain to the temple still rise in sombre ruin, disclosing only the rough core masonry, across which the modern village of Kafr is now built. Further south is a section of the wall which surrounded the town on the plain below, probably the place of Khufu's residence, and perhaps the residence of the dynasty. In leaving the tomb of Khufu our admiration for the monument, whether stirred by its vast dimensions or by the fineness of its masonry, should not obscure its real and final significance; for the great pyramid is the earliest and most impressive witness surviving from the ancient world, to the final emergence of organized society from prehistoric chaos and local conflict, thus coming for the first time completely under the power of a far-reaching and comprehensive centralization effected by one controlling mind.

100. Khufu's name has been found from Desuk in the northwestern and Bubastis in the eastern Delta, to Hieraconpolis in the south, but we know almost nothing of his other achievements. He continued operations in the peninsula of Sinai (BAR, I, 176); perhaps opened for the first time, and in any case kept workmen in the alabaster quarry of Hatnub; and Ptolemaic tradition also made him the builder of a Hathor temple at Dendereh (DD, p. 15). But we know nothing further of his great and prosperous reign.

101. It is uncertain whether his successor, Khafre, was his son or not. But the new king's name, which means "His Shining is Re," would indicate the political influence of the priests of Re at Heliopolis. He built a pyramid beside that of Khufu, but it is somewhat smaller and distinctly inferior in workmanship. Scanty remains of the pyramid-temple on the east side are still in place, from which the usual causeway leads down to the margin of the plateau and terminates in a splendid granite building, which served as the gateway to the causeway and the pyramid enclosure above. This imposing entrance stands beside the Great Sphinx, and is still usually termed the "temple of the sphinx," with which it had, however, nothing to do. Whether the sphinx itself is the work of Khafre is not yet deter-

mined. The Great Sphinx, like other Egyptian sphinxes, is the portrait of a Pharaoh, and an obscure reference to Khafre in an inscription between its forepaws, dated fourteen hundred years later in the reign of Thutmose IV, perhaps shows that in those times he was considered to have had something to do with it (BAR, II, 815). Beyond these buildings we know nothing of Khafre's deeds, but these show clearly that the great state which Khufu had done so much to create was still firmly controlled by the Pharaoh.

102. Under Khafre's successor, Menkure, however, if the size of the royal pyramid is an adequate basis for judgment, the power of the royal house was no longer so absolute. The third pyramid of Gizeh, which we owe to him, is less than half as high as those of Khufu and Khafre; its ruined temple, recently excavated by Reisner, was evidently unfinished at his death, and his successor put in only sun-dried brick instead of the granite facing it was intended to receive. Besides this, the causeway, still submerged in sand, and three small pyramids of Menkure's family, are all that remains of his splendour. Of his immediate successors we possess contemporary monuments only from the reign of Shepseskaf. Although we have a record that he selected the site for his pyramid in his first year (BAR, I, 151), he was unable to erect a monument sufficiently large and durable to survive, and we do not even know where it was located; while of the achievements of this whole group of kings at the close of the Fourth Dynasty, including several interlopers, who may now have assumed the throne for a brief time, we know nothing whatever.

103. The cause of the fall of the Fourth Dynasty, while not clear in the details, is in the main outlines

tolerably certain. The priests of Re at Heliopolis, whose influence is also evident in the names of the kings following Khufu, had succeeded in organizing their political influence, becoming a party of sufficient power to overthrow the old line. The state theology had always represented the king as the successor of the sun-god, and he had borne the title "Horus," a sun-god, from the beginning; but the priests of Heliopolis now demanded that he be the bodily son of Re, who henceforth would appear on earth to become the father of the Pharaoh. A folk-tale (PW), of which we have a copy, some nine hundred years later than the fall of the Fourth Dynasty, relates how Khufu, while enjoying an idle hour with his sons, learned from an ancient wiseman that the three children soon to be borne by the wife of a certain priest of Re were begotten of Re himself, and that they should all become kings of Egypt. The names given these children by the disguised divinities who assisted at their birth were: Userkaf, Sahure and Kakai, the names of the first three kings of the Fifth Dynasty. In this folk-tale we have the popular form of what is now the state fiction: every Pharaoh is the bodily son of the sun-god, a belief which was thereafter maintained throughout the history of Egypt (BAR, II, 187–212).

104. The kings of the Fifth Dynasty, who continued to reside in the vicinity of Memphis, began to rule about 2750 B. C. They show plain traces of the origin ascribed to them by the popular tradition; the official name which they assume at the coronation must invariably contain the name of Re. Before this name must now be placed a new title, "Son of Re." Besides the old "Horus" title and another new title representing the Horus-hawk trampling upon the

symbol of Set, this new designation "Son of Re" was the fifth title peculiar to the Pharaohs, later producing the complete Pharaonic titulary as it remained throughout their history. Their adherence to the cult of Re as the state religion *par excellence* found immediate and practical expression in the most splendid form. By the royal residence near later Memphis each king erected a magnificent temple to the sun, each bearing a name like "Favourite Place of Re," or "Satisfaction of Re," and having in place of a holy of holies at the rear an enclosure in which rose a tall obelisk exposed to the sky. On either side of the sanctuary on a brick foundation were set up two ships representing the two celestial barques of the sun-god, as he sailed the heavens morning and evening. The sanctuary was richly endowed and its service was maintained by a corps of priests (BAR, I, 159, 8). in whose titles we can follow these temples, one for each king, at least into the reign of Isesi, the eighth monarch of the line (FE, p. 13). Enjoying wealth and distinction such as had been possessed by no official god of earlier times, Re gained a position of influence which he never again lost. Through him the forms of the Egyptian state began to pass over into the world of the gods, and the myths from now on were dominated and strongly coloured by him, if indeed some of them did not owe their origin to the exalted place which Re now occupied. In the sun-myth he became king of Upper and Lower Egypt and, like a Pharaoh, he had ruled Egypt with Thoth as his vizier.

105. The change in the royal line is also evident in the organization of the government. The eldest son of the king is no longer the most powerful officer in the state, but the position which he held in the Fourth Dynasty as vizier and chief judge is now the preroga-

tive of another family, with whom it remains hereditary. Each incumbent, through five generations, bore the name Ptahhotep. This hereditary succession, so striking in the highest office of the central government, was now common in the nomes also, and the local governors were each gaining stronger and stronger foothold in his nome as the generations passed, and son succeeded father in the same nome (BAR, I, 213 *ff.*).

106. While Userkaf, as the founder of the new dynasty, may have had enough to do to make secure the succession of his line, he has left his names on the rocks at the first cataract, the earliest of the long series of rock-inscriptions there, which from now on will furnish us many hints of the career of the Pharaohs in the south (MMD, 54 e). Sahure, who followed Userkaf, continued the development of Egypt as the earliest known naval power in history. He dispatched a fleet against the Phœnician coast, and a relief just discovered in his pyramid-temple at Abusir shows four of the ships, with Phœnician captives among the Egyptian sailors. This is the earliest surviving representation of sea-going ships (c. 2750 B. C.), and the oldest known picture of Semitic Syrians. Another fleet was sent by Sahure to still remoter waters, on a voyage to Punt, the Somali coast at the south end of the Red Sea, and along the south side of the gulf of Aden. From this region, which, like the whole east, was termed the "God's-Land," were obtained the fragrant gums and resins so much desired for the incense and ointments indispensable in the life of the Oriental. Intercourse with this country had been carried on for centuries (BAR, II, 247), but Sahure was the first Pharaoh of whom the monuments record the dispatch of a special expedition thither. This ex-

pedition brought back 80,000 measures of myrrh, probably 6,000 weight of electrum (gold-silver alloy), besides 2,600 staves of some costly wood, presumably ebony (BAR, I, 161, 8). We find his officials at the first cataract also, one of whom left the *earliest* of the long series of inscriptions on the rocks there (MCM, I, 88), while an expedition to Sinai returned richly laden (BAR, I, 161, 7; 236).

107. We can only discern enough of the next four reigns to gain faint impressions of a powerful and cultured state, conserving all its internal wealth and reaching out to distant regions around it for the materials which its own natural resources do not furnish. Toward the end of the dynasty, in the second half of the twenty-seventh century B. C., Isesi opened the quarries of the Wadi Hammamat in the eastern desert, three days' journey from the Nile, and two days from the Red Sea port, from which the Isesi's fleet sailed for Punt on the second voyage thither known to us (BAR, I, 351, 353). His successor, Unis, must have been active in the south, for we find his name at the frontier of the first cataract, followed by the epithet "lord of countries" (PS. xii, No. 312).

108. Under Isesi we perceive more clearly the rising power of the officials, who from now on never fail to make themselves increasingly prominent in all records of the royal achievements (BAR, I, 264, 266). It is a power with which the Pharaoh will find more and more difficulty in dealing as time passes. There is now perhaps another evidence of declining power in the comparatively diminutive size and poorer workmanship of the Fifth Dynasty pyramids, ranged along the desert margin south of Gizeh, at Abusir and Sakkara. The centralized power of the earlier Pharaohs was thus

visibly weakening, and it was indeed in every way desirable that there should be a reaction against the totally abnormal absorption by the Pharaoh's tomb of such a large proportion of the national wealth.

109. The transitional period of the Fifth Dynasty, lasting probably a century and a quarter, during which nine kings reigned, was therefore one of significant political development, and in material civilization one of distinct progress. Architecture passed from the massive, unadorned, rectangular granite pillars of the Fourth Dynasty at Gizeh to the graceful papyrus and palm-crowned columns and colonnades of the sun- and pyramid-temples at Abusir. Art thus flourished as before, and great works of Egyptian sculpture were produced; while in literature Ptahhotep, King Isesi's vizier and chief judge composed his proverbial wisdom, which we have already discussed. The state religion received a form worthy of so great a nation, the temples throughout the land enjoyed constant attention, and the larger sanctuaries were given endowments commensurate with the more elaborate daily offerings on the king's behalf (BAR, I, 154–167). It is this period which has preserved our first religious literature of any extent, as well as our earliest lengthy example of the Egyptian language. In the pyramid of Unis, the last king of the dynasty, is recorded the collection of mortuary ritualistic utterances, the so-called Pyramid Texts which we have before discussed (p. 68). As most of them belong to a still earlier age, and some of them originated in predynastic times, they represent a much earlier form of language and belief than those of the generation to which the pyramid of Unis belongs.

VII

THE SIXTH DYNASTY: THE DECLINE OF THE OLD KINGDOM

110. IN the fullest of the royal lists, the Turin Papyrus, there is no indication that the line of Menes was interrupted until the close of the reign of Unis. That a new dynasty arose at this point there can be no doubt. As the reader has probably already perceived (sect. 105), the movement which brought in this new dynasty was due to a struggle of the local governors for a larger degree of power and liberty. The establishment of the Fifth Dynasty by the influence of the Heliopolitan party had given them the opportunity they desired. They gained hereditary hold upon their offices, and the kings of that family had never been able to regain the complete control over them maintained by the Fourth Dynasty. Gradually the local governors had then shaken off the restraint of the Pharaoh; and when about 2625 B. C., after the reign of Unis, they succeeded in overthrowing the Fifth Dynasty, they became landed barons, each firmly entrenched in his nome, or city, and maintaining an hereditary claim upon it. The old title of "local governor" disappeared as a matter of course, and the men who had once borne it now called themselves "great chief" or "great lord" of this or that nome. They continued the local government as before, but as princes with a large degree of indepen-

dence, not as officials of the central government. We have here the first example traceable in history of the dissolution of a centralized state by a process of aggrandizement on the part of local officials of the crown, like that which resolved the Carlovingian empire into duchies, landgraviates, or petty principalities. The new lords were not able to render their tenure unconditionally hereditary, but here the monarch still maintained a powerful hold upon them; for at the death of a noble his position, his fief and his title must be conferred upon the inheriting son by the gracious favour of the Pharaoh. These nomarchs or "great lords" are loyal adherents of the Pharaoh, executing his commissions in distant regions, and displaying the greatest zeal in his cause; but they are no longer his officials merely; nor are they so attached to the court and person of the monarch as to build their tombs around his pyramid. They now have sufficient independence and local attachment to erect their tombs near their homes. They devote much attention to the development and prosperity of their great domains, and one of them even tells how he brought in emigrants from neighbouring nomes to settle in the feebler towns and infuse new blood into the less productive districts of his own nome (BAR, I, 281).

111. The chief administrative bond which united the nomes to the central government of the Pharaoh will have been the treasury as before; but the Pharaoh found it necessary to exert general control over the great group of fiefs which now comprised his kingdom, and already toward the end of the Fifth Dynasty he had therefore appointed over the whole of the valley above the Delta a "governor of the South," through whom he was able constantly to exert governmental

pressure upon the southern nobles; there seems to have been no corresponding "governor of the North," and we may infer that the lords of the North were less aggressive. Moreover, the kings still feel themselves to be kings of the South governing the North.

112. The seat of government, the chief royal residence, was, as before, in the vicinity of Memphis, still called the "White Wall"; but after the obscure reign of Teti II, and possibly Userkere, the first two kings of the new dynasty, the pyramid-city of his successor, the powerful Pepi I, was so close to the "White Wall" that the name of his pyramid, "Men-nofer," corrupted by the Greeks to Memphis, rapidly passed to the city, and "White Wall" survived only as an archaic and poetic designation of the place. The administration of the residence had become a matter of sufficient importance to demand the attention of the vizier himself. He henceforth assumed its immediate control, receiving the title "governor of the pyramid-city" or "governor of the city" merely, for it now became customary to speak of the residence as the "city." Notwithstanding thorough-going changes, the new dynasty continued the official cult maintained by their predecessors. Re remained supreme, and the old foundations were respected.

113. In spite of the independence of the new nobles, it is evident that Pepi I possessed the necessary force to hold them well in hand. His monuments, large and small, are found throughout Egypt. Now began also the biographies of the officials of the time, affording us a picture of the busy life of the self-satisfied magnates of that distant age; while to these we may fortunately add also the records at the mines and in the quarries. Loyalty now demands no more than a relief showing

the king as he worships his gods or smites his enemies; and this done, the vanity of the commander of the expedition and his fellows may be gratified in a record of their deeds or adventures, which becomes longer and longer as time passes. In the quarries of Hammamat and Hatnub, as well as in Wady Maghara in Sinai the officials of Pepi I have left their records with full lists of their names and titles (BAR, I, 295-301; 304-305; 302-303). We have a very interesting and instructive example of this official class under the new régime in Uni, a faithful adherent of the royal house, who has fortunately left us his biography. Under king Teti II he had begun his career at the bottom as an obscure under-custodian in the royal domains. Pepi I now appointed him as a judge, at the same time giving him rank at the royal court, and an income as a priest of the pyramid-temple. He was soon promoted to a superior custodianship of the royal domains, and in this capacity he had so gained the royal favour that when a conspiracy against the king arose in the harem he was nominated with one colleague to prosecute the case. Pepi I thus strove to single out men of force and ability with whom he might organize a strong government, closely attached to his fortunes and to those of his house. In the heart of the southern country he set up among the nobles the "great lord of the Hare-nome," and made him governor of the South; while he married as his official queens the two sisters of the nomarch of Thinis, both bearing the same name, Enekhnes-Merire, and they became the mothers of the two kings who followed him (BAR, I, 294, 307, 310, 344-349).

114. The foreign policy of Pepi I was more vigorous than that of any Pharaoh of earlier times. In Nubia

THE DECLINE OF THE OLD KINGDOM

he gained such control over the negro tribes that they were obliged to contribute quotas to his army in case of war. When such war was in the north, where safety permitted these negro levies were freely employed, and in Egypt they formed a regular contingent of gensdarmes in state service (AZ, 42, 1 *ff.*). The Beduin tribes of the north, having become too bold in their raiding of the eastern Delta, or having troubled his mining expeditions in Sinai, Pepi commissioned Uni to collect such an army among the negroes, supplemented by levies throughout Egypt. On five successive punitive expeditions Pepi I sent him against the tribes of this country; while a sixth carried him in troop-ships along the coast of Palestine, to punish the Asiatics as far north as the highlands of Palestine, and Phœnicia, a naval expedition like that of Sahure some two centuries earlier (sect. 106). The naïve account of these wars left by Uni in his biography is one of the most characteristic evidences of the totally unwarlike spirit of the early Egyptian (BAR, I, 311–315).

115. Having thus firmly established his family at the head of the state, the fact that Pepi I's death, after a reign of probably twenty years, left his son, Mernere, to administer the kingdom as a mere youth, seems not in the least to have shaken its fortunes. Mernere immediately appointed Uni, the old servant of his house, as governor of the South, under whose trusty guidance all went well (BAR, I, 320). The powerful nobles of the southern frontier were also zealous in their support of the young king. They were a family of bold and adventurous barons, living on the island of Elephantine, just below the first cataract. The valley at the cataract was now called the "Door of the South," and its defense against the turbulent tribes of northern Nubia

was placed in their hands, so that the head of the family bore the title "Keeper of the Door of the South." They made the place so safe that when the king dispatched Uni to the granite quarries at the head of the cataract to procure the sarcophagus and the finer fittings for his pyramid, the noble was able to accomplish his errand with "only one war-ship," an unprecedented feat (BAR, I, 322). The enterprising young monarch then commissioned Uni to establish unbroken connection by water with the granite quarries by opening a succession of five canals through the intervening granite barriers of the cataracts; and the faithful noble completed this difficult task, besides the building of seven boats, launched and laden with great blocks of granite for the royal pyramid in only one year (BAR, I, 324).

116. Now that the first cataract was passable for Nile boats at high water, a closer control, if not the conquest of northern Nubia was quite feasible. *Northern* Nubia was not of itself a country which the agricultural Egyptian could utilize. The strip of cultivable soil between the Nile and the desert on either hand is here so scanty, even in places disappearing altogether, that its agricultural value is slight. But the high ridges and valleys in the desert on the east contain rich veins of gold-bearing quartz, and iron ore is plentiful also, although no workings of it have been found there. The country was furthermore the only gateway to the regions of the south, with which constant trade was now maintained. Besides gold, the Sudan sent down the river ostrich feathers, ebony logs, panther skins and ivory; while along the same route, from Punt and the countries further east, came myrrh, fragrant gums and resins and aromatic woods. It was therefore imperative that

the Pharaoh should command this route. We know little of the negro and negroid tribes who inhabited the cataract region at this time. Immediately south of the Egyptian frontier dwelt the tribes of Wawat, extending well toward the second cataract, above which the entire region of the upper cataracts was known as Kush, although the name does not commonly occur on the monuments until the Middle Kingdom. In the northern loop of the huge "S" formed by the course of the Nile between the junction of the two Niles and the second cataract, was included the territory of the powerful Mazoi, who afterward appeared as auxiliaries in the Egyptian army in such numbers that the Egyptian word for soldier ultimately became "Matoi," a late (Coptic) form of Mazoi. In this northern loop of the "S" too, between the Third and the Fourth Cataracts, the Nile Valley widens into broad fields, of the greatest productivity and enjoying the finest climate. But the conquest of this Nubian paradise by the Pharaohs was still a thousand years away. Probably on the west of the Mazoi was the land of Yam, and between Yam and Mazoi on the south and Wawat on the north were distributed several tribes, of whom Irthet and Sethut were the most important. The last two, together with Wawat, were sometimes united under one chief (BAR, I, 336). All these tribes were still in the barbarous stage. They dwelt in squalid settlements of mud huts along the river, or beside wells in the valleys running up country from the Nile; and besides the flocks and herds which they maintained, they also lived upon the scanty produce of their small grain-fields.

117. Doubtless utilizing his new canal, Mernere now devoted special attention to the exploitation of these regions. His power was so respected by the chiefs of

Wawat, Irthet, Mazoi and Yam that they furnished the timber for the heavy cargo-boats built by Uni for the granite blocks which he took out at the first cataract. In his fifth year Mernere did what no Pharaoh before him had ever done, in so far as we are informed. He appeared at the first cataract in person to receive the homage of the southern chiefs, and left upon the rocks a record of the event, accompanied by a relief depicting the Pharaoh leaning upon his staff, while the Nubian chiefs bow down in his presence (BAR, I, 324, 316–318).

118. Mernere now utilized the services of the Elephantine nobles in tightening his hold upon the southern chiefs. Harkhuf, who was then lord of Elephantine, was also appointed governor of the South, perhaps as the successor of Uni, who was now too old for active serivce, or had meantime possibly died (BAR, I, 332); although the title had now become a mere epithet of honour worn by more than one deserving noble at this time. It was upon Harkhuf and his relatives, a family of daring and adventurous nobles, that the Pharaoh now depended as leaders of the arduous and dangerous expeditions which should intimidate the barbarians on his frontiers and maintain his prestige and his trade connections in the distant regions of the south. These men are the earliest known explorers of inner Africa and the southern Red Sea. At least two of the family perished in executing the Pharaoh's hazardous commissions in these far-off lands, a significant hint of the hardships and perils to which they were all exposed. Besides their princely titulary as lords of Elephantine they all bore the title "caravan-conductor, who brings the products of the countries to his lord," which they proudly display upon their tombs, excavated high in

the front of the cliffs facing modern Assuan, where they still look down upon the island of Elephantine, the one-time home of the ancient lords who occupy them. Here Harkhuf has recorded how Mernere dispatched him on three successive expeditions to distant Yam. These dangerous journeys consumed from seven to eight months each, and from the last he returned with the rich proceeds of his royal trafficking loaded upon three hundred asses (BAR, I, 333-336).

119. These operations for the winning of the extreme south were interrupted by the untimely death of Mernere. He was buried behind Memphis in the granite sarcophagus procured for him by Uni, in the pyramid for which Uni had likewise laboured so faithfully, and here his remains survived, in spite of vandals and tomb-robbers, until their removal to the museum at Gizeh in 1881—the oldest royal body, interred 4,500 years ago. As Mernere reigned only four years and died early in his fifth year without issue, the succession devolved upon his half-brother, who, although only a child, ascended the throne as Pepi II. His accession and successful rule speak highly for the stability of the family, and the faithfulness of the influential nobles attached to it. Pepi II was the son of Enekhnes-Merire, one of the two sisters of the Thinite nomarch, whom Pepi I first had taken as his queens. Her brother Zau, Pepi II's uncle, who was now nomarch of Thinis, was appointed by the child-king as vizier, chief judge and governor of the residence city. He thus had charge of the state during his royal nephew's minority, and as far as we can now discern, the government proceeded without the slightest disturbance (BAR, I, 344-349).

120. Pepi II, or in the beginning, of course, his ministers, immediately resumed the designs of the royal

house in the south. In the young king's second year Harkhuf was for the fourth time dispatched to Yam, whence he returned bringing a rich pack train and one of those uncouth, bandy-legged dwarfs from one of the pigmy tribes of inner Africa, so highly prized for the dances by which the king's leisure hours were diverted. The delighted letter of thanks written by the child-king on hearing of the dwarf was recorded by the gratified Harkhuf on the front of his tomb and thus preserved (BAR, I, 350–354).

Not all of these hardy lords of Elephantine, who adventured their lives in the tropical fastnesses of inner Africa in the twenty-sixth century before Christ, were as fortunate as Harkhuf. One of them, a governor of the South, named Sebni, suddenly received news of the death of his father, Prince Mekhu, who perished while on an expedition south of Wawat. Thereupon Sebni undertook the dangerous mission of recovering his father's remains. Returning in safety, he was shown every mark of royal favour for his pious deed in rescuing his father's body. Splendid gifts and the "gold of praise" were showered upon him, and later an official communication from the vizier conveyed to him a parcel of land (BAR, I, 362–374).

121. A loose sovereignty was now extended over the Nubian tribes, and Pepinakht, one of the Elephantine lords, was placed in control with the title "governor of foreign countries." In this capacity Pepi II twice sent him against Wawat and Irthet, where he finally captured the two chiefs of these countries themselves, besides their two commanders and plentiful spoil from their herds. Expeditions were pushed far into the upper cataract region, which is once called Kush in the Elephantine tombs, and, in general, the preliminary

THE DECLINE OF THE OLD KINGDOM

work was done which made possible the complete conquest of lower Nubia in the Middle Kingdom. Indeed that conquest would now have been begun had not internal causes produced the fall of the Sixth Dynasty (BAR, I, 356, 358, 359, 361).

122. The responsibility for the development of Egyptian commerce with the land of Punt and the region of the southern Red Sea also fell upon the lords of Elephantine. Evidently they had charge of the whole south from the Red Sea to the Nile. There was no waterway connecting the Nile with the Red Sea (*cf.* p. 159), and these leaders were obliged to build their ships at the eastern terminus of the Coptos caravan route from the Nile, in one of the Red Sea harbours like Kosêr or Leucos Limên. While so engaged, Enenkhet, Pepi II's naval commander, was fallen upon by the Beduin, who slew him and his entire command. Pepinakht was immediately dispatched by the Pharaoh to rescue the body of the unfortunate noble (BAR, I, 360). In spite of these risks, the communication with Punt was now active and frequent, and at least one man had made the voyage probably eleven times (BAR, I, 361). It will be seen that the usually accepted seclusion of the Old Kingdom can no longer be maintained. The commerce of the Old Kingdom Pharaohs extended from the gate of the Indian Ocean on the south, to the forests of Lebanon, and the pre-Mycenæan civilization of the Greek islands on the north. (See Note xi.)

123. The tradition of Manetho states that Pepi II was six years old when he began to reign, and that he continued until the hundredth year, doubtless meaning of his life. The list preserved by Eratosthenes avers that he ruled a full century. The Turin Papyrus of kings supports the first tradition, giving him over

ninety years, and there is no reason to doubt its truth. His was thus the longest reign in history. Several brief reigns followed, among them possibly that of the Queen Nitocris, to whose name were attached the absurdest legends.

124. But after the death of Pepi II all is uncertain, and impenetrable obscurity veils the last days of the Sixth Dynasty. When it had ruled something over one hundred and fifty years the power of the landed barons had become a centrifugal force, which the Pharaohs could no longer withstand, and the dissolution of the state resulted. The nomes gained their independence, the Old Kingdom fell to pieces, and for a time was thus resolved into the petty principalities of prehistoric times. Nearly a thousand years of unparalleled development since the rise of a united state, thus ended, in the twenty-fifth century B.C., in political conditions like those which had preceded it.

125. It had been a thousand years of inexhaustible fertility when the youthful strength of a people of boundless energy had for the first time found the organized form in which it could best express itself. In every direction we see the products of a national freshness and vigour which are never spent; the union of the country under a single guiding hand which had quelled internal dissensions and directed the combined energies of a great people toward harmonious effort, had brought untold blessing. The Pharaohs, to whom the unparalleled grandeur of this age was due, not only gained a place among the gods in their own time, but two thousand years later, at the close of Egypt's history as an independent nation, in the Twenty-sixth Dynasty, we still find the priests who were appointed to maintain their worship. And at the end of her

career, when the nation had lost all that youthful elasticity and creative energy which so abounded in the Old Kingdom, the sole effort of her priests and wise men was to restore the unsullied religion, life and government which in their fond imagination had existed in the Old Kingdom, as they looked wistfully back upon it across the millennia. To us it has left the imposing line of temples, tombs and pyramids, stretching for many miles along the margin of the western desert, the most eloquent witnesses to the fine intelligence and Titanic energies of the men who made the Old Kingdom what it was; not alone achieving these wonders of mechanics and internal organization, but building the earliest known sea-going ships and exploring unknown waters, or pushing their commercial enterprises far up the Nile into inner Africa. In plastic art they had reached the highest achievement; in architecture their tireless genius had created the column and originated the colonnade; in government they had elaborated an enlightened and highly developed state, with a large body of just law; in religion they were already dimly conscious of a judgment in the hereafter, and they were thus the first men whose ethical intuitions made happiness in the future life dependent upon character. Everywhere their unspent energies unfolded in a rich and manifold culture which left the world such a priceless heritage as no nation had yet bequeathed it. It now remains to be seen, as we stand at the close of this remarkable age, whether the conflict of local with centralized authority shall exhaust the elemental strength of this ancient people; or whether such a reconciliation can be effected as will again produce harmony and union, permitting the continuance of the marvellous development of which we have witnessed the first fruits.

PART III

THE MIDDLE KINGDOM:
THE FEUDAL AGE

VIII

THE DECLINE OF THE NORTH AND THE RISE OF THEBES

126. The internal struggle which caused the fall of the Old Kingdom developed at last into a convulsion, in which the destructive forces were for a time completely triumphant. Exactly when and by whom the ruin was wrought is not now determinable, but the magnificent mortuary works of the greatest of the Old Kingdom monarchs fell victims to a carnival of destruction in which many of them were annihilated. The temples were not merely pillaged and violated, but their finest works of art were subjected to systematic and determined vandalism, which shattered the splendid granite and diorite statues of the kings into bits, or hurled them into the well in the monumental gate of the pyramid-causeway. Thus the foes of the old régime wreaked vengeance upon those who had represented and upheld it. The nation was totally disorganized. From the scanty notes of Manetho it would appear that an oligarchy, possibly representing an attempt of the nobles to set up their joint rule, assumed control for a brief time at Memphis. Manetho calls them the Seventh Dynasty. He follows them with an Eighth Dynasty of Memphite kings, who are but the lingering shadow of ancient Memphite power. Their names as preserved in the Abydos list show that they

134 THE MIDDLE KINGDOM: THE FEUDAL AGE

regarded the Sixth Dynasty as their ancestors; but none of their pyramids has ever been found, nor have we been able to date any tombs of the local nobility in this dark age. In the mines and quarries of Sinai and Hammamat, where records of every prosperous line of kings proclaim their power, not a trace of these ephemeral Pharaohs can be found. A generation after the fall of the Sixth Dynasty a family of Heracleopolitan nomarchs wrested the crown from the weak Memphites of the Eighth Dynasty, who may have lingered on, claiming royal honours for nearly another century.

127. Some degree of order was finally restored by the triumph of the nomarchs of Heracleopolis. This city, just south of the Fayum, had been the seat of a temple and cult of Horus from the earliest dynastic times. Akhthoes, who, according to Manetho, was the founder of the new dynasty, must have taken grim vengeance on his enemies, for all that Manetho knows of him is that he was the most violent of all the kings of the time, and that, having been seized with madness, he was slain by a crocodile. The new house is known to Manetho as the Ninth and Tenth Dynasties, but its kings were still too feeble to leave any enduring monuments; neither have any records contemporary with the family survived except during the last three generations, when the powerful nomarchs of Siut were able to excavate cliff-tombs in which they fortunately left records of the active and successful career of their family, furnishing us a hint of the disorganized state from which the country had been rescued (BAR, I, 391–414).

128. These Siut nomarchs enjoyed the most intimate relations with the royal house at Heracleopolis, and we see them digging canals, reducing taxation, reaping

rich harvests, maintaining large herds, while there were always in readiness a body of troops and a fleet. Such was the wealth and power of these Siut nobles that they soon became a buffer state on the south of inestimable value to the house of Heracleopolis, and one of them was made military "commander of Middle Egypt" (BAR, I, 410).

129. Meantime among the nobles of the South a similar powerful family of nomarchs was slowly rising into notice. Some four hundred and forty miles above Memphis, and less than one hundred and forty miles below the first cataract, along the stretch of Nile about forty miles above the great bend, where the river approaches most closely to the Red Sea before turning abruptly away from it, the scanty margin between river and cliffs expands into a broad and fruitful plain, in the midst of which now lie the mightiest ruins of ancient civilization to be found anywhere in the world. They are the wreck of Thebes, the world's first great monumental city. At this time it was an obscure provincial town and the neighbouring Hermonthis was the seat of a family of nomarchs, the Intefs and Mentuhoteps. Toward the close of the Heracleopolitan supremacy, Thebes had gained the lead in the South, and its nomarch, Intef, was "keeper of the Door of the South." His successors were finally able to detach the whole south as far northward as his own Theban nome, and organized an independent kingdom, with Thebes at its head. This Intef was ever after recognized as the ancestor of the Theban line, and the monarchs of the Middle Kingdom set up his statue in the temple at Thebes among those of their royal predecessors who were worshipped there (BAR, I, 420, 419).

130. At this juncture, the unshaken fidelity of the

Siut princes was the salvation of the house of Heracleopolis. We can now vaguely discern a protracted struggle, in which they bore the brunt, continuing with varying fortune, as the Intefs pushed northward from Thebes, till Wahenekh-Intef gained Abydos and fixed his northern boundary there. His southern frontier was at the cataract. His son and successor, another Intef, maintained this southern kingdom till the accession of a line of five Mentuhoteps, probably a collateral branch of the Theban family, who established the universal supremacy of Thebes, and the sovereignty of Egypt passed from the north to the south. Heracleopolis disappears, after we have gained but a fleeting glimpse of her kings in the tombs of the Siut lords (BAR, I, 396, 398, 403, 1. 23; 401). We then find the last three Mentuhoteps controlling all Egypt, and reviving building operations, for which the first of them (Nibtowere) dispatched a great expedition to Hammamat for the necessary stone. The second (Nibhepetre) erected a terraced mortuary temple against the cliffs of Der el-Bahri, now the oldest surviving building at Thebes. He even resumed the absorption of Nubia, and sent a fleet against Wawat. He was later regarded as the great founder of the dynasty.

131. After his reign of half a century Senekhkere-Mentuhotep continued to hold the undivided sovereignty of all Egypt. This Mentuhotep was able to resume the distant foreign enterprises of the Pharaohs for the first time since the Sixth Dynasty, five hundred years before. He dispatched his chief treasurer, Henu, to the Red Sea by the Hammamat road with a following of three thousand men. Such was the efficiency of his organization that each man received two jars

of water and twenty small biscuit-like loaves daily, involving the issuance of six thousand jars of water and sixty thousand such loaves by the commissary every day during the desert march and the stay in the quarries of Hammamat. Everything possible was done to make the desert route thither safe and passable. Henu dug fifteen wells and cisterns, and settlements of colonists were afterward established at the watering stations. Arriving at the Red Sea end of the route, Henu built a ship which he dispatched to Punt, while he himself returned by way of Hammamat, where he secured and brought back with him fine blocks for the statues in the royal temples. In such efficient organization we discern slowly emerging from centuries of anarchy and civil strife the great state which we shall soon meet as the Middle Kingdom. After a rule of a little over one hundred and sixty years the Eleventh Dynasty was brought to a close with the reign of Senekhkere-Mentuhotep, about 2000 B. C. They left few monuments; their modest pyramids of sun-dried brick on the western plain of Thebes were in a perfect state of preservation a thousand years later, but they barely survived into modern times, and their vanishing remains were excavated by Mariette (Note I; BAR, I, 419–459; iv, 514).

132. It was not without hostilities that the last Mentuhotep gave way before the new line. With the advent of its founder, the unknown Theban, Amenemhet, we hear of a campaign on the Nile with a fleet of twenty ships of cedar, followed by the expulsion of some unknown enemy from Egypt. The development of local power among the landed nobility which had become so evident in the Fifth Dynasty had now reached its logical issue; Amenemhet could only ac-

cept the situation and deal with it as best he might. He now achieved the conquest of the country and its reorganization only by skilfully employing in his cause those noble families whom he could win by favour and fair promises. We see him rewarding Khnumhotep, one of his noble partisans, with the gift of the Oryx-nome, and personally going about determining the just boundaries and erecting landmarks. To suppress these landed barons entirely was impossible. The utmost that the monarch could now accomplish was the appointment in the nomes of nobles favourably inclined toward his house. The state which the unprecedented vigour and skill of this great statesman finally succeeded in thus erecting, again furnished Egypt with the stable organization which enabled her about 2000 B. C. to enter upon her second great period of productive development, the Middle Kingdom (BAR, I, 465, 688 *f*., 625, 619-639).

IX

THE MIDDLE KINGDOM OR THE FEUDAL AGE: STATE, SOCIETY AND RELIGION

133. It had been but natural that the kings of the Eleventh Dynasty should reside at Thebes, where the founders of the family had lived during the long war for the conquest of the North. But Amenemhet was evidently unable to continue this tradition. All the kings of Egypt, since the passing of the Thinites a thousand years before, had lived in the North, except the Eleventh Dynasty which he had supplanted. The spot which he selected was on the west side of the river some miles south of Memphis, near the place now called Lisht, where the ruined pyramid of Amenemhet has been discovered. From this stronghold, bearing the significant name Ithtowe, "Captor of the Two Lands," Amenemhet swayed the destinies of a state which required all the skill and political sagacity of a line of unusually strong rulers in order to maintain the prestige of the royal house.

The nation was made up of an aggregation of small states or petty princedoms, the lords of which owed the Pharaoh their loyalty, but they were not his officials or his servants. Some of these local nobles were "great lords" or nomarchs, ruling a whole nome; others were only "counts" of a smaller domain with its fortified town. It was thus a feudal state, not essentially different from that of later Europe, which Amenemhet had organized. We are dependent for our knowledge of these barons upon their surviving tombs and mortuary monuments. All such remains in the Delta have perished, so that we can speak with certainty only of the conditions in the South, and even here it is only in Middle Egypt that we are adequately informed.

134. Through long generations of possession the nomarch had now become a miniature Pharaoh in his little realm. On a less sumptuous scale his residence was surrounded by a *personnel* not unlike that of the Pharaonic court and harem; while his government demanded a chief treasurer, a court of justice, with offices, scribes, and functionaries, and all the essential machinery of government which we find at the royal residence. The nomarch collected the revenues of his domain, was high priest or head of the sacerdotal organization, and commanded the militia of his realm which was permanently organized. His power was thus considerable. Such lords were able to build temples, erect public buildings, and set up massive and pretentious monuments in their principal towns (BAR, I, 520 *f.*; 466, note c; 694–706, 403, 637 and note a.) The nomarch devoted himself to the interests of his people, and was concerned to leave to posterity a reputation as a merciful and beneficent ruler. After making all due allowance for a natural desire to record the most favourable aspects of his government, it is evident that the paternal character of the nomarch's local and personal rule, in a community of limited numbers, with which he was acquainted by almost daily contact, had proved an untold blessing to the country and population at large (BAR, I, 638, 408, 407, 459, 523).

135. The domains over which the nomarch thus ruled were not all his unqualified possessions. His wealth consisted of lands and revenues of two classes: the "paternal estate," received from his ancestors and entailed in his line; and the "count's estate" (BAR, I, 536), over which the dead hand had no control; it was conveyed as a fief by the Pharaoh anew at the nomarch's death. It was this fact which to some extent enabled the Pharaoh to control the feudatories and to secure the appointment of partisans of his house throughout the country. Nevertheless he could not ignore the natural line of succession, which was through the eldest daughter; and she might even rule the domain after the death of her father until her son was old enough to assume its government (BAR, I, 414). The history of the lords of Benihasan through four generations, which their tomb records, enable us to follow, shows that the Pharaoh could not overlook the claims of the heir of a powerful family, and the deference which he showed them evidently limited the control which he might exert over a less formidable dynasty of nobles (BAR, I, 619 *ff.*).

136. To what extent these lords felt the restraint of the royal hand in their government and administration it is not now possible to determine. A royal commissioner, whose duty it was to look to the interests of the Pharaoh, seems to have resided in the nome, and there were "overseers of the crown-possessions" (probably under him), in charge of the royal herds in each nome; but the nomarch himself was the medium through whom all revenues from the nome were conveyed to the treasury (BAR, I, 522). "All the imposts of the king's house passed through my hand," says Ameni of the Oryx nome. The treasury was the organ of the

central government, which gave administrative cohesion to the otherwise loose aggregation of nomarchies. It had its income-paying property in all the nomes. Some of this property was administered by government overseers, while to a large extent it was entrusted to the noble, probably as part of the "count's estate" (BAR, I, 522, and note a). We have no means of even conjecturing the amount or proportion of property held by the crown in the nomes and "count's estates," but it is evident that the claims of these powerful feudatories must have seriously curtailed the traditional revenues of the Pharaoh. He no longer had the resources of the country at his unconditional disposal as in the Old Kingdom. Other resources of the treasury were, however, now available, and, if not entirely new, were henceforth more energetically exploited. Besides his internal revenues, including the tribute of the nomes and the Residence, the Pharaoh received a regular income from the gold-mines of Nubia, and those on the Coptos road to the Red Sea. The traffic with Punt and the southern coasts of the Red Sea seems to have been the exclusive prerogative of the crown, and must have brought in a considerable return; while the mines and quarries of Sinai, and perhaps also the quarries of Hammamat, had also been developed as a regular source of profit. The conquest of lower Nubia, and now and then a plundering expedition into Syria-Palestine, also furnished not unwelcome contributions to the treasury.

137. The central organization and the chief functionaries of the treasury were the same as in the Old Kingdom, and the vigorous administration of the time is evident in the frequent records of these active officials, showing that notwithstanding their rank, they often

personally superintended the king's interests in Sinai, Hammamat, or on the shores of the Red Sea at the terminus of the Coptos road. It is evident, however, that the treasury had become a more highly developed organ since the Old Kingdom. The army of subordinates, stewards, overseers and scribes filling the offices under the heads of sub-departments was obviously larger than before. They began to display an array of titles, of which many successive ranks, heretofore unknown, were being gradually differentiated. Such condition made possible the rise of an official middle class.

138. Justice, as in the Old Kingdom, was still dispensed by the administrative officials (BAR, I, 618). The six "Great Houses," or courts of justice, with the vizier at their head, sat in Ithtowe (SEI, I, 100). There was, besides, a "House of Thirty," which evidently possessed judicial functions, and was also presided over by the vizier, but its relation to the six "Great Houses" is not clear. There was now more than one "Southern Ten," and "Magnates of the Southern Tens" were frequently entrusted with various executive and administrative commissions by the king. The law which they administered, while it has not survived, had certainly attained a high devlopment, and was capable of the finest distinctions. A nomarch at Siut makes a contract between himself as count, and himself as high priest in the temple of his city, showing the closest differentiation of the rights which he possessed in these two different capacities (BAR, I, 568 *ff.*).

139. The scanty records of the time throw but little light upon the other organs of government, like the administration of lands, the system of irrigation and the like. The country was divided into two adminis-

trative districts of the South and the North, and the "Magnates of the Southern Tens" served in both districts, showing that they were not confined to the South alone. The office of the governor of the South had disappeared, and already before the close of the Old Kingdom the title had become merely an honourable predicate, if used at all. An elaborate system of registration was in force. Every head of a family was enrolled as soon as he had established an independent household, with all the members belonging to it, including serfs and slaves (GKP, pl. ix, *f.*, pp. 19-29). The office of the vizier was the central archives of the government as before, and all records of the land-administration with census and tax registration were filed in his bureaus. His powers were the same as in the Old Kingdom, and that he might prove dangerous to the crown is evident in the history of Amenemhet's I probable rise from the viziership.

140. It was therefore now more necessary than ever that the machinery of government should be in the hands of men of unquestioned loyalty. Young men were brought up in the circle of the king's house that they might grow up in attachment to it. Discreet conduct toward the Pharaoh was the condition of a career, and the wise praise him who knows how to be silent in the king's service (BAR, I, 665, 514, 532, 748).

141. Under such conditions the Pharaoh could not but surround himself with the necessary power to enforce his will when obliged to do so. A class of military "attendants," or, literally, "followers of his majesty" therefore arose, the first professional soldiers of whom we have any knowledge in ancient Egypt. In companies of a hundred men each they garrisoned the

palace and the strongholds of the royal house from Nubia to the Asiatic frontier. They formed at least the nucleus of a standing army, although it is evident that they were not as yet in sufficient numbers to be dignified by this term. They were probably of the same social class as the feudatory militia, forming the great mass of the army employed by the Pharaoh at this time. This feudatory militia was composed of the free born citizens of the middle class on the estate of the nomarch, who at the king's summons placed himself at their head and led them in the wars of his liege-lord. The army in time of war was therefore made up of contingents furnished and commanded by the feudatories. In peace they were also frequently drawn upon to furnish the intelligent power applied to the transportation of great monuments or employed in the execution of public works. All free citizens, whether priests or not, were organized and enrolled in "generations," a term designating the different classes of youth, who were to become successively liable to draught for military or public service. As in the Old Kingdom, war continues to be little more than a series of loosely organized predatory expeditions, the records of which clearly display the still unwarlike character of the Egyptian.

142. The detachment of the nobles from the court since the Sixth Dynasty had resulted in the rise of a provincial society, of which we gain glimpses especially at Elephantine, Bersheh, Benihasan and Siut, where the tombs of the nomarchs are still preserved, and at Abydos, where all other classes now desired to be buried or to erect a memorial stone. The life of the nobles therefore no longer centred in the court, and the aristocracy of the time, being scattered throughout the

country, took on local forms. The nomarch, with his large family circle, his social pleasures, his hunting and his sports, is an interesting and picturesque figure of the country nobleman, with whom we would gladly tarry if space permitted. Characteristic of this age is the prominence of the middle class. To some extent this prominence is due to the fact that a tomb, a tombstone and mortuary equipment have become a necessity also for a large proportion of this class, who felt no such necessity and left no such memorial of their existence in the Old Kingdom. In the cemetery at Abydos, among nearly eight hundred men of the time having tombstones there, one in four bore no title either of office or of rank (CC, Nos. 20001-20780). Some of these men were tradesmen, some land-owners, others artisans and artificers; but among them were men of wealth and luxury. In the Art Institute at Chicago there is a fine coffin belonging to such an untitled citizen, which he had made of costly cedar imported from Lebanon. Of the people bearing titles of office on these Middle Kingdom tombstones of Abydos the vast majority were small office-holders, displaying no title of rank and undoubtedly belonging to this same middle class. The government service now offered a career to the youth of this station in life. The inheritance by the son of his father's office, already not uncommon in the Old Kingdom, was now general. Such a custom must necessarily lead to the formation of an official middle class. Their ability to read and write also raised them above those of their own social station who were illiterate, and from this time on we shall find the scribe constantly glorying in his knowledge and despising all other callings (P Sall., II). For the first time therefore we now discern a prosperous and often well-to-do middle class in the provinces, sometimes owning their own slaves and lands and bringing their offerings of first fruits to the temple of the town as did the nomarch himself (BAR, I, 536). At the bottom of the social scale were the unnamed serfs, the toiling millions who produced the agricultural wealth of the land—the despised class whose labour nevertheless formed the basis of the economic life of the nation. In the nomes they were also taught handicrafts, and we see them depicted in the tombs at Benihasan and elsewhere engaged in the production of all sorts of handiwork. Whether their output was solely for the use of the nomarch's estates or also on a large scale for traffic in the markets with the middle class throughout the country, is entirely uncertain.

143. In no element of their life are there clearer evidences of change and development than in the religion of the Middle Kingdom Egyptians. Here again we are in a new age. The official supremacy of Re, so marked since the rise of the Fifth Dynasty, was now complete. The other priesthoods, desirous of securing for their own, perhaps purely local deity, a share of the sun-god's glory, gradually discovered that their god was but a form and name of Re; and some of them went so far that their theologizing found practical expression in the god's name. Thus, for example, Amon, hitherto an obscure local god of Thebes, who had attained some prominence by the political rise of the city, was from now on a solar-god, and was commonly called by his priests Amon-Re. There were in this movement the beginnings of a tendency toward a pantheistic solar monotheism, which we shall yet trace to its remarkable culmination. While the temples had probably somewhat increased in size, the official cult was

not materially altered, and there was still no large class of priests (AZ, 1900, 94).

144. The triumph of Re was largely due to his political prominence; but that of Osiris, which is now equally evident, had no connection with the state, but was a purely popular victory. That his priests contributed to his triumph by persistent propaganda is nevertheless probable, but their field of operations will have been among the people. At Abydos the Osiris-myth was wrought into a series of dramatical presentations in which the chief incidents of the god's life, death and final triumph were annually enacted before the people by the priests. Indeed in the presentation of some portions of it the people were permitted to participate; and this ancient passion play was unquestionably as impressive in the eyes of the multitude as were the miracle and passion plays of the Christian age (BAR, I, 662, 669; SU, ix, 2). Among the incidents enacted was the procession bearing the god's body to his tomb for burial, a custom which finally resulted in identifying as the original tomb of Osiris the place on the desert behind Abydos, which in this scene served as the tomb. Thus the tomb of King Zer of the First Dynasty, who had ruled over a thousand years before, was in the Middle Kingdom already regarded as that of Osiris (*ibid.*). As veneration for the spot increased, it became a veritable holy sepulchre, and Abydos gained a sanctity possessed by no other place in Egypt. All this wrought powerfully upon the people; they came in pilgrimage to the place, and the ancient tomb of Zer was buried deep beneath a mountain of jars containing the votive offerings which they brought. If possible the Egyptian was now buried at Abydos; from the vizier himself down to the humblest

cobbler we find them crowding this most sacred cemetery of Egypt. But the masses to whom this was impossible erected memorial tablets and small false or model tombs there for themselves and their relatives, calling upon the god in prayer and praise to remember them in the hereafter. Royal officials and emissaries of the government, whose business brought them to the city, failed not to improve the opportunity to erect such a tablet, and the date and character of their commissions which they sometimes add furnish us with invaluable historical facts, of which we should otherwise never have gained any knowledge (BAR, 1, 671–672).

145. As the destiny of the dead became more and more identified with that of Osiris, the judgment which he had been obliged to undergo was supposed to await also all who departed to his realms. The heart of the deceased is weighed over against a feather, the symbol of truth, while he pleads "not guilty" to forty-two different sins. These sins are such as to show that the ethical standard was high; moreover in this judgment the Egyptian introduced for the first time in the history of man the fully developed idea that the future destiny of the dead must be dependent entirely upon the ethical quality of the earthly life, the idea of future accountability, of which we found the first traces in the Old Kingdom. The whole conception is notable; for a thousand years or more after this no such idea was known among other peoples, and in Babylonia and Israel good and bad alike descended together at death into gloomy Sheol, where no distinction was made between them. The blessed dead, who successfully sustained the judgment each received the predicate "true of speech," a term which was interpreted as meaning "triumphant," and from now on so employed. Every

deceased person, when spoken of by the living, received this predicate; it was always written after the names of the dead, and finally also after those of the living in anticipation of their happy destiny.

146. In one important respect the beliefs of the Egyptian regarding his future state have suffered a striking change. He is now beset with innumerable dangers in the next world. Besides the serpents common in the Pyramid Texts, the most uncanny foes and the most terrifying dangers await him. Against all these the deceased must now be forewarned and forearmed, and hence a mass of magical formularies has arisen, by the proper utterance of which the dead may overcome all these foes and live in triumph and security. These charms, with many others securing many blessings to the dead, were written for the use of the deceased on the inside of his coffin, and although no canonical selection of these texts yet existed, they formed the nucleus of what afterward became the Book of the Dead or, as the Egyptian later called it, "The Chapters of Going Forth by Day," in reference to their great function of enabling the dead to leave the tomb. It will be seen that in this class of literature there was offered to an unscrupulous priesthood an opportunity for gain, of which in later centuries they did not fail to take advantage. Already they attempted what might be termed a "guide-book" of the hereafter, a geography of the other world, with a map of the two ways along which the dead might journey. This "Book of the Two Ways" was probably composed for no other purpose than for gain; and the tendency of which it is an evidence will meet us in future centuries as the most baleful influence of Egyptian life and religion. In the material equipment of the dead, the mastaba, while it

has not entirely disappeared, has largely been displaced by the excavated cliff-tomb, already found so practical and convenient by the nobles of Upper Egypt in the Old Kingdom. The kings, however, continue to build pyramids, as we shall see.

X

THE TWELFTH DYNASTY

147. THE difficult and delicate task of reorganization doubtless consumed a large part of Amenemhet I's reign, but when it was once thoroughly accomplished his house was able to rule the country for over two centuries. It is probable that at no other time in the history of Egypt did the land enjoy such widespread and bountiful prosperity as now ensued.

148. In the midst of all this, when Amenemhet fancied that he had firmly established himself and his line upon the throne of the land which owed him so much, a foul conspiracy to assassinate him was conceived among the official members of his household. The palace halls rang with the clash of arms, and the king's life was in danger, though he finally escaped (BAR, I, 479 *f.*). In the twentieth year of his reign (1980 B.C.), probably no long time after this incident, and doubtless influenced by it, Amenemhet appointed his son Sesostris, the first of the name, to share the throne as coregent with him. It was during this coregency that Egypt again resumed a policy of expansion. In spite of the achievements of the Sixth Dynasty in the South the country below the first cataract as far north as Edfu was still reckoned as belonging to Nubia and still bore the name Tapedet, "Bow-Land," usually applied to Nubia (BAR, I, 500, l. 4). In the twenty-ninth year

of the old king the Egyptian forces penetrated Wawat to Korusko, the termination of the desert route, cutting off the great westward bend of the Nile, and captured prisoners among the Mazoi in the country beyond. We can hardly doubt that the young Sesostris was the leader of this expedition. Work was also resumed in the quarries of Hammamat, while in the North "the Troglodytes, the Asiatics and Sand-dwellers" on the east of the Delta were punished. This eastern frontier was strengthened at the eastern terminus of the Wady Tumilat by a fortification, perhaps that already in existence under the Old Kingdom Pharaohs; and a garrison, with its sentinels constantly upon the watch towers, was stationed there. Thus in North and South alike an aggressive policy was maintained, the frontiers made safe and the foreign connections of the kingdom carefully regarded (BAR, I, 500, l. 4; 472 *f*., 466–468, 469–471, 483, l. 3; 493, ll. 17–19, 474–483).

149. As the old king felt his end approaching, he delivered to his son brief instructions embodying the ripe wisdom which he had accumulated during his long career. The modern reader may clearly discern in these utterances the bitterness with which the attempt upon his life by his own immediate circle had imbued the aged Amenemhet (BAR, I, 474–483). It was probably not long after this that Sesostris was dispatched at the head of an army to chastise the Libyans on the western frontier. During the absence of the prince on this campaign in 1970 B.C. Amenemhet died, after a reign of thirty years (BAR, I, 487 *ff*.).

150. The achievements of the house of Amenemhet outside of the limits of Egypt: in Nubia, Hammamat and Sinai, have left more adequate records in these regions than their beneficent and prosperous rule in

Egypt itself; and the progress of the dynasty, at least in inscribed records, can be more clearly traced abroad than at home. It will therefore be easier to follow the foreign enterprises of the dynasty before we dwell upon their achievements at home. We follow the feudatories like Ameni, later nomarch of the Oryx-nome, under the leadership of their liege, Sesostris I, as they penetrate above the second cataract into the great region known as Kush, which now for the first time becomes common in the monumental records. The campaign is notable as the first in a foreign country ever led by the Pharaoh personally, in so far as we know (BAR, I, 519). Eight years after the death of his father, Sesostris I dispatched Mentuhotep, one of his commanders, on a further campaign into Kush. Mentuhotep left a large stela at Wady Halfa, just below the first cataract, recording his triumph and giving us the first list of conquered foreign districts and towns which we possess. Mentuhotep made himself so prominent on his triumphant stela that his figure was erased and that of a god placed over it. All appearances would indicate that the successful commander was deposed and disgraced (BAR, I, 510–514). Nubian gold now began to flow into the treasury, and Ameni of the Oryx-nome was dispatched to Nubia at the head of four hundred troops of his nome to bring back the output. The king improved the occasion to send with Ameni the young crown prince, who afterwards became Amenemhet II, in order that he might familiarize himself with the region where he should one day be called upon to continue his father's enterprises (BAR, I, 520). Similarly the gold country on the east of Coptos was now exploited, and the faithful Ameni was entrusted with the mission of convoying it. It is under the energetic Sesostris I also, that we first hear of intercourse with the oases (BAR, I, 521, 524–528).

151. It was doubtless the realization of the evident advantage which he had enjoyed by ten years' association with his father as coregent that induced Sesostris I to appoint his own son in the same way. When he died in 1935 B. C., after a reign of thirty-five years, his son, Amenemhet II had already been coregent for three years, and assumed the sole authority without difficulty. This policy was also continued by Amenemhet II, and his son Sesostris II had also ruled three years in conjunction with his father at the latter's death (BAR, I, 460). For fifty years under these two kings in succession the nation enjoyed unabated prosperity. The mines of Sinai were reopened, and the traffic with Punt resumed by Amenemhet II was continued under his son. The distant shores of Punt gradually became more familiar to Egyptian folk, and a popular tale narrates the marvellous adventures of a shipwrecked seaman in these waters (AZ, 43). The Nubian goldmines continued to be a source of wealth to the royal house, and Egyptian interests in Nubia were protected by fortresses in Wawat, garrisoned and subject to periodical inspection. With the death of Sesostris II in 1887 B. C., all was ripe for the complete and thorough conquest of the two hundred miles of Nile valley that lie between the first and second cataracts (BAR, I, 602, 604–606, 616–618).

152. Immediately on his accession Sesostris III took the preliminary step toward the completion of the great task in Nubia, viz., the establishment of unbroken connection by water with the country above the first cataract. What had become of the canal made by Uni, six hundred years before, we cannot say (see p. 122).

At the most difficult point in the granite barrier the engineers of Sesostris III cut a channel through the rock, and many a war-galley of the Pharaoh must have been drawn up through it during the early campaigns of this king, of which we unfortunately have no records (BAR, I, 642–644). By the eighth year the subjugation of the country had made such progress that Sesostris III was able to select a favourable strategic position as his frontier at modern Kummeh and Semneh, situated on opposite banks of the river in the heart of the second cataract country forty miles above the lower end. This point he formally declared to be the southern boundary of his kingdom. He erected on each side of the river a stela marking the boundary-line, and one of these two important landmarks has survived (BAR, I, 651 *f*.). It was of course impossible to maintain the new frontier without a constant display of force. Sesostris III therefore erected a strong fortress on each side of the river at this point, each with its temple and barracks within the enclosure. These two strongholds of Kummeh and Semneh still survive, and although in a state of ruin, they show remarkable skill in the selection of the site and unexpected knowledge of the art of constructing effective defenses.

153. Later disturbances among the turbulent Nubian tribes south of the new frontier three times recalled the king into Nubia, the last time in his nineteenth year (BAR, I, 653 *f*., 661). Although Egypt did not claim sovereignty in Kush, the country above the second cataract, it was nevertheless necessary for the Pharaoh to protect the trade-routes leading through it to his new frontier, from the extreme south—routes along which the products of the Sudan were now constantly passing into Egypt. The declaration of the frontier

on the boundary-stela permitted the passage of any negro who came to trade, or bore a matter of business from some southern chief (BAR, I, 652). From now on it was more often south of his frontier that the Pharaoh was obliged to appear in force than in the country between the first two cataracts. Moreover, there was rich plunder to be had on these campaigns over the border, so that the maintenance of the southern trade-routes was not without its compensations. Sesostris III was able to send his chief treasurer, Ikhernofret, to restore the cultus image of Osiris at Abydos with gold captured in Kush (BAR, I, 665).

154. In the campaign of the sixteenth year he renewed his declaration of the southern boundary at Semneh, erecting a stela in the temple there bearing his second proclamation of the place of the frontier, and exhorting his descendants to maintain it where he had established it. He also erected on the boundary a statue of himself, as if to awe the natives of the region by his very presence (BAR, I, 653–660). At the same time he strengthened the frontier defenses by three more fortresses in the vicinity. His vigorous policy so thoroughly established the supremacy of the Pharaoh in the newly won possessions that the Empire regarded him as the real conqueror of the region. He was worshipped already in the Eighteenth Dynasty as the god of the land, while his feast of victory was still celebrated and his calendar of offerings renewed at the same time (BAR, II, 167 *ff.*). Thus the gradual progress of the Pharaohs southward, which had begun in prehistoric times at El Kab (Nekhen) and had absorbed the first cataract by the beginning of the Sixth Dynasty, had now reached the second cataract, and had added two hundred miles of the Nile valley to the kingdom.

158 THE MIDDLE KINGDOM: THE FEUDAL AGE

155. It is under the aggressive Sesostris III also that we hear of the first invasion of Syria by the Pharaohs. Sebek-khu, commandant of the residence city, mentions on his memorial stone at Abydos that he accompanied the king on a campaign into a region called Sekmem in Retenu (Syria). The Asiatics were defeated in battle, and Sebek-khu took a prisoner. He narrates with visible pride how the king rewarded him, and we discern a trace of the military enthusiasm which two centuries and a half later achieved the conquest of the Pharaoh's empire in the same region. While we do not know the location of Sekmem in Syria, it is highly improbable that this was the only expedition of the Twelfth Dynasty kings into that country. In some degree the Pharaohs of the Middle Kingdom were thus preparing the way for the conquest in Asia, as those of the Sixth Dynasty had done in Nubia. Already in Sesostris I's time regular messengers to and from the Pharaonic court were traversing Syria and Palestine: Egyptians and the Egyptian tongue were not uncommon there, and the dread of the Pharaoh's name was already felt. At Gezer, between Jerusalem and the sea, the stela of an Egyptian official of this age and the statue of another have been found. The port of Byblos, whence Snefru had brought cedar a thousand years before, was well known in Egypt, and Egyptian women were now named after her goddess (AZ, 42, 109). Khnumhotep of Menat-Khufu depicts in his well-known Benihasan tomb the arrival there of thirty-seven Semitic tribesmen, who evidently came to trade. Their leader was a "ruler of the hill-country, Absha," a name well known in Hebrew as Abshai. The unfortunate noble, Sinuhe, who fled to Syria at the death of Amenemhet I, found not far over the border a friendly

sheik who had been in Egypt; in Syria he found Egyptians abiding. While a fortress existed at the Delta frontier to keep out the marauding Beduin, there can be no doubt that it was no more a hindrance to legitimate trade and intercourse than was the blockade against the negroes maintained by Sesostris III at the second cataract. A canal connected the Nile with this fortress and the Bitter Lakes of the Isthmus of Suez, thus joining the Nile and the Red Sea. The needs of the Semitic tribes of neighbouring Asia were already those of highly civilized peoples and gave ample occasion for trade. Already the red pottery produced by the Hittite peoples in Cappadocia, of Asia Minor, was possibly finding its way to the Semites of southern Palestine. Undoubtedly the commerce along this route, through Palestine, over Carmel and northward to the trade-routes leading down the Euphrates to Babylon, while not yet heavy, was already long existent. Commerce with southern Europe had also begun. The peoples of the Ægean, whose civilization had now developed into that of the early Mycenæan age, were not unknown in Egypt at this time. Their pottery has been found at Kahun in burials of this age, and the Ægean decorative art of the time, especially in its use of spirals, is influenced by that of Egypt. Europe thus emerges more clearly upon the horizon of the Nile people during the Middle Kingdom (BAR, I, 676–687; 496, l. 94; 620, note d; 493 *f*.; 428; PEFQS, 1903, 37, 125; 1905, 317; 1906, 121; II, Sam. x, 10; AZ, 43, 72 *f*.).

156. For thirty-eight years Sesostris III continued his vigorous rule of a kingdom which now embraced a thousand miles of Nile valley. The regard in which he was held is evident in the extraordinary hymn in his honour composed before his death (GKP). To the

name Sesostris tradition attached the first foreign conquests of the Pharaohs. Around this name clustered forever after the stories of war and conquest related by the people, and in Greek times Sesostris had long since become but a legendary figure which cannot be identified with any particular king. As old age drew on, Sesostris III appointed his son as coregent, and an account of the appointment was recorded on the walls of the temple at Arsinoe in the Fayum. At Sesostris III's death in 1849 B. C., this coregent son Amenemhet, the third of the name, seems to have assumed the throne without difficulty.

157. A number of peaceful enterprises for the prosperity of the country and the increase of the royal revenues were successfully undertaken by Amenemhet III. Operations in the mines of Sinai had been resumed as early as the reign of Sesostris I. It remained for Amenemhet III to develop the equipment of the stations in the peninsula, so that they might become more permanent than the mere camp of a brief expedition. These expeditions suffered great hardships, and an official of the time describes the difficulties which beset him when some unlucky chance had decreed that he should arrive there in summer (BAR, I, 733–740). Amenemhet III therefore made the mines at Sarbut el-Khadem a well equipped station (BAR, I, 725–727; 717 *f.*, 738). The mines were placed each under charge of a foreman, after whom it was named, and at periodic visits of the treasury officials a fixed amount of ore was expected from each mine. Here Egyptians died and were buried in the burning valley with all the equipment customary at home, and the ruins still surviving show that what had before been but an intermittent and occasional effort had now become

a permanent and uninterrupted industry (BAR, I, 731).

158. While forced to seek new sources of wealth outside of the country, the Twelfth Dynasty monarchs, as we have before intimated, raised the productive capacity of the homeland to an unprecedented level. Unfortunately, the annals or records of these achievements have not survived. We find the officials of Amenemhet III in the fortress of Semneh in the second cataract recording the height of the Nile on the rocks there, which thus in a few years became a nilometer, recording the maximum level of the high water from year to year. These records, still preserved upon the rocks, are from twenty-five to thirty feet higher than the Nile rises at the present day. Such observations, communicated without delay to the officials of Lower Egypt in the vizier's office, enabled them to estimate the crops of the coming season, and the rate of taxation was fixed accordingly (LD, II, 139; SBA, 1844, 374 *ff.*).

159. In Lower Egypt a plan was also devised for extending the time during which the waters of the inundation could be made available by an enormous scheme of irrigation. A glance at the map will show the reader at a point about sixty-five miles above the southern apex of the Delta a great depression of the Libyan desert known as the Fayum, a basin some forty miles across, which does not differ from those of the western oases, and is indeed an extensive oasis close to the Nile valley, with which it is connected by a gap in the western hills. In prehistoric times the high Nile had filled the entire Fayum basin, producing a considerable lake. The kings of the Twelfth Dynasty conceived the plan of controlling the inflow and outflow for the benefit of the irrigation system then in

force. At the same time they undertook vast retention walls inside the Fayum at the point where the waters entered, in order to reclaim some of the area of the Fayum for cultivation. The earlier kings of the Twelfth Dynasty began this process of reclamation, but it was especially Amenemhet III who so extended this vast wall that it was at last probably about twenty-seven miles long, thus reclaiming a final total of twenty-seven thousand acres. These enormous works at the point where the lake was most commonly visited gave the impression that the whole body of water was an artificial product, excavated, as Strabo says, by King "Lamares," a name in which we recognize with certainty the throne name of Amenemhet III. This was the famous lake Moeris of the classic geographers and travellers. Modern calculations have shown that enough water could have been accumulated to double the volume of the river below the Fayum during the hundred days of low Nile from the first of April on (BFLM).

160. The rich and flourishing province recovered from the lake was doubtless royal domain, and there are evidences that it was a favourite place of abode with the kings of the latter part of the Twelfth Dynasty. A prosperous town, known to the Greeks as Crocodilopolis, or Arsinoe, with its temple to Sobk, the crocodile-god, arose in the new province, and remains of imposing monuments of the time still lie near. In the gap, on the north bank of the inflowing canal, was a vast building, some eight hundred by a thousand feet, which formed a kind of religious and administrative centre for the whole country, with a set of halls for each nome where its gods were enshrined and worshipped, and the councils of its government gathered from time to time.

THE TWELFTH DYNASTY

It would seem from the remarks of Strabo that the building was the Pharaoh's seat of government for the entire country. It was still standing in Strabo's time, when it had already long been known as the "Labyrinth," one of the wonders of Egypt, famous among travellers and historians of the Græco-Roman world, who compared its intricate complex of halls and passages with the Cretan Labyrinth of Greek tradition. The town which had grown up around this remarkable building was seen by Strabo; but both have now completely disappeared. Sesostris II had also founded a town just outside the gap called Hotep-Sesostris, "Sesostris is contented," and he later built his pyramid beside it. Under these circumstances the Fayum had become the most prominent centre of the royal and governmental life of this age; and its great god Sobk was rivalling Amon in the regard of dynasty, whose last representative bore the name Sobk-nefru-Re, which contains that of the god. The name of the god also appeared in a whole series of Sobk-hoteps of the next dynasty.

For nearly half a century the beneficent rule of Amenemhet III maintained peace and prosperity throughout his flourishing kingdom (BAR, I, 747). Business was on a sound basis, values were determined in terms of weight in copper, and it was customary to indicate the value of an article when mentioned in a document, by appending to it the words "of x deben [of copper]," a deben being 1414 grains. From the frontier forts in the second cataract to the Mediterranean, the evidences of this prosperity under Amenemhet III and his predecessors still survive in the traces of their extensive monuments and building enterprises, although these have so suffered from the rebuilding under the Empire that they are but a tithe of what was once to be seen. Moreover the vandalism of the Nineteenth Dynasty, especially under Ramses II, obliterated priceless records of the Middle Kingdom by the most reckless appropriation of its monuments as building material. Besides the great works of the kings, it should not be forgotten that the wealthier and more powerful of the nomarchs also erected temples and considerable buildings for purposes of government; and, had the various structures due to these great lords survived, there is no doubt that they would have added materially to our impressions of the solidity and splendour with which the economic life of the nation was developing on every hand (BAR, I, 484, 488 *f.*; 741 *f.*, 534, note b; 674 *f.*, 498–506, 503, 637, note a; 706).

161. Such impressions are also strengthened by the tombs of the time, which are indeed the only buildings which have survived from the feudal age; and even these are in a sad state of ruin. The chapel-hall in the cliff-tombs of the nobles, with its scenes from the life and activity of the departed lords, are our chief source for the history and life of the feudal age. The tombs of the Twelfth Dynasty kings show that the resources of the nation are no longer absorbed by the pyramid as in the Old Kingdom. Amenemhet I built his pyramid at Lisht of brick protected by casing masonry of limestone (GJL). The custom was continued by all the kings of the dynasty with one exception. Their pyramids are scattered from the mouth of the Fayum northward to Dahshur, just south of Memphis. All these pyramids show the most complicated and ingenious arrangements of entrance and passages in order to baffle the tomb-robbers. Nevertheless all were entered and robbed in antiquity, doubt-

less with the connivance of later officials, or even of the later kings themselves. The failure of these magnificent structures to protect the bodies of their builders must have had something to do with the gradual discontinuance of pyramid building which now ensued. Henceforward, with the exception of a few small pyramids at Thebes, we shall meet no more of these remarkable tombs, which, stretching in a desultory line along the margin of the western desert for sixty-five miles above the southern apex of the Delta, are the most impressive surviving witnesses to the grandeur of the civilization which preceded the Empire.

162. Unfortunately the buildings of the Middle Kingdom are so fragmentary that we can gain little idea of their architecture. Plastic art had made a certain kind of progress since the Old Kingdom. Sculpture had become much more ambitious and attempted works of the most impressive size. The statues of Amenemhet III, which overlooked Lake Moeris, were probably forty or fifty feet high, and we find the royal sculptors furnishing ten or even sixteen colossal portrait statues of the king at once (BAR, I, 601; GJL). Fragments of such colossi in massive granite are scattered over the ruins of Tanis and Bubastis, and we recall that Sesostris III erected his statue on the southern Nubian border (BAR, I, 660). Under such circumstances the royal sculptors could not but betray to some extent the mechanical and imitative spirit in which they worked. Their figures do not so often possess the striking vivacity and the strong individuality which are so characteristic of the Old Kingdom sculpture. There is, however, now and then a portrait of surprising strength and individuality (BH, Figs. 89, 90). The chapels in the cliff-tombs of

the nomarchs were elaborately decorated with paintings depicting the life of the deceased and the industries on his great estates. It cannot be said that these paintings, excellent as many of them unquestionably are, show any progress over those of the Old Kingdom, while as flat relief they are for the most part distinctly inferior to the earlier work.

163. The close and familiar oversight of the nomarch lent a distinct impetus to the arts and crafts, and the provinces developed large numbers of skilled craftsmen throughout the country (BAR, I, 638). Naturally the artisans of the court were unsurpassed. We discern in their work the result of the development which had been going on since the days of the early dynasties. The magnificent jewelry of the princesses of the royal house displays both technical skill and refined taste, quite beyond our anticipations. Little ever produced by the later goldsmiths of Europe can surpass either in beauty or in workmanship the regal ornaments worn by the daughters of the house of Amenemhet nearly two thousand years before Christ (MD, I).

164. It is literature to which we must look for the most remarkable monuments of this age. A system of uniform orthography, hitherto lacking, was now developed and followed by skilled scribes with consistency. The language of the age and its literary products were in later times regarded as classic, and in spite of its excessive artificialities, the judgment of modern study confirms that of the Empire. Although it unquestionably existed earlier, it is in Egypt and in this period that we first find a literature of entertainment. The unfortunate noble, Sinuhe, who fled into Syria on the death of Amenemhet I, returned to Egypt in his old age, and told the story of his flight, of his life and ad-

ventures in Asia till it became a favourite tale (BAR, I, 486 *ff.*), which attained such popularity that it was even written on sherds and flags of stone to be placed in the tomb for the entertainment of the dead in the hereafter. A prototype of Sindbad the Sailor, who was shipwrecked in southern waters on the voyage to Punt, returned with a tale of marvellous adventures on the island of the serpent queen where he was rescued, and loaded with wealth and favours, was sent safely back to his native land (AZ, 43). The life of the court and the nobles found reflection among the people in folk-tales, narrating the great events in the dynastic transitions, and a tale of the rise of the Fifth Dynasty was now in common circulation, although our surviving copy was written a century or two after the fall of the Twelfth Dynasty (PW). The ablest literati of the time delighted to employ the popular tale as a medium for the exercise of their skill in the artificial style now regarded as the aim of all composition. A story commonly known at the present day as the Tale of the Eloquent Peasant was composed solely in order to place in the mouth of a marvellous peasant a series of speeches in which he pleads his case against an official who had wronged him, with such eloquence that he is at last brought into the presence of the Pharaoh himself, that the monarch may enjoy the beauty of the honeyed rhetoric which flows from his lips (PKM). We have already had occasion to notice the instruction left by the aged Amenemhet I for his son, which was very popular and has survived in no less than seven fragmentary copies (BAR, I, 474 *ff.*). The instruction concerning a wise and wholesome manner of life, which was so prized by the Egyptians, is represented by a number of compositions of this age, like the advice of the father to his son on the value of the ability to write (P Sall.); or the wisdom of the viziers of the Old Kingdom; although there is no reason why the Wisdom of Ptahhotep and Kegemne (PP), preserved in a papyrus of the Middle Kingdom, should not be authentic compositions of these old wise men. A remarkable philosophizing treatise represents a man weary of life involved in a long dialogue with his reluctant soul as he vainly attempts to persuade it that they should end life together and hope for better things beyond this world (EG). A strange and obscure composition of the time represents a Sibylline prophet named Ipuwer, standing in the presence of the king and delivering grim prophecies of coming ruin, in which the social and political organization shall be overthrown, until there shall come a saviour, who shall be "the shepherd of all the people," and shall save them from destruction. Specimens of this remarkable class of literature, of which this is the earliest example, may be traced as late as the early Christian centuries, and we cannot resist the conclusion that it furnished the Hebrew prophets with the form and to a surprising extent also with the content of Messianic prophecy. It remained for the Hebrew to give this old form a higher ethical and religious significance (SBA, xxvii, 601–610).

165. So many of the compositions of the Egyptian scribe are couched in poetic language that it is often difficult to distinguish between poetry and prose. But even among the common people there were compositions which are distinctively poems: the song of the threshers as they drive their cattle to and fro upon the threshing-floor, a few simple lines breathing the wholesome industry of the people; or the lay of the harper as he sings to the banqueters in the halls of the rich—

a song burdened with premonitions of the coming darkness and admonishing to unbridled enjoyment of the present ere the evil day come.

166. The earliest known example of poetry exhibiting rigid strophic structure and all the conscious aritficialities of literary art is a remarkable hymn of six strophes, singing the praises of Sesostris III, and written during that king's lifetime. The dramatic presentation of the life and death of Osiris at Abydos undoubtedly demanded much dialogue and recitation, which must at least have assumed permanent form and have been committed to writing. Unfortunately this, the earliest known drama, has perished. It is characteristic of this early world that in neither the art nor the literature, of which we have a considerable mass from the Middle Kingdom, can we discern any individuals to whom these great works should be attributed. Among all the literary productions which we have enumerated it is only of the wisdom, the "instruction," that we know the authors. Of the literature of the age, as a whole, we may say that it now displays a wealth of imagery and a fine mastery of *form* which five hundred years earlier, at the close of the Old Kingdom, was but just emerging. The *content* of the surviving works does not display evidence of constructive ability in the larger sense, involving both form and content. It is possible, however, that the Osirian drama, which offered greater constructive opportunity, might have altered this verdict if it had survived.

167. It was thus over a nation in the fulness of its powers, rich and productive in every avenue of life, that Amenemhet III ruled; and his reign crowned the classic age which had dawned with the advent of his family. This may perhaps have been due to the fact

that already in the reign of the mighty Sesostris III the power of the feudal barons had been broken; we find no tombs of these rich country nobles from the accession of Sesostris III on. The Pharaoh's power had suppressed them almost to disappearance. Thus Amenemhet III had a free hand. But when he passed away in 1801 B. C. the strength of the line was waning. As Prammares, god of the Fayum, the worship of the great king survived far into Greek days. A fourth Amenemhet, after a short coregency with the old king, succeeded at the death of Amenemhet III, but his brief reign of a little over nine years has left few monuments, and the decline of the house, to whom the nation owed two centuries of imperishable splendour, was evident. Amenemhet IV left no son, for he was succeeded by the Princess Sebek-nefru-Re, the Skemiophris of Manetho. After struggling on for nearly four years she too, the last of her line, disappeared. The family had ruled Egypt two hundred and thirteen years, one month and some days (AZ, 42, 111 *ff.*; 43, 84 *ff.*; BAR, I, 64).

PART IV

THE HYKSOS:

THE RISE OF THE EMPIRE

XI

THE FALL OF THE MIDDLE KINGDOM. THE HYKSOS

168. WHILE the transition of authority to another dynasty (the Thirteenth) had seemingly taken place without disturbance, its first king, Sekhemre-Khutowe, was early overthrown after a reign of but five years. Rapid dissolution followed, as the provincial lords rose against each other and strove for the throne. Pretender after pretender struggled for supremacy; now and again one more able than his rivals would gain a brief advantage and wear his ephemeral honours, only to be quickly supplanted by another. Private individuals contended with the rest and occasionally won the coveted goal, only to be overthrown by a successful rival. A Sebekemsaf of this time ruled long enough to build a modest pyramid for himself and his queen at Thebes, where their bodies were found violated and robbed six hundred and fifty years later, by the Ramessid inspectors (BAR, IV, 517). At one time a usurper named Neferhotep succeeded in overthrowing one of the many Sebekhoteps of the time, and established stable government. He made no secret of his origin, and on the monuments added the names of his untitled parents without scruple (BAR, I, 753-765). He reigned eleven years, when he was succeeded by his son, Sihathor, who shortly gave way to his father's brother, Neferkhere-Sebekhotep (Note II; TP,

Frag. No. 80; P Scar., No. 309). It was, however, but a brief restoration, and the monuments which have survived bear no records to inform us of its character.

169. The darkness which followed is only the more obscure by contrast. Foreign adventurers took advantage of the opportunity, and one of the pretenders who achieved a brief success was a Nubian. Within a century and a quarter after the fall of the Twelfth Dynasty sixty of these ephemeral Theban rulers had held the throne, forming Manetho's Thirteenth Dynasty. They left little behind them. Here and there a fragment of masonry, a statue, or sometimes only a scarab bearing a royal name, furnishes contemporary testimony to the brief reign of this or that one among them. There was neither power, nor wealth, nor time for the erection of permanent monuments; king still followed king with unprecedented rapidity, and for most of them our only source of knowledge is therefore the bare name in the mutilated Turin list, the disordered fragments of which have not even preserved for us the order of these ephemeral rulers except as we find groups upon one fragment. Where preserved at all, the length of the reign is usually but a year or two, while in two cases we find after a king's name but three days.

170. Economically the condition of the country must have rapidly degenerated. The lack of a uniform administration of the irrigation system, oppressive taxation and the tyranny of warring factions in need of funds sapped the energies and undermined the prosperity of the past two centuries. The hapless nation was thus an easy prey to foreign aggression. About 1657 B. C., before the close of the Thirteenth Dynasty,

THE FALL OF THE MIDDLE KINGDOM 175

there now poured into the Delta from Asia a possibly Semitic invasion such as that which in prehistoric times had stamped the language with its unmistakable form; and again in our own era, under the influence of Mohammed's teaching, had overwhelmed the land (MNC 34). These invaders, now generally called the Hyksos, after the designation applied to them by Josephus (quoting Manetho), themselves left so few monuments in Egypt that even their nationality is still the subject of much difference of opinion; while the exact length and character of their supremacy, for the same reason, are equally obscure matters. The documentary materials bearing on them are so meagre and limited in extent that the reader may easily survey them and judge the question for himself, even if this chapter is thereby in danger of relapsing into a "laboratory note-book." The late tradition regarding the Hyksos, recorded by Manetho and preserved to us in the essay of Josephus against Apion, is but the substance of a folk-tale like that narrating the fall of the Fourth Dynasty (above, p. 112). The more ancient and practically contemporary evidence should therefore be questioned first.

Two generations after the Hyksos had been expelled from the country, the great queen, Hatshepsut, narrating her restoration of the temples they had desecrated, calls them "Asiatics" and "barbarians" dwelling in Avaris, and ruling "in ignorance of Re" (BAR, II, 303). The still earlier evidence of a soldier in the Egyptian army that expelled the Hyksos shows that a siege of Avaris was necessary to drive them from the country; and, further, that the pursuit of them was continued into southern Palestine, and ultimately into Phœnicia or Cœlesyria (BAR, II, 8–10; 12 *f.*, 20). Some four hundred years after their expulsion a folk-tale, narrating the cause of the final war against them, was circulating among the people. It gives an interesting account of them:

"Now it came to pass that the land of Egypt was the possession of the polluted, no lord being king at the time when it happened; but King Sekenenre, he was ruler of the Southern City [Thebes] . . . King Apophis was in Avaris, and the whole land was tributary to him; the [Southland] bearing their impost, and the Northland likewise bearing every good thing of the Delta. Now King Apophis made Sutekh his lord, serving no other god, who was in the whole land, save Sutekh. He built the temple in beautiful and everlasting work. . . ." (P Sall., I, ll. 1-3).

171. From these earlier documents it is evident that the Hyksos were an Asiatic people who ruled Egypt from their stronghold of Avaris in the Delta. The exact site of Avaris is still undetermined. The later tradition as quoted from Manetho by Josephus in the main corroborates the above more trustworthy evidence, and is as follows:

"There was a king of ours whose name was Timaios, in whose reign it came to pass, I know not why, that God was displeased with us, and there came unexpectedly men of ignoble birth out of the eastern parts, who had boldness enough to make an expedition into our country, and easily subdued it by force without a battle. And when they had got our rulers under their power, they afterward savagely burnt down our cities and demolished the temples of the gods, and used all the inhabitants in a most hostile manner, for they slew some and led the children and wives of others into slavery. At length they made one of themselves king, whose name was Salatis, and he lived at Memphis and made both Upper and Lower Egypt pay tribute, and left garrisons in places that were most suitable for them. And he made the eastern part especially strong, as he foresaw that the Assyrians, who had then the greatest power, would covet their kingdom and invade them. And as he found in the Saite [read Sethroite] nome a city very fit for his purpose—which lay east of the arm of the Nile near Bubastis, and with regard to a certain theological notion was called Avaris—he rebuilt it and made it very strong by the walls he built around it and by a numerous garrison of two hundred and forty thousand armed men, whom he put into it to keep it. There Salatis went every summer, partly to gather in his corn and pay his soldiers their wages, and partly to train his armed men and so to awe foreigners" (Contra Apion, I, 14).

172. If we eliminate the absurd reference to the Assyrians and the preposterous number of the garrison at Avaris, the tale may be credited as in general a probable narrative. The further account of the Hyksos in the same essay shows clearly that the late tradition was at a loss to identify them as to nationality and origin. Still quoting from Manetho, Josephus says: "All this nation was styled Hyksos, that is, Shepherd Kings; for the first syllable 'hyk' in the sacred dialect denotes a king, and 'sos' signifies a shepherd, but this is only according to the vulgar tongue; and of these was compounded the term Hyksos. Some say they were Arabians." According to his epitomizers, Manetho also called them Phœnicians. Turning to the designations of Asiatic rulers as preserved on the Middle Kingdom and Hyksos monuments, there is no such term to be found as "ruler of shepherds," and Manetho wisely adds that the word "sos" only means shepherd in the

late vulgar dialect. There is no such word known in the older language of the monuments. "Hyk" (Egyptian *Hk'*), however, is a common word for ruler, as Manetho says, and Khian, one of the Hyksos kings, often gives himself this title upon his monuments, followed by a word for "countries," which by slight and very common phonetic changes might become "sos"; so that "Hyksos" is a not improbable Greek spelling for the Egyptian title "Ruler of Countries."

173. Looking further at the scanty monuments left by the Hyksos themselves, we discover a few vague but nevertheless significant hints as to the character of these strange invaders, whom tradition called Arabians and Phœnicians; and contemporary monuments designated as "Asiatics," "barbarians," and "rulers of countries." An Apophis, one of their kings, fashioned an altar, now at Cairo, and engraved upon it the dedication: "He [Apophis] made it as his monument for his father Sutekh, lord of Avaris, when he [Sutekh] set all lands under his [the king's] feet" (MMD, 38). General as is the statement, it would appear that this Apophis ruled over more than the land of Egypt. More significant are the monuments of Khian, the most remarkable of this line of kings. They have been found from Gebelen in southern Egypt to the northern Delta; but they do not stop here. Under a Mycenæan wall in the palace of Cnossos in Crete an alabaster vaselid bearing his name was discovered by Mr. Evans (Annual of British School at Athens, VII, 65, Fig. 21); while a granite lion with his cartouche upon the breast, found many years ago at Bagdad, is now in the British Museum. One of his royal names was "Encompasser [literally 'embracer'] of the Lands," and we recall that his constant title upon his scarabs and cylinders is "ruler of

THE FALL OF THE MIDDLE KINGDOM 179

countries." Scarabs of the Hyksos rulers have been turned up by the excavations in southern Palestine. Meagre as these data are, one cannot contemplate them without seeing conjured up before him the vision of a vanished empire which once stretched from the Euphrates to the first cataract of the Nile, an empire of which all other evidence has perished, for the reason that Avaris, the capital of its rulers, was in the Delta where, like so many other Delta cities, it suffered a destruction so complete that we cannot even locate the spot on which it once stood. There was, moreover, every reason why the victorious Egyptians should annihilate all evidence of the supremacy of their hated conquerors. In the light of these developments it becomes evident why the invaders did not set up their capital in the midst of the conquered land, but remained in Avaris, on the extreme east of the Delta, close to the borders of Asia. It was that they might rule not only Egypt, but also their Asiatic dominions. Accepting the above probabilities, we can also understand how the Hyksos could retire to Asia and withstand the Egyptian onset for three years in southern Palestine, as we know from contemporary evidence they did (BAR, II, 13). It then becomes clear also how they could retreat to Syria when beaten in southern Palestine; these movements were possible because they controlled Palestine and Syria.

174. If we ask ourselves regarding the nationality, origin and character of this mysterious Hyksos empire, we can hazard little in reply. Manetho's tradition that they were Arabians and Phœnicians, if properly interpreted, may be correct. Such an overflow of southern Semitic emigration into Syria, as we know has since then taken place over and over again, may well have

180 THE HYKSOS: THE RISE OF THE EMPIRE

brought together these two elements; and a generation or two of successful warrior-leaders might weld them together into a rude state. The wars of the Pharaohs in Syria immediately after the expulsion of the Hyksos show the presence of civilized and highly developed states there. Now, such an empire as we believe the Hyksos ruled could hardly have existed without leaving its traces among the peoples of Syria-Palestine for some generations after the beginning of the Egyptian supremacy in Asia which now followed. It would therefore be strange if we could not discern in the records of the subsequent Egyptian wars in Asia some evidence of the surviving wreck of the once great Hyksos empire which the Pharaohs demolished.

175. For two generations after the expulsion of the Hyksos we can gain little insight into the conditions in Syria. At this point the ceaseless campaigns of Thutmose III, as recorded in his Annals, enable us to discern which nation was then playing the leading rôle there. The great coalition of the kings of Palestine and Syria, with which Thutmose III was called upon to contend at the beginning of his wars, was led and dominated throughout by the powerful king of Kadesh on the Orontes. It required ten years of constant campaigning by Thutmose III to achieve the capture of the stubborn city and the subjugation of the kingdom of which it was the head; but with power still unbroken it revolted, and Thutmose III's twenty years of warfare in Syria were only crowned with victory when he finally succeeded in again defeating Kadesh, after a dangerous and persistent struggle. The leadership of Kadesh from the beginning to the end of Thutmose III's campaigns is such as to show that many Syrian and Palestinian kinglets, especially in southern

THE FALL OF THE MIDDLE KINGDOM 181

Lebanon, were its vassals. It is in this Syrian domination of the king of Kadesh that we should probably recognize the last nucleus of the Hyksos empire, finally annihilated by the genius of Thutmose III. Hence it was that Thutmose III, the final destroyer of the Hyksos empire, became also the traditional hero who expelled the invaders from Egypt; and as Misphragmouthosis he thus appears in Manetho's story as the liberator of his country. That it was an empire of some Semitic elements we cannot doubt, in view of the Manethonian tradition and the subsequent conditions in Syria-Palestine. Moreover the scarabs of a Pharaoh who evidently belonged to the Hyksos time give his name as Jacob-her or possibly Jacob-El, and it is not impossible that some chief of the Jacob-tribes of Israel for a time gained the leadership in this obscure age. Such an incident would account surprisingly well for the entrance of these tribes into Egypt, which on any hypothesis must have taken place at about this age; and in that case the Hebrews in Egypt will have been but a part of the Beduin allies of the Kadesh or Hyksos empire, whose presence there brought into the tradition the partially correct impression that the Hyksos were shepherds, and led Manetho to his untenable etymology of the second part of the word. Likewise the naïve assumption of Josephus, who identifies the Hyksos with the Hebrews, may thus contain a kernel of truth, however accidental. But such precarious combinations should not be made without a full realization of their hazardous character.

176. Of the reign of these remarkable conquerors in Egypt we know no more than of their contemporaries, the Egyptian dynasts of this age. Shortly after the invasion of the Hyksos, the Thirteenth Dynasty at

Thebes died out about 1665 B. C. The local Fourteenth Dynasty at Xois in the Delta had probably already arisen as ephemeral vassals of the Hyksos. Similar vassals doubtless continued to rule in Thebes and probably throughout Upper Egypt. Both the account in Manetho and the folk-tale above quoted state that the Hyksos kings laid the whole country under tribute, and we have already observed that Hyksos monuments have been found as far south as Gebelen. The beginning of their rule may have been a gradual immigration without hostilities, as Manetho relates. It is perhaps in this epoch that we should place one of their kings, a certain Khenzer, who seems to have left the affairs of the country largely in the hands of his vizier, Enkhu, so that the latter administered and restored the temples (BAR, I, 781–787). As this vizier lived in the period of Neferhotep and the connected Sebekhoteps, it is evident that we should place the gradual rise of Hyksos power in Egypt just after that group of Pharaohs.

177. From the contemporary monuments we learn the names of three Apophises and of Khian, besides possibly Khenzer and Jacob-her, whom we have already noted. Among the six names preserved from Manetho by Josephus we can recognize but two, an Apophis and Iannas, who is certainly the same as Khian of the contemporary monuments. The only contemporary date is that of the thirty-third year of an Apophis, in the mathematical papyrus of the British Museum. The Manethonian tradition in which we find three dynasties of shepherds or Hyksos (the Fifteenth to Seventeenth) is totally without support from the contemporary monuments in the matter of the duration of the Hyksos supremacy in Egypt. A hundred years is

ample for the whole period. Even if it was actually much longer, this fact would not necessarily extend the length of the period from the fall of the Twelfth Dynasty to the end of the Hyksos rule; for it is evident that many of the numerous kings of this period, enumerated in the Turin Papyrus, ruled as vassals of the Hyksos, like the Sekenenre, whom the folk-tale makes the Theban vassal of one of the Apophises.

178. What occasioned the unquestionable barbarities on the part of the conquerors, it is now impossible to discern; but it is evident that hostilities must have eventually broken out, causing the destruction of the temples, later restored by Hatshepsut. Their patron god Sutekh is of course the Egyptianized form of some Syrian Baal; Sutekh being an older form of the well-known Egyptian Set. The Hyksos kings themselves must have been rapidly Egyptianized; they assumed the complete Pharaonic titulary, and they appropriated statues of their predecessors in the Delta cities, wrought, of course, in the conventional style peculiar to the Pharaohs. Civilization did not essentially suffer; a mathematical treatise dated under one of the Apophises is preserved in the British Museum. We have already seen one of the Apophises building a temple in Avaris, and a fragment of a building inscription of an Apophis at Bubastis says that he made "numerous flag-staves tipped with copper for this god," such flag-staves flying a tuft of gaily coloured pennants being used to adorn a temple front (NB, I, pl. 35 c.). Having once gained the upper hand, the Hyksos Dynasty evidently slowly decayed to become at last much like their own Egyptian vassals. The country was now broken up into petty kingdoms, of which Thebes was evidently the largest in the South. Nubkheprure-Intef, one of a group of

three Intefs who ruled there, frankly discloses the conditions in a decree of banishment, naïvely declaring that no other king or ruler showing mercy to a banished traitor shall become Pharaoh of the whole country (BAR, I, 773–780). These Intefs were buried at Thebes, where the pyramids of two of them were inspected five hundred years later by the Ramessid commissioners, who found that one of them had been tunnelled into by tomb robbers (BAR, IV, 514 *f.*; 517, 538). The influence upon Egypt of such a foreign dominion, including both Syria-Palestine and the lower Nile valley, was epoch making, and had much to do with the fundamental transformation which began with the expulsion of these aliens. It brought the horse into the Nile valley and taught the Egyptians warfare on a large scale. Whatever they may have suffered, the Egyptians owed an incalculable debt to their conquerors.

XII

THE EXPULSION OF THE HYKSOS AND THE TRIUMPH OF THEBES

179. It must have been about 1600 B.C., nearly two hundred years after the fall of the Twelfth Dynasty, that the Sekenere of the folk-tale was ruling in Thebes under the suzerainty of a Hyksos Apophis in Avaris (see p. 176). This tale, as current four hundred years later in Ramessid days, is our only source for the events that immediately followed. After its account of the Hyksos, which the reader will recall as quoted above, there finally follows a council of Apophis and his wise men; but what took place at this council is quite uncertain. It concerned a plot or design against King Sekenenre, however, for the story then recounts how Apophis sent a messenger to complain to King Sekenenre in Thebes, that the noise of the hippopotami there disturbed his sleep in Avaris. Here the tantalizing bit of papyrus is torn off, and we shall never know the conclusion of the tale (P Sall., I, II, l. 1–III, l. 3). However, what we have in it is the popular and traditional version of an incident, doubtless regarded as the occasion of the long war between the Theban princes and the Hyksos in Avaris. The preposterous *casus belli*, is folk-history, a wave mark among the people, left by the tide which the Hyksos war set in motion. Manetho corroborates the general situation depicted in

the tale; for he says that the kings of the Thebaid and other parts of Egypt made a great and long war upon the Hyksos in Avaris. His use of the plural "kings" immediately suggests the numerous local dynasts, whom we have met before, each contending with his neighbour and effectually preventing the country from presenting a united front to the northern foe. There were three Sekenenres. The mummy of the last of the three discovered in the great find at Der el-Bahri, and now at the Cairo museum, exhibits frightful wounds in the head, so that he doubtless fell in battle, not improbably in the Hyksos war. They were followed by a King Kemose who probably continued the war. This Theban family, who form the latter part of Manetho's Seventeenth Dynasty, were obliged to maintain themselves not merely against the Hyksos, but also against numerous rival dynasts, especially in the extreme South above El Kab. Here, removed from the turmoil of northern war, and able to carry on a flourishing internal commerce, the local princes enjoyed great prosperity, while those of the North had doubtless in many instances perished. We shall later find these prosperous dynasts of the South holding out against the rising power of Thebes while the latter was slowly expelling the Hyksos.

180. Following Kemose's short reign, Ahmose I, possibly his son, the first king of Manetho's Eighteenth Dynasty, assumed the leadership of the Theban house, about 1580 B. C., and became the deliverer of Egypt from her foreign lords. He succeeded in holding the valuable support of the powerful El Kab princes, already won by Sekenenre III, and he employed them against both the Hyksos and the obstinate local dynasts of the upper river, who constantly threatened his rear.

Ahmose thus made El Kab a buffer, which protected him from the attacks of his Egyptian rivals south of that city. No document bearing on the course of the war with the Hyksos in its earlier stages has survived to us, nor have any of Ahmose's royal annals been preserved, but one of his El Kab allies, named Ahmose, son of Ebana, has fortunately left an account of his own military career on the walls of his tomb at El Kab (BAR, II, 17 *ff.*). He tells how he was taken from El Kab and given service in the northern fleet against the Hyksos in Avaris. After three battles before the city, the siege of Avaris was interrupted by an uprising of one of Ahmose's southern enemies, a hostile dynasty above El Kab—a danger which was regarded as so serious by the king that he himself went south to meet it, and took Ahmose, son of Ebana, with him. Having sufficiently quelled his southern rivals, Ahmose resumed the siege of Avaris, for at this point our naval officer abruptly announces its capture: "One captured Avaris; I took captive there one man and three women, total four heads. His majesty gave them to me for slaves." The city thus fell on the fourth assault after the arrival of Ahmose, son of Ebana, but it is quite uncertain how many such assaults had been made before his transference thither, for the siege had evidently lasted many years and had been interrupted by a rebellion in Upper Egypt (BAR, II, 7–12).

181. Ahmose I pursued the Hyksos fleeing into Asia after being driven from Avaris, and they took refuge in Sharuhen, probably in southern Judah (Josh., 19, 6). Our biographer now says: "One besieged Sharuhen for three years and his majesty took it. Then I took captive there two women and one hand. One gave to me the gold of bravery besides giving me the captives

for slaves" (Note III; BAR, II, 13). This is the earliest siege of such length known in history, and it is surprising evidence of the stubbornness of the Hyksos defence and the tenacity of King Ahmose in dislodging them from a stronghold in such dangerous proximity to the Egyptian frontier. Ahmose then pursued the Hyksos northward from Sharuhen, forcing them back to at least a safe distance from the Delta frontier. Returning to Egypt, now entirely free from all fear of its Hyksos lords, he gave his attention to the recovery of the Egyptian possessions in Nubia.

182. During the long period of disorganization following the Middle Kingdom, the Nubians had naturally taken advantage of their opportunity and fallen away. How far Ahmose penetrated it is impossible to determine, but he was no sooner well out of the country on the Nubian campaign than his inveterate rivals south of El Kab again arose against him. Totally defeated in a battle on the Nile, they rose yet again and Ahmose was obliged to quell one more rebellion before he was left in undisputed possession of the throne. Our old friend Ahmose, son of Ebana, was rewarded for his valour in these actions with five slaves and five stat (nearly three and a half acres) of land in El Kab, and again he says: "There were given to me three heads [slaves] and five stat of land in my city." His comrades were treated with equal generosity (BAR, II, 14-16). We thus see how king Ahmose bound his supporters to his cause. He did not stop, however, with gold, slaves and land, but in some cases even granted the local princes, the descendants of the great feudal lords of the Middle Kingdom, high and royal titles like "first king's son," which, while perhaps conveying few or no prerogatives, satisfied the vanity of old and illustri-

ous families, like that of El Kab, who deserved well at his hands. There were but few of the local nobles who thus supported Ahmose and gained his favour; the larger number opposed both him and the Hyksos and perished in the struggle. Their more fortunate fellows, being now nothing more than court and administrative officials, the feudal lords, who had survived the repressive hand of the Pharaoh during the second half of the Middle Kingdom, thus practically disappeared. The lands which formed their hereditary possessions were confiscated and passed to the crown, where they permanently remained. There was one notable exception; the house of El Kab, to which the Theban dynasty owed so much, was allowed to retain its lands, and two generations after the expulsion of the Hyksos, the head of the house appears as lord, not only of El Kab but also Esneh and all the intervening territory. Besides this he was given administrative charge, though not hereditary possession, of the lands of the south from the vicinity of Thebes (Per-Hathor) to El Kab. Yet this exception serves but to accentuate more sharply the total extinction of the landed nobility, who had formed the substance of the governmental organization under the Middle Kingdom. We do indeed find a handful of barons still wearing their old feudal titles, but they resided at Thebes and were buried there (BAR, II, 329, note e). All Egypt was now the personal estate of the Pharaoh just as it was after the destruction of the Mamlukes by Mohammed Ali early in the nineteenth century. It is this state of affairs which in Hebrew tradition was represented as the direct result of Joseph's sagacity (Gen. xlvii: 19–20).

PART V

THE EMPIRE: FIRST PERIOD

XIII

THE NEW STATE: SOCIETY AND RELIGION

183. THE task of building up a state, which now confronted Ahmose I, differed materially from the reorganization accomplished at the beginning of the Twelfth Dynasty by Amenemhet I. The latter dealt with social and political factors no longer new in his time, whereas Ahmose had now to begin with the erection of a fabric of government out of elements so completely divorced from the old forms as to have lost their identity, being now in a state of total flux. The course of events, which culminated in the expulsion of the Hyksos, determined for Ahmose the form which the new state was to assume. He was now at the head of a strong army, effectively organized and welded together by long campaigns and sieges protracted through years, during which he had been both general in the field and head of the state. The character of the government followed involuntarily out of these conditions. Egypt became a military state. It was quite natural that it should remain so, in spite of the usually unwarlike character of the Egyptian. The long war with the Hyksos had now educated him as a soldier, the large army of Ahmose had spent years in Asia and had even been for a longer or shorter period among the rich cities of Syria. Having thoroughly learned war and having perceived the enormous wealth to be gained by it in Asia, the

whole land was roused and stirred with a lust of conquest, which was not quenched for several centuries. The wealth, the rewards and the promotion open to the professional soldier were a constant incentive to a military career, and the middle classes, otherwise so unwarlike, now entered the ranks with ardour. In the biographies which they have left in their tombs at Thebes the survivors of the noble class narrate with the greatest satisfaction the campaigns which they went through at the Pharaoh's side, and the honours which he bestowed upon them (BAR, II, 1–16; 17–25 *et passim*). Many a campaign, all record of which would have been irretrievably lost, has thus come to our knowledge through one of these military biographies, like that of Ahmose, son of Ebana, from which we have quoted (Ibid). The sons of the Pharaoh, who in the Old Kingdom held administrative offices, are now generals in the army (BAR, II, 350; 362). For the next century and a half the story of the achievements of the army will be the story of Egypt, for the army is now the dominant force and the chief motive power in the new state. In organization it quite surpassed the militia of the old days, if for no other reason than that it was now a standing army. It was organized into two grand divisions, one in the Delta and the other in the upper country (BAR, III, 56). In Syria it had learned tactics and proper strategic disposition of forces, the earliest of which we know anything in history. We shall now find partition of an army into divisions, we shall hear of wings and centre, we shall even trace a flank movement and define battle lines. All this is fundamentally different from the disorganized plundering expeditions naïvely reported as wars by the monuments of the older periods. Besides the old bow and spear, the troops henceforth carry also a war axe. They have learned archery fire by volleys and the dreaded archers of Egypt now gained a reputation which followed and made them feared even in classic times. But more than this, the Hyksos having brought the horse into Egypt, the Egyptian armies now for the first time possessed a large proportion of chariotry. Cavalry in the modern sense of the term was not employed. The deft craftsmen of Egypt soon mastered the art of chariot-making, while the stables of the Pharaoh contained thousands of the best horses to be had in Asia. In accordance with the spirit of the time, the Pharaoh was accompanied on all public appearances by a bodyguard of élite troops and a group of his favourite military officers.

184. This new state is revealed to us more clearly than that of any other period of Egyptian history under native dynasties. The supreme position occupied by the Pharaoh meant a very active participation in the affairs of government. He was accustomed every morning to meet the vizier, still the mainspring of the administration, to consult with him on all the interests of the country and all the current business which necessarily came under his eye. Immediately thereafter he held a conference with the chief treasurer. These two men headed the chief departments of government: the treasury and the judiciary. The Pharaoh's office, in which they made their daily reports to him, was the central organ of the whole government where all its lines converged. Even in the limited number of such documents preserved to us, we discern the vast array of detailed questions in practical administration which the busy monarch decided, going on frequent journeys to examine new buildings and check all sorts of official

abuses. Besides numerous campaigns in Nubia and Asia, he visited the quarries and mines in the desert or inspected the desert routes, seeking suitable locations for wells and stations. The official cults in the great temples, too, demanded more and more of the monarch's time and attention as feasts and ritual were multiplied. Early in the Eighteenth Dynasty, however, the business of government and the duties of the Pharaoh had so increased that he appointed a second vizier. One resided at Thebes, for the administration of the South, from the cataract as far as the nome of Siut; while the other, who had charge of all the region north of the latter point, lived at Heliopolis (GIM).

For administrative purposes the country was divided into irregular districts, of which there were at least twenty-seven between Siut and the cataract, and the country as a whole must have been divided into over twice that number. The head of government in the old towns still bore the feudal title "count," but it now indicated solely administrative duties and might better be translated "mayor" or "governor." Each of the smaller towns had a "town-ruler," but in the other districts there were only recorders and scribes, with one of their number at their head (BAR, II, 716–745).

185. The great object of government was to make the country economically strong and productive. To secure this end, its lands, now chiefly owned by the crown, were worked by the king's serfs, controlled by his officials, or entrusted by him as permanent and indivisible fiefs to his favourite nobles, his partisans and relatives. Divisible parcels might also be held by tenants of the untitled classes. Both classes of holdings might be transferred by will or sale in much the same way as if the holder actually owned the land. For purposes of

taxation all lands and other property of the crown, except that held by the temples, were recorded in the tax-registers of the White House, as the treasury was still called (BAR, II, 916, l, 31). On the basis of these, taxes were assessed. They were still collected in naturalia: cattle, grain, wine, oil, honey, textiles and the like. Besides the cattle-yards, the "granary" was the chief sub-department of the White House, and there were innumerable other magazines for the storage of its receipts. If we may accept Hebrew tradition as transmitted in the story of Joseph, such taxes comprised one fifth of the produce of the land (Gen. xlvii, 23-27). The chief treasurer, through the local officials above noticed, collected all such taxes; he was however, under the authority of the vizier, to whom he made a report every morning, after which he received permission to open the offices and magazines for the day's business (BAR, II, 679). The collection of a second class of revenue, that paid by the local officials themselves as a tax upon their offices, was exclusively in the hands of the viziers. The southern vizier was responsible for all the officials of Upper Egypt in his jurisdiction from Elephantine to Siut; and in view of this fact the other vizier doubtless bore a similar responsibility in the North. This tax on the officials consisted chiefly of gold, silver, grain, cattle and linen, a stately sum in the annual revenues. All foreign tribute was reported to the southern vizier at Thebes. We can unfortunately form no estimate of the total of all revenues. Of the royal income from all sources in the Eighteenth Dynasty the southern vizier had general charge. The amount of all taxes to be levied and the distribution of the revenue when collected were determined in his office, where a constant balance sheet was kept. In order to control both income and outgo, a monthly fiscal report was made to him by all local officials, and thus the southern vizier was able to furnish the king from month to month with a full statement of prospective resources in the royal treasury (BAR, II, 708; 716–745; 709; 746–751; 760 *f.*).

186. In the administration of justice the southern vizier played even a greater rôle than in the treasury. Here he was supreme. The old magnates of the Southern Tens, once possessed of important judicial functions, have sunk to a mere attendant council at the vizier's public audiences, where they seem to have retained not even advisory functions (BAR, II, 712). The six "great houses" or courts of justice have evidently disappeared save in the title of the vizier. All petitioners for legal redress applied first to him in his audience hall; if possible in person, but in any case in writing. Every morning the people crowded into the "hall of the vizier," where the ushers and bailiffs jostled them into line that they might "be heard," in order of arrival, one after another. All crimes in the capital city were denounced and tried before him, and he maintained a criminal docket of prisoners awaiting trial or punishment, which strikingly suggests modern documents of the same sort. All this, and especially the land cases, demanded rapid and convenient access to the archives of the land. They were therefore all filed in his office. No one might make a will without filing it in the "vizier's hall." Copies of all nome archives, boundary records and all contracts were deposited with him or with his colleague in the North. Every petitioner to the king was obliged to hand in his petition in writing at the same office (BAR, II, 675; 714 *f.*; 683; 688; 703; 691; GIM).

187. Besides the vizier's "hall," also called the

"great council," there were local councils throughout the land, not primarily of a legal character. There was, as heretofore, no class of judges with *exclusively* legal duties, and these local courts were merely the body of administrative officials in each district, who were corporately empowered to try cases with full competence. They were the "great men of the town," or the local "council," and acted as the local representatives of the "great council." The number of these local courts is entirely uncertain, but the most important two known were at Thebes and Memphis. At Thebes its composition varied from day to day; it was appointed by the vizier or the Pharaoh, according to the nature of the case. All courts were largely made up of priests. They did not, however, always enjoy the best reputation among the people, for the bribe of the rich was often stronger than the justice of the poor man's cause, as it frequently is at the present day (BAR, II, 705; IV, 423 *f*.; SS; PA, II, 8, 6).

The law to which the poor appealed was undoubtedly just. The vizier was obliged to keep it constantly before him, contained in forty rolls which were laid out before his dais at all his public sessions where they were doubtless accessible to all. Unfortunately the code which they contained has perished, but of its justice we have ample evidence. Even conspirators against the king's life were not summarily put to death, but were handed over to a legally constituted court to be properly tried, and condemned only when found guilty. While the great body of this law was undoubtedly very old, it continued to grow; thus Haremhab's regulations were new law enacted by him. The social, agricultural and industrial world of the Nile-dwellers under the Empire was therefore not at the mercy of arbitrary whim on the part of either king or court, but was governed by a large body of long respected law, embodying the principles of justice and humanity (BAR, II, 675; 712 *f.*; 715; III, 51 *f.*; 65; I, 531; SS).

188. The southern vizier was the motive power behind the organization and operation of this ancient state. We recall that he went in every morning and took council with the Pharaoh on the affairs of the country; and the only other check upon his untrammelled control of the state was a law constraining him to report the condition of his office to the chief treasurer. His office was the Pharaoh's means of communication with the local authorities, who reported to him in writing on the first day of each season, that is, three times a year. It is in his office that we discern with unmistakable clearness the complete contralization of all local government in all its functions. He was minister of war for both army and navy, and in the Eighteenth Dynasty at least, "when the king was with the army," he conducted the administration at home. He had legal control of the temples throughout the country, or, as the Egyptian put it, "he established laws in the temples of the gods of the South and the North," so that he was minister of ecclesiastical affairs. He exercised advisory functions in all the offices of the state; so long as his office was undivided with a vizier of the North he was grand steward of all Egypt, and there was no prime function of the state which did not operate immediately or secondarily through his office. He was a veritable Joseph and it must have been this office which the Hebrew narrator had in mind as that to which Joseph was appointed. He was regarded by the people as their great protector and no higher praise could be proffered to Amon when addressed by a worshipper than

to call him "the poor man's vizier who does not accept the bribe of the guilty" (PA, II, 6, 5 *f.*). His appointment was a matter of such importance that it was conducted by the king himself, and the instructions given him by the monarch display a spirit of kindness and humanity, and exhibit an appreciation of statecraft surprising in an age so remote. They may perhaps be epitomized in the Pharaoh's own words on that occasion, "Lo, the true dread of a prince is to do justice. . . . Be not known to the people and they shall not say, 'He is only a man.'" The viziers of the Eighteenth Dynasty desired the reputation of hard working, conscientious officials, who took the greatest pride in the proper administration of the office. Several of them have left a record of their installation, with a long list of the duties of the office, engraved and painted upon the walls of their Theban tombs, and it is from these that we have drawn our account of the vizier (BAR, II, 671 *ff.*; 665 *ff.*).

189. Such was the government of the imperial age in Egypt. In society the disappearance of the landed nobility, and the administration of the local districts by a vast army of petty officials of the crown, opened the way more fully than in the Middle Kingdom for innumerable careers among the middle class. These opportunities must have worked a gradual change in their condition. Thus one official relates his obscure origin thus: "I was one whose family was poor and whose town was small, but the king recognized me. . . . He exalted me more than the royal companions, introducing me among the princes" (Leyden, Stela V, I). Such possibilities of promotion and royal favour awaited success in local administration, for in some local office the career of this unknown official in the small town

must have begun. There thus grew up a new official class. As there was no longer a feudal nobility, the great government officials became the nobles of the Empire, surrounding the person of the Pharaoh. At the bottom the masses who worked the fields and estates, the serfs of the Pharaoh, formed so large a portion of the inhabitants, that the Hebrew scribe, evidently writing from the outside, knew only this class of society besides the priests (Gen. xlvii, 21). These lower strata passed away and left little or no trace, but the middle class was now able to erect tombs and mortuary stelæ in such surprising numbers that they furnish us a vast mass of materials for reconstructing the life and customs of the time. The soldier in the standing army has now also become a social class. The free middle class, liable to military service, are called "citizens of the army," a term already known in the Middle Kingdom, but now very common; so that liability to military service becomes the significant designation of this class of society. Politically the soldier's influence grows with every reign and he soon becomes the involuntary reliance of the Pharaoh in the execution of numerous civil commissions where formerly the soldier was never employed (BAR, II, 274; p. 165, note a; 681).

190. Side by side with the soldier appears another new and powerful class, that of the priesthood. As a natural consequence of the great wealth of the temples under the Empire, the priesthood becomes a profession, no longer merely an incidental office held by a layman, as in the Old and Middle Kingdoms. All the priestly communities were now for the first time united in a great sacerdotal organization embracing the whole land. The head of the state temple at Thebes, the High Priest of Amon, was the supreme head of this greater

THE NEW STATE: SOCIETY AND RELIGION 203

body also and his power was thereby increased far beyond that of his older rivals at Heliopolis and Memphis. The temples grew into vast and gorgeous palaces, each with its community of priests, and the high priest of such a community in the larger centres was a veritable sacerdotal prince, ultimately wielding considerable political power.

191. The triumph of a Theban family had brought with it the supremacy of Amon. Transformed by the solar theology into Amon-Re, and with some attributes borrowed from his neighbour, Min of Coptos, he now rose to a unique and supreme position of unprecedented splendour as the state god. But the fusion of the old gods had not deprived Amon alone of his individuality, for in the general flux almost any god might possess the qualities and functions of the others, although the dominant position was still occupied by the sun-god.

192. The mortuary beliefs of the time are the outgrowth of tendencies already plainly observable in the Middle Kingdom (see p. 150). The magical formulæ by which the dead are to triumph in the hereafter become more and more numerous, so that it is no longer possible to record them on the inside of the coffin. They must be written on papyrus and the roll placed in the tomb. As the selection of the most important of these texts came to be more and more uniform, the "Book of the Dead" began to take form. But magic achieved still more. The luxurious lords of the Empire no longer look forward with pleasure to the prospect of plowing, sowing and reaping in the happy fields of Yaru; a magical statuette placed in the tomb arises and does the work otherwise falling upon the deceased. Such "Ushebtis," or "respondents," as they were termed, were now placed in the necropolis by scores and hun-

dreds. A sacred beetle or scarabæus is cut from stone and inscribed with a charm, beginning with the significant words, "O my heart, rise not up against me as a witness;" and thus an evil life is masked in the judgment hall of Osiris. Likewise the rolls of the Book of the Dead containing, besides all the other charms, also the scene of judgment, and especially the welcome verdict of acquital, are now sold by the priestly scribes to anyone with the means to buy; and the fortunate purchaser's name is then inserted in the blanks left for this purpose throughout the document; thus securing for himself the certainty of such a verdict, before it was known whose name should be so inserted. The invention of these devices by the priests was undoubtedly as subversive of moral progress in religion as the sale of indulgences in Luther's time, and as the priestly literature on the hereafter continued to grow, it stifled the moral aspirations which had come into the religion of Egypt with the ethical influences so potent in the Osiris-myth.

193. The tomb of the noble consists as before of chambers hewn in the face of the cliff. In accordance with the prevailing tendency it is now filled with imaginary scenes from the next world, while at the same time the tomb has become more a personal monument to the deceased, and the walls of the chapel bear many scenes from his life, especially from his official career, particularly as a record of the honours which he received from the king. Thus the cliffs opposite Thebes, honeycombed as they are with the tombs of the lords of the Empire, contain whole chapters of the life and history of the period, with which we shall now deal. In a solitary valley behind these cliffs, as we shall see, the kings now likewise excavate their tombs in the limestone

walls and the pyramid is no longer employed. Vast galleries are pierced into the mountain, and, passing from hall to hall, they terminate many hundreds of feet from the entrance in a large chamber, where the body of the king is laid in a huge stone sarcophagus. On the western plain of Thebes, the plain east of this valley, as on the east side of the pyramid, arose the splendid mortuary temples of the emperors, of which we shall later have occasion to say more. But these elaborate mortuary customs are now no longer confined to the Pharaoh and his nobles; the necessity for some equipment in preparation for the hereafter is now felt by all classes. The manufacture of such materials, resulting from the gradual extension of these customs, has become an industry; the embalmers, undertakers and manufacturers of coffins and tomb furniture occupy a quarter at Thebes, forming almost a guild by themselves, as they did in later Greek times.

194. Out of the chaos which the rule of foreign lords had produced, the new state and the new conditions slowly emerged as Ahmose I gradually gained leisure from his arduous wars. With the state religion, the foreign dynasty had shown no sympathy and the temples lay wasted and deserted in many places. We find Ahmose therefore in his twenty-second year undertaking the repair and equipment of the temples. His greatest work, however, remains the Eighteenth Dynasty itself, for whose brilliant career his own achievements had laid so firm a foundation. Notwithstanding his reign of at least twenty-two years, Ahmose must have died young (1557 B. C.) for his mother was still living in the tenth year of his son and successor, Amenhotep I. By him he was buried in the old Eleventh Dynasty cemetery at the north end of the western Theban plain

in a masonry tomb, which has now long perished. The famous jewelry of his mother, stolen from her neighbouring tomb at a remote date, was found by Mariette concealed in the vicinity. The body of Ahmose I, as well as this jewelry, are now preserved in the Museum at Cairo (BAR, II, 26–8; 33 *ff.*; 49–51; Masp. Mom. roy. 534).

XIV

THE CONSOLIDATION OF THE KINGDOM; THE RISE OF THE EMPIRE

195. THE time was not yet ripe for the great achievements which awaited the monarchs of the new dynasty in Asia. The old Nubian dominion of the Middle Kingdom, from the first to the second cataract, was still far from final pacification. The Troglodytes, who later harassed the Romans on this same frontier, now possessed a leader, and Ahmose's campaign against them had not been lasting in its effects. Amenhotep I, Ahmose's successor, was therefore obliged to invade Nubia in force. He captured the rebellious leader, and penetrated to the old landmarks of the Middle Kingdom frontier at the second cataract. Northern Nubia was now placed under the administration of the mayor or governor of the old city of Nekhen, which now became the northern limit of a southern administrative district, including all the territory on the south of it, controlled by Egypt, at least as far as northern Nubia, or Wawat. From this time the new governor was able to go north with the tribute of the country regularly every year (BAR, II, 38 f.; 41, 47 f.).

196. The wars of the Hyksos had given the Libyans the opportunity, which they always improved, of pushing in and occupying the rich lands of the Delta, and the new Pharaoh was now suddenly called northward

to expel them. This mission successfully concluded, Amenhotep was at liberty to turn his arms toward Asia. Unfortunately we have no records of his Syrian war, but he possibly penetrated far to the north, even to the Euphrates. In any case he accomplished enough to enable his successor to boast of ruling as far as the Euphrates, before the latter had himself undertaken any Asiatic conquests (BAR, II, 39, ll. 27 *f*.; 42, 22; 73).

197. After a reign of at least ten years Amenhotep I's richly wrought buildings at Thebes were interrupted by his death (BAR, II, 45 *f*.; IV, 513; B, I, 4, No. 3, 164 *f*.). Whether he left a son entitled to the throne or not, we do not know. His successor, Thutmose I, was the son of a woman not of royal blood. Her great son evidently owed his accession to the kingship to his marriage with a princess of the old line, named Ahmose, through whom he could assert a valid claim to the throne. It is to him that Egypt owed the conquest of Upper Nubia, over four hundred miles beyond the old frontier of the Middle Kingdom, to Napata at the foot of the Fourth cataract where the southern frontier remained for nearly eight hundred years. The forward movement began already in the king's second year. In the battle which probably took place between the second and third cataracts, the Pharaoh himself transfixed the opposing chief with his lance. He now pushed on through the exceedingly difficult country of the second and third cataracts, where his scribes and officers have left a long trail of names and titles scratched on the rocks. At the Island of Tombos, he emerged from the desolate and precipitous cataract country upon the wide and fertile valley of the Dongola Province winding along a wide curve of uninterrupted river, two hundred and fifty miles to the foot of the fourth cataract. At Tombos,

therefore, on the threshold of the new province he engraved upon the rocks five triumphant stelæ, one of them bearing a long inscription. These are the earliest records above the third cataract. Here also at the head of the third cataract, he erected a fortress, and garrisoned it with troops from the army of conquest. It was now August and he had left Egypt in February or March. When he repassed the first cataract, with the Nubian chief, whom he had slain, hanging head downward at the prow of his royal barge, he had been absent over a year. But undoubtedly he had reorganized the country as a province under a viceroy, and Thure, the first viceroy of Nubia, now cleared the ancient canal of stones for the return passage of the king through the first cataract (BAR, II, 54–60; 67–77; 80; 75; 84 1020–25).

198. Nubia having now been thoroughly pacified, henceforth the Pharaoh looks northward. The character of the country along the eastern end of the Mediterranean, which we may call Syria-Palestine, is not such as to favor the gradual amalgamation of small and petty states into one great nation, as that process took place in the valleys of the Nile and the Euphrates. The Orontes valley, stretching northward between the two Lebanons, is the only extensive region in Syria-Palestine not cut up by the hills and mountains, where a strong kingdom might develop. The coast is completely isolated from the interior by the ridge of Lebanon, while in the south, Palestine with its harbourless coast and its large tracts of unproductive soil, hardly furnished the economic basis for the development of a strong nation. Along almost its entire eastern frontier, Syria-Palestine merges into the northern extension of the Arabian desert, save in the extreme north, where the valley of the Orontes and that of the Euphrates almost blend.

199. The country was settled chiefly by Semites, the descendants of an early overflow of population from the deserts of Arabia, such as has occurred in historic times over and over again. In the north these were Aramæans, while in the south they may be most conveniently designated as Canaanites. In general these peoples showed little genius for government, and were totally without any motives for consolidation. Divided, moreover, by the physical conformation of the country, they were organized into numerous city-kingdoms, each having not only its own kinglet, but also its own god, a local ba'al (Baal) or "lord," with whom was often associated a ba'lat or "lady," a goddess like her of Byblos. These miniature kingdoms were embroiled in frequent wars with one another, each dynast endeavouring to unseat his neighbour and absorb the latter's territory and revenues. Exceeding all the others in size was the kingdom of Kadesh, in the Orontes valley, in which we should, in the author's opinion, recognize the nucleus of the Hyksos empire as already indicated (pp. 180 f.). We shall now discern it for two generations, struggling desperately to maintain its independence, and only crushed at last by twenty years of warfare under Thutmose III.

200. Some of these kingdoms possessed a high degree of civilization. Masters of the art of metal-working they made metal vessels, weapons and chariots a great industry. Woolen textiles of the finest dye, rich and sumptuous in design, issued from their looms. These Semites were already inveterate traders, and an animated commerce was passing from town to town, where the market place was a busy scene of traffic as it is today. On the scanty shoreward slopes of Lebanon some of them, crossing from the interior, had early gained

a footing, to become the Phœnicians of historic times. They rapidly subdued the sea and soon developed into hardy mariners. In every favourable harbour they established their colonies, in Cyprus and Rhodes, along the southern litoral of Asia Minor, throughout the Ægean, and here and there on the mainland of Greece. Everywhere throughout the regions which they reached, their wares were prominent in the markets. As their wealth increased, every harbour along the Phœnician coast was the seat of a rich and flourishing city, among which Tyre, Sidon, Byblos, Arvad and Simyra were the greatest, each being the seat of a dynasty. Thus it was that in the Homeric poems the Phœnician merchant and his wares were proverbial, for the commercial and maritime power enjoyed by the Phœnicians at the rise of the Egyptian Empire continued into Homeric times and later.

201. The civilization which they found in the northern Mediterranean was that of the Mycenæan age. Its people are termed by the Egyptian monuments Keftyew, and so regular was the traffic with these regions that the Phœnician craft plying on these voyages were known as "Keftyew ships" (BAR, II, 492). All this northern region was known to the Egyptians as the "Isles of the Sea," for having no acquaintance with the interior of Asia Minor, they supposed it to be but island coasts, like those of the Ægean.

202. Much more highly organized than the neighbouring peoples of Asia, the mature civilization of the mighty kingdom on the Nile had from time immemorial exerted a powerful influence upon the politically feeble states there. There was little or no native art among these peoples of the western Semitic world, but they were skilful imitators, and the products which their fleets marketed throughout the eastern Mediterranean,

212   THE EMPIRE: FIRST PERIOD

if not original Egyptian work, were therefore tinctured through and through with Egyptian elements. In these Phœnician galleys the material civilization of the Orient was being gradually disseminated through southern Europe and the west. Babylonian influences, while not so noticeable in the art of Syria-Palestine, were nevertheless sufficiently powerful to have introduced there the cuneiform system of writing, even among the non-Semitic Hittites. Thus Syria-Palestine became common ground, where the forces of civilization from the Nile and the Euphrates mingled at first in peaceful rivalry, but ultimately to meet upon the battlefield. The historical significance of this region is found in the inevitable struggle for its possession between the kingdom of the Nile on the one hand and those of the Tigro-Euphrates valley and Asia Minor on the other. It was in the midst of this struggle that Hebrew national history fell, and in its relentless course the Hebrew monarchies perished.

203. Other non-Semitic peoples were also beginning to appear on Egypt's northern horizon. A group of warriors of Iran, now appearing for the first time in history, had by 1500 B.C. pushed westward to the upper Euphrates and established an Aryan dynasty, ruling the kingdom of Mitanni in the great westward bend of the river, where it approaches most closely to the Mediterranean. It was the earliest and westernmost outpost of the Aryan race. They formed a powerful and cultivated state, which, planted thus on the road leading westward from Babylon along the Euphrates, effectively cut off the latter from her profitable western trade, and doubtless had much to do with the decline in which Babylon, under her foreign Kassite dynasty, now found herself. Everything thus conspired to favour the permanence of Egyptian power in Asia (MAAG).

THE RISE OF THE EMPIRE

204. Under these conditions Thutmose I prepared to quell the perpetual revolt in Syria and bring it into such complete subjection as he had achieved in Nubia. Without serious opposition, the Pharaoh reached Naharin, or the land of the "rivers," as the name signifies, which was the designation of the country from the Orontes to the Euphrates and beyond, merging into Asia Minor. The battle resulted in a great slaughter of the Asiatics, followed by the capture of large numbers of prisoners. Somewhere along the Euphrates at its nearest approach to the Mediterranean, Thutmose now erected a stone boundary-tablet, marking the northern and at this point the eastern limit of his Syrian possessions. Two Pharaohs had now seen the Euphrates, the Syrian dynasts were fully impressed with the power of Egypt, and their tribute, together with that of the Beduin and other inhabitants of Palestine, began to flow into the Egyptian treasury. Thus Thutmose I was able to begin the restoration of the temples so neglected since the time of the Hyksos. The modest old temple of the Middle Kingdom monarchs at Thebes was no longer in keeping with the Pharaoh's increasing wealth and pomp. His chief architect, Ineni, was therefore commissioned to erect two massive pylons, or towered gateways, in front of the old Amon-temple, and between these a columned hall, which was later to be intimately identified with the family history of the dynasty (BAR, II, 81; 85; 478; 98; 101; 103 *f*.; 92-97).

XV

THE FEUD OF THE THUTMOSIDS AND THE REIGN OF QUEEN HATSHEPSUT

205. How long Thutmose I's Asiatic war may have occupied him, we do not now know, but at about the time of his thirty years' jubilee—the 30th anniversary of his appointment to the heirship of the throne—his claim upon it was probably weakened by the death of his queen, Ahmose, through whom alone he had any valid title to the crown. She was a descendant of the old Theban princes who had expelled the Hyksos, and there was a strong party who regarded the blood of this line as alone entitled to royal honours. Her only surviving child was a daughter, Makere-Hatshepsut, and so strong was the party of legitimacy, that they had forced the king, years before, at about the middle of his reign, to proclaim her his successor, in spite of the general disinclination to submit to the rule of a queen. Among other children, Thutmose I had also two sons by other queens: one, who afterward became Thutmose II, was the son of a princess Mutnofret; while the other, later Thutmose III, had been born to the king by an obscure concubine named Isis. The close of Thutmose I's reign is involved in deep obscurity, and the following reconstruction is not without its difficulties. When the light finally breaks, Thutmose III is on the throne for a long reign, the beginning of which had been interrupted

for a short time by the ephemeral rule of Thutmose II. Thus, although Thutmose III's reign really began before that of Thutmose II, seven-eighths of it falls after Thutmose II's death, and the numbering of the two kings is most convenient as it is. As a young prince of no prospects, Thutmose III had been placed in the Karnak temple as a priest with the rank of prophet. Meantime he had in some way gained the hand of the beautiful and gifted Hatshepsut, the sole princess of the old line. He now had a claim upon the throne, by inheritance through his wife. To this legal right the priesthood of Amon, who supported him, agreed to add that of divine sanction, and under the most dramatic circumstances secured his call to the kingship by the god himself during state ceremonies in the temple hall of Thutmose I. Thutmose III's five-fold name and titulary were immediately published, and on the third of May, in the year 1501, B. C., he suddenly stepped from the duties of an obscure prophet of Amon into the palace of the Pharaohs (BAR, II, 105; 86-8; 64, l. 11; 307; 128-136; 138-148).

206. Thutmose I was evidently not regarded as a source of serious danger, for he was permitted to live on. Thutmose III early shook off the party of legitimacy. Indeed he allowed Hatshepsut no more honourable title than "great or chief royal wife." But the party of legitimacy was not to be so easily put off. As a result of their efforts Thutmose III was forced to acknowledge the coregency of his queen and actually to give her a share in the government. Before long her partisans had become so strong that the king was seriously hampered, and eventually even thrust into the background, and the conventions of the court were all warped and distorted to suit the rule of a woman. Hardly had she

begun her independent works and royal monuments, especially the great temple of Der el-Bahri, when the priestly party of Thutmose III and the party of legitimacy fell victims of a third party, that of Thutmose II, who, allying himself with the old dethroned king, Thutmose I, succeeded in thrusting aside Thutmose III and Hatshepsut and seizing the crown. Then Thutmose I and II, father and son, began a bitter persecution of the memory of Hatshepsut, cutting out her name on the monuments and placing both their own over it wherever they could find it.

207. News of the enmities within the royal house had probably now reached Nubia, and on the very day of Thutmose II's accession, the report of a serious outbreak there was handed to him. One of his commanders quelled the rising, however, and another insurrection in southern Palestine was also successfully put down. At this juncture it is probable that the death of the aged Thutmose I so weakened the position of the feeble and diseased Thutmose II that he made common cause with Thutmose III, then apparently living in retirement, but of course secretly seeking to reinstate himself. In any case we find them together for a brief coregency, which was terminated by the death of Thutmose II, after a reign of not more than three years at most (Note IV; BAR, II, 119–125; 593–5; MMR, 547).

208. Thutmose III thus held the throne again, although the partisans of Hatshepsut forced him to a compromise, by which the queen was recognized as coregent. Matters did not stop here; her party was so powerful, that, although they were unable to dispose of Thutmose III entirely, he was again relegated to the background, while the queen played the leading rôle in the state. Both she and Thutmose III numbered the

years of their joint reign from the first accession of Thutmose III, as if it had never been interrupted by the short reign of Thutmose II. The queen now entered upon an aggressive career as the first great woman in history of whom we are informed. Her partisans had now installed themselves in the most powerful offices, from that of the vizier, chief treasurer, chief architect and High Priest of Amon downward. The whole machinery of the state was thus in the hands of these partisans of the queen. It is needless to say that the fortunes, and probably the lives of these men were identified with the success and the dominance of Hatshepsut; they therefore took good care that her position should be maintained. In every way they were at great pains to show that the queen had been destined for the throne by the gods from the beginning. In her temple at Der el-Bahri, where work was now actively resumed, they had sculptured on the walls a long series of reliefs showing the birth of the queen. Here all the details of the old state fiction that the sovereign should be the bodily child of the sun-god were elaborately depicted. The artist who did the work followed the current tradition so closely that the new-born child appears as a *boy*, showing how the introduction of a woman into the situation was wrenching the inherited forms. Thutmose I was depicted appointing and acknowledging her as queen, or praying for a prosperous reign for his daughter. With such devices as these it was sought to overcome the prejudice against a queen upon the throne of the Pharaohs (BAR, II, 341; 344; 363 *ff.*; 348; 388 *ff.*; 369 *ff.*; 290; 187 *ff.*; 198; 215; 237, ll. 15–16; 243 *ff.*).

209. Hatshepsut's first enterprise was, as we have intimated, to continue the building of her magnificent

temple against the western cliffs at Thebes, where her father and brother had inserted their names over hers. The building was in design quite unlike the great temples of the age. It resembled the little terraced temple of Nibhepetre-Mentuhotep in a neighbouring bay of the cliffs. In a series of three colonnaded terraces it rose from the plain to the level of an elevated court, flanked by the massive yellow cliffs, into which the holy of holies was cut. The queen found especial pleasure in the design of the temple, seeing in it a paradise of Amon, and conceived its terraces as the "myrrh-terraces" of Punt, the original home of the gods. To carry out the design fully it was further necessary to plant the terraces with the myrrh trees from Punt, and resuming the Red Sea traffic interrupted by the Hyksos wars, she dispatched a fleet to Punt to secure the myrrh trees (BAR, II, 351, ll. 6 *f.*; 375; 295; 287; 285, ll. 5–6; 288). It was the largest expedition thither of which we know. Passing from the Nile to the Red Sea by means of a canal in the eastern Delta, the fleet reached Punt in safety. Besides Egyptian merchandise they carried with them a statue of the queen, which they erected in Punt (AZ, 42, 91 *ff.*). After a fair return voyage, and without mishap, the fleet of fine vessels finally moored again at the docks of Thebes. Probably the Thebans had never before been diverted by such a sight as now greeted them, when the motley array of Puntites and the strange products of their far-off country passed through the streets to the queen's palace, where the Egyptian commander presented them to her majesty. Having planted the trees in the temple, the queen boasted, "It was done. . . . I have made for him a Punt in his garden, just as he commanded me. . . . It is large enough for him to walk abroad in it." Thus the splendid temple was made a terraced myrrh-garden for the god, though the energetic queen was obliged to send to the end of the known world to do this for him. She had all the incidents of the remarkable expedition recorded in a series of splendid reliefs on the upper terrace, where they still form one of the great beauties of her temple (BAR, II, 290; 252 *f.*; 292; 254; 257; 259; 246–295).

210. This unique temple was in its function the culmination of a new development in the arrangement and architecture of the royal tomb. As we have seen, the Pharaoh had gradually abandoned the construction of a pyramid, and he now, like his nobles, excavated a cliff-tomb with the mortuary temple against the face of the cliff before it. Probably for purposes of safety Thutmose I then took the radical step of separating the cliff-tomb from the mortuary chapel before it. The chapel was left upon the plain at the foot of the western cliffs, but the burial chamber, with the passage leading to it was hewn into the rocky wall of a wild and desolate valley lying behind the cliffs, some two miles in a direct line westward from the river, and accessible only by a long detour northward, involving nearly twice that distance. It is evident that the exact spot where the king's body was entombed was intended to be kept secret, that all possibility of robbing the royal burial might be precluded. The new arrangement was such that the sepulchre, as in pyramid days, was still behind the chapel or temple, which thus continued to be on the east of the tomb as before, although the two were now separated by the intervening cliffs. The valley, now known as the "Valley of the Kings' Tombs," rapidly filled with the vast excavations of Thutmose I's successors. It continued to be the cemetery of the

Eighteenth, Nineteenth and Twentieth Dynasties, and over forty tombs of the Theban kings were excavated there. Forty-two now accessible form one of the wonders which attract the modern Nile-tourists to Thebes, and Strabo speaks of forty which were worthy to be visited in his time. Hatshepsut's terraced sanctuary was therefore her mortuary temple, dedicated also to her father. As the tombs multiplied in the valley behind, there rose upon the plain before it temple after temple endowed for the mortuary service of the departed gods, the emperors who had once ruled Egypt. Hatshepsut's tomb has in recent times been discovered behind her terraced temple, and that of her father is near by (BAR, II, 513; 106; 552; 389).

211. Meanwhile Hatshepsut was receiving tribute from her wide empire, extending from the upper cataracts of the Nile to the Euphrates. Evidently no serious trouble in Asia had as yet resulted from the fact that there was no longer a warrior upon the throne of the Pharaohs. This energetic woman therefore began to employ her new wealth in the restoration of the old temples, which, although two generations had elapsed, had not yet recovered from the neglect which they had suffered under the Hyksos (BAR, II, 321; 296 *ff.*; 303).

212. It was now seven or eight years since she and Thutmose III had regained the throne, and fifteen years since they had first seized it. Thutmose III had never been appointed heir to the succession, but his queen had enjoyed that honour, and at the thirtieth anniversary of her appointment she celebrated her jubilee by the erection of a pair of obelisks, which were the customary memorial of such jubilees. The queen chose an extraordinary location for these monuments, namely, the very colonnaded hall of the Karnak temple erected by

her father, where her husband Thutmose III had been named king by oracle of Amon; although this necessitated the removal of many of her father's cedar columns, besides, of course, unroofing the hall. Sumptuously overlaid with gold-silver alloy, they towered so high above the dismantled hall of Thutmose I that the queen recorded a long oath, swearing by all the gods that they were each of one block. They were indeed the tallest shafts ever erected in Egypt up to that time, being ninety seven and a half feet high and weighing nearly three hundred and fifty tons each. Nevertheless they had been quarried at the first cataract in only seven months. One of them still stands, an object of constant admiration to the modern visitor at Thebes. Two, and possibly four, more of the queen's obelisks have perished (BAR II, 317, ll. 6 *f.*; 318; 376, l. 28; 319, l. 3; 377, ll. 36–38; 315; 304–336; 322 *ff.*).

213. With these splendid works at home Hatshepsut's power, or that of her party, was drawing to a close. In Sinai her mining works went on until her twentieth year. Some time between this date and the close of the year twenty-one, when we find Thutmose III ruling alone, the great queen must have died. Great though she was, her rule was a distinct misfortune, falling, as it did, at a time when Egypt's power in Asia had not yet been seriously tested, and Syria was only too ready to revolt. Thutmose III was not chivalrous in his treatment of her when she was gone. He had suffered too much. Burning to lead his forces into Asia, he had been assigned to puerile temple functions or his restless energies were spent on building his mortuary temple of the western plain of Thebes. Around her obelisks in her father's hall at Karnak he now had a masonry sheathing built, covering her name and the record of her erection of them

on the base. Everywhere from the cataracts to the Delta, on the walls of all buildings both her figure and her name have been hacked out. Her partisans doubtless all fled. If not they must have met short shrift. In all the records of the time, and even in their tombs and on their statues, their names and their figures were ruthlessly chiselled away. And these mutilated monuments stand to this day, grim witnesses of the great king's vengeance. But in Hatshepsut's splendid temple her fame still lives, and the masonry around her Karnak obelisk has fallen down, displaying her name and records, and exposing the gigantic shaft, to proclaim to the modern world the greatness of Hatshepsut (BAR, II, 337; 338, note *f*; 348; PPS, p. 19).

XVI

THE CONSOLIDATION OF THE EMPIRE: THE WARS OF THUTMOSE III

214. In the year fifteen Hatshepsut and Thutmose III still controlled their Asiatic dependencies as far north as the Lebanon. From that time until we find him marching into Asia, late in the year twenty-two, we are not informed of what took place there; but the condition which then confronted him, and the course of his subsequent campaigns, makes it evident how matters had gone with Egyptian supremacy during the interim. Not having seen an Egyptian army for many years, the Syrian dynasts grew continually more restless, and finding that their boldness called forth no response from the Pharaoh, the king of Kadesh had stirred all the city-kings of northern Palestine and Syria to accept his leadership in a great coalition, in which they at last felt themselves strong enough to begin open revolt. Kadesh thus assumed its head with a power in which we should evidently recognize the surviving prestige of her old-time more extended suzerainty. Only southern Palestine held aloof and remained true to the Pharaoh. Not only were "all the allied countries of Zahi," or western Syria, in open rebellion against the Pharaoh, but it is also evident that the great kingdom of Mitanni, on the east of the Euphrates, had done all in her power to encourage the rebellion and to support it when once in

progress. Against such formidable resources as these, then, Thutmose III was summoned to contend, and no Pharaoh before his time had ever undertaken so great a task. In what condition the long unused Egyptian army may have been, or how long it took Thutmose to reorganize and prepare it for service, we have no means of knowing. The armies of the early Orient were not large, and it is not probable that any Pharaoh ever invaded Asia with more than twenty-five or thirty thousand men, while less than twenty thousand is probably nearer the usual figure (BAR, II, 137; 162; 416; 616; BK, 8–11).

215. Late in his twenty-second year we find Thutmose with his army ready to take the field. He marched from Tharu, the last Egyptian city on the northeastern frontier, about the 19th of April, 1479 B. C. On the 10th of May he camped on the southern slopes of the Carmel range. Meantime the army of the Asiatic allies, under the command of the king of Kadesh, had pushed southward and had occupied the strong fortress of Megiddo, in the plain of Esdraelon, on the north slope of the Carmel ridge. This place, which here appears in history for the first time, was not only a powerful stronghold, but occupied an important strategic position, commanding the road from Egypt between the two Lebanons to the Euphrates; hence its prominent rôle in Oriental history from this time on (BAR, II, 409; 415; 417–419; 439).

216. Learning now of the enemy's occupation of Megiddo, Thutmose called a council of his officers to ascertain the most favourable route for crossing the ridge and reaching the plain of Esdraelon. Thutmose characteristically favoured the direct route, but his officers urged that two other roads, involving long detours to north or south, were more open, while the

middle one was a narrow pass. Their objections showed a good military understanding of the dangers of the pass; but Thutmose swore a round oath that he would move against his enemies by the most direct route, and they might follow or not as they pleased. Accordingly, making his preparations very deliberately, he moved into the pass on the thirteenth of May. To prevent surprise and also to work upon the courage of his army, he personally took the head of the column, vowing that none should precede him, but that he would go "forth at the head of his army himself, showing the way by his own footsteps." Having met only a forepost of the enemy on the heights, he disengaged his army in safety from the pass, and emerged upon the plain of Esdraelon without opposition on the south of Megiddo. The Asiatics had thus lost an inestimable opportunity to destroy him in detail. Late in the afternoon of the same day (the fourteenth), or during the ensuing night, Thutmose drew his line around the west side of Megiddo and boldly threw out his left wing on the northwest of the city. He thus secured, in case of necessity, a safe and easy line of retreat westward along the northernmost of the three roads crossing Carmel, while at the same time his extreme left might cut off the enemy from flight northward (BAR, II, 420–428).

217. Early the next morning, the fifteenth of May, Thutmose gave orders to form and move out in order of battle. In a glittering chariot of electrum he took up his position with the centre; his right or southern wing rested on a hill southwest of Megiddo; while, as we have seen, his left was northwest of the city. The Asiatics in a north and south line barred his way to the city. He immediately attacked them, leading the onset himself "at the head of his army." The enemy gave

way at the first charge, "they fled headlong to Megiddo in fear, and many, finding the gates closed against them, were drawn up the wall by their friends within. The discipline of an Oriental army cannot to this day withstand a rich display of plunder; much less could the host of Egypt in the fifteenth century B. C. resist the spoil of the combined armies of Syria, although by pushing quickly forward they might have captured Megiddo at once. It is evident that in the disorganized rout the camp of the king of Kadesh fell into the hands of the Egyptians, and they brought its rich and luxurious furniture to the Pharaoh (BAR, II, 429–433; 413; 616; 414).

218. But the stern Thutmose was not to be placated by these tokens of victory; he saw only what had been lost, and gave orders for the instant investment of the city. The season was far enough advanced so that the Egyptians foraged on the grain-fields of the plain of Esdraelon, while its herds furnished them the fat of the land. They were the first host, of whom we have knowledge, to ravage this fair plain, destined to be the battle-ground of the east and west from Thutmose III to Napoleon. But within the walls all was different; proper provision for a siege had not been made, and famine finally wrought its customary havoc in the beleaguered town, which, after sustaining the siege for some weeks, at length surrendered. But the king of Kadesh was not among the prisoners. To compensate for the failure to capture the dangerous king of Kadesh himself they secured his family as hostages; for Thutmose says, "Lo, my majesty carried off the wives of that vanquished one, together with his children, and the wives of the chiefs who were there, together with their children." Rich as had been the spoil on the

battle-field, it was not to be compared with the wealth of the allied kings which awaited the Pharaoh in the captured city: nine hundred and twenty-four chariots, including those of the kings of Kadesh and Megiddo, two thousand two hundred and thirty-eight horses, two hundred suits of armour, again including those of the same two kings, the gorgeous tent of the king of Kadesh, his magnificent household furniture, and among it his royal sceptre, a silver statue, perhaps of his god, and an ebony statue of himself, wrought with gold and lapis-lazuli, besides prodigious quantities of gold and silver (BAR, II, 433–437; 441 *f.*; 596; I Kings, xv, 23).

219. Thutmose lost no time in marching as far northward as the hostile strongholds and the lateness of the season would permit. He captured three cities on the southern slopes of Lebanon. They quickly succumbed. Here, in order to prevent another southward advance of the still unsubmissive king of Kadesh and to hold command of the important road northward between the Lebanons, he now built a fortress. He then began the reorganization of the conquered territory, supplanting the old revolting dynasts, of course, with others who might be expected to show loyalty to Egypt. These new rulers were allowed to govern much as they pleased, if only they regularly and promptly sent in the yearly tribute to Egypt. In order to hold them to their obligations Thutmose carried off their eldest sons with him to Egypt, where they were educated and so treated as to engender feelings of friendliness toward Egypt; and whenever a king of one of the Syrian cities died "his majesty would cause his son to stand in his place." The Pharaoh now controlled all Palestine as far north as the southern end of Lebanon, and, further inland, also Damascus (BAR, II, 548; 434; 402; 467; 436).

Early in October Thutmose had reached Thebes. It was less than six months since he had left Egypt, and he had done all within the limits of the dry season in Palestine. With what difficulties such an achievement was beset we may learn by a perusal of Napoleon's campaign from Egypt through the same country against Akko, which is almost exactly as far from Egypt as Megiddo. We may then understand why it was that Thutmose immediately celebrated three "Feasts of Victory" in his capital, each five days long. These feasts were made permanent, endowed with an annual income of plentiful offerings. At the feast of Opet, Amon's greatest annual feast, lasting eleven days, he presented to the god the three towns captured in southern Lebanon, besides a rich array of magnificent vessels of gold, silver and costly stones from the Asiatic spoil, and also extensive lands in Upper and Lower Egypt, equipped with plentiful herds and with hosts of peasant serfs taken from among his Asiatic prisoners. Thus was established the foundation of that vast fortune of Amon, which now began to grow out of all proportion to the increased wealth of other temples (BAR, II, 409; 549; 550–553; 557 *f.*; 543–547; 555; 596).

220. The great task of properly consolidating the empire was now fairly begun; but Egyptian power in Asia during the long military inactivity of Hatshepsut's reign had been so thoroughly shaken that Thutmose III was far from ready, as a result of the first campaign, to march immediately upon Kadesh, his most dangerous enemy. Moreover, he desired properly to organize and render perfectly secure the states already under the power of Egypt. In the year twenty-four therefore he marched in a wide curve through the conquered territory of northern Palestine and southern Syria, while

Israel

<u>Assyria</u> (brute force) has left little gain to posterity. no art, literature, Its art was either Babylonian or Egy.
Assyria only great in army — and provincial government. Usually puts in governor of Ass. blood — contrary to method of Egypt.

Meet Assyrian 2500 BC. About 1400 BC Egy acknowledges Ass. a power — thus giving offence to Babylon — Who claims in

Ass. captures Babylon 1250

In 745 — Assyria becomes a world power under Tiglath-pileser III.

Fall of Ass. — <u>606.</u> This is the only permanent gov. in the Tigris Eu. Valley.
Babylon never possessed (A) permanent culture —

Egy. world power from 1600 to 1200 BC
    "   "   for two centuries
    great power for 5

Plan IV.—THE TE

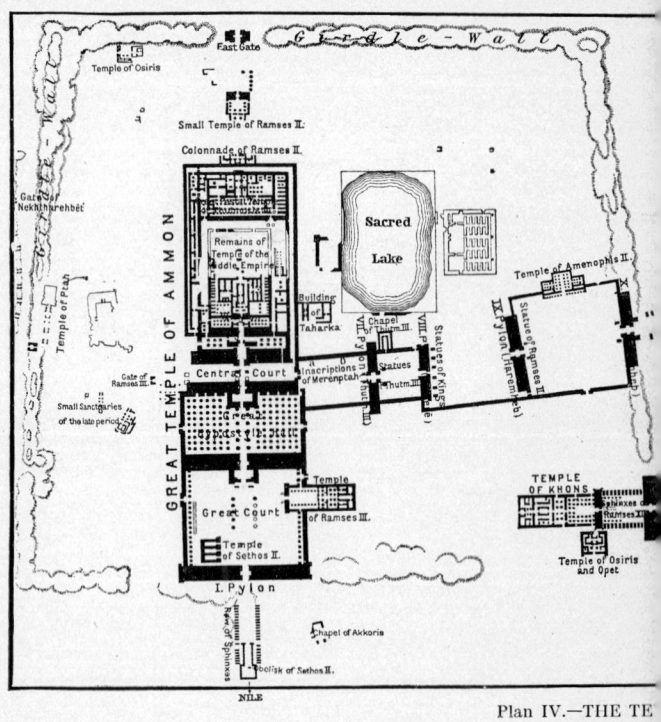

PLAN OF KARNAK.

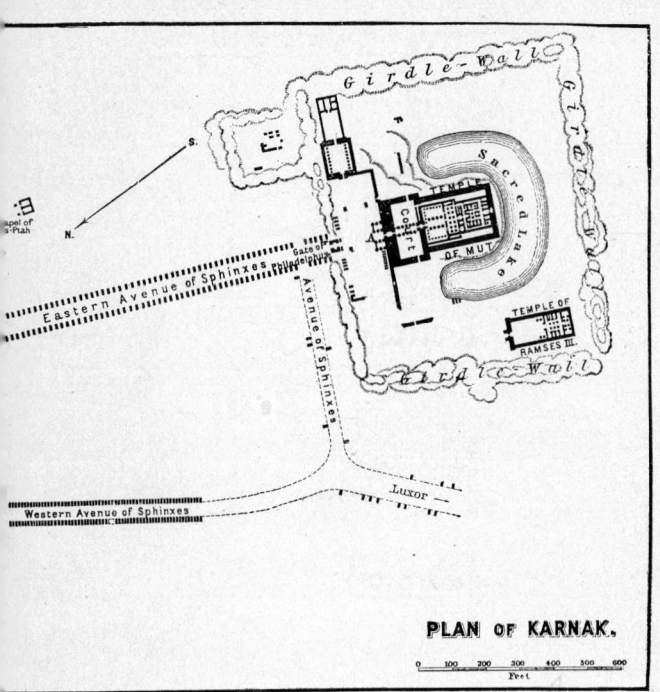

PLES OF KARNAK.

1800 yrs in building
about 1/4 mi long
2000 yrs B.C. to 200 BC
Use of hypostyle
Notre Dame could be
placed inside hall —
Large part fell in 1897 —
Columns 11 ft diameter
65 ft high

Israel -

Damascus - a buffer state between
Egy. and Assyria,
Damascus citizen Aramaeans -
akin to Israellis.

Assurnaser pal - about 900 B C -
king of Assyria pushes W. to Med.
receives tribute from Israel, Syria
Shalmaneser II. Real conquest of Israel
About 850. - For first time in history
Arabs are mentioned - called by
other names suti - bedui[n] arabs
854 the date of their first mention of arab -
856 - Shalmaneser goes S - to conquest
and meets the madai - (Medes)
Israel was divided under Saul.
David succeeded in combining some
what -

Tiglath-pileser III is the Asy. who
makes Palestine a Ass. Provinces
Israel gains her mighty conception of
God - from the trials and tribulations
arising from Assyrians - Philistines &
& - Herodotus - merely childish tales of history
Assyria - "organized brute force" - an axe
Israel not built in this way: higher thing
Assyria - "brute force" could do nothing
without a great leader. Egy different
one great king could and did follow
another. Peaceful development of
national life in Egypt
see pg 228

the dynasts came to pay their tribute and do him homage in "every place of his majesty's circuit where the tent was pitched." The news of his great victory of the year before had by this time reached Assyria, now just rising on the eastern horizon, with her career as yet all before her. Her king naturally desired to be on good terms with the great empire of the west, and the gifts of costly stone, chiefly lapis-lazuli from Babylon, and the horses which he sent to Thutmose, so that they reached him while on this campaign, were, of course, interpreted by the Egyptians as tribute. In all probability no battles were fought on this expedition.

221. Returning to Thebes as before, in October, the king immediately planned for the enlargement of the Karnak temple, to suit the needs of the empire of which he dreamed. As the west end, the real front of the temple, was marred by Hatshepsut's obelisks, rising from his father's dismantled hall, Thutmose III laid out his imposing colonnaded halls at the other, or east end, of the temple, where they to-day form one of the great architectural beauties of Thebes (Map IV; BAR, II, 100; 306; 772; 600; 602; 608 *ff.*; 447, l. 25; 446; 599 *ff.*; 604 *f.*).

222. The third campaign, of the next year (twenty-five) was evidently spent like the first, in organizing the southern half of the future Asiatic empire, the northern half being still unsubdued (BAR, II, 450–452). No records of the fourth campaign have survived, but the course of his subsequent operations was such that it must have been confined like the others to the territory already regained. It had now become evident to Thutmose that he could not march northward between the Lebanons and operate against Kadesh, while leaving his flank exposed to the

unsubdued Phœnician cities of the coast. It was likewise impossible to strike Naharin and Mitanni without first destroying Kadesh, which dominated the Orontes valley. He therefore planned a series of campaigns, directed first against the northern coast, which he might then use as a base of operations against Kadesh; and this being once disposed of, he could again push in from the coast against Mitanni and the whole Naharin region. He therefore organized a fleet and placed in command of it a trusty officer named Nibamon, who had served with his father. Employing the new fleet, he transported his army by sea, and in the year twenty-nine, on his fifth campaign, he moved for the first time against the northern coast cities, the wealthy commercial kingdoms of Phœnicia. The name of the wealthy city which Thutmose first took is unfortunately lost, but it was on the coast opposite Tunip, which sent it reinforcements. It must have been a place of considerable importance, for it brought him rich spoils; and there was in the town a temple of Amon, erected by one of Thutmose III's predecessors. Thence the Pharaoh moved his army southward against the powerful city of Arvad. A short siege sufficed to bring the place to terms, and with its surrender a vast quantity of the wealth of Phœnicia fell into the hands of the Egyptians, who spent days of feasting and drunkenness in the rich Phœnician vineyards and gardens. The dynasts along the coast now came in with their tribute and offered submissions. Thutmose had thus gained a secure footing on the northern coast, easily accessible by water from Egypt, and forming an admirable base for operations inland, as he had foreseen. He then returned to Egypt, possibly not for the first time, by water (BAR, II, 779; 457–459; 460–464).

223. All was now in readiness for the long planned advance upon Kadesh. It had taken five campaigns to gain the south and the coast; the sixth was at last directed against his long invulnerable enemy. In the year thirty the close of the spring rains found Thutmose disembarking his army from the fleet at Simyra, by the mouth of the Eleutheros, up the valley of which he immediately marched upon Kadesh. The city lay on the west side of the Orontes river, surrounded by its waters and those of a tributary at this point, at the north end of the high valley between the two Lebanons (Map II). An inner moat encircling the high curtain-walls within the banks of the rivers reinforced the natural water-defences, so that, in spite of its location in a perfectly level plain, it was probably the most formidable fortress in Syria and commanded the Orontes valley, the only route northward in inner Syria. It will be remembered, furthermore, that it also dominated the Eleutheros valley, the only road inland from the coast for a long distance both north and south (BK, 13–21; 49). The capture of such a place by siege was an achievement of no slight difficulty, but the scanty sources permit us to discern only that it was taken after a difficult siege, lasting from early spring to harvest time, during which at least one assault was made. The siege continued long enough to encourage the coast cities in the hope that Thutmose had suffered a reverse. Before the long planned advance into Naharin could be undertaken the revolting cities of the coast had therefore again to be chastised. The rest of this season and all the next, the seventh campaign (year 31), were spent in punishing the obstinate Arvad, and its neighbour Simyra. Thutmose then sailed from harbour to harbour along the coast, displaying his force and thoroughly organizing

the administration of the cities. In particular he saw to it that every harbour-town should be liberally supplied with provisions for his coming campaign in Naharin. On his return to Egypt he found envoys from the extreme south, probably eastern Nubia, bringing to the Pharaoh their tribute, showing that he was maintaining an aggressive policy in the far south while at the same time so active in the north (BAR, II, 465; 585; 467; 470-475).

224. Preparations for the great campaign delayed Thutmose until the spring of the year thirty-three, when we find him on the march down the Orontes on his eighth campaign. Having captured Ketne, he fought a battle at the city of Senzar, which he also took. Entering Naharin no serious force confronted him until he had arrived at "The Height of Wan, on the west of Aleppo," where a considerable battle was fought. Aleppo itself must have fallen, for the Pharaoh could otherwise hardly have pushed on without delay, as he evidently did. "Behold his majesty went north, capturing the towns and laying waste the settlements of that foe of wretched Naharin," who was, of course, the king of Mitanni. Egyptian troops were again plundering the Euphrates valley, a license which they had not enjoyed since the days of their fathers under Thutmose I, some fifty years before (BAR, II, 476; 598; 584; 581 *f.*; 479).

225. As he advanced northward Thutmose now turned slightly toward the Euphrates, in order to reach Carchemish. In the battle fought at that city it must have been his long unscathed foe, the king of Mitanni, whose army Thutmose scattered far and wide, "not one looked behind him, but they fled forsooth like a herd of mountain goats." This battle at last enabled Thutmose

to do what he had been fighting ten years to attain, for he now crossed the Euphrates into Mitanni and set up his boundary tablet on the east side, an achievement of which none of his fathers could boast. But the season was now far advanced; a winter in Naharin was impossible. He therefore returned unmolested to the west shore, where he found the boundary tablet of his father, Thutmose I, and with the greatest satisfaction he set up another of his own alongside it. But one serious enterprise still awaited him before he could return to the coast. After the capture of the city of Niy, a little further down the Euphrates, the object of the campaign had been accomplished and its arduous duties were past. It is now that we behold the great king diverting himself in an elephant hunt, in which, but for the bravery and adroitness of Amenemhab, a favourite general, he would probably have lost his life (BAR, II, 479; 583; 478; 481; 656, ll, 7 *f.*; 480 *f.*; 588).

226. Meantime all the local princes and dynasts of Naharin appeared at his camp and brought in their tribute as a token of their submission. Even far off Babylon was now anxious to secure the good-will of the Pharaoh, and its king sent him gifts wrought of lapis-lazuli. But what was still more important, the mighty people of the Kheta, whose domain stretched far away into the unknown regions of Asia Minor, sent him a rich gift. Thus the Kheta, probably the Biblical Hittites, emerge for the first time, as far as we know, upon the stage of Oriental history (Note V). On Thutmose's arrival at the coast he laid upon the chiefs of the Lebanon the yearly obligation to keep the Phœnician harbours supplied with the necessary provision for his campaigns. From any point in this line of harbours, which he could reach from Egypt by ship in a

few days, he was then able to strike inland without delay and bring delinquents to an immediate accounting. His sea power was such that the king of Cyprus became practically a vassal of Egypt, as later in Saitic times. Moreover, his fleet made him so feared in the islands of the north that he was able to exert a loose control over the eastern Mediterranean, westward an indefinite distance toward the Ægean. Likewise the Pharaoh's treasury was now receiving the richest contributions from his trade with Punt; and it is at some time during these wars that Thutmose is also found in possession of the entire oasis region on the west of Egypt (BAR, II, 482-486; 763).

227. The great object for which Thutmose had so long striven was now achieved; he had followed his fathers to the Euphrates. The kings whom they had been able to defeat singly and in succession, he had been obliged to meet united, and against the combined military resources of Syria and northern Palestine he had, in ten years' warfare, forced his way through to the north. He might pardonably permit himself some satisfaction in the contemplation of what he had accomplished. A pair of enormous obelisks, which had been in preparation for his second jubilee, were now erected at the Karnak temple and one of them bore the proud words "Thutmose, who crossed the great 'Bend of Naharin' [the Euphrates] with might and with victory at the head of his army." The other obelisk of this pair has perished, but this one now stands in Constantinople. Indeed, all of the great king's obelisks in Egypt have either perished or been removed, while the modern world possesses a line of them reaching from Constantinople, through Rome and London to New York (BAR II, 382-384; 629-636).

228. With such monuments as these before them the people of Thebes soon forgot that he who erected them was once a humble priest in the very temple where his giant obelisks now rose. On its walls, moreover, they saw long annals of his victories in Asia, endless records of the plunder he had taken, with splendid reliefs picturing the rich portion which fell to Amon. In the garden of Amon's temple grew the strange plants of Syria-Palestine, while animals unknown to the hunter of the Nile valley wandered among trees equally unfamiliar. Envoys from the north and south were constantly appearing at the court. Phœnician galleys, such as the upper Nile had never seen before, delighted the eyes of the curious crowd at the docks of Thebes; and from these landed whole cargoes of the finest stuffs of Phœnicia, gold and silver vessels of magnificent workmanship, from the cunning hand of the Tyrian artificer or the workshops of distant Asia Minor, Cyprus, Crete and the Ægean islands; exquisite furniture of carved ivory, delicately wrought ebony, chariots mounted with gold and electrum, and bronze implements of war; besides these, fine horses for the Pharaoh's stables and untold quantities of the best that the fields, gardens, vineyards, orchards and pastures of Asia produced. Under heavy guard emerged from these ships, too, the annual tribute of gold and silver in large commercial rings, some of which weighed as much as twelve pounds each, while others for purposes of daily trade were of but a few grains weight. The amount of wealth which thus came into Egypt must have been enormous for those times, and on one occasion the treasury was able to weigh out some eight thousand nine hundred and forty-three pounds of gold-silver alloy. Nubia also, under the Egyptian viceroy, was rendering with great regu-

larity her annual impost of gold, negro slaves, cattle, ebony, ivory and grain; much of the gold in the above hoard must have come from the Nubian mines. Similar sights diverted the multitudes of the once provincial Thebes, when every autumn Thutmose's war-galleys moored in the harbour of the town; and the unhappy Asiatic captives, bound one to another in long lines, were led down the gang planks to begin a life of slave-labour for the Pharaoh. With their strange speech and uncouth postures the poor wretches were the subject of jibe and merriment on the part of the multitude; while the artists of the time could never forbear caricaturing them, in the gorgeous paintings in which the vizier and treasury officials loved to perpetuate such scenes on the inner walls of their tomb chapels. Many of them found their way into the houses of the Pharaoh's favourites and generals; but the larger number were immediately employed on the temple estates, the Pharaoh's domains, or in the construction of his great monuments and buildings. We shall later see how this captive labour transformed Thebes (BAR, II, 402 *f*.; 760 *f*.; 773; 756–759).

229. The return of the king every autumn began for him a winter, if not so arduous, at least as busily occupied as the campaigning season in Asia. Immediately after his return Thutmose made a tour of inspection throughout Egypt for the purpose of suppressing corruption and oppression in the local administration. On these journeys, too, he had opportunity of observing the progress on the noble temples which he was either erecting, restoring or adorning at over thirty different places of which we know, and many more which have perished. He revived the long neglected Delta, and from there to the third cataract his buildings were rising, strung like

gems, along the river. Besides the Nubian sources of gold, he organized the other gold country, that on the Coptos road, placing it under a "governor of the gold country of Coptos." It is evident that every resource of his empire was being thus exploited. The increasing wealth of the Amon temple demanded reorganization of its management, which the king personally accomplished. As the fruit of a moment's respite from the cares of state, he even handed to his chief of artificers designs sketched by his own royal hand for vessels which he desired for the temple service (BAR, III, 58; II, 774 *f*. 571; 545).

230. His campaigning was now as thoroughly organized as the administration at Thebes. As soon as the spring rains in Syria and Palestine had ceased, he regularly disembarked his troops in some Phœnician or north Syrian harbour. Here his permanent officials had effected the collection of the necessary stores from the neighbouring dynasts, who were obligated to furnish them. His herald or marshal, Intef, accompanied him on all his marches, and as Thutmose advanced inland Intef preceded him, sought out the palace of the local dynast in each town, and prepared it for Thutmose's reception. Had it been preserved, the life of these warriors of Thutmose would form a stirring chapter in the history of the early East. The career of his general, Amenemhab, who rescued the king in the elephant hunt, is but a hint of the life of the Pharaoh's followers in bivouac and on battlefield, a life crowded to the full with perilous adventure and hard-won distinction. Such incidents, of course, found their way among the common people, and many a stirring adventure from the Syrian campaigns took form in folk-tales, told with eager interest in the market-places and the streets

of Thebes. A lucky chance has rescued one of these tales written by some scribe on a page or two of papyrus. It concerns one Thutiy, a great general of Thutmose, and his clever capture of the city of Joppa by introducing his picked soldiers into the town, concealed in panniers, borne by a train of donkeys. But Thutiy was not a creation of fancy, and some of his splendid tomb equipment, especially a golden dish given him by his king, still survives. But the daily records of Thutmose's scribal annalist which might have enabled us to follow not only the whole romance of Thutmose's personal adventures on the field and those of his commanders, but also the entire course of his campaigns, have all perished. From these, we have upon the wall at Karnak only the capricious extracts of a temple scribe, more anxious to set forth the spoil and Amon's share therein than to perpetuate the story of his king's great deeds. How much he has passed over, the biography of Amenemhab shows only too well; and thus all that we have of the wars of Egypt's greatest commander has filtered through the shrivelled soul of an ancient bureaucrat, who little dreamed how hungrily future ages would ponder his meagre excerpts (BAR, II, 763–771; 577; 392).

231. The conquest in Asia was not yet complete. The spring of the thirty-fourth year therefore found Thutmose again in Zahi on his ninth campaign, punishing some disaffection, probably in the Lebanon region. This year evidently saw the extension of his power in the south also; for he secured the son of the chief of Irem, the neighbour of Punt, as a hostage; and the combined tribute of Nubia amounted to over one hundred and thirty-four pounds of gold alone, besides the

usual ebony, ivory, grain, cattle and slaves (BAR, II, 489-495). It was now nearly two years since he had seen Naharin, and in so short a time its princes had ceased to fear his power. They formed a coalition, with some prince at its head, possibly the king of Aleppo, whom Thutmose's Annals call "that wretched foe of Naharin," and together revolted. Thutmose's continual state of preparation enabled him to appear promptly on the plains of Naharin in the spring of the year thirty-five. He engaged the allies in battle at a place called Araina, which we are unable to locate with certainly, but it was probably somewhere in the lower Orontes valley. Here the alliance of the Naharin dynasts was completely shattered, and its resources for future resistance destroyed or carried off by the victorious Egyptians (BAR, II, 587; 498-501).

232. Thutmose's annals for the next two years are lost, and we know nothing of the objective of his eleventh and twelfth campaigns; but the year thirty-eight found him on his thirteenth campaign, chastising southern Lebanon, while the next expedition (fourteenth campaign) carried him from southern Palestine to Syria, setting his house in order. On the march the envoys of Cyprus and Arrapakhitis met him with gifts. The tribute seems to have come in regularly for the next two years (forty and forty-one), and again the king of "Kheta the Great" sent gifts, which Thutmose, as before, records among the "tribute" (BAR, II, 507; 511 *f.*; 517; 580; 520-527).

233. The princes of Syria, sorely chastised as they had been, were nevertheless unwilling to relinquish finally their independence. Incited by Kadesh, Thutmose's inveterate enemy, they again rose in a final united effort to shake off the Pharaoh's strong hand. All

Naharin, especially the king of Tunip, and also some of the northern coast cities, had been induced to join the alliance. The great king was now an old man, probably over seventy years of age, but with his accustomed promptitude he appeared with his fleet off the north coast of Syria in the spring of the year forty-two. It was his seventeenth and last campaign. Like his first, it was directed against his arch enemy, Kadesh, which he now isolated by approaching from the north and capturing Tunip first. He then accomplished the march up the Orontes to Kadesh without mishap and wasted the towns of the region. The king of Kadesh knowing that his all was lost unless he could defeat Thutmose's army, made a desperate resistance, but in spite of stratagem, lost the battle before the city. Thutmose's siege-lines now closed in on the doomed city, the wall was breached, and the strongest fortress of Syria was again at the Pharaoh's mercy.

234. Never again as long as the old king lived did the Asiatic princes make any attempt to shake off his yoke. In seventeen campaigns, during a period of nineteen years, he had beaten them into submission, until there was no spirit for resistance left among them. With the fall of Kadesh disappeared the last vestige of that Hyksos power which had once subdued Egypt. Thutmose's name became a proverb in their midst, and when, four generations later, his successors failed to shield their faithful vassals in Naharin from the aggression of the Kheta, the forsaken unfortunates remembered Thutmose's great name, and wrote pathetically to Egypt: "Who formerly could have plundered Tunip without being plundered by Manakhbiria (Thutmose III)?" But even now, at three score and ten or more,

THE WARS OF THUTMOSE III

the indomitable old warrior had the harbours equipped with the necessary supplies, and there is little doubt that if it had been necessary he would have led his army into Syria again. For the last time in Asia he received the envoys of the tribute-paying princes in his tent, and then returned to Egypt. There the Nubian envoys brought him over five hundred and seventy-eight pounds of gold from Wawat alone (AL, 41, 6-8; BAR, II, 531; 533-539; 590).

235. Twelve years more were vouchsafed the great king after he had returned from his last campaign in Asia. He still continued his attention to Nubia, sending out an expedition thither in the fiftieth year of his reign. It was now paying him six to eight hundred pounds of gold each year, and his great viceroy, Nehi, was carrying on his buildings there at a number of points. A list of one hundred and fifteen places which he conquered in Nubia is twice displayed on the walls of Karnak (BAR, II, 772 *ff.*; 526 *f.*; 649-652).

As Thutmose felt his strength failing he made coregent his son, Amenhotep II, born to him by Hatshepsut-Meretre, a queen of whose origin we know nothing. About a year later, on the 17th of March, in the year 1447 B. C., when he was within five weeks of the end of his fifty-fourth year upon the throne, he closed his eyes upon the scenes among which he had played so great a part (BAR, II, 184; 592). He was buried in his tomb in the Valley of the Kings by his son, and his body still survives.

236. The character of Thutmose III stands forth with more of colour and individuality than that of any king of early Egypt, except Ikhnaton. We see the man of a tireless energy unknown in any Pharaoh before or since; the man of versatility designing exquisite vases

in a moment of leisure; the lynx-eyed administrator, who launched his armies upon Asia with one hand and with the other crushed the extortionate tax-gatherer; the astute politician of many a court crisis, and the first great military strategist of the early East (BAR, II, 664; 570; 452). His reign marks an epoch not only in Egypt, but in the whole East as we know it in his age. Never before in history had a single brain wielded the resources of so great a nation and wrought them into such centralized, permanent and at the same time mobile efficiency, that for years they could be brought to bear with incessant impact upon another continent. The genius which rose from an obscure priestly office to accomplish this for the first time in history reminds us of an Alexander or a Napoleon. He built the first real empire, and is thus the first character possessed of universal aspects, the first world-hero. From the fastnesses of Asia Minor, the marshes of the upper Euphrates, the islands of the Ægean, the swamps of Babylonia, the distant shores of Libya, the oases of the Sahara, the terraces of the Somali coast and the upper cataracts of the Nile, the princes of his time rendered their tribute to his greatness. He thus made not only a world wide impression upon his age, but an impression of a new order. His commanding figure, towering like an embodiment of righteous penalty among the trivial plots and treacherous schemes of the petty Syrian dynasts, must have clarified the atmosphere of Oriental politics as a strong wind drives away miasmic vapours. The inevitable chastisement of his strong arm was held in awed remembrance by the men of Naharin for three generations. His name was one to conjure with, and centuries after his empire had crumbled to pieces it was placed on amulets as a word of power. It should be a

THE WARS OF THUTMOSE III 243

matter of gratification to us of the western world that on either shore of the western ocean, one of this king's greatest monuments now rises as a memorial of the world's first empire-builder.*

* Of his two Heliopolitan obelisks, one is on the Thames Embankment in London, and the other in Central Park, New York City.

Obelisks were always erected in pairs —

both — Removed to Alexandria

One removed to Thames embankment in London

One sent to N-Y.

Khedive had no idea U.S. would accept the obelisk. All Europe tried to prevent its removal. Khedive amazed that the U.S. accepted his offer immediately and sent a naval commander to remove it. —

Much trouble with officials in regard to removal

XVII

THE EMPIRE AT ITS HEIGHT

237. THE imperial age was now at its full noontide in the Nile valley. The old seclusiveness had totally disappeared, the wall of partition between Asia and Africa, already shaken by the Hyksos, was now completely broken down by the wars of Thutmose III. Traditional limits disappeared, the currents of life eddied no longer within the landmarks of tiny kingdoms, but pulsed from end to end of a great empire, embracing many kingdoms and tongues, from the upper Nile to the upper Euphrates. The wealth of Asiatic trade, circulating through the eastern end of the Mediterranean, which once flowed down the Euphrates to Babylon, was thus diverted to the Nile Delta, now united by canal with the Red Sea. All the world traded in the Delta markets. Assyria was still in her infancy and Babylonia no longer possessed any political influence in the west. The Pharaoh looked forward to an indefinite lease of power throughout the vast empire which he had conquered.

Of his administration in Asia we know very little. The whole region was under the general control of a "governor of the north countries." To bridle the turbulent Asiatic dynasts it was necessary permanently to station troops throughout Syria-Palestine in strongholds named after the Pharaoh, under deputies with power to act as the Pharaoh's representatives. Remains of an Egyptian temple found by Renan at Byblos doubtless belong to this period. As we have seen, the city-kings were allowed to rule their little states with great freedom as long as they paid the annual tribute with promptness and regularity. When such a ruler died, his son, who had been educated at Thebes, was installed in the father's place. The Asiatic conquests were therefore rather a series of tributary kingdoms than provinces, which indeed represent a system of foreign government only roughly foreshadowed in the rule of the viceroy of Kush (AL; BAR, II, 457–458; 548; 787; Rougé, Revue Arch, n. s. vii, 1863, pp. 194 *ff.*).

238. As so often in similar empires of later age, when the great king died, the tributary princes revolted. Thus Amenhotep II had reigned as coregent but a year when his father died, and the storm broke. All Naharin, including the Mitanni princes, and probably also the northern coast cities, were combined, or at least simultaneous, in the uprising. With all his father's energy the young king prepared for the crisis and marched into Asia against the allies, who had collected a large army. The south had evidently not ventured to rebel, but from northern Palestine on the revolt was general. Leaving Egypt with his forces in April of his second year (1447 B.C.), Amenhotep was in touch with the enemy in northern Palestine early in May, and immediately fought an action at Shemesh-Edom against the princes of Lebanon. In this encounter he led his forces in person, as his father before him had so often done, and mingled freely in the hand-to-hand fray. With his own hand he took eighteen prisoners and sixteen horses. The enemy was routed. By early June he had dispersed the allies

of Naharin, captured seven of their dynasts in Tikhsi, retaken Niy, and rescued his beleaguered garrison in Ikathi. As he reached his extreme advance, which probably surpassed his father's, he set up a boundary tablet, as his father and grandfather had done. His return was a triumphal procession as he approached Memphis, driving before him over five hundred and fifty of the north Syrian lords, with their women, horses and chariots, and a treasure of nearly sixteen hundred and sixty pounds of gold in the form of vases and vessels, besides nearly one hundred thousand pounds of copper. Proceeding to Thebes the seven kings of Tikhsi were hung head downward on the prow of his royal barge as he approached the city. He personally sacrificed them in the presence of Amon and hanged their bodies on the walls of Thebes, reserving one for a lesson to the Nubians, as we shall see (BAR, II, 184; 780–790; 792, l. 4; 796 *f.*; 800, ll. 4–5; 804, ll. 2–3).

239. The young Pharaoh now directed his attention to the other extremity of his empire. He dispatched an expedition into Nubia, bearing the body of the seventh king of Tikhsi, which was hung up on the wall of Napata, just below the fourth cataract, in the region of Karoy, the southern limit of Egyptian administration. Here Amenhotep set up tablets marking his southern frontier, and beyond these there was no more control of the rude Nubian tribes than was necessary to keep open the trade-routes from the south and prevent the barbarians from becoming so bold as to invade the province in plundering expeditions. Thenceforth, as far as we know, he was not obliged to invade either Asia or Nubia again (BAR, II, 1025; 800; 791–798).

240. Personally, we are able to discern little of Amenhotep II, but he seems to have been a worthy son

THE EMPIRE AT ITS HEIGHT

of the great king. Physically he was a very powerful man, and claims in his inscriptions that no man could draw his bow, which curiously enough was found in his tomb. It is this circumstance which furnished Herodotus with the legend that Cambyses was unable to draw the bow of the king of Ethiopia. Few or no remnants of his fine buildings at Karnak, Memphis and Heliopolis have survived, but in Nubia, especially at Kummeh and Amada, more has escaped. Dying about 1420 B.C., after a reign of some twenty-six years, Amenhotep II was interred like his ancestors in the valley of the kings' tombs, where his body rests to this day, though even now a prey to the clever tomb-robbers of modern Thebes, who in November, 1901, forced the tomb and cut through the wrappings of the mummy in their search for royal treasure on the body of their ancient ruler. Their Theban ancestors in the same craft, however, had three thousand years ago taken good care that nothing should be left for their descendants (BAR, II, 803–806; 792, note d; 507 *f.*; IV, 499 *ff.*).

241. Amenhotep II was followed by his son, Thutmose IV. It is possible that this prince was not at first designed to be his father's successor, if we may believe a folk-tale, in circulation some centuries later, and now recorded on the huge granite stela between the forelegs of the Great Sphinx. He was early called upon to maintain the empire in Asia, and invaded Naharin, returning with the usual captives and plunder, besides a cargo of cedar for the sacred barge of Amon at Thebes. His nobles now called him "Conqueror of Syria," and the tribute of the Syrian princes was regularly sent in. To confirm his position there, Thutmose evidently desired a friend in the north, for he sent to Artatama, the Mitannian king, and secured his daughter

in marriage. She probably received an Egyptian name, Mutemuya, and became the mother of the next king of Egypt, Amenhotep III. A firm alliance with Mitanni was thus formed, which forbade all thought of future conquest by the Pharaoh east of the Euphrates. A friendly alliance was also cemented with Babylonia. The suppression of a serious revolt in northern Nubia, in his eighth year, concludes the known wars of Thutmose IV. It is probable that he did not long survive this war, and his most notable monument from this period is the greatest of all obelisks, a monument left unfinished by his grandfather Thutmose III, at Thebes, and now standing before the Lateran in Rome (BAR, II, 810–815; 819–822; 824; 826; 829; 830 ff.; 838; AL, I, l. 63; 21, 16–18).

242. The son who succeeded him was the third of the Amenhoteps and the last of the great emperors. He was but the great grandson of Thutmose III, but with him the high tide of Egyptian power was already slowly on the ebb, and he was not the man to stem the tide. Already as crown prince, or at least early in his reign, he married a remarkable woman of untitled parentage, named Tiy. There is not a particle of evidence to prove her of foreign birth, as is so often claimed. In celebration of the marriage, Amenhotep issued a large number of scarabs, or sacred beetles, carved in stone and engraved with a record of the event, in which the untitled parentage of his queen frankly follows her name. From the beginning the new queen exerted a powerful influence over Amenhotep, and he immediately inserted her name in the official caption placed at the head of royal documents. Her power continued throughout his reign, and was the beginning of a remarkable era, characterized by the prominence of the queens in state

affairs and on public occasions, a peculiarity which we find only under Amenhotep III and his immediate successors. The significance of these events we shall later dwell upon (BAR, II, 861 *f*.)

243. In the administration of his great empire Amenhotep III began well. The Asiatics gave him no trouble at his accession, and he ruled in security and unparalleled splendour. Towards the close of his fourth year, however, trouble in Nubia called him south. It was so far up river that he was able to levy forces for its suppression among the northern Nubians, a striking evidence of the very Egyptianized character of lower Nubia. Amenhotep marched southward for a month, taking captives and spoil as he went, and arriving finally at the land of Uneshek, perhaps above the cataracts. This marked his extreme southern advance. His frontier, however, was certainly not essentially in advance of that of his father. This was the last great invasion of Nubia by the Pharaohs. As far as the fourth cataract the country was completely subjugated, and as far as the second cataract largely Egyptianized, a process which now went steadily forward. Egyptian temples had now sprung up at every larger town, and the Egyptian gods were worshipped therein; the Egyptian arts were learned by the Nubian craftsmen, and everywhere the rude barbarism of the upper Nile was receiving the stamp of Egyptian culture. Nevertheless the native chieftains, under the surveillance of the viceroy, were still permitted to retain their titles and honours, and doubtless continued to enjoy at least a nominal share in the government (BAR, II, 852–854; 850; 847 *f*.; 889; 845; 1037; 1035–1041).

244. In Asia Amenhotep enjoyed unchallenged supremacy. All the powers: Babylonia, Assyria, Mitan-

ni and Alasa-Cyprus, were exerting every effort to gain the friendship of Egypt. A scene of world politics, such as is unknown before in history, now unfolds before us. From the Pharaoh's court as the centre radiate a host of lines of communication with all the great peoples of the age. The Tell el-Amarna letters, perhaps the most interesting mass of documents surviving from the early East, have preserved to us this glimpse across the kingdoms of hither Asia as one might see them on a stage, each king playing his part before the great throne of the Pharaoh. The letters, some three hundred in number, written on clay tablets in the Babylonian cuneiform, were discovered in 1888 at Tell el-Amarna, from which the correspondence takes its name. They date from the reign of Amenhotep III and that of his son and successor, Amenhotep IV, or Ikhnaton, being correspondence of a strictly official character between these Pharaohs on the one hand, and on the other the kings of Babylonia, Nineveh, Mitanni, Alasa (Cyprus) and the Pharaoh's vassal kings of Syria-Palestine. Five letters survive from the correspondence of Amenhotep III with Kadashman-Bel (Kallimma-Sin), king of Babylonia, one from the Pharaoh and the others from Kadashman-Bel. The Babylonian king is constantly in need of gold and insistently importunates his brother of Egypt to send him large quantities of the precious metal, which he says is as plentiful as dust in Egypt according to the reports of the Babylonian messengers. Considerable friction results from the dissatisfaction of Kadashman-Bel at the amounts with which Amenhotep favours him. He refers to the fact that Amenhotep had received from his father a daughter in marriage, and makes this relationship a reason for further gifts of gold. As the correspondence goes on another marriage is negotiated between a daughter of Amenhotep and Kallimma-Sin or his son.

245. Similarly Amenhotep enjoys the most intimate connection with Shuttarna, the king of Mitanni, the son of Artatama, with whom his father, Thutmose IV, had sustained the most cordial relations. Indeed Amenhotep was perhaps the nephew of Shuttarna, from whom he now, in his tenth year, received a daughter, named Gilukhipa, in marriage. On the death of Shuttarna the alliance was continued under his son, Dushratta, from whom Amenhotep later received, as a wife for his son and successor, a second Mitannian princess, Tadukhipa, the daughter of Dushratta (AL, 7; 1–5; 17; BAR, II, 866 *f.*).

246. Similarly Amenhotep sent a gift of twenty talents of gold to the king of Assyria, and gained his friendship also. The vassalship of the king of Alasa-Cyprus continued, and he regularly sent the Pharaoh large quantities of copper, save when on one occasion he excuses himself because his country had been visited by a pestilence. So complete was the understanding between Egypt and Cyprus that even the extradition of the property of a citizen of Cyprus who had died in Egypt was regarded by the two kings as a matter of course (AL, 23, 30 *ff.*; 25, 30 *ff.*).

247. Thus courted and flattered, the object of diplomatic attention from all the great powers, Amenhotep found little occasion for anxiety regarding his Asiatic empire. The Syrian vassals were now the grandsons of the men whom Thutmose III had conquered; they had grown thoroughly habituated to the Egyptian allegiance, and it was not without its advantages. An Egyptian education at the Pharaoh's capital had, moreover, made him many a loyal servant among the

children of the dynasts. They protest their fidelity to the Pharaoh on all occasions, and their letters were introduced by the most abject and self-abasing adulation. They are "the ground upon which thou treadest, the throne upon which thou sittest, the foot-stool of thy feet"; even "thy dog"; and one is pleased to call himself the groom of the Pharaoh's horse. The garrisons in the larger towns, consisting of infantry and chariotry, are no longer solely native Egyptians, but to a large extent Nubians and Sherden, perhaps the ancestors of the historical Sardinians. From now on they took service in the Egyptian army in ever larger and larger numbers. These forces of the Pharaoh were maintained by the dynasts, and one of their self-applied tests of loyalty in writing to the Pharaoh was their readiness and faithfulness in furnishing supplies. Syria thus enjoyed a stability of government which had never before been hers. The roads were safe from robbers, caravans were convoyed from vassal to vassal, and a word from the Pharaoh was sufficient to bring any of his subject princes to his knees. The payment of tribute was as regular as the collection of taxes in Egypt itself. But in case of any delay a representative of the Pharaoh, who was stationed in the various larger towns, needed but to appear in the delinquent's vicinity to recall the unfulfilled obligation. Amenhotep himself was never obliged to carry on a war in Asia. On one occasion he appeared at Sidon, but one of the vassal princes later wrote to Amenhotep's son: "Verily, thy father did not march forth, nor inspect the lands of his vassal princes" (AL, 138, 4–13; 149, 1–7; 87, 62–64).

248. Under such circumstances Amenhotep was at leisure to devote himself to those enterprises of peace which have occupied all emperors under similar condi-

tions. Trade now developed as never before. The
Nile was alive with the freight of all the world, flowing
into it from the Red Sea fleets and from long caravans
passing back and forth through the Isthmus of Suez,
bearing the rich stuffs of Syria, the spices and aromatic
woods of the East, the weapons and chased vessels of
the Phœnicians, and a myriad of other things, which
brought their Semitic names into the hieroglyphic and
their use into the life of the Nile-dwellers. Parallel
with the land traffic through the isthmus were the routes
of commerce on the Mediterranean, thickly dotted with
the richly laden galleys of Phœnicia, converging upon
the Delta from all quarters and bringing to the markets
of the Nile the decorated vessels of damascened bronzes
from the Mycenæan industrial settlements of the
Ægean. The products of Egyptian industry were likewise in use in the palace of the sea-kings of Cnossos, in
Rhodes, and in Cyprus, where a number of Egyptian
monuments of this age have been found. Scarabs and
bits of glazed ware with the names of Amenhotep II,
Amenhotep III or Queen Tiy have also been discovered
on the mainland of Greece at Mycenæ. The northern
Mediterranean peoples were feeling the impact of
Egyptian civilization with more emphasis than ever
before. In Crete, Egyptian religious forms had been
introduced, in one case under the personal leadership
of an Egyptian priest bearing an Egyptian sistrum.
Mycenæan artists were powerfully influenced by the in-
coming products of Egypt. Egyptian landscapes appear in their metal work, and the lithe animal forms in
instantaneous postures, caught by the pencil of the
Theban artist, were now common in Mycenæ. The
superb decorated ceilings of Thebes likewise appear in
the tombs of Mycenæ and Orchomenos. Even the pre-

Greek writing of Crete shows traces of the influence of the hieroglyphics of the Nile. The men of the Mycenæan world, the Keftyew, were now a familiar sight upon the streets of Thebes, where the wares which they offered were also modifying the art of Egypt. The plentiful silver of the north now came in with the northern strangers in great quantities, and, although under the Hyksos the baser metal had been worth twice as much as gold, the latter now and permanently became the more valuable medium. The ratio was now about one and two-thirds to one, and the value of silver steadily fell until Ptolemaic times (third century B. C. on), when the ratio was twelve to one. Such trade required protection and regulation. Against the bold Lycian pirates Amenhotep was obliged to develop a marine police which constantly patrolled the coast of the Delta. Here and at all frontiers custom houses were also maintained, and all merchandise not consigned to the king was dutiable (AL, 87, 62–64; 28; 29; 32;. 33; BAR, II, 916, ll. 33 *f.*).

249. The influx of slaves, chiefly of Semitic race, still continued, and the king's chief scribe distributed them throughout the land and enrolled them among the tax-paying serfs. As this host of foreigners intermarried with the natives, the large infusion of strange blood began to make itself felt in a new and composite type of face, if we may trust the artists of the day. The incalculable wealth which had now been converging upon the coffers of the Pharaoh for over a century also began to exert a profound influence, which, as under like conditions, in later history, was far from wholesome. On New Year's Day the king presented his nobles with a profusion of costly gifts which would have amazed the Pharaohs of the pyramid-age. The luxury and display

of the metropolis supplanted the old rustic simplicity and sturdy elemental virtues. A noble of the landed class from the time of the Amenemhets or the Sesostrises, could he have walked the streets of Thebes in Amenhotep III's reign, would almost have been at a loss to know in what country he had suddenly found himself; while his own antiquated costume, which had survived only among the priests, would have awakened equal astonishment among the fashionable Thebans of the day. He would not have felt less strange than a noble of Elizabeth's reign upon the streets of modern London. Where once was a provincial village he would now have found elegant châteaus and luxurious villas, with charming gardens and summer-houses grouped about vast temples, such as the Nile-dweller had never seen before (BAR, II, 916, ll. 31-33, 36; 801 *ff.*).

250. The wealth and the captive labour of Asia and Nubia were being rapidly transmuted into noble architecture, on a scale of size and grandeur surpassing all precedent, and at Thebes a new fundamental chapter in the history of the world's architecture was being daily written. Amenhotep supported his architects with all his unparalleled resources. There were among them men of the highest gifts, like "Amenhotep, son of Hapu," whose wisdom circulated in Greek some twelve hundred years later among the "Proverbs of the Seven Wise Men," till it gained him a place among the gods. (BAR, II, 911). Despite the vast dimensions of the imperial buildings, the smaller of the two forms of temple which now developed is not less effective than the larger. It was a simple rectangular cella or holy of holies, thirty or forty feet long and fourteen feet high, with a door at each end, surrounded by colonnades, the whole

being flat-roofed and raised upon a base of about half the height of the temple walls. With the door looking out between two graceful columns, and the façade happily set in the retreating vistas of the side colonnades, the whole is so finely proportioned and boldly conceived that the trained eye immediately recognizes the hand of a master who appreciated and depended upon simple, fundamental lines of *structural* origin and significance. The other and larger type of temple, which now found its highest development, differs strikingly from the one just discussed; and perhaps most fundamentally in the fact that its colonnades are all within and not visible from the outside. The holy of holies at the rear is surrounded, as of old, by a series of chambers, now larger than before, as rendered necessary by the rich and elaborate ritual which had arisen. Before it is a large colonnaded hall, often called the hypostyle, while in front of this hall lies an extensive forecourt surrounded by a columned portico. In front of this court rise two towers (together called a "pylon"), which form the façade of the temple. Their outer walls incline inward, they are crowned by a hollow cornice, and the great door of the temple opens between them. While the masonry, which is of sandstone or limestone, does not usually contain large blocks, huge architraves, thirty or forty feet long and weighing one or two hundred tons, are not unknown. Nearly all the surfaces, except those on the columns, are carved with reliefs, the outside showing the king in battle, while on the inside he appears in the worship of the gods, and all surfaces with slight exception were highly coloured. Before the vast double doors of cedar of Lebanon mounted in bronze, rose, one on either side, a pair of obelisks, towering high above the pylon-towers, while colossal statues of the king, each

THE EMPIRE AT ITS HEIGHT

hewn from a single block, were placed with backs to the pylon, on either side of the door. In the use of these elements and this general arrangement of the parts, already common before Amenhotep's reign, his architects now created a radically new type, destined to survive in frequent use to this day as one of the noblest forms of architecture.

251. At Luxor, the old southern suburb of Thebes, his architects laid out a superb forecourt of the temple of Amon, in front of which they planned a new and more ambitious hall than had ever been attempted before. The great hall was laid out with a row of gigantic columns, yet displaying faultless proportions ranged on either side the central axis. These, the loftiest columns yet attempted, with capitals of the graceful spreading papyrus-flower type, were higher than those ranged on both sides of the middle, thus producing a higher roof over a central aisle or nave and a lower roof over the side aisles, the difference in level to be filled with grated stone windows in a clear-story. Thus were produced the fundamental elements in basilica and cathedral architecture. Unfortunately the vast hall was unfinished at the death of the king, and the whole stands to-day a mournful wreck of an unfinished work of art, the first example of a now universal type of great architecture, for which we are indebted to Egypt and the Theban architects of Amenhotep III.

252. Amenhotep now proceeded to give the great buildings of the city a unity which they had not before possessed. Approaching the gorgeous pylon which he set up in front of the Karnak temple, an avenue led up from the river between two tall obelisks, which flanked a colossal portrait statue of the Pharaoh, hewn from a single block sixty-seven feet long. Through the beauti-

ful gardens, with which he united Karnak and Luxor, avenues of sculptured rams connected the great temples. The general effect must have been imposing in the extreme; the brilliant hues of the polychrome architecture, with columns and gates overwrought in gold, and floors overlaid with silver, the whole dominated by towering obelisks clothed in glittering metal, rising high above the rich green of the nodding palms and tropical foliage which framed the mass, or mirrored in the surface of the temple lake—all this must have produced an impression both of gorgeous detail and overwhelming grandeur, of which the sombre ruins of the same buildings, impressive as they are, offer little hint at the present day (BAR, II, 903; 917).

253. Thebes was thus rapidly becoming a worthy seat of empire, the first monumental city of antiquity. Nor did the western plain on the other side of the river, behind which the conquerors slept, suffer by comparison with the new glories of Karnak and Luxor. Along the foot of the rugged cliffs, from the modest chapel of Amenhotep I on the north, there stretched southward in an imposing line the mortuary temples of the emperors. At the south end of this line, but a little nearer the river, Amenhotep III now erected his own mortuary sanctuary, the largest temple of his reign, the prodigal magnificence of which defies description. But this sumptuous building, probably the greatest work of art ever wrought in Egypt, has vanished utterly. Only the two weather-beaten colossi which guarded the entrance still look out across the plain, one of them still bearing the scribblings in Greek of curious tourists in the times of the Roman Empire who came to hear the marvellous voice which issued from it every morning (BAR, II, 904 *ff.*; 878 *ff.*).

254. Adorned with such works as these the western

plain of Thebes was a majestic prospect as the observer advanced from the river, ascending Amenhotep's avenue of sculptured jackals, between the two seven-hundred ton colossi of the king, towering above the temple. On the left, behind the temple and nearer the cliffs, appeared a palace of the king of rectangular wooden architecture in bright colours; very light and airy, and having over the front entrance a gorgeous cushioned balcony with graceful columns, in which the king showed himself to his favourites on occasion. Innumerable products of the industrial artist which fill the museums of Europe indicate with what tempered richness and delicate beauty such a royal château was furnished and adorned. Magnificent vessels in gold and silver, with figures of men and animals, plants and flowers rising from the rim, glittered on the king's table among crystal goblets, glass vases, and gray porcelain vessels inlaid with pale blue designs. The walls were covered with woven tapestry which skilled judges have declared equal to the best modern work. Besides painted pavements depicting animal life, the walls also were adorned with blue glazed tiles, the rich colour of which shone through elaborate designs in gold leaf, while glazed figures were employed in encrusting larger surfaces. All this was done with fine and intelligent consideration of the whole colour scheme. The fine taste and the technical skill required for all such supplementary works of the craftsman were now developed to a point of classical excellence, beyond which Egyptian art never passed.

255. Sculpture also flourished under such circumstances as never before. While there now developed an attention to details which required infinite patience and nicety, such arduous application did not hamper the

fine feeling of which these Eighteenth Dynasty sculptors were capable. They thus interpreted and expressed individuality with a keen insight, a subtle refinement and an individual power, which endued their portraits with a personality and a winning grace far surpassing all earlier works. The perfection attained in the sculpture of animal forms by the artists of this time marks the highest level of achievement attained by Egyptian art herein, and Ruskin has even insisted with his customary conviction that the two lions of Amenhotep's reign, now in the British Museum, are the finest embodiment of animal majesty which has survived to us from any ancient people. Especially in relief were the artists of this age masters. In a fragment now in the Berlin Museum, the abandoned grief of the two sons of the High Priest of Memphis as they follow their father's body to the tomb, is effectively contrasted with the severe gravity and conventional decorum of the great ministers of state behind them, who themselves are again in striking contrast with a Beau Brummel of that day, as he affectedly arranges the perfumed curls of his elaborate wig. Here across thirty-five centuries there speaks to us a maturity in the contemplation of life which finds a sympathetic response in every cultivated observer. This fragmentary sketch belongs to a class of work totally lacking in other lands in this age. It is one of the earliest examples of sculpture exhibiting that interpretation of life and appreciation of individual traits (often supposed to have arisen first among the sculptors of Greece), in which art finds its highest expression.

256. Now, too, the Pharaoh's deeds of prowess inspired the sculptors of the time to more elaborate compositions than had ever before been approached.

The battle scenes on the noble chariot of Thutmose IV exhibit a complexity in drawing and composition unprecedented, and this tendency continues in the Nineteenth Dynasty. Of the painting of the time, the best examples were in the palaces, and these being of wood and sun-dried brick, have perished, but a fine perception, which enabled the artist in his representation of animals and birds to depict instantaneous postures, is already observable, reaching its highest expression in the next reign. In such an age literature doubtless throve, but chance has unfortunately preserved to us little of the literature of the Eighteenth Dynasty. There is a triumphant hymn to Thutmose III, and we shall read the remarkable sun-hymn of Ikhnaton; but of narrative, song and legend, which must have flourished from the rise of the Empire, our surviving documents date almost exclusively from the Nineteenth Dynasty.

257. Near his palace in western Thebes Amenhotep laid out an exclusive quarter which he gave to his queen Tiy. He excavated a large lake in the enclosure about a mile long and over a thousand feet wide, and at the celebration of his coronation anniversary in his twelfth year he opened the sluices for filling it, and sailed out upon it in the royal barge with his queen, in a gorgeous festival "fantasia." Such festivals were now common in Thebes, and enriched the life of the fast growing metropolis with a kaleidoscopic variety which may be only compared with similar periods in Babylon or in Rome under the emperors. The religious feasts of the seventh month were celebrated with such opulent splendour that the month quickly gained the epithet, "That of Amenhotep," a designation which still survives among the natives of modern Egypt, who employ

it without the faintest knowledge of the imperial ruler, their ancestor, whose name is perpetuated in it.

258. Among the king's favourite diversions was the hunt, which he practised on an unprecedented scale. He slew as many as seventy-six wild cattle in one expedition, and in the first ten years of his reign he had slain one hundred and two lions. In celebration of these exploits and of such events as the dedication of the sacred lake the king issued each time a series of commemorative scarabs (see p. 248). It will be seen that in these things a new and modern tendency was coming to its own. The divine Pharaoh is constantly being exhibited in common human relations, the affairs of the royal house are made public property, the name of the queen, not even a woman of royal birth, is constantly appearing at the head of official documents side by side with that of the Pharaoh. In constant intercourse with the nations of Asia he is gradually forced from his old superhuman state, suited only to the Nile, into less provincial and more modern relations with his neighbours of Babylon and Mitanni, who in their letters call him "brother." This lion-hunting, bull-baiting Pharaoh is far indeed from the godlike and unapproachable immobility of his divine ancestors. Whether consciously or not he had assumed a modern stand-point, which must inevitably lead to sharp conflict with the almost irresistible inertia of tradition in an Oriental country (BAR, II, 865; 868 *f.*; 863 *f.*; 880, note a; 893 *ff.*).

259. Presiding over the magnificence of Thebes, the now aging Amenhotep had celebrated his third jubilee when ominous signs of trouble appeared on the northern horizon. Mitanni was invaded by the Hittites (Kheta), and the provinces of Egypt on the lower Orontes were not spared. The situation was complicated by the

connivance of treacherous vassals of the Pharaoh, who were themselves attempting the conquest of territory on their own account, even threatening Ubi, the region of Damascus. While the Hittites thus secured a footing in northern Naharin of the greatest value in their further plans for the conquest of Syria, an invasion of the Khabiri, desert Semites, such as had periodically inundated Syria and Palestine from time immemorial, was also now taking place. It was of such proportions that it may fairly be called an immigration. Before Amenhotep III's death it had become threatening, and thus Ribaddi of Byblos later wrote to Amenhotep III's son: "Since thy father returned from Sidon, since that time the lands have fallen into the hands of the Khabiri" (BAR, II, 870–873; AL, 16, 30–37; 138 rev. ll. 5, 18–31, 37; 83, 28–33; 94, 13–18; 69, 71–73).

260. Under such ominous conditions as these the old Pharaoh, whom we may well call "Amenhotep the Magnificent," drew near his end. His brother of Mitanni, with whom he was still on terms of intimacy, probably knowing of his age and weakness, sent the captured image of Ishtar of Nineveh for the second time to Egypt, doubtless in the hope that the far-famed goddess might be able to exorcise the evil spirits which were causing Amenhotep's infirmity and restore the old king to health. But all such means were of no avail, and about 1375 B. C., after nearly thirty-six years upon the throne, "Amenhotep the Magnificent" passed away, and was buried with the other emperors, his fathers, in the Valley of the Kings' Tombs (AL, 20).

XVIII

THE RELIGIOUS REVOLUTION OF IKHNATON

261. No nation ever stood in direr need of a strong and practical ruler than did Egypt at the death of Amenhotep III. Yet she chanced to be ruled at this fatal crisis by a young dreamer, who, in spite of unprecedented greatness in the world of ideas, was not fitted to cope with a difficult situation demanding an aggressive man of affairs and a skilled military leader. The conflict of new forces with tradition was, as we have seen, already felt by his father. The task before him was such manipulation of these conflicting forces as might eventually give reasonable play to the new and modern tendency, but at the same time to conserve enough of the old to prevent a catastrophe. It was a problem of practical statesmanship. His mother, Tiy, and his queen, Nofretete, perhaps a woman of Asiatic birth, and a favourite priest, Eye, the husband of his childhood nurse, formed his immediate circle. The first two were given a prominent share in the government, and in a manner quite surpassing his father's similar tendency, he constantly appeared in public with both his mother and his wife. With such effeminate counsellors about him, instead of gathering the army so sadly needed in Naharin, Amenhotep IV immersed himself heart and soul in the thought of the time, and the philosophizing theology of the priests was of more importance to him

THE RELIGIOUS REVOLUTION OF IKHNATON 265

than all the provinces of Asia. In such contemplations he gradually developed ideals and purposes which make him the most remarkable of all the Pharaohs, and the first *individual* in human history.

262. The profound influence of Egypt's imperial position had not been limited to the externals of life, to the manners and customs of the people, to the rich and prolific art, but had extended likewise to the thought of the age. Even before the conquests in Asia the priests had made great progress in the interpretation of the gods, and they had now reached a stage in which, like the Greeks, they were importing semi-philosophical significance into the myths, such as these had of course not originally possessed. The interpretation of a god was naturally suggested by his place or function in the myth. Thus Ptah, the artificer-god of Memphis, had been from the remotest ages the god of the architect and craftsman, to whom he communicated plans and designs for architectural works and the products of the industrial arts. Contemplating this god, the Memphite priest, little used as his mind was to abstractions, found a tangible channel, moving along which he gradually gained a rational and with certain limitations a philosophical conception of the world. The workshop of the Memphite temple, where, under Ptah's guidance, were wrought the splendid statues, utensils and offerings for the temple, expands into a world, and Ptah, its lord, grows into the master-workman of the universal workshop. As he furnishes all designs to the architect and craftsman, so now he does the same for all men in all that they do; he becomes the supreme mind; he is mind, and all things proceed from him. Gods and men, the world and all that is in it first existed as thought in his mind; and his thoughts, like his plans for buildings

and works of art, needed but to be expressed in spoken words to take concrete form as material realities. Thus the efficient force by which this intelligence put his designs into execution was his spoken "word," and this primitive "logos" is undoubtedly the incipient germ of the later logos-doctrine which found its origin in Egypt. Early Greek philosophy may also have drawn upon it (AZ, 39, 39 *ff.*).

263. Similar ideas were now being propagated regarding all the greater gods of Egypt, but the activity of such a god had been limited, in their thinking, to the confines of the Pharaoh's domain, and the world of which they thought meant no more. From of old the Pharaoh was the heir of the gods and ruled the two kingdoms of the upper and lower river which they had once ruled. Thus they had not in the myths extended their dominion beyond the river valley. But under the Empire all this is changed, the god goes where the Pharaoh's sword carries him; the advance of the Pharaoh's boundary-tablets in Nubia and Syria is the extension of the god's domain. Thus, for king and priest alike, the world was becoming only a great domain of the god. The theological theory of the state is simply that the king receives the world that he may deliver it to the god, and he prays for extended conquests that the dominion of the god may be correspondingly extended. It can be no accident that the notion of a practically universal god arose in Egypt at the moment when he was receiving universal tribute from the world of that day. Similarly the analogy of the Pharaoh's power unquestionably operated powerfully with the Egyptian theologian at this time; for as in the myth-making days the gods were conceived as Pharaohs ruling the Nile valley, because the myth-makers lived under Pharaohs

THE RELIGIOUS REVOLUTION OF IKHNATON 267

who so ruled; so now, living under Pharaohs who ruled a world-empire, the priest of the imperial age had before him in tangible form a world-dominion and a world-concept, the prerequisite of the notion of the world-god. Conquered and organized and governed, it had now been before him for two hundred years, and out of the Pharaoh-ruled world he gradually began to see the world-god (BAR, II, 770; 959, l. 3; 1000; III, 80).

264. While many local gods, especially Amon claimed precedence as the state god, none of the old divinities of Egypt had been proclaimed the god of the Empire, although in fact the priesthood of Heliopolis had gained the coveted honour for their revered sun-god, Re, who indeed enjoyed the best historical title to the distinction. Already under Amenhotep III an old name for the material sun, "Aton," had come into prominent use, where the name of the sun-god might have been expected. The sun-god, too, had now and again been designated as "the sole god" by Amenhotep III's contemporaries. Under the name of Aton, Amenhotep IV introduced the worship of the supreme god. While he made no attempt to conceal the identity of his new deity with the old sun-god, Re, it was not merely sun-worship; the word Aton was employed in place of the old word for "god" (nuter), and the god is clearly distinguished from the material sun. To the old sun-god's name is appended the explanatory phrase "under his name: 'Heat which is in the Sun [Aton],'" and he is likewise called "lord of the sun [Aton]." The king, therefore, was deifying the vital heat which he found accompanying all life. Thence, as we might expect, the god is stated to be everywhere active by means of his "rays." In his age of the world it is perfectly certain that the king could not have had the vaguest notion of

the physico-chemical aspects of his assumption any more than had the early Greeks in dealing with a similar thought. The outward symbol of his god, a disk in the heavens, darting earthward numerous diverging rays which terminate in hands, each grasping the symbol of life, broke sharply with tradition, but it was capable of practical introduction in the many different nations making up the empire, and could be understood at a glance by any intelligent foreigner (BAR, II, 869; 945; 934, l. 2; 987, note e).

265. The new god could not dispense with a temple, and early in the new king's reign arose a stately sanctuary of Aton called "Gem-Aton" between Karnak and Luxor, in a new quarter now called "Brightness of Aton the Great." Although the other gods were still tolerated as of old, it was nevertheless inevitable that the priesthood of Amon should view with growing jealousy the brilliant rise of a strange god in their midst. The priesthood of Amon was now a rich and powerful body. Besides being supreme head of the national sacerdotal organization, their High Priest was often grand vizier and wielded the widest political power. They had installed Thutmose III as king, and could they have supplanted with one of their own tools the young dreamer who now held the throne they would of course have done so at the first opportunity. But besides the prestige of his great line, Amenhotep IV possessed unlimited personal force of character, and he was of course supported in his opposition of Amon by the older priesthoods of the north at Memphis and Heliopolis, long jealous of this interloper, the obscure Theban god, who had never been heard of in the north before the rise of the Middle Kingdom. A conflict to the bitter end, with the most disastrous results to the Amonite

THE RELIGIOUS REVOLUTION OF IKHNATON

priesthood ensued. Exasperated by opposition the young Pharaoh broke with the priesthoods; including that of Amon, they were dispossessed, the official temple-worship of the various gods throughout the land ceased, and their names were erased wherever they could be found upon the monuments. Even the word "gods" was not permitted to appear anywhere, and the walls of the temples at Thebes were painfully searched that wherever the compromising word appeared it might be blotted out. What was worse, as the name of the king's father, Amenhotep, contained the name of Amon, the young king was placed in the unpleasant predicament of being obliged to cut out his own father's name in order to prevent the name of Amon from appearing "writ large" on all the temples of Thebes. And then there was the embarrassment of the king's own name, likewise Amenhotep, "Amon rests," which could not be spoken or placed on a monument. It was of necessity also banished, and the king assumed in its place the name "Ikhnaton," which means "Spirit of Aton" (BAR, II, 935; 942, note b; 937; 944-947).

266. Thebes was now compromised by too many old associations to be a congenial place of residence for so radical a revolutionist. As he looked across the city and beheld the vast monuments raised to Amon by his fathers, the sight could hardly have stirred pleasant memories in the heart of the young reformer. A doubtless long contemplated plan was therefore undertaken. Aton, the god of the empire, should possess exclusively his own city in each of the three great divisions of the empire: Egypt, Asia and Nubia, and the god's Egyptian city should be made the royal residence. It must have been an enterprise requiring some time, but the three cities were duly founded. The

Aton-city of Nubia was located on the west side of the river at the foot of the third cataract, in the heart of the Egyptian province (Note VI). It was named "Gem-Aton" after the Aton-temple in Thebes. In Syria the Aton-city is unknown, but Ikhnaton will not have done less for Aton there than his fathers had done for Amon. In the sixth year, shortly after he had changed his name, the king was already living in his own Aton-city in Egypt. He chose as its site a fine bay in the cliffs about one hundred and sixty miles above the Delta and nearly three hundred miles below Thebes. He called it Akhetaton, "Horizon of Aton," and it is known in modern times as Tell el-Amarna. In addition to the town, the territory around it was demarked as a domain belonging to the god, and included the plain on both sides of the river. In the cliffs on either side, fourteen large stelas, one of them no less than twenty-six feet in height, were cut into the rock, bearing inscriptions determining the limits of the entire sacred district around the city. As thus laid out the district was about eight miles wide from north to south, and from twelve to over seventeen miles long from cliff to cliff. Besides this sacred domain the god was endowed with revenues from other lands in Egypt and Nubia, and probably also in Syria. The royal architect, Bek, was sent to the first cataract to procure stone for the new temple, or we should rather say temples, for no less than three were now built in the new city, one for the queen mother, Tiy, and another for the Princess Beketaton ("Maid-servant of Aton"), beside the state temple of the king himself. Around the temples rose the palace of the king and the châteaus of his nobles. Many a scene of splendour is now discernible in the beautiful city, as when the king publicly demits the office of High Priest of Aton and confers it with rich gifts upon Merire, one of the royal favourites. Again we behold the king proceeding to the temple in his chariot, accompanied by his four daughters and a gorgeous retinue, while he receives there the first dues from its revenues (BAR, II, 949–972; 973 ff.; 1016–1018; 1000; 982; AZ, 40, 106 ff.).

267. It becomes more and more evident that all that was devised and done in the new city and in the propagation of the Aton faith is directly due to the king and bears the stamp of his individuality. A king who was deliberately attempting the annihilation of the gods—one who did not hesitate to erase his own father's name on the monuments in order to destroy Amon, the great foe of his revolutionary movement, was not one to stop half way, and the men about him must have been involuntarily carried on at his imperious will. But Ikhnaton understood enough of the old policy of the Pharaohs to know that he must hold his party by practical rewards, and the leading partisans of his movement, like Merire, enjoyed liberal bounty at his hands. The reason which they give, as they boast of his favour, is significant. Thus the general of the king's army, Mai, says: "My lord has advanced me because I have carried out his teaching, and I hear his word without ceasing. . . . . How prosperous is he who hears thy teaching of life!" On state occasions, instead of the old stock phrases, with innumerable references to the traditional gods (which it must have been very awkward for them to cease using), every noble who would enjoy the king's favour was evidently obliged to show his familiarity with the Aton faith and the king's position in it by a liberal use of its current phrases and allusions. Even the Syrian vassals were wise enough to make their dispatches pleasant reading

by glossing them with appropriate recognition of the supremacy of the sun-god. Although there must have been a nucleus of men who really appreciated the ideal aspects of the king's teaching, it is evident that many were chiefly influenced by "the loaves and the fishes" (BAR, II, 994, ll. 17 *f.;* 995, ll. 21 *f.;* 985; 987; 994, ll. 16 *f.;* 1002 *f.*).

268. Indeed there was one royal favour which must have been welcome to them all without exception. This was the beautiful cliff-tomb which the king commanded his craftsmen to hew out of the eastern cliffs for each one of his favourites. The "eternal house" was no longer disfigured with hideous demons and grotesque monsters which should confront the dead in the future life; and the magic paraphernalia necessary to meet and vanquish the dark powers of the nether world, which filled the tombs of the old order at Thebes, were completely banished. The tomb now became a monument to the deceased; the walls of its chapel bore fresh and natural pictures from the life of the people in Akhetaton, particularly the incidents in the official career of the dead man, and preferably his intercourse with the king. Thus the city of Akhetaton is now better known to us from its cemetery than from its ruins. Throughout these tombs the nobles take delight in reiterating, both in relief and inscription, the intimate relation between Aton and the king. Over and over again they show the king and the queen together standing under the disk of Aton, whose rays, terminating in hands, descend and embrace the royal pair (BAR, II, 996; 1012; 1000, l. 5; 991, l. 3; 1010, l. 3; AL, 149, 6 *ff.* and often).

269. It is in these tombs that the nobles have engraved the two hymns to Aton composed by the king.

THE RELIGIOUS REVOLUTION OF IKHNATON 273

Of all the monuments left by this unparalleled revolution, these hymns are by far the most remarkable; and from them we may gather an intimation of the doctrines which the speculative young Pharaoh had sacrificed so much to disseminate. The titles of the separate strophes are the addition of the present author, and in the translation no attempt has been made to do more than to furnish an accurate rendering. The one hundred and fourth Psalm of the Hebrews shows a notable similarity to our hymn both in the thought and the sequence, so that it seems desirable to place the most noticeably parallel passages side by side.

THE SPLENDOUR OF ATON

Thy dawning is beautiful in the horizon of heaven,
O living Aton, Beginning of life!
When thou risest in the eastern horizon of heaven,
Thou fillest every land with thy beauty;
For thou art beautiful, great, glittering, high over the earth;
Thy rays, they encompass the lands, even all thou hast made,
Thou art Re, and thou hast carried them all away captive;
Thou bindest them by thy love.
Though thou art afar, thy rays are on earth;
Though thou art on high, thy footprints are the day.

NIGHT

When thou settest in the western horizon of heaven,
The world is in darkness like the dead.
They sleep in their chambers,
Their heads are wrapt up,
Their nostrils stopped, and none seeth the other.
Stolen are all their things, that are under their heads,
While they know it not.
Every lion cometh forth from his den,
All serpents, they sting.
Darkness reigns (?),
The world is in silence,
He that made them has gone to rest in his horizon.

Thou makest darkness and it is night,
Wherein all the beasts of the forest do creep forth.
The young lions roar after their prey;
They seek their meat from God.
(Psalm 104, 20–21.)

Day and Man

Bright is the earth,
When thou risest in the horizon,
When thou shinest as Aton by day.
The darkness is banished,
When thou sendest forth thy rays,
The Two Lands [Egypt] are in daily festivity,
Awake and standing upon their feet,
For thou hast raised them up.
Their limbs bathed, they take their clothing;
Their arms uplifted in adoration to thy dawning.
Then in all the world, they do their work.

The sun ariseth, they get them away,
And lay them down in their dens.
Man goeth forth unto his work,
And to his labour until the evening.

(Psalm 104, 22-23.)

Day and the Animals and Plants

All cattle rest upon their herbage,
All trees and plants flourish,
The birds flutter in their marshes,
Their wings uplifted in adoration to thee.
All the sheep dance upon their feet,
All winged things fly,
They live when thou hast shone upon them.

Day and the Waters

The barques sail up-stream and down-stream alike.
Every highway is open because thou hast dawned.
The fish in the river leap up before thee,
And thy rays are in the midst of the great sea.

Yonder is the sea, great and wide,
Wherein are things creeping innumerable
Both small and great beasts.
There go the ships;
There is leviathan, whom thou hast formed to sport with him.

(Psalm 104, 25-26.)

Creation of Man

Thou art he who createst the man-child in woman,
Who makest seed in man,
Who givest life to the son in the body of his mother,
Who soothest him that he may not weep,
A nurse [even] in the womb.
Who giveth breath to animate every one that he maketh.

When he cometh forth from the body,
. . . on the day of his birth,
Thou openest his mouth in speech,
Thou suppliest his necessities.

Creation of Animals

When the chicklet crieth in the egg-shell,
Thou givest him breath therein, to preserve him alive.
When thou hast perfected him
That he may pierce the egg,
He cometh forth from the egg,
To chirp with all his might;
He runneth about upon his two feet,
When he hath come forth therefrom.

The Whole Creation

How manifold are all thy works!
They are hidden from before us,
O thou sole god, whose powers no other possesseth.*
Thou didst create the earth according to thy desire,
While thou wast alone:
Men, all cattle large and small,
All that are upon the earth,
That go about upon their feet;
All that are on high,
That fly with their wings.
The countries of Syria and Nubia,
The land of Egypt;
Thou settest every man in his place,
Thou suppliest their necessities.
Every one has his possessions,
And his days are reckoned.
Their tongues are divers in speech,
Their forms likewise and their skins,
For thou divider, hast divided the peoples.

O lord, how manifold are thy works!
In wisdom hast thou made them all;
The earth is full of thy creatures.

(Psalm 104, 24.)

Watering the Earth

Thou makest the Nile in the Nether World,
Thou bringest it at thy desire, to preserve the people alive.

---

*The other hymns frequently say, "O thou sole god, beside whom there is no other."

O lord of them all, when feebleness is in them,
O lord of every house, who risest for them,
O sun of day, the fear of every distant land,
Thou makest [also] their life.
Thou hast set a Nile in heaven,
That it may fall for them,
Making floods upon the mountains, like the great sea;
And watering their fields among their towns.

How excellent are thy designs, O lord of eternity!
The Nile in heaven is for the strangers,
And for the cattle of every land, that go upon their feet;
But the Nile, it cometh from the Nether World for Egypt.

Thus thy rays nourish every garden,
When thou risest they live, and grow by thee.

The Seasons

Thou makest the seasons, in order to create all thy works:
Winter bringing them coolness,
And the heat [of summer likewise].
Thou hast made the distant heaven to rise therein,
In order to behold all that thou didst make,
While thou wast alone,
Rising in thy form as living Aton,
Dawning, shining afar off and returning.

Beauty Due to Light

Thou makest the beauty of form, through thyself alone.
Cities, towns and settlements,
On highway or on river,
All eyes see thee before them,
For thou art Aton of the day over the earth.

Revelation to the King

Thou art in my heart,
There is no other that knoweth thee,
Save thy son Ikhnaton.
Thou hast made him wise in thy designs
And in thy might.
The world is in thy hand,
Even as thou hast made them.
When thou hast risen, they live;
When thou settest, they die.
For thou art duration, beyond thy mere limbs,
By thee man liveth,
And their eyes look upon thy beauty,
Until thou settest.

THE RELIGIOUS REVOLUTION OF IKHNATON

All labour is laid aside,
When thou settest in the west;
When thou risest, they are made to grow
. . . . . for the king.
Since thou didst establish the earth,
Thou hast raised them up for thy son,
Who came forth from thy limbs,
The king, living in truth,
The lord of the Two Lands Nefer-khepru-Re, Wan-Re,
The son of Re, living in truth, lord of diadems,
Ikhnaton, whose life is long;
[And for] the great royal wife, his beloved,
Mistress of the Two Lands, Nefer-nefru-aton, Nofretete,
Living and flourishing for ever and ever.

270. In this hymn the universalism of the Empire finds full expression, and the royal singer sweeps his eye from the far-off cataracts of the Nubian Nile to the remotest lands of Syria. He grasped the idea of a world-dominator, as the creator of nature, in which the king saw revealed the creator's beneficent purpose for all his creatures, even the meanest; the birds fluttering about in the lily-grown Nile-marshes to him seemed to be uplifting their wings in adoration of their creator; and even the fish in the stream leaped up in praise to God. It is his voice that summons the blossoms and nourishes the chicklet or commands the mighty deluge of the Nile. He called Aton, "the father and the mother of all that he had made," and he saw in some degree the goodness of that All-Father as did he who bade us consider the lilies. He perceived the universal sway of God in his fatherly care of all men alike, irrespective of race or nationality, and to the proud and exclusive Egyptian he pointed to the all-embracing bounty of the common father of humanity, even placing Syria and Nubia before Egypt in his enumeration. It is this aspect of Ikhnaton's mind which is especially remarkable; he is alike the first prophet and the first wise-man of history.

271. While Ikhnaton thus recognized clearly the power, and to a surprising extent, the beneficence of God, there is not here a very spiritual conception of the deity nor any attribution to him of ethical qualities beyond those already long attributed to the gods. Nevertheless, there is in this "teaching," a constant emphasis upon "truth" such as is not found before nor since. The king always attaches to his name the phrase "living in truth," and that this phrase was not meaningless is evident in his daily life. Thus his family life was open and unconcealed before the people. He took the greatest delight in his children and appeared with them and the queen, their mother, on all possible occasions, as if he had been but the humblest scribe in the Aton-temple. He had himself depicted on the monuments while enjoying the most familiar and unaffected intercourse with his family, and whenever he appeared in the temple to offer sacrifice, the queen and the daughters she had borne him participated in the service. All that was natural was to him "true," and he never failed practically to exemplify this belief, however radically he was obliged to disregard tradition.

272. Such a principle unavoidably affected the art of the time in which the king took great interest. Bek, his chief sculptor, appended to his title the words, "whom his majesty himself taught." Thus the artists of his court were taught to make the chisel and the brush tell the story of what they actually saw. The result was a simple and beautiful realism that saw more clearly than ever any art had seen before. They caught the instantaneous postures of animal life; the coursing hound, the fleeing game, the wild bull leaping in the swamp; for all these belonged to the "truth," in which Ikhnaton lived. The king's person, as we have inti-

THE RELIGIOUS REVOLUTION OF IKHNATON 279

mated, was no exception to the law of the new art, and the monuments of Egypt now bore what they had never borne before, a Pharaoh not frozen in the conventional posture demanded by the traditions of court propriety, but as he actually was. There are now portraits of the king that might have been done by a Donatello. The modelling of the human figure at this time was so plastic that at the first glance one is sometimes in doubt whether he has before him a product of the Greek age. More than this, complex compositions of grouped figures in the round were now first conceived. Fragments recently discovered show that in the court of the king's palace at Akhetaton there stood a group wrought in stone depicting the king in his chariot in full career, pursuing the wounded lion. This was indeed a new chapter in the history of art, even though so soon to perish. It was in some things an obscure chapter; for the strange treatment of the lower limbs by Ikhnaton's artists is a problem which still remains unsolved and cannot be wholly accounted for by supposing a malformation of the king's own limbs. It is one of those unhealthy symptoms which are visible too in the body politic, and to these last we must now turn if we would learn how fatal to the material interests of the state this violent break with tradition has been (BAR, II, 975).

> *It is not certain what became of the Hittites as their nation disappeared.*

XIX

THE FALL OF IKHNATON, AND THE DISSOLUTION OF THE EMPIRE

273. WHOLLY absorbed in the exalted religion to which he had given his life, with difficulty stemming the tide of tradition that was daily as strong against him as at first, Ikhnaton was beset with too many problems at home to give much attention to the affairs of the Empire abroad. On his accession his sovereignty in Asia had immediately been recognized by the Hittites and the powers of the Euphrates valley. Dushratta of Mitanni and Burraburyash of Babylon sent assurances of sympathy on Amenhotep III's death, and both sought the favour of the new Pharaoh. A son of Burraburyash later sojourned at Ikhnaton's court and married a daughter of the latter. But such intercourse did not last long, as we shall see (AL, 22; 21; 14; 8, 41.)

274. Meantime the power of the Hittites in northern Syria was ever increasing, constantly reinforced by the southern movement of their countrymen behind them. The remains of this remarkable race, one of the greatest problems in the study of the early Orient, have been found from the western coast of Asia Minor eastward to the plains of Syria and the Euphrates, and southward as far as Hamath. They were a non-Semitic people, or rather peoples, of uncertain racial affinities, but evidently distinct from, and preceding, the Indo-

Germanic influx after 1200 B. C. which brought in the Phrygians. The Hittite pictographic records are still in course of decipherment, and enough progress has not yet been made to enable the scholar to do more than recognize a word here and there. For correspondence they employed the Babylonian cuneiform, and therefore maintained scribes and interpreters who were masters of Babylonian speech and writing. Large quantities of cuneiform tablets in the Hittite tongue have been found at Boghaz-köi. In war they were formidable opponents. The infantry, among which foreign mercenaries were plentiful, fought in close phalanx formation, very effective at close quarters; but their chief power consisted of heavy chariotry. As far back as the eighteenth century they had pushed eastward, invaded Mesopotamia, and plundered Babylon, probably causing the fall of the First Dynasty there (KSEH, II, 72, 148). One of the Hittite dynasts had consolidated a kingdom beyond the Amanus, which Thutmose III regularly called "Great Kheta," as probably distinguished from the less important independent Hittite princes. His capital was a great fortified city called Khatti, near modern Boghaz-köi, east of Angora in eastern Asia Minor (Note X). Active trade and intercourse between this kingdom and Egypt had been carried on from that time or began not long after. When Ikhnaton ascended the throne Seplel, the king of the Hittites, wrote him a letter of congratulation, and to all appearances had only the friendliest intentions toward Egypt. Even after Ikhnaton's removal to Akhetaton his new capital, a Hittite embassy appeared there with gifts and greetings. But Ikhnaton must have regarded the old relations as no longer desirable, for the Hittite king asks him why he has ceased the correspondence which his father had maintained. If he realized the situation, Ikhnaton had good reason indeed for abandoning the connection; for the Hittite empire now stood on the northern threshold of Syria, the most formidable enemy which had ever confronted Egypt, and the greatest power in Asia (MAAG; AL, 35; 25, 49 *f.*; BAR, II, 981).

275. Immediately on Ikhnaton's accession the disaffected dynasts who had been temporarily suppressed by his father resumed their operations against the faithful vassals of Egypt. The Hittites were steadily advancing up the Orontes, with the coöperation of the unfaithful Egyptian vassals, Abd-ashirta and his son Aziru, who were at the head of an Amorite kingdom on the upper Orontes; together with Itakama, a Syrian prince, who had seized Kadesh as his kingdom. Aziru of Amor finally succeeded in capturing all the Phœnician and north Syrian coast cities except Simyra and Byblos which held out. Then, as the Hittites pushed up the Orontes, Aziru coöperated with them and captured Niy, whose king he slew. Tunip was now in such grave danger that her elders wrote the Pharaoh a pathetic letter beseeching his protection. They ask: "Who formerly could have plundered Tunip without being plundered by Manakhbiria [Thutmose III]?" and they conclude with lamentation: "And when Aziru enters Simyra, Aziru will do to us as he pleases, in the territory of our lord, the king, and on account of these things our lord will have to lament. And now, Tunip, thy city weeps, and her tears are flowing, and there is no help for us. For twenty years we have been sending to our lord, the king, the king of Egypt, but there has not come to us a word, no not one" (AL, 88; 119; 125; 131–133; 123; 86; 119; 120; 41).

276. During all this, Rib-Addi, a faithful vassal of Byblos, where there was an Egyptian temple, repeatedly writes to the Pharaoh the most urgent appeals, stating what is going on, and asking for help to drive away Aziru's people from Simyra, knowing full well that if it falls his own city of Byblos is likewise doomed. But no help comes. Several Egyptian deputies had been charged with the investigation of affairs at Simyra, but they did not succeed in doing anything, and the city finally fell. Aziru had no hesitation in slaying the Egyptian deputy resident in the place, and having destroyed it, was now free to move against Byblos. Rib-Addi wrote in horror of these facts to the Pharaoh, stating that the Egyptian deputy, resident in Kumidi in northern Palestine, was now in danger. But the wily Aziru, skilful in specious excuses, so uses his friends at court that he escapes. Ikhnaton is reassured by Aziru's promises to pay the same tribute as the cities which he has taken formerly paid. Such acknowledgment of Egyptian suzerainty by the turbulent dynasts everywhere must have left in the Pharaoh a feeling of security which the situation by no means justified ((AL, 150 *f.*; 85; 119; 120; 94; 44–47; 49, 36–40; 50 *f.*).

277. During all this time Rib-Addi is in sore straits in Byblos, and sends dispatch after dispatch to the Egyptian court, appealing for aid against Aziru. The claims of the hostile dynasts, however, are so skilfully made that the resident Egyptian deputies actually do not seem to know who are the faithful vassals and who the secretly rebellious. Thus Bikhuru, the Egyptian deputy in Galilee, not understanding the situation in Byblos, sent his Beduin mercenaries thither, where they slew all of Rib-Addi's Sherden garrison. The unhappy

Rib-Addi, now at the mercy of his foes, sent off two dispatches beseeching the Pharaoh to take notice of his pitiful plight; while, to make matters worse, the city raised an insurrection against him because of the wanton act of the Egyptian resident. He has now sustained the siege for three years, he is old and burdened with disease; fleeing to Berût to secure help from the Egyptian deputy there, he returns to Byblos to find the city closed against him, his brother having seized the government in his absence and delivered his children to Aziru. As Berût itself is soon attacked and falls, he forsakes it, again returns to Byblos and in some way regains control and holds the place for a while longer. Although Aziru, his enemy, was obliged to appear at court and finally did so, no relief came for the despairing Rib-Addi. All the cities of the coast were held by his enemies and their ships commanded the sea, so that provisions and reinforcements could not reach him. His wife and family urge him to abandon Egypt and join Aziru's party, but still he is faithful to the Pharaoh and asks for three hundred men to undertake the recovery of Berût, and thus gain a little room. The Hittites are plundering his territory and the Khabiri, or Beduin mercenaries of his enemy Aziru, swarm under his walls; his dispatches to the court soon cease, his city of course fell, he was probably slain like the kings of the other coast cities, and in him the last vassal of Egypt in the north had perished (AL, 51; 77; 100; 71; 23; 96; 65; 67; 104; 68; 102; 104).

278. Similar conditions prevailed in the south, where the advance of the Khabiri, among whom we must recognize bands of Hebrews and Aramæans, was steadily absorbing Palestine. Knots of their warriors are now appearing everywhere and taking service as mercenary

THE DISSOLUTION OF THE EMPIRE 285

troops under the dynasts on both sides. Under various adventurers the Khabiri are frequently the real masters, and Palestinian cities like Megiddo, Askalon and Gezer write to the Pharaoh for succour against them. The last named city, together with Askalon and Lachish, united against Abdkhiba, the Egyptian deputy in Jerusalem, already at this time an important stronghold of southern Palestine, and the faithful officer sends urgent dispatches to Ikhnaton explaining the danger and appealing for aid against the Khabiri and their leaders. Fleeing in terror before the Khabiri, who burned and laid waste everywhere, many of the Palestinians forsook their towns and took to the hills, or sought refuge in Egypt, where the Egyptian officer in charge of some of them said of them: "They have been destroyed and their town laid waste, and fire has been thrown [into their grain?]. . . . Their countries are starving, they live like goats of the mountain. . . . A few of the Asiatics, who knew not how they should live, have come [begging a home in the domain?] of Pharaoh, after the manner of your father's fathers since the beginning." The last tribute from Asia, of which we are informed, was received at Akhetaton in the twelfth year. Some time thereafter, both in Syria and Palestine the provinces of the Pharaoh passed entirely out of Egyptian control (AL, 102; 104; 146; 179–185; 180, 55 *f*,; 94; 182; 97; 11; BAR, III, 11; II, 1014 *f*.).

279. Ikhnaton's faithful vassals had showered dispatches upon him, had sent special ambassadors, sons and brothers to represent to him the seriousness of the situation; but they had either received no replies at all, or an Egyptian commander with an entirely inadequate force was dispatched to make futile and desultory attempts to deal with a situation which demanded the

Pharaoh himself and the whole available army of Egypt. At Akhetaton, the new and beautiful capital, the splendid temple of Aton resounded with hymns to the new god of the Empire, while the Empire itself was no more. The habit of generations and fast vanishing apprehension lest the Pharaoh might appear in Syria with his army, still prompted a few sporadic letters from the dynasts, assuring him of their loyalty, which perhaps continued in the mind of Ikhnaton the illusion that he was still lord of Asia.

280. The storm which had broken over his Asiatic empire was not more disastrous than that which threatened the fortunes of his house in Egypt. But he was as steadfast as before in the propagation of his new faith. At his command temples of Aton had now risen all over the land. He devoted himself to the elaboration of the temple ritual and the tendency to theologize somewhat dimmed the earlier freshness of the hymns to the god. Meantime the suppression of the most cherished beliefs of the people, like their faith in Osiris, their old-time protector and friend in the world of darkness, was producing a national convulsion. The people could understand nothing of the refinements involved in the new faith, and in the course of such attempted changes in the customs and traditional faith of a whole people, as we see in the similar attempt of Theodosius eighteen hundred years later, the span of one man's life is insignificant indeed. The Aton-faith remained but the cherished theory of the idealist, Ikhnaton, and a little circle which formed his court; it never really became the religion of the people (BAR, II, 1014–15; 1017–18; AZ, 40, 110–113).

281. Added to the secret resentment and opposition of the people, we must consider also a far more danger-

THE DISSOLUTION OF THE EMPIRE 287

ous force, the hatred of the old priesthoods, particularly that of Amon. The neglect and loss of the Asiatic empire must have turned against the king many a strong man, and aroused indignation in the hearts of the military class, whose grandfathers had served under Thutmose III. One such man, an officer named Harmhab, now in the service of Ikhnaton and enjoying the royal favour, not only contrived to win the support of the military class, but also gained the favour of the priests of Amon, who were of course looking for some one who could bring them the opportunity they coveted. Thus both the people and the priestly and military classes, alike, were fomenting plans to overthrow the hated dreamer in the palace of the Pharaohs, of whose thoughts they understood so little. To increase his danger, fortune had decreed him no son, and he was obliged to depend for support as the years passed, upon his son-in-law a noble named Sakere, who had married his eldest daughter, Meritaton, "Beloved of Aton." Ikhnaton had probably never been physically strong; his spare face, with the lines of an ascetic, shows increasing traces of the cares which weighed so heavily upon him. He finally nominated Sakere as his successor and appointed him at the same time coregent. He survived but a short time after this, and about 1358 B. C., having reigned some seventeen years he succumbed to the overwhelming forces that were against him. In a lonely valley some miles to the east of his city he was buried in a tomb which he had excavated in the rock for himself and family, and where his second daughter, Maketaton, already rested (BAR, III, 22 *ff*.).

282. Thus disappeared the most remarkable figure in earlier oriental history; or indeed in the history of the world before the Hebrews. To his own nation he was

afterward known as "the criminal of Akhetaton;" but, however much we may censure him, we see in him at the same time such a spirit as the early world had never known before. Among the Hebrews, seven to eight hundred years later, we look for such men; but the modern world has yet adequately to value or even acquaint itself with this man, who in an age so remote and under conditions so adverse, became the world's first idealist and the world's first *individual*.

283. Sakere quickly disappeared, to be followed by Tutenkhaton ("Living image of Aton"), another son-in-law of Ikhnaton, who was soon forced by the priests of Amon to forsake Akhetaton and reside at Thebes which had not seen a Pharaoh for twenty years. The Aton-temples fell a prey to the vengeance of the Theban party, and the once beautiful city of Aton was gradually transformed into a desolate ruin. Here in a low brick room, which had served as an archive-chamber for Ikhnaton's foreign office, were found in 1885 some three hundred letters and dispatches, the Tell el-Amarna letters, in which we have traced his intercourse and dealings with the kings and rulers of Asia and the gradual disintegration of his empire there. Here were the more than sixty dispatches of the unfortunate Rib-Addi of Byblos. All the other Aton-cities likewise perished utterly; but Gem-Aton, safe from the first burst of wrath in far-off Nubia, survived for a thousand years, and—strange irony!—there was afterward a temple there to "Amon, lord of Gem-Aton!" (AZ, 40, 106–108).

284. On reaching Thebes, Tutenkhaton continued the worship of Aton, but Amon slowly regained his own, till the king was obliged even to change his name to Tutenkhamon, "Living image of Amon," showing that

THE DISSOLUTION OF THE EMPIRE 289

he was now completely in the hands of the priestly party. The empire which he ruled was still no mean one, extending as it did from the Delta through Nubia to the fourth cataract, and even still enjoying an occasional installment of traditional tribute from Palestine. Tutenkhaton was quickly succeeded by Eye, another of the worthies of the Akhetaton court, who had married Ikhnaton's nurse, Tiy. He was sufficiently imbued with Ikhnaton's ideas feebly to strive for a short time against the priests of Amon; but ere long he too passed away and it would appear that one or two other ephemeral pretenders gained the ascendancy either now or before his accession. Anarchy ensued. Thebes was a prey of plundering bands, who forced their way into the royal tombs and robbed the tomb of Thutmose IV. The prestige of the old Theban line which had been dominant for two hundred and fifty years; the illustrious family which two hundred and thirty years before had cast out the Hyksos and built the greatest empire the east had ever seen, was now totally eclipsed (1350 B.C.). Manetho places Harmhab, the restorer who now gained the throne, at the close of the Eighteenth Dynasty; but in so far as we know he was not of royal blood nor any kin of the now fallen house. He marks the complete restoration of Amon, the resumption of the old order and the beginning of a new epoch (AZ, 34, 135; BAR, II, 896; 1019; 1034 ff.; 1027 ff.; III, 20, ll. 2, 5, 8; 32 A ff.).

PART VI

THE EMPIRE: SECOND PERIOD

XX

THE TRIUMPH OF AMON AND THE REORGANIZATION OF THE EMPIRE

285. THE officer Harmhab, whom we have already noticed in the service of Ikhnaton, was an able organizer and skilful man of affairs quite after the manner of Thutmose III. He belonged to an old family once nomarchs of Alabastronpolis; he had successfully executed important royal commissions and had served with distinction in Asia. During the precarious times incident to the rapid succession of weak kings following Ikhnaton's death, he had skilfully maintained himself and gradually gained a position of such influence, that he was now the real power of the throne. This continued for some years, until 1350 B. C., and the next step was but to receive the titles and insignia of royalty. With the army behind him and the support of the priesthood of Amon at Thebes, it was only necessary to proceed thither to be recognized by Amon as the ruling Pharaoh. This was done, amid great splendour at the feast of Opet. Harmhab at the same time contracted a purely formal marriage with one of the princesses of the old line, to secure the semblance of legitimacy, and the new reign then began (BAR, III, 5–13; 25–30).

286. The energy which had brought Harmhab his exalted office was immediately evident in his administra-

tion of it. He was untiring in restoring to the land the orderly organization which it had once enjoyed. At the same time he did not forget the temples, which had been so long closed under the Aton régime. He restored the temples from the pools of the Delta marshes to Nubia. He shaped all their images in number more than before. The priesthoods were everywhere restored, Amon received again his old endowments and even "gold-country" of his own in Nubia, while the incomes of all the other disinherited temples were likewise restored. The people resumed in public the worship of the innumerable gods which they had practised in secret during the supremacy of Aton. The sculptors of the king were sent throughout the land, reinserting on the monuments defaced by Ikhnaton, the names of the gods which he had erased. Everywhere the name of the hated Ikhnaton was treated as he had those of the gods. At Akhetaton his tomb was wrecked and its reliefs chiselled out; while the tombs of his nobles there were violated in the same way. Every effort was made to annihilate all trace of the reign of such a man; and when in legal procedure it was necessary to cite documents or enactments from his reign he was designated as "that criminal of Akhetaton." The triumph of Amon was complete; the priests exulted in the overthrow of his enemies: "Woe to him who assails thee! Thy city endures but he who assails thee is overthrown. Fie upon him who sins against thee in any land. . . . The sun of him who knew thee not has set, but he who knows thee shines. The sanctuary of him who assailed thee is overwhelmed in darkness, but the whole earth is in light" (BAR, III, 22–32; 71 *f*.; II, p. 383, notes a, b; BTLN, p. 20; AZ, 42, 106–109; GIM).

THE REORGANIZATION OF THE EMPIRE 295

287. There were other directions in which the restoration of what Harmhab regarded as normal conditions was not merely yielding to the inertia of tradition. Gross laxity in the oversight of the local administration had characterized the reign of Ikhnaton and his successors. Everywhere the local officials, long secure from close inspection on the part of the central government, had revelled in extortions, practised upon the long-suffering masses. To ameliorate these conditions Harmhab first informed himself thoroughly as to the extent and character of the evils, and then in his private chamber he dictated to his personal scribe a remarkable series of special and highly particularized laws to suit every case of which he had learned. The penalties were severe. A tax-collector for example, if found guilty of thus practising upon the poor man, was sentenced to have his nose cut off, followed by banishment to Tharu, the desolate frontier city far out in the sands of the Arabian desert toward Asia. The discovery of such local misgovernment was very difficult owing to collusion with the local officials by inspecting officers sent out by the central government. These corrupt superiors, for a share in the plunder, would overlook the extortions which they had been sent from the court to discover and prevent. This evil, rooted out in the days of the aggressive Thutmose III, was now rampant again, and Harmhab apparently revived the methods of Thutmose III for controlling it. In order to lift his executive officials above all necessity of accepting any income from a corrupt source, Harmhab had them provided for with great liberality. They went out on inspection several times a month, and on these occasions either just before their departure or immediately after their return, the king gave them a

sumptuous feast in the palace court, appearing himself
upon the balcony, addressing each man by name and
throwing down gifts among them. In the introduction
and application of the new laws Harmhab went personally from end to end of the kingdom, improving also the
administration of justice. Besides the appointment of
good viziers and stringent laws against bribery, in
order to discourage the latter among the local judges, he
took an unprecedented step. He remitted the tax of
gold and silver levied upon judicial officers, permitting
them to retain the entire income of their offices, in order
that they might have no excuse for illegally enriching
themselves. These sane and philanthropic reforms
give Harmhab a high place in the history of humane
government; especially when we remember that even
since the occupation of the country by the English,
the evils at which he struck have been found exceedingly persistent and difficult to root out (BAR, III,
45–67).

288. If Harmhab had any ambition to leave a reputation as a foreign conqueror, the times were against him.
His accession fell at a time when all his powers and all
his great ability were necessarily employed exclusively
in reorganizing the kingdom. He probably reached an
understanding with the Hittites, he kept Nubia well in
hand, and he sent out a successful expedition to Punt. He
performed his task at home with a strength and skill not
less than were required for great conquest abroad;
and, although a soldier, with all the qualities which that
calling implies in the early east, he could truly say:
"Behold, his majesty spent the whole time seeking the
welfare of Egypt." He probably reigned some thirty-
five years, and was buried in his old Memphite tomb,
erected before his coronation and still bearing his old

titles (BAR, III, 64-67; 45 *ff*.; 34; 377; 40 *ff*.; 37 *ff*.; 50; 1-21; 157; 78; 74 *ff*.; GIM).

289. The fruits of Harmhab's reorganization were destined to be enjoyed by his successors. Whether or not he succeeded in founding a dynasty we do not know. It is impossible to discover any certain connection between him and Ramses I, an old man, who now (1315 B.C.) succeeded him. Too old to accomplish anything, Ramses I was after a short coregency followed by his son, Seti I, then probably about thirty years old (1313 B.C.). During his short coregency of not more than a year, Seti I must have already laid all his plans and organized his army in readiness for an attempt to recover the lost empire in Asia. The information which Seti I now received as to the state of Palestine betrays a condition of affairs quite such as we should expect would have resulted from the tendency evident in the letters of Abdkhiba of Jerusalem to Ikhnaton (p. 285). They showed us the Beduin of the neighbouring desert pressing into Palestine and taking possession of the towns, whether in the service of the turbulent dynasts or on their own responsibility. We saw these letters corroborated by Egyptian monuments, portraying the panic-stricken Palestinians fleeing into Egypt before these foes. Seti I's messengers now bring him information of the very same character regarding the Beduin. It was among these desert invaders of Palestine that the movement of the Hebrews resulting in their settlement there took place (BAR, III, 157; 84; 86; II, 409; III, 101, ll. 3-9).

290. In his first year Seti was able to march out from Tharu and lead his expedition along the desert road, past the stations which he had already restored. Having subdued the Beduin of southern Palestine, he pushed

rapidly northward, capturing the towns of the plain of Esdraelon (Jezreel), pushing eastward across the valley of the Jordan and erecting his tablet of victory in the Hauran, and westward to the southern slopes of Lebanon, where the neighbouring dynasts immediately came to him and offered their allegiance. They had not seen a Pharaoh at the head of his army in Asia for over fifty years,—not since Amenhotep III had left Sidon (See p. 263). It is remotely possible that he advanced as far north as Simyra and Ullaza, and that the prince of Cyprus sent in his gifts as of old. However that may be, Tyre and Othu submitted in any case, and having thus secured the coast and restored the water route between Syria and Egypt for future operations, Seti returned to Egypt, where a triumph awaited him as he passed the frontier and on his arrival at Thebes, such as the grandees of the realm had not witnessed for two generations (BAR, III, 83 *f.*; 85 *f.*; 87 *f.*; 81; 89–94; 98–113).

291. This campaign was quite sufficient to restore southern Palestine to the kingdom of the Pharaoh, and probably also most of northern Palestine. Seti's operations in Asia were now interrupted by a campaign against the Libyans west of the Nile mouths who never failed to improve the opportunity of lax government in Egypt to push into the Delta and settle there. The next season we find him in Galilee, storming the walled city of Kadesh (not to be confused with Kadesh on the Orontes), in the Amorite kingdom, founded by Abdashirta and Aziru (p. 282), now forming a kind of buffer state in the Orontes valley between Palestine on the south and the southern Hittite frontier on the north. After harrying its territory and probably taking Kadesh, Seti pushed northward against the Hittites, now

under their king, Merasar (cuneiform Mursili), son of Seplel (cuneiform Shubbiluliuma), who had entered into treaty relations with Egypt toward the close of the Eighteenth Dynasty. Somewhere in the Orontes valley Seti came into contact with them and the first battle between the Hittites and a Pharaoh occurred. It is, not probable that he met the main army of the Hittites; certain it is that he did not shake their power in Syria; Kadesh on the Orontes remained in their hands, and at most, Seti could not have accomplished more than to check their southern advance. The boundary which he had established in Asia roughly coincided inland with the northern limits of Palestine, and must have included also Tyre and the Phœnician coast south of the mouth of the Litâny. Though much increasing the territory of Egypt in Asia, it represented but a small third of what she had once conquered there. Under these circumstances, it would have been quite natural for Seti to continue the war in Syria. For some reason, however, he did not, in so far as we know, ever appear with his forces in Asia again; and either at this time or later, he negotiated a treaty of peace with the Hittite king, Metella, who had succeeded his father, Merasar (BAR, III, 82, 2; 120–152; 375; 377).

292. Returning to Egypt, he devoted himself to the interests of peace, especially to restoring the temples of the gods defaced during the Aton revolution, only partially repaired by Harmhab. At all the great sanctuaries of the old gods his buildings were now rising on a scale unprecedented in the palmiest days of the Empire. In front of the pylon of Amenhotep III, forming the façade of the state temple at Karnak, Seti continued the vast colonnaded hall planned and begun by his father, and surpassing in size even the enormous

unfinished hypostyle of Amenhotep III at Luxor. He completed some of the columns of the northern aisles as well as the north wall, on the outside of which his sculptors engraved a colossal series of reliefs portraying his campaigns. Mounting from the base to the coping they cover the entire wall (over two hundred feet long). Similar works existed in the Eighteenth Dynasty temples, but they have all perished, and Seti's battle-reliefs therefore form the most imposing work of the kind now surviving in Egypt. Like his fathers of the Eighteenth Dynasty, he erected a great mortuary temple on the western plain of Thebes, and another yet more splendid at Abydos, having a side chapel for the services of the old kings, especially of the First and Second Dynasties, whose tombs still lie in the desert behind the temple. The list of their names which he engraved upon the walls still forms one of the most important sources for our chronological arrangement and assignment of the Pharaohs. A temple at Memphis, probably another at Heliopolis, with doubtless others in the Delta of which we know nothing, completed the series of Seti's greater buildings (Note VII; BAR, III, 200–221; 225–243; 80–156; 495).

293. These works drew heavily upon his treasury, and he personally explored the road leading to the gold mines of Gebel Zebâra, finally digging a well and establishing a station on this road thirty-seven miles from the river (just above Edfu). Then Seti established the income from the mines thus reached as a permanent endowment for his temple at Abydos, and called down terrifying curses on any posterity who should violate his enactments. Yet within a year after his death they had ceased to be effective and had to be renewed by his son. In a similar attempt further south

on the road to the Wady Alâki, a well two hundred feet deep failed to reach water (BAR, III, 170–195; 263; 289).

294. The art developed in connection with Seti's buildings was hardly less strong, virile and beautiful than that prevailing during the Eighteenth Dynasty. His battle-reliefs are the most ambitious attempt at elaborate composition left by the surviving school of the Eighteenth Dynasty, although the finest reliefs of the time are to be found in Seti's temple at Abydos, in which there is a rare combination of softness and refinement, with bold and sinuous lines and exquisite modelling.

295. Beyond Seti's ninth year we know practically nothing of his reign. He seems to have spent his energies upon his extensive buildings, and among these he did not forget the excavation of the largest tomb yet made in the valley of the kings at Thebes. It descends into the mountain through a series of galleries and extensive halls no less than four hundred and seventy feet in oblique depth. His last days were clouded with conflicts over the succession between his eldest son and a younger brother, Ramses, son of the queen Tuya. Some time before his approaching jubilee, while the obelisks for it were still unfinished, Seti died (about 1292 B. C.), having reigned over twenty years since his own father's death. The body, still preserved by happy accident, shows him to have been one of the stateliest figures that ever sat upon the throne of Egypt.

296. On Seti's death Prince Ramses brushed aside his eldest brother without a moment's hesitation and seized the throne. But the usual court devices were immediately resorted to. He lost no time, however, in making himself strong at Thebes, the seat of power.

Thither he immediately hastened, probably from the Delta, and celebrated in the state temple the great annual Feast of Opet. Having gained the priests of Amon, he devoted himself with great zeal to pious works in memory of his father, whose magnificent mortuary temple at Abydos had been left unfinished by Seti. This sumptuous building having been completed, he restored its endowments already violated, and generously furnished it. These and similar works required him to continue his father's efforts to increase the revenue from the Nubian gold countries, and he succeeded where Seti had failed, in supplying with water the road to the mines of the Wadi Alâki. Such enterprises of internal exploitation were but preparatory in the plans of Ramses. His ambition held him to greater purposes; and he contemplated nothing less than the recovery of the great Asiatic empire, conquered by his predecessors of the Eighteenth Dynasty (BAR, II, 251-293).

XXI

THE WARS OF RAMSES II

297. WE have seen that the Nineteenth Dynasty had inherited a very dangerous situation in Syria. When Ramses II ascended the throne the Hittites had remained in undisputed possession of their Syrian conquests for probably more than twenty years since the only attempt by Seti I to dislodge them. The long peace probably concluded with Seti gave their king, Metella (cuneiform Muttallu), an opportunity, of which he made good use, to render their position in Syria impregnable, by pushing southward and seizing Kadesh, the key to the Orontes valley and the strongest fortress in Syria.

298. Ramses's plan for the war was like that of his great ancestor, Thutmose III: he first gained the coast, that he might use one of its harbours as a base, enjoying quick and easy communication with Egypt by water. An illegible limestone stela cut into the face of the rocks overlooking the Nahr el-Kelb (Dog River) near Berût, our only source for this event, shows that it took place in the "year four." Meantime Metella was collecting probably the largest force that Egypt had ever met, containing probably not less than twenty thousand men. We find among them the old enemies of Egypt in Syria: the kings of Naharin, Arvad, Carchemish, Kode, Kadesh, Nuges, Ekereth (Ugarit) and Aleppo. Besides

these, Mettella's subject kingdoms in Asia Minor, like Kezweden and Pedes, were drawn upon; and not content with the army thus collected, he emptied his treasury to tempt the mercenaries of Asia Minor and the Mediterranean islands: Lycian pirates, Mysians, Cilicians, and Dardanians took service in the Hittite ranks.

299. Ramses on his part had not been less active in securing mercenary support. Nubian levies, not unknown in the Egyptian army since the remote days of the old Kingdom, and especially the "Sherden" or Sardinians, long ago employed in the Pharaoh's Syrian garrisons (p. 252), were now a recognized contingent. Thus Ramses likewise commanded a force of not less than twenty thousand men all told. He divided these troops into four divisions, each named after one of the great gods: Amon, Re, Ptah and Sutekh; and himself took personal command of the division of Amon (BAR, III, 297; 306 *f.*; 491).

300. About the end of April of his fifth year (1288 B. C.), when the rains of Syria had ceased, Ramses marched out of Tharu, on his northeastern frontier, at the head of these troops. The division of Amon, with whom the Pharaoh was, formed the advance, and the other divisions, Re, Ptah and Sutekh, followed in the order mentioned. A month later we find him marching down the Orontes, northward, till he camped on a height overlooking the vast plain in which lay Kadesh, only a day's march distant, with its battlements probably visible on the northern horizon, toward which the Orontes wound its way across the plain (BAR, III, 491; BK).

301. Day after day Ramses' officers had reported to him their inability to find any trace of the enemy, and

had added their impression that he was still far in the north. At this juncture two Beduin of the region appeared and stated that they had deserted from the Hittite ranks, and that the Hittite king had retreated northward to the district of Aleppo, north of Tunip. In view of the failure of his scouting parties to find the enemy, Ramses readily believed this story, broke camp early, crossed the river with the division of Amon and pushed rapidly on to Kadesh, which he reached by noon, while the divisions of Re, Ptah and Sutekh, marching in the order named, straggled far behind. Meantime the crafty Metella, seeing that the story of his two Beduin, whom he has sent out for the very purpose of deceiving Ramses, has been implicitly accepted, quickly transfers his entire army from the northwest of the city to the east side of the river, and while Ramses passes northward along the west side of Kadesh, Metella deftly dodges him, moving southward along the east side of the city, always keeping it between him and the Egyptians to prevent his troops from being seen. As he draws in on the east and southeast

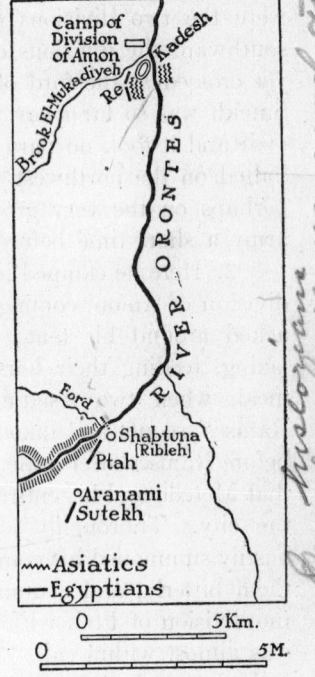

THE BATTLE OF KADESH.
Positions of the opposing forces at the time of the Asiatic attack.

of the city he has secured a position on Ramses' flank, from which he can completely isolate the Pharaoh from his southern divisions, threatening the destruction of Ramses and his army. The Egyptian forces were now roughly divided into two groups: near Kadesh were the two divisions of Amon and Re, while far southward the divisions of Ptah and Sutekh have not yet crossed at the ford of Shabtuna. The division of Sutekh was so far away that nothing more was heard of it and it took no part in the day's action. Ramses halted on the northwest of the city, not far from and perhaps on the very ground occupied by the Asiatic army a short time before.

302. Here he camped in the early afternoon, and the division of Amon, coming up shortly afterward, bivouacked around his tent. The weary troops were relaxing, feeding their horses and preparing their own meal, when two Asiatic spies were brought in by Ramses' scouts and taken to the royal tent. Brought before Ramses after a merciless beating, they confessed that Metella and his entire army were concealed behind the city. Thoroughly alarmed, the young Pharaoh hastily summoned his commanders and officials, chided them bitterly, and commanded the vizier to bring up the division of Ptah with all speed, supposing that Re was almost within call. He therefore at this juncture little dreamed of the desperate situation into which he had been betrayed, nor of the catastrophe which at that very moment was overtaking the unfortunate division of Re. Already Metella's chariotry had issued from the south side of Kadesh and quickly crossing the river, struck the unsuspecting division of Re while on the march, cut it in two and scattered the two portions far and wide. Some fled northward toward Ramses'

camp in a wild rout, and the first intimation received by the Pharaoh of the appalling disaster which now faced him was the headlong flight of these fugitives of the annihilated division, among whom were two of his own sons. As they burst over the barricade into the astonished camp, with the Hittite chariotry in hot pursuit close upon their heels, they inevitably swept along with them northward the surprised and defenseless division of Amon. The bulk of Ramses' available force was thus in flight, his southern divisions were miles away and separated from him by the whole mass of twenty-five hundred of the enemy's chariotry, whose wings now rapidly swelled out on either hand and enfolded the camp. The disaster was complete.

303. Taken with but short shrift for preparation, the young Pharaoh hesitated not a moment in attempting to cut his way out and to reach his southern columns.

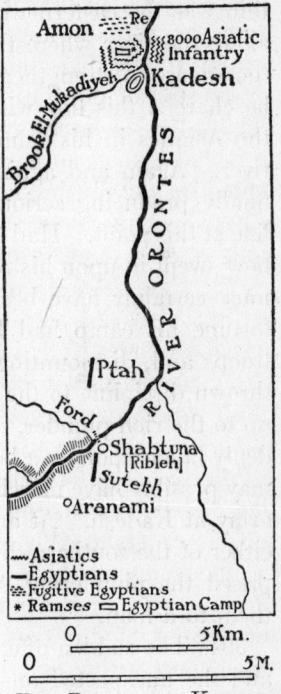

THE BATTLE OF KADESH.

Showing Ramses II's divided forces and his envelopment by the enemy in the second stage of the battle.

With only his household troops, his immediate followers and the officers, who happened to be at his side, he mounted his waiting chariot and boldly charged into the advance of the Hittite pursuit as it poured into his camp on the west side; but perceiving how heavily the enemy was massed before him, immediately understood that further onset in that direction was hopeless. Retiring into the camp again, he must have noted how thin was the eastern wing of the surrounding chariots along the river where there had not yet been time for the enemy to strengthen their line. As a forlorn hope he charged this line with an impetuousity that hurled the Asiatics in his immediate front pell-mell into the river. Again and again Ramses renewed the charge, finally producing serious discomfiture in the enemy's line at this point. Had the mass of the Hittite chariotry now swept in upon his rear from the west and south he must certainly have been lost. But to his great good fortune his camp had fallen into the hands of these troops and, dismounting from their chariots, they had thrown discipline to the winds as they gave themselves up to the rich plunder. Thus engaged, they were suddenly fallen upon by a body of Ramses' "recruits" who may possibly have marched in from the coast to join his army at Kadesh. At any rate, they did not belong to either of the southern divisions. They completely surprised the plundering Asiatics in the camp and slew them to a man.

304. The sudden offensive of Ramses along the river and the unexpected onslaught of the "recruits" must have considerably dampened the ardour of the Hittite attack, giving the Pharaoh an opportunity to recover himself. These newly arrived "recruits," together with the returning fugitives from the unharmed but scattered division of Amon, so augmented his power, that even though Metella now sent in his reserves of a thousand chariots, the Pharaoh, by prodigies of personal valour, still kept his scanty forces together, till the be-

THE WARS OF RAMSES II

lated division of Ptah arrived on the field as evening drew on. Caught between the opposing lines, the Hittite chariotry was driven into the city, probably with considerable loss, and Ramses was saved. What made the issue a success for Ramses was his salvation from utter destruction, and that he eventually held possession of the field added little practical advantage. His losses were doubtless much heavier than those of the enemy, and he was glad enough to lead his shattered forces back to Egypt. None of his records makes any claim that he captured Kadesh, as is so frequently stated in the current histories (BAR, III, 298-351; BK).

305. Once safely extricated from the perilous position into which his rashness had betrayed him, Ramses was very proud of his exploit at Kadesh. On the temple walls at Abu Simbel, at the Ramesseum, his mortuary temple at Thebes, at Luxor, Karnak, Abydos and probably on other buildings now perished, his artists executed a vast series of vivacious reliefs depicting Ramses' camp, the flight of his sons, the Pharaoh's furious charge down to the river, and the arrival of the recruits who rescued the camp, all accompanied by numerous explanatory inscriptions. These sculptures are better known to modern travellers in Egypt than any other like monuments in the country. They are twice accompanied by a report on the battle which reads like an official document. There early arose a poem on the battle, of which we shall later have more to say. These sources have enabled us to trace with certainty the maneuvres which led up to the battle of Kadesh, the first battle in history which can be so studied. We see that already in the thirteenth century B. C. the commanders of the time understood the value of placing troops advantageously before battle. The immense

*Humor seen in Egyptian art,
not found in Babylon or Assyria.*

superiority to be gained by clever maneuvres masked, from the enemy, was clearly comprehended by the Hittite king when he executed the first flank movement of which we hear in the early orient; and the plains of Syria, already at that remote epoch, witnessed notable examples of that supposedly modern science, which was brought to such perfection by Napoleon,—the science of winning the victory before the battle (BAR, III, 298–351; BK).

306. Arrived in Thebes, Ramses enjoyed the usual triumph in the state temple, but the moral effect of his return to Egypt immediately after the battle without even laying siege to Kadesh, was immediately evident among the dynasts of Syria and Palestine, who now revolted. The rising spread southward to the very gates of Ramses' frontier forts in the northeastern Delta. We see him, therefore, obliged to begin again at the very bottom to rebuild the Egyptian empire in Asia and recover by weary campaigns even the territory which his father had won. It was not until his eighth year, after three years spent in recovering Palestine, that Ramses was again pushing down the valley of the Orontes, where he must have finally succeeded in dislodging the Hittites. In Naharin he conquered the country as far as Tunip, which he also reduced and placed a statue of himself there. But the Hittites soon stirred the region to further revolt, and Ramses again found them in Tunip, which he retook by storm. His lists credit him with having subdued Naharin, Lower Retenu (North Syria), Arvad, the Keftyew, and Ketne in the Orontes valley. It is thus evident that Ramses' ability and tenacity as a soldier had now really endangered the Hittite empire in Syria, although it is very uncertain whether he succeeded in holding

THE WARS OF RAMSES II

these northern conquests (BAR, III, 355–360; 364–366).

307. When he had been thus campaigning probably some fifteen years, Metella, the Hittite king, either died in battle or at the hands of a rival, and his brother, Khetasar (cuneiform Hattusil), who succeeded him, proposed to the Pharaoh a permanent peace and a treaty of alliance. In Ramses' twenty-first year (1272 B. C.) Khetasar's messengers bearing the treaty reached the Egyptian court, now in the Delta. Having been drafted in advance and accepted by representatives of the two countries, it was now in its final form, in eighteen paragraphs inscribed on a silver tablet. It then proceeded to review the former relations between the two countries, passed then to a general definition of the present pact, and thus to its special stipulations. Of these the most important were: the renunciation by both rulers of all projects of conquest against the other, the reaffirmation of the former treaties existing between the two countries, a defensive alliance involving the assistance of each against the other's foes; co-operation in the chastisement of delinquent subjects, probably in Syria; and the extradition of political fugitives and immigrants. A codicil provides for the humane treatment of these last. Two transcripts of the treaty have been found at Thebes, engraved upon temple walls, and last summer (1906) the Hittite copy in Babylonian cuneiform on a clay tablet, was found at Boghaz-Köi in Asia Minor (Note X; BAR, III, 375, l. 10; 373; 367–391).

308. It will be noticed that the treaty nowhere refers to the boundary recognized by both countries in Syria. It is difficult to form any idea of the location of this boundary. It is not safe to affirm that Ramses had

permanently advanced the boundary of his father's kingdom in Asia, save probably on the coast, where he carved two more stelæ on the rocks near Berut, beside that of his fourth year (p. 303). Thirteen years later (1259 B. C.) the Hittite king himself visited Egypt to consummate the marriage of his eldest daughter as the wife of Ramses. His visit was depicted before Ramses' temple at Abu Simbel, with accompanying narrative inscriptions, while the Hittite princess was given a prominent position at court and a statue beside her royal husband in Tanis. Court poets celebrated the event and pictured the Hittite king as sending to the king of Kode and summoning him to join in the journey to Egypt that they might do honour to the Pharaoh. The occurrence made a popular impression also, and a tale, which was not put into writing, so far as we know, until Greek times, began with the marriage and told how afterward, at the request of her father, an image of the Theban Khonsu was sent to the land of the princess, that the god's power might drive forth the evil spirits from her afflicted sister. The friendly relations between the two kingdoms prospered, and it is even probable that Ramses received a second daughter of Khetasar in marriage. Throughout Ramses' long reign the treaty remained unbroken and the peace continued at least into the reign of his successor, Merneptah (BAR, III, 392; 394–424; 416 *f.*; 425 *f.*; 427 *f.*; 429–447).

309. From the day of the peace compact with Khetasar, Ramses was never called upon to enter the field again. Unimportant revolts in Nubia, and a Libyan campaign, often vaguely referred to on his monuments, did not require the Pharaoh's personal leadership.

310. With the Asiatic campaigns of Ramses II the military aggressiveness of Egypt which had been awak-

Ramses II spent 16 yrs in conquest of Hittites – Syrians etc

ened under Ahmose I in the expulsion of the Hyksos was completely exhausted. Nor did it ever revive. Henceforward for a long time the Pharaoh's army is but a weapon of defense against foreign aggression; a weapon, however, which he was himself unable to control,—and before which the venerable line of Re was finally to disappear (BAR, III, 448–491).

Kings of that time – the greatest merchants

Treaty at this time also between Hittites and Babylonians. Many letters regarding it. Much diplomacy. Read "Lord of Canaan"(?).

Hittites encouraged Babylon to attack Assyria – a rival

XXII

THE EMPIRE OF RAMSES II

311. The dominance of Egypt in Asiatic affairs had irresistibly drawn the centre of power on the Nile from Thebes to the Delta. Thebes remained the religious capital of the state and at the greater feasts in its temple calendar the Pharaoh was often present, but his permanent residence was in the north. His constant presence here resulted in a development of the cities of the eastern Delta such as they had never before enjoyed. Tanis became a great and flourishing city, with a splendid temple, while in the Wady Tumilât, the natural approach to Egypt from Asia, Ramses built a "store-city," which he called Pithom, or "House of Atum" (Ex. I, 11). At the western end of the Wady he and Seti founded a city just north of Heliopolis, now known as Tell el-Yehudîyeh. Somewhere in the eastern Delta he founded a residence city, Per-Ramses, or "House of Ramses." Its situation is not certain, although it has often been thought to be identical with Tanis; but it was close to the eastern frontier, and was also accessible to seafaring traffic. It was familiar to the Hebrews as "Raamses" (Ex. I, 11), and through this Pharaoh's other great enterprises here, this region became known as "the land of Ramses," a name so completely identified with it that Hebrew tradition read it back into the days of Joseph, before any Ramses had ever sat on the throne. In

THE EMPIRE OF RAMSES II

Memphis and Abydos little has survived. At Thebes he spent enormous resources in the completion of his father's mortuary temple, another beautiful sanctuary for his own mortuary service, known to all visitors at Thebes as the Ramesseum; a large court and pylon in enlargement of the Luxor temple; while, surpassing in size all buildings of the ancient or modern world, his architects completed the colossal colonnaded hall of the Karnak temple, already begun under the first Ramses, the Pharaoh's grandfather. Few of the great temples of Egypt have not some chamber, hall, colonnade or pylon which bears his name, in perpetuating which the king stopped at no desecration or destruction of the ancient monuments of the country. But in spite of this fact, his own legitimate building was on a scale quite surpassing in size and extent anything that his ancestors had ever accomplished. The buildings which he erected were filled with innumerable supplementary monuments, especially colossal statues of himself and obelisks. The former are the greatest monolithic statues ever executed; one at Tanis having been ninety feet in height, of a single block weighing nine hundred tons, while another, still lying in fragments in the Ramesseum, weighed about a thousand tons. As the years passed and he celebrated jubilee after jubilee the obelisks which he erected in commemoration of these festivals rapidly rose among his temples. At Tanis alone he erected no less than fourteen, all of which are now prostrate; three at least of his obelisks are in Rome; and of the two which he erected in Luxor, one is in Paris. The generous endowment necessary for the erection of each such temple, must have been a serious economic problem (BAR, III, 82, 2; 492–537; 543–549; PT, I, 22–24;

AS, III, 29; PI, p. 4; PKGH, p. 22; NA, pp. 2, 9-11, pl. I).

312. Notwithstanding the shift of the centre of gravity northward, the south was not neglected. In Nubia Ramses became the patron deity; no less than seven new temples arose there, dedicated to the great gods of Egypt, to the Pharaoh and his queen, Nefretiri. Nubia became more and more Egyptianized, and between the first and second cataracts the old native chiefs had practically disappeared, the administrative officials of the Pharaoh were in complete control, and there was even an Egyptian court of justice, with the viceroy as chief judge (ELAE, 504).

313. Ramses' great building enterprises were not achieved without vast expense of resources, especially those of labour. There is probably little question of the correctness of the Hebrew tradition in attributing the oppression of some tribe of their ancestors to the builder of Pithom and Ramses; that they should have fled the country to escape such labour is quite in accord with what we know of the time. Intercourse with Palestine and Syria was now more inimate than ever. A letter of a frontier official, dated in the reign of Ramses II's successor, tells of passing a body of Edomite Beduin through a fortress in the Wady Tumilât, that they might pasture their herds by the pools of Pithom as the Hebrews had done in the days of Joseph. In the rough memoranda of a commandant's scribe, probably of the frontier fortress of Tharu, in the Isthmus of Suez, we find also noted the people whom he had allowed to pass: messengers with letters for the officers of the Palestinian garrisons, for the king of Tyre, and for officers with the king (Merneptah) then campaigning in Syria, besides officers bearing reports,

or hurrying out to Syria to join the Pharaoh. Although there was never a continuous fortification of any length across the Isthmus of Suez, there was a line of strongholds, of which Tharu was one and probably Ramses another, stretching well across the zone along which Egypt might be entered from Asia. This zone did not extend to the southern half of the isthmus, which was well nigh impassable, but was confined to the territory between Lake Timsah and the Mediterranean, whence the line of fortresses therefore extended southward, passed the lake and bent westward into the Wady Tumilât. Hence Hebrew tradition depicts the escape of the Israelites across the southern half of the isthmus south of the line of defences, which might have stopped them. The tide of commerce that ebbed and flowed through the Isthmus of Suez was even fuller than under the Eighteenth Dynasty, while on the Mediterranean the Egyptian galleys must have whitened the sea (BAR, III, 636–638; 630–635).

314. On the Pharaoh's table were rarities and delicacies from Cyprus, the land of the Hittites and of the Amorites, Babylonia and Naharin. Elaborately wrought chariots, weapons, whips and gold-mounted staves from the Palestinian and Syrian towns filled his magazine, while his stalls boasted fine horses of Babylon and cattle of the Hittite country. The appurtenances of a rich man's estate included a galley plying between Egypt and the Syrian coast to bring to the pampered Egyptian the luxuries of Asia; and even Seti I's mortuary temple at Abydos possessed its own sea-going vessels, given by Ramses, to convey the temple offerings from the east. The country swarmed with Semitic and other Asiatic slaves, while Phœnician and other alien merchants were so numerous that there was a foreign quarter in Mem-

phis, with its temples of Baal and Astarte; and these and other Semitic gods found a place in the Egyptian pantheon. The dialects of Palestine and vicinity, of which Hebrew was one, lent many a Semitic word to the current language of the day, as well as select terms with which the learned scribes were fond of garnishing their writings. We find such words commonly in the Nineteenth Dynasty papyri four or five centuries before they appear in the Hebrew writings of the Old Testament. The royal family was not exempt from such influence; Ramses' favourite daughter was called "Bint-Anath," a Semitic name, which means "Daughter of Anath" (a Syrian goddess), and one of the royal steeds was named "Anath-herte," "Anath is Satisfied."

315. The effect of the vast influx of Asiatic life, already apparent under the Eighteenth Dynasty, was now profound, and many a foreigner of Semitic blood found favour and ultimately high station at the court or in the government. A Syrian named Ben-'Ozen was chief herald or marshal of Merneptah's court, but he was never regent as sometimes stated. The commercial opportunities of the time also brought them wealth and power; a Syrian sea-captain named Ben-Anath was able to secure a son of Ramses II as a husband for his daughter. In the army great careers were open to such foreigners, although the rank and file of the Pharaoh's forces were replenished from western and southern peoples rather than from Asia. In a body of five thousand of Ramses' troops not a single native Egyptian was to be found; over four thousand of them were Sherden and Libyans and the remainder were Nubians. The dangerous tendencies inherent in such a system had already shown themselves and were soon felt by the royal house, although powerless to make head against

them. The warlike spirit which had made Egypt the first world power had endured but a few generations, and a naturally peaceful people were returning to their accustomed peaceful life; while at the very moment when this reversion to their old manner of living was taking place, the eastern Mediterranean and the Libyan tribes offered the Pharaoh an excellent class of mercenary soldiery which under such circumstances he could not fail to utilize (PA, IV, 15, 2–17=III, 8; Ibid. IV, 3, 10 f; BAR, III, 274; MA, II, 50; MC d'Ab., No. 1136, p. 422; RIH, 32; BT, VI, 437; Ostracon, Louvre, Inv., 2262; Devér., Cat., p. 202; Rec., 16, 64; BK, 9).

316. While the wars in Asia had not recovered the empire of Thutmose III, all Palestine and possibly some of southern Syria continued to pay tribute to the Pharaoh, while on the south the boundary of the Empire was as before at Napata, below the fourth cataract. The wealth thus gained still served high purposes. Art, though now decadent, still lived. Nothing better was ever produced by the Egyptian sculptor than the superb statue of the youthful Ramses, which forms the chef d'œuvre of the Turin Museum; and even colossal statues like those of Abu Simbel are sometimes fine portraits. However much the refinement of the Eighteenth Dynasty may be wanting in the great hall at Karnak, it is nevertheless the most impressive building in Egypt, and at the last, as even Ruskin admits, size does tell. Nor should it be forgotten that the same architects produced Ramses' mortuary temple, the Ramesseum, a building not inferior in refined beauty to the best works of the Eighteenth Dynasty. Again no visitor to the temple of Abū Simbel will ever forget the solemn grandeur of this lonely sanctuary looking out upon the river from the sombre cliffs. But among the

host of buildings which Ramses exacted from his architects, there were unavoidably many which were devoid of all life and freshness, or like his addition to the Luxor temple, heavy, vulgar and of very slovenly workmanship. All such buildings were emblazoned with gayly coloured reliefs, interesting as compositions, but often badly drawn, depicting the valiant deeds of the Pharaoh in his various wars, especially, as we have already noticed, his desperate defence at the battle of Kadesh.

317. This last incident was not only influential in graphic art; it also wrought powerfully upon the imagination of the court poets, one of whom produced a prose poem on the battle, which displays a good deal of literary skill, and is the nearest approach to the epic to be found in Egyptian literature. A copy of this composition on papyrus was made by a scribe named Pentewere (Pentaur), who was misunderstood by early students of the document to be the author of the poem. The real author is unknown, although "Pentaur" still commonly enjoys the distinction. In manner this heroic poem strikes a new note; but it came at a period too late in the history of the nation to be the impulse toward a really great epic. The martial age and the creative spirit were passed in Egypt (ELAE; GLWBL; BAR, III, 305–315).

In the tale, however, the Nineteenth Dynasty really showed great fertility, combined with a spontaneous naturalism, which quite swept away all trace of the artificialities of the Middle Kingdom. Already in the Middle Kingdom and probably earlier, there had grown up collections of artless folk-tales woven often about a historical motive, and such tales, clothed in the simple language of the people, had early in the Eighteenth Dynasty gained sufficient literary respectability to be put into writing. While the Eighteenth Dynasty possessed such tales as these, yet by far the larger part of our surviving manuscripts of this class date from the Nineteenth Dynasty and later. It is now that we find the story of the conflict between the Hyksos king, Apophis, and Sekenenre at Thebes, a tale of which the lost conclusion doubtless contained a popular version of the expulsion of the Hyksos (p. 176). The people now loved to dwell upon the exploits of Thutmose III's commanders, like the tale of Thutiy and his capture of Joppa, perhaps the prototype of "Ali Baba and the Forty Thieves" (p. 238). But the artless charm of the story of the doomed prince quite surpasses such historical tales. It furnishes the earliest known example of that almost universal motive in which a youth must pass through some ordeal or competition in order to win a wife. A pastoral tale of idyllic simplicity represents two brothers as living together, the elder being married and a householder, while the younger dwells with him much after the manner of a son. At the hands of his elder brother's wife, there then befell the younger an adventure later appropriated for the Hebrew hero, Joseph. The number of such tales must have been legion, and in Greek times they furnished all that many Greek writers, or even the priest, Manetho, knew of early Egyptian kings.

While much of such literature is poetic in content and spirit, it lacks poetic form. Such form, however, was not wanting. Besides the prescribed and formal poems in praise of the Pharaoh or the gods, there were many love-songs, the oldest in the world, which belong among the best contributed by the early East. Religious poems, songs and hymns are now very numerous, and some of them display distinct literary character. We shall revert to them again in discussing the religion of this age. Numerous letters from scribes and officials of the time, exercises and practice letters composed by pupils of the scribal schools, bills, temple records and accounts,—all these serve to fill in the colour and detail in a picture of unusual fullness and interest (ELAE; GLWBL; MCP; PTAG).

318. In religion the age was moving rapidly. The state, always closely connected with religion, was becoming more and more a religious institution, designed to exalt and honour the gods through its head, the Pharaoh. The state was thus being gradually distorted to fulfill one function at the expense of all the rest, and its wealth and economic resources were being slowly engulfed, until its industrial processes should become but incidents in the maintenance of the gods. The priesthood of Amon was the strongest influence in this direction. The High Priest of Amon, as head of the sacerdotal organization embracing all the priesthoods of the country, controlled a most influential political faction. Hence it was that under Merneptah (Ramses II's son and successor), and possibly already under Ramses himself, the High Priest of Amon was able to go further and to install his son as his own successor, a very dangerous precedent. Thus there was gradually arising the sacerdotal state described by Diodorus, upon which the Egyptian priests of Greek times looked back as upon a golden age. As the inward content of the prevailing religion had already long been determined by the dominant priesthood, so now its outward manifestations were being elaborated by them into a vast and inflexible system, and the popularity of every Pharaoh with the priesthood was determined by the

degree of his acquiescence in its demands (BAR, III, 618; 640; IV, 4).

319. Though the state religion was made up of formalities, the Pharaohs were not without their own ethical standards, and these were not wholly a matter of appearances. The things for which these kings prayed, however, were not character nor the blameless life. It is material things which they desire. A higher type of personal religion was developing among the better class of the people. A fine hymn to Amon, popular at this time, contains many of the old ideas prevalent in the Aton-faith, while other religious poems show that a personal relation is gradually growing up between the worshipper and his god, so that he sees in his god the friend and protector of men. Man feels also the sense of sin and cries out: "Punish me not for my many sins." The proverbial wisdom of the time shows much of the same spirit. Whereas it formerly inculcated only correct behaviour, it now exhorts to hate evil, and to abhor what the god abhors. Prayer should be the silent aspiration of the heart and to Thoth the wise man prays, "O thou sweet Well for the thirsty in the desert! It is closed up for him who speaks, but it is open for him who keeps silence. When he who keeps silence comes, lo he finds the Well." The poisonous power of the magical literature now everywhere disseminated by the priests gradually stifled these aspirations of the middle class, and these the last symptoms of ethical and moral life in the religion of Egypt slowly disappeared (BAR, IV, 470; BIHC, XXVI; PA, II, 8, 6; Ibid, 6, 5–6; EHEL; PSall., I, 8, 2 *ff.*).

It is at this time that we gain our sole glimpse into the religious beliefs of the common people. The poor man had no place amid the magnificence of the state temples, nor could he offer anything worthy the attention of a god of such splendour. He could only resort to the host of minor genii or spirits of mirth and music, the demi-gods, who, frequenting this or that limited region, had local interest and inclination to assist the humble in their daily cares and needs. Besides these and the old kings, the foreign gods of Syria, brought in by the hosts of Asiatic slaves, appear also among those to whom the folk appeal; Baal, Kedesh, Astarte, Reshep, Anath and Sutekh are not uncommon names upon the votive tablets of the time. Animal worship now also begins to appear both among the people and in official circles (EHEL).

320. The young Pharaoh under whom these momentous transitions were slowly taking place was too plastic in dealing with them for us to discover the manner of man he was. His unscrupulous appropriation of the monuments of his ancestors does not prepossess us in his favour. In person he was tall and handsome, with features of dreamy and almost effeminate beauty, in no wise suggestive of the manly traits which he certainly possessed. After his nearly fifteen years of arduous campaigning, in which he more than redeemed the almost fatal blunder at Kadesh, he was quite ready to enjoy the well earned peace. He was inordinately vain and made far more ostentatious display of his wars on his monuments than was ever done by Thutmose III. He loved ease and pleasure and gave himself up without restraint to voluptuous enjoyments. He had an enormous harem, and the descendants of his nearly two hundred children became a Ramessid class of nobles whom we still find over four hundred years later bearing among their titles the name Ramses, not as a patronymic, but as the designation of

a class or rank. The sons of his youth accompanied him in his wars, and according to Diodorus one of them was in command of each of the divisions of his army. His favourite among them was Khamwese, whom he made High Priest of Ptah at Memphis (Diod., I, 47; BK, 34).

321. As the years passed Ramses celebrated no less than nine jubilees, erecting a forest of obelisks to commemorate them. His was the sunset glory of the venerable line which he represented. One by one the sons of his youth were taken from him until twelve were gone, and the thirteenth was the eldest and heir to the throne. Yet still the old king lived on. He lost the vitality for aggressive rule. The Libyans and the maritime peoples allied with them, Lycians, Sardinians and the Ægean races, whom he had once swept from his coasts or impressed into the service of his army, now entered the western Delta with impunity, or even pushed forward and settled there. Amid the splendours of his magnificent residence in the eastern Delta the threatening conditions at its opposite extremity never roused him from the lethargy into which he had fallen. Finally, having ruled for sixty-seven years, and being over ninety years of age, he passed away (1225 B. C.) none too soon for the redemption of his empire. We are able to look into the withered face of the hoary nonogenarian, evidently little changed from what he was in those last days of splendour in the city of Ramses, and the resemblance to the face of the youth in the noble Turin statue is still very marked (BAR, III, 543–560).

322. Probably no Pharaoh ever left a more profound impression upon his age. A quarter of a century later began a line of ten kings bearing his name. One of

them prayed that he might be granted a reign of sixty-seven years like that of his great ancestor, and all of them with varying success imitated his glory. He had set his stamp upon them all for a hundred and fifty years, and it was impossible to be a Pharaoh without being a Ramses (BAR, IV, 471).

Ramses II ideal Pharaoh

XXIII

THE FINAL DECLINE OF THE EMPIRE: MERNEPTAH AND RAMSES III

323. EGYPT was now on the defensive. This was the result of conditions both within and without. Within, the spirit which had stirred the heroes of the Asiatic conquests had now vanished; without all was turbulence and unrest. The restless maritime peoples of the northern Mediterranean, creeping along the coasts, sought plunder or places for permanent settlement, and together with the Libyans on the one hand and the peoples of remoter Asia Minor on the other, they broke in wave on wave upon the borders of the Pharaoh's empire. Egypt was inevitably thrown on the defensive. For the next sixty years after the death of Ramses II we shall be able to watch the struggle of the Pharaohs merely to *preserve* the empire, which it had been the ambition of their great ancestors rather to *extend*. At this crisis in the affairs of the nation, the enfeebled Ramses was succeeded by his thirteenth son, Merneptah, now far advanced in years. Thus one old man succeeded another upon the throne. The death of Ramses was not at once followed by any disturbance in the Asiatic dominions. The northern border in Syria was still as far north as the upper Orontes valley, including at least part of the Amorite country. With the Hittite kingdom he enjoyed undisturbed peace, even sending

them shiploads of grain in time of famine. By the end of his second year, however, he had reason to rue the good will shown his father's ancient enemy, whom he now discovered to be involved in the incursions of the maritime peoples in the western Delta in alliance with the Libyans. Thereupon the year three (about 1223 B. C.) found widespread revolt against Merneptah in Asia from Askalon at the very gates of Egypt, to the tribes of Israel and all western Syria-Palestine as far as it was controlled by the Pharaoh; all these rose against their Egyptian overlord. We have nothing but a song of triumph to tell us of the ensuing war; but it is evident that Merneptah appeared in Asia with his army in his third year. The revolting cities were severely punished and all Palestine was again humiliated and brought completely under the yoke, including some of the tribes of Israel, who had now secured a footing in Palestine, as we saw at the close of the Eighteenth and opening of the Nineteenth Dynasty (pp. 284 *ff.*). They were sufficiently amalgamated to be referred to as "Israel," and they here make their first appearance in history as a people (BAR, III, 580, l. 24; 606; 603; 617; 629-35).

324. Meantime the situation in the west was serious in the extreme; the hordes of Tehenu-Libyans were pushing further into the Delta from their settlements along the northern coast of Africa west of Egypt. It is possible that some of their advance settlers had even reached the canal of Heliopolis. Little is known of the Libyans at this time. Immediately upon the Egyptian border seems to have been the territory of the Tehenu; further west came the tribes known to the Egyptians as Lebu or Rebu, the Libyans of the Greeks, by which name also the Egyptians designated these western peoples as a whole. On the extreme west, and extend-

ing far into then unknown regions, lived the Meshwesh, or Maxyes of Herodotus. They were all doubtless the ancestors of the Berber tribes of North Africa. They were far from being totally uncivilized barbarians, but were skilled in war, well armed and capable of serious enterprises against the Pharaoh. Now rapidly consolidating under good leadership, they gave promise of becoming an aggressive and formidable state, with its frontier not ten days' march from the Pharaoh's residence in the eastern Delta. The whole western Delta was strongly tinctured with Libyan blood and Libyan families were now constantly crossing into it. Others had penetrated to the two northern oases which lie southwest of the Fayum. Meryey, king of the Libyans, forced the Tehenu to join him and, supported by roving bands of maritime adventurers from the coast, he invaded Egypt. He brought his wife and his children with him, as did also his allies, and the movement was clearly an immigration as well as an invasion. The allies were the now familiar Sherden or Sardinians; the Shekelesh, possibly the Sikeli natives of early Sicily; Ekwesh, perhaps Achæans, the Lycians, who had preyed on Egypt since the days of Amenhotep III; and the Teresh, doubtless the Tyrsenians or Etruscans. It is with these wandering marauders that the peoples of Europe emerge for the first time upon the arena of history, although we have seen them in their material documents since the Middle Kingdom. This crossing to Africa by the northern Mediterranean peoples is but one of many such ventures which in prehistoric ages brought over the white race whom we know as Libyans. Judging from the numbers who were afterward slain or captured, the Libyan king must have commanded at least some twenty thousand men or more (BAR, III, 576; 579 *f.*; 595).

325. Merneptah, at last aroused to the situation, was fortifying Heliopolis and Memphis, when news of the danger reached him late in March of his fifth year. In fourteen days his forces were ready to move, and on the morning of April fifteenth, near the Pharaoh's château at Periere in the western Delta, battle was joined. The contest lasted six hours when the Egyptian archers drove the allies from the field with immense loss. King Meryey had fled as soon as he saw the action going against him. He made good his escape, but all his household furniture and his family fell into the hands of the Egyptians. The energetic pursuit resulted in a great slaughter and many prisoners. No less than nine thousand of the invaders fell, of whom at least one-third were among the maritime allies of the Libyans; while propably as many more were taken prisoner. Among the dead were six sons of the Libyan king. The booty was enormous. The hostile camp was burned; and with the booty came news to the Pharaoh, that the Libyans had repudiated and dethroned their discomfited king and chosen another in his place who was hostile to him and would fight him. It was evident therefore that the aggressive party in Libya had fallen and that no further trouble from that quarter need be apprehended during the reign of Merneptah at least (BAR, III, 569–617).

326. The constant plundering at the hands of Libyan hordes, which the people of the western Delta had endured for nearly a generation was now ended. Not only was a great national danger averted, but an intolerable situation was relieved. The people sang:

The kings are overthrown, saying, "Salâm!"
Not one holds up his head among the nine nations of the bow.
Wasted is Tehenu,

THE DECLINE: MERNEPTAH AND RAMSES III 331

> The Hittite Land is pacified,
> Plundered is the Canaan, with every evil,
> Carried off is Askalon,
> Seized upon is Gezer,
> Yenoam is made as a thing not existing.
> Israel is desolated, her seed is not,
> Palestine has become a [defenceless] widow for Egypt.
> All lands are united, they are pacified;
> Every one that is turbulent is bound by king Merneptah.
>
> (BAR, III, 616-617; 603 ff.)

327. It is this concluding song, reverting also to Merneptah's triumphs in Asia, which tells us nearly all that we know of his Asiatic war. It is a kind of summary of all his victories, and forms a fitting conclusion of the rejoicing of the people.

328. Thus the sturdy old Pharaoh, although bowed down with years, had repelled from his empire the first assault, premonitory of the coming storm. He reigned at least five years longer, apparently enjoying profound peace in the north. He strengthened his Asiatic frontier with a fortress bearing his name, and in the south he quelled a rebellion in Nubia. Too old to gather from the quarries the blocks for great buildings, Merneptah brutally destroyed the monuments of his forefathers. He made a quarry of the noble sanctuary of Amenhotep III on the western plain, ruthlessly tore down its walls and split up its superb statues to serve as blocks in his own mortuary temple. We even find Merneptah's name constantly on the monuments of his father, who in this respect had set him a notorious example (PA, VI, pl. 4, l. 13–pl. 5, l. 5; BAR, III, 606, note a; II, 878 ff.; III, 602-617).

329. After a reign of at least ten years Merneptah passed away (1215 B. C.) and was buried at Thebes in the valley with his ancestors. His body has recently

been found there. However much we may despise him for his shameful destruction of the greatest works of his ancestors, it must be admitted that at an advanced age, when such responsibility must have sat heavily, he manfully met a grave crisis in the history of his country, which might have thrown it into the hands of a foreign dynasty.

330. The laxity which had accompanied the successive rule of two old men gave ample opportunity for intrigue, conspiracy and the machinations of rival factions. The death of Merneptah was the beginning of a conflict for the throne which lasted for many years. As in the Roman Empire, we discern the influence of provincial power, as the viceroy of Nubia, one Seti, probably thrusts aside the second of the two pretenders Amenmeses and Memeptah-Siptah, who now followed each other. This Seti, the second of the name, seems to have ruled with some success; but his lease of power was brief; the long uncurbed nobility, the hosts of mercenaries in the armies, the powerful priesthoods, the numerous foreigners in positions of rank at court, ambitious pretenders and their adherents,—all these aggressive and conflicting influences demanded for their control a strong hand and unusual qualities of statesmanship in the ruler. These qualities Seti II did not possess, and he fell a victim to conditions which would have mastered many a stronger man than he (BAR, III, 640–644; 651).

331. With the disappearance of Seti II those who had overthrown him were unable to gain the coveted power of which they had deprived him. Complete anarchy ensued. The whole country fell into the hands of the nobles, chiefs and rulers of towns; famine and violence were supreme. Profiting by the helplessness of the

people and the preoccupation of the native rulers, one of those Syrians who had held an official position at the court seized the crown, or at least the power, and ruled in tyranny and violence (BAR, IV, 398).

332. As might have been expected the Libyans were not long in perceiving the helplessness of Egypt. Immigration across the western frontier of the Delta began again; plundering bands wandered among the towns from the vicinity of Memphis to the Mediterranean. At this juncture, about 1200 B. C., there arose one Setnakht, a strong man of uncertain origin, but possibly a descendant of the old line of Seti I and Ramses II. Although he ruled but a year or two, he succeeded in exterminating the pretenders and restoring order. Before he died (1198 B. C.) he named as his successor his son, Ramses, the third of the name, who had already been of assistance to him in the government (BAR, IV, 40, ll. 20-22; 405; 399).

333. With the Ramessid line, now headed by Ramses III, Manetho begins a new dynasty, the Twentieth, although the old line was evidently already interrupted after Merneptah. Ramses III immediately perfected the organization for military service, depending more and more upon the foreign mercenaries as the permanent element in his army. The Libyan question and the situation in the western Delta were now more serious even than in Merneptah's day. The northern Mediterranean peoples, whom the Egyptians designated the "peoples of the sea," were showing themselves there in ever increasing numbers. Among these, two in particular whom we have not met before, the Thekel and the Peleset, better known as the Philistines of Hebrew history, were prominent. The Peleset were one of the early tribes of Crete, and the Thekel may have been an-

other branch of the pre-Greek Sikeli or Sicilians. These, accompanied by contingents of Denyen (Danaoi), Sherden, Weshesh and Shekelesh, had begun a southward movement, some of them impelled by pressure of Indo-Germanic peoples (among them the later Phrygians), pushing into Asia Minor in their rear. Their own racial affinities are unknown. Moving gradually southward in Syria, some of these immigrants had now advanced perhaps as far as the upper waters of the Orontes and the kingdom of Amor; while the more venturesome of their ships were coasting along the Delta and stealing into the mouths of the river on plundering expeditions. They readily fell in with the plans of Themer, the Libyan king, to invade and plunder the rich and fertile Delta. By land and water they advanced into the western Delta where Ramses III promptly met and overthrew them. Their ships were destroyed or captured and their army beaten back with enormous loss. Over twelve thousand five hundred were slain upon the field and at least a thousand captives were taken. Of the killed a large proportion were from the ranks of the sea-rovers. To strengthen his frontier against the Libyans, Ramses now built a town and stronghold named after himself upon the western road where it left the Delta (MAAG; BAR, IV, 402; 44; 39; 52–55; 42; 57 *f.*; 47, l. 73; 102; 107; III, 588; 600).

334. Meanwhile the rising tide from the north was threatening gradually to overwhelm the Egyptian Empire; we have seen its outermost waves breaking on the shores of the Delta. It was now in full motion southward through Syria. Its hosts were approaching both by land, with their families in curious, heavy, two-wheeled ox-carts, and by sea in a numerous fleet that skirted the Syrian coast. Well armed and skilled in

warfare as the invaders were, the Syrian city-states were unable to withstand their onset. They overran all the Hittite country of northern Syria as far as Carchemish on the Euphrates, past Arvad on the Phœnician coast, and up the Orontes valley to the kingdom of Amor, which they devastated. The Syrian dominions of the Hittites must have been lost and the Hittite power in Syria completely broken. The fleet visited Alasa, or Cyprus; and nowhere was an effective resistance offered them. In Amor they established a central camp and apparently halted for a time (BAR, IV, 64; 77).

335. Ramses III threw himself with great energy into the preparations for repelling the attack. He fortified his Syrian frontier and rapidly gathered a fleet, which he distributed in the northern harbours. He then set out for Syria to lead the campaign himself. Where the land-battle took place we are unable to determine, but as the Northerners had advanced to Amor, it was at most not further north than that region. We learn nothing from Ramses III's records concerning it beyond vague and general statements of the defeat of the enemy, although in his reliefs we see his Sherden mercenaries breaking through the scattered lines of the enemy and plundering their ox-carts, bearing the women and children and the belongings of the Northerners. Ramses was also able to reach the scene of the naval battle, probably in one of the northern harbours on the coast of Phœnicia, early enough to participate in the action from the neighbouring shore. He had manned his fleet with masses of the dreaded Egyptian archers, whose fire was so effective that the ranks of the heavy armed Northerners were completely decimated before they could approach within boarding distance. As the

336   THE EMPIRE: SECOND PERIOD

Egyptians then advanced to board, the enemy's ships were thrown into confusion and many were capsized. Those who escaped the fleet and swam ashore were captured by the waiting Egyptians on the beach. The Pharaoh's suzerainty, at least as far north as Amor, could not now be questioned by the invaders. They continued to arrive in Syria, only to become vassals of Egypt, paying tribute into the treasury of the Pharaoh. The Egyptian Empire in Asia had again been saved and Ramses returned to his Delta residence to enjoy a well-earned triumph (BAR, IV, 59–82; 403).

336. He was now given but a short respite, for another migration of the peoples in the far west caused an overflow which again threatened the Delta in the eleventh year of the king. The Meshwesh, a tribe living behind the Libyans, invaded the Libyan country and laid it waste, thus forcing the unfortunate Libyans, already twice punished, into another alliance against Egypt. The leader of the movement was Meshesher, son of Keper, king of the Meshwesh, whose firm purpose was to migrate and settle in the Delta. Ramses attacked the allies under the walls of Hatsho, his frontier fortress, and put them to flight. Meshesher, the chief of the Meshwesh, was slain and his father Keper was captured, two thousand one hundred and seventy-five of their followers fell, while two thousand and fifty-two, of whom over a fourth were females, were taken captive. The western tribes had thus been hurled back from the borders of the Delta for the third successive time, and Ramses had no occasion to apprehend any further aggressions from that quarter. The expansive power of the Libyan peoples, although by no means exhausted, now no longer appeared in united national action, but as they had done from prehistoric times they continued

These peoples of N— and S— unable to conquer Ramses III— came in as settlers, and in this way he could not repel them.

THE DECLINE: MERNEPTAH AND RAMSES III 337

to sift gradually into the Delta in scattered and desultory migration, not regarded by the Pharaoh as a source of danger (BAR, IV, 83–114; 405; 224; 145).

337. Following closely upon the last Libyan campaign, Ramses found it necessary again to appear in Amor with his army. The limits and the course of the campaign are but obscurely hinted at in the meagre records now surviving. He stormed at least five strong cities, one of which was in Amor; another was perhaps Kadesh; and two, one of which was called Ereth, were defended by Hittites. He probably did not penetrate far into the Hittite territory, although its cities were rapidly falling away from the Hittite king and much weakened by the attacks of the sea-peoples. It was the last hostile passage between the Pharaoh and the Hittites; both empires were swiftly declining to their fall, and in the annals of Egypt we never again hear of the Hittites in Syria. He now organized the Asiatic possessions of Egypt as stably as possible, the boundary very evidently not being any further north than that of Merneptah, that is, just including the Amorite kingdom on the upper Orontes. To ensure the stability which he desired he built new fortresses wherever necessary in Syria and Palestine; somewhere in Syria he also erected a temple of Amon, containing a great image of the state god, before which the Asiatic dynasts were obliged to declare their fealty to Ramses by depositing their tribute in its presence every year. Only a revolt of the Beduin of Seir interrupted the peaceful government of the Pharaoh in Asia from this time forth (BAR, IV, 115–135; 141; 219; 406; 404).

338. The influence of Egyptian commerce and administration in Syria was evident in one important particular especially, for it was now that the cumbrous

and inconvenient clay tablet was gradually supplemented in Syria by the handy papyrus. With the papyrus paper, the hand customarily written upon it in Egypt now made its way into Phœnicia, where before the tenth century B. C. it developed into an alphabet of consonants, which was quickly transmitted to the Ionian Greeks and thence to Europe (BAR, IV, 576; 582).

339. The suppression of occasional disorders in Nubia, caused no disturbance of the profound peace, which now settled down upon the Empire. Intercourse and commerce with the outside world were now fostered by the Pharaoh as in the great days. The temples of Amon, Re, and Ptah had each its own fleet upon the Mediterranean or the Red Sea, transporting to the god's treasury the products of Phœnicia, Syria and Punt. Other fleets of the Pharaoh brought copper and malachite from Sinai and its now familiar wealth from Punt. Navigation was now perhaps on a larger scale than ever before. Ramses tells of a sacred barge of Amon at Thebes, which was two hundred and twenty-four feet long, built in his yards, of enormous timbers of cedar of Lebanon (BAR, IV, 211; 270; 328; 407–409; 209).

340. The Pharaoh's wealth now enabled him to undertake buildings and works of public utility. Throughout the kingdom, and especially in Thebes and the royal residence, he planted numerous trees, offering grateful shade, in a land devoid of natural forests. He also resumed building, at a standstill since the death of Ramses II. On the western plain of Thebes, at the point now called Medinet Habu, he began a large and splendid temple to Amon, which, as it grew from year to year, became a vast record of the king's achievements

in war which the modern visitor may read, tracing it from year to year as he passes from the earliest halls in the rear to the latest courts and pylon at the front. Here he may see the hordes of the North in battle with Ramses' Sherden mercenaries. The first naval battle on salt water, of which we know anything, is here depicted, and in these reliefs we may study the armour, clothing, weapons, war-ships and equipment of these northern peoples with whose advent Europe for the first time emerges upon the stage of the early world. Other buildings of his have for the most part perished; a small temple of Amon at Karnak, and a sanctuary for Khonsu, only begun by Ramses III, still survive. In the residence city he laid out a magnificent quarter and garden for Amon, possessing nearly eight thousand slaves for its service. He also erected in the city a temple of Sutekh in the temonos of Ramses II's temple. The art displayed by these buildings, in so far as they have survived, is clearly in a decadent stage. The lines are heavy and indolent, the colonnades have none of the old-time soaring vigour; they visibly labour under the burden imposed upon them, expressing the sluggish spirit of the decadent architect. The work also is careless and slovenly in execution. The reliefs which cover the vast surfaces of the Medinet Habu temple are with few exceptions but weak imitations of the fine sculptures of Seti I at Karnak, badly drawn and executed without feeling. Only here and there do we find a flash of the old-time power (BAR, IV, 213; 215; 410; 195–215; 1–26; 69–82; 250–265; 311–328; 225; 362; 369).

341. The imitation so evident in the art of Ramses III's reign is characteristic of the time in all respects. The inspiring figure of a young and active Pharaoh

hurrying his armies from frontier to frontier of his empire and repeatedly hurling back the most formidable invasions Egypt had ever suffered, awoke no response in the conventional soul of the priestly scribe, whose lot it was to write the record of these things for the temple wall. He possessed only the worn and long spent currency of the older dynasties from which he drew whole hymns, songs and lists to be furbished up and made to do service again in perpetuating the glory of a really able and heroic ruler. Even the king himself considered it his highest purpose to restore and reproduce the times of Ramses II.

342. This was especially evident in his attitude toward the religious conditions inherited from the Nineteenth Dynasty. He made no effort to shake off the priestly influences with which the crown was encumbered. The temples were fast becoming a grave political and economic menace. In the face of this fact Ramses III continued the policy of his ancestors, and with the most lavish liberality poured the wealth of the royal house into the sacred coffers. The opulent splendour with which the rituals of the great gods were daily observed beggars description. In making the great temple balances for weighing the offerings to Re at Heliopolis nearly two hundred and twelve pounds of gold and four hundred and sixty-one pounds of silver were consumed. The reader may peruse pages of such descriptions in the great Papyrus Harris, of which we shall later give some account. Such magnificence, while it might frequently be due to incidental gifts of the king, must nevertheless be supported by an enormous income, derived from a vast fortune in lands, slaves and revenues. The records of Ramses III for the first and only time in the course of Egyptian history,

THE DECLINE: MERNEPTAH AND RAMSES III 341

enable us to determine the total amount of property owned and controlled by the temples. They owned not less than one and a quarter and very probably two per cent. of the population as slaves. In lands we find the sacred endowments amounting to fifteen per cent. of the available land of the country. These are the only items in the temple estates which can be safely compared with the total national wealth and resources; but they by no means complete the list of property held by the temples. They owned nearly a half million head of large and small cattle; their combined fleets numbered eighty-eight vessels, some fifty-three workshops and ship-yards consumed a portion of the raw materials, which they received as income; while in Syria, Kush and Egypt they owned in all one hundred and sixty-nine towns. When we remember that all this vast property in a land of less than ten thousand square miles and some five or six million inhabitants was entirely exempt from taxation it will be seen that the economic equilibrium of the state was endangered (BAR, IV, 363; 199; 202; 198–210; 256; 285; 151–412; 146–150; 166 *f*.).

343. These extreme conditions were aggravated by the fact that no proper proportion had been observed in the distribution of gifts to the gods. By far too large a share of them had fallen to the lot of the insatiable Amon, the demands for whose innumerable temples far exceeded those of all others put together. In his festal calendar, now introduced by Ramses III, we find that there was an annual feast day of Amon on an average every three days, not counting the monthly feasts. Yet Ramses III later lengthened even the feasts of this calendar. As in the days of the Eighteenth Dynasty conquerors, the bulk of the spoil from his wars went into the treasury of Amon. The result of this

This disproportion in wealth of Gods commenced in 18 dynasty

342   THE EMPIRE: SECOND PERIOD

long continued policy was inevitable. Of the nearly three quarters of a million acres of land held by the temples, Amon owned over five hundred and eighty-three thousand, over five times as much as his nearest competitor, Re of Heliopolis. Of the fifteen per cent. of the lands of the entire country held by all the temples, Amon thus owned over two-thirds. In other items of Amon's wealth the same proportion is observable. His estate and his revenues, second only to those of the king, now assumed an important economic rôle in the state, and the political power wielded by a community of priests who controlled such vast wealth was from now on a force which no Pharaoh could ignore. Other similar prerogatives also now came to Amon. His High Priest had in the Eighteenth Dynasty become head of all the priesthoods of Egypt; now his Theban temple became the sacerdotal capital, where the records of the other temples were kept, and the furtive power of Amon was thus gradually extended over all the sacred estates in the land (BAR, IV, 164; 146; 189–226; 219; 218; 139–145; 236–237; 25–34; 190; 224; 405; 167; 165; 170 f.).

Amon

Karnak

344. It is a mistake to suppose, as is commonly done, that Ramses III was solely or even chiefly responsible for these conditions. They began in the enormous gifts to the temples, especially to Amon, by the conquerors of the Eighteenth Dynasty. By generations of this policy the vast wealth of the temples had gradually been accumulated, and against the insatiable priesthoods long accustomed to the gratification of unlimited exactions, Ramses III was unable and indeed did not attempt to make a stand. Yet the treasury, with its income gradually shrinking, must have sorely felt the draughts upon it. It was now with the greatest diffi-

culty that day-labourers for the state could wring their wages of grain from the complacent scribal overseer. Thus while the poor in the employ of the state were starving at the door of an empty treasury, the storehouses of the gods were groaning with plenty, and Amon was yearly receiving over two hundred and five thousand bushels of grain for the offerings at his annual feasts alone (BAR, IV, 202; 157 *f.*; 174; ELAE, 124–126).

345. The only forces which Ramses III and his contemporaries could bring into play against the powerful priestly coteries were the numerous foreigners among the slaves owned by the crown. These slaves were now largely natives of Syria, Asia Minor and Libya, especially Syria, and as the king found them more and more useful, they gradually gained high office in the state and at the court, especially as "royal butlers." It was a situation, as Erman has remarked, precisely like that at the court of the Egyptian sultans of the Middle Ages. While all was outwardly splendour and tranquillity and the whole nation was celebrating the king who had saved the Empire, the forces of decay which had for generations been slowly gathering in the state were rapidly reaching the acute stage. An insatiable and insidious priesthood commanding enormous wealth, a foreign army ready to serve the master who paid most liberally, a personal following of alien slaves, and a host of royal relatives and dependants,— these were the factors which Ramses III was constantly forced to manipulate and employ, each against the others in a situation of ever increasing difficulty and complication (BAR, IV, 405; 419 *ff.*).

346. The first serious trouble discernible was the insubordination of one of the viziers. This past, the

first royal jubilee was celebrated with the usual splendour at Memphis. Something over a year after this stately commemoration, as the old king was beginning to feel his years, a more serious crisis developed. In order to crown a pretender from the numerous harem children, a conspiracy against the Pharaoh's life was formed. Involved in it were no less than eleven harem officials of various ranks, five royal butlers, the commander of archers in Nubia, an overseer of the treasury, a general in the army named Peyes, three royal scribes in various offices, and several subordinate officials.

347. At the critical moment the king's party gained full information of the conspiracy, and the people involved in the treason were all seized. The old Pharaoh, sorely shaken by the ordeal, and possibly suffering bodily injury from attempted assassination, lived to appoint a special court for the trial of the conspirators with the most impartial justice. Even now there was a bold attempt by the accused to influence two of the judges, who were guilty of such indiscretion that they were tried and condemned to lose nose and ears. The trials of the conspirators proceeded with regularity, and from the records of three different prosecutions we are able to trace the conviction of thirty-two officials of all ranks, including the unhappy young pretender himself. Meantime the thirty-second anniversary of the Pharaoh's accession was celebrated with the gorgeous twenty days' feast customary since his twenty-second year. But the old king survived only twenty days more and before the prosecution of his would-be assassins was ended he passed away (1167 B. C.), having ruled thirty-one years and forty days (BAR, IV, 361; 335; 413–415; 416–456; 237).

Goodspeed p 133 to Assyria & Bab
end of chapter

Babylon established cuneiform.
Nineveh took it up. Hebrew archaeology
has been attempted by Philologists,
not archaeologists — and must be false
Not a document in Palestine (in its height)
written in cuneiform
By gau[?] line
Hebrews of inferior culture at time of their conquest.

PART VII
THE DECADENCE OF ANCIENT EGYPT

The Semites have had reasons
of pushing westward — migrations —
since the beginning of time +

"The permanent" and abiding
power of art — is oriental — not Greek,
that the Greek was only temporary
a flaming up, and then a rapid
decay — and will probably always
continue. It once almost took the
world (Mohammedans) it may again

Into Assyria — Babylon — Serla[?]
"Pan Babylonian" — Babylon dominated the sur-
neighboring states. Astral Religion —
Gods deified in stars & planets &c

Israel.

Lack of material for study of history of early Israel

The Hebrews fortunately had time to develope and combine (11 Cen B C) because Assyria and Babylon were quiescent — at that time weak.

Israel lived in midst of historical forces — just as any other nation

according to the Old testament Moses had 4 father-in laws Ex - 1, 18 - 1
                                     Ex 11 - 18
                                     Judges. 1 - 16

Even Solomon little more than a vassal of Egypt. Not a free king

Israel unified by its religion — (Jahweh) God of Israel — Volcanic Fire spirit

Israelites — at first. Some settled down — some could not. Clash between nomadic life and town life — with class distinctions.

Jakweh finally developes from a terrible — war like god — as the Is. advance becomes a much loftier god —

So called "Prophets — Elijah etc
Gov. of I. tribal — adjusted to kingship
Econ omic — disorganized & meagre
     compared with Eg. & Babylon. etc.
Artisans — few; Commerce — little
Art — no art surviving no Architecture
No Literature — Religion strong — Songs

Had a notion of law

Read this chapter

Breasted – read wonderful prayer of Ramses IV. He argues with God – telling God that he had done more in his four years reign than Ramses III in 6 yrs.

XXIV

THE FALL OF THE EMPIRE

348. The death of Ramses III introduced a long line of nine weaklings all of whom bore the great name Ramses. They were far from bearing it worthily, and under them the waning power of the Pharaohs declined swiftly to its fall in a few decades. We see Ramses IV, the son of Ramses III, struggling feebly with the hopeless situation which he inherited about 1167 B. C. Immediately on his accession the new king prepared one of the most remarkable documents which has reached us from the civilization of ancient Egypt, a huge list of his father's good works. It contained an enormous inventory of Ramses III's gifts to the three chief divinities of the nation, besides a statement of his achievements in war and of his benefactions toward the people of his empire. All this recorded on papyrus formed a huge roll one hundred and thirty feet long, now called Papyrus Harris, the largest document which has descended to us from the early orient. Accompanied by this extraordinary statement of his benefactions toward gods and men, Ramses III was laid in his tomb. In its efficacy in securing him unlimited favour with the gods there could be no doubt; and it contained so many prayers placed in the mouth of Ramses III on behalf of his son and successor, that the gods, unable to resist the appeals of the favourite to whom they

Perfectly preserved now in British Museum

Did they produce ghost wailed tales of old.

The Arabs who found the Papyrus Harris told Harris that they had found a huge amt. of other papyrus rolls but burned them for the sake of the sweet odor

347

owed so much, would certainly grant his son a long reign. Indeed it is clear that to this motive was due the production of the document. In this decadent age the Pharaoh was more dependent upon such means for the maintenance of his power than upon his own strong arm, and the huge papyrus thus becomes a significant sign of the times. With fair promises of a long reign the insatiable priesthoods were extorting from the impotent Pharaoh all they demanded, while he was satisfied with the assured favour of the gods (BAR, IV, 151–412; 471).

349. Naturally the only work of Ramses IV, of which we know, is an enterprise for the benefit of the gods, involving the dispatch of nine thousand men to secure building stone from the quarries of Hammamat, which he himself first visited. After an inglorious reign of six years he was succeeded in 1161 B. C. by the fifth Ramses, probably his son. The exploitation of the mines of Sinai now ceased, and the last Pharaonic name found there is that of Ramses IV. The Empire still maintained by Ramses III in Asia must have rapidly declined; that in Nubia was still maintained. In quick succession these feeble Ramessids now followed each other. They all excavated tombs in the Valley of the Kings, but we know nothing of their deeds. Now and again the obscurity lifts, and we catch fleeting glimpses of a great state tottering to its fall (BAR, IV, 457–485).

350. From the close of Ramses III's reign to the first years of Ramses IX, only some twenty-five or thirty years elapsed. The high priesthood of Amon which had at least once descended from father to son in the Nineteenth Dynasty had since become permanently hereditary, and now while it was passing from the hands

THE FALL OF THE EMPIRE

of Ramsesnakht to his son Amenhotep, with a single transmission of authority, six feeble Ramessids succeeded each other, with ever lessening power and prestige. Meanwhile Amenhotep, the High Priest of Amon, flourished. He sumptuously restored the refectory and kitchen of the priests in the temple of his god at Karnak built eight hundred years before by Sesostris I. We see the crafty priest manipulating the pliant Pharaoh as he pleases, and obtaining golden decorations and every honour at his hands. The days when such distinctions were the reward of valour on the battle-fields of Syria are long passed; and skill in priest-craft is the surest guarantee of preferment. As the king delivered the rich gifts to the High Priest he accompanied them with words of praise such that one is in doubt whether they are delivered by the sovereign to the subject or by the subject to his lord. All these honours were twice recorded by Amenhotep, on the walls of the Karnak temple, in a large relief showing Amenhotep receiving his gifts from the king, and depicting his figure in the same heroic stature as that of the king. In all such scenes from time immemorial the official appearing before the king had been represented as a pigmy before the towering figure of the Pharaoh; but the High Priest of Amon was now rapidly growing to measure his stature with that of the Pharaoh himself, both on the temple wall and in the affairs of government (BAR, IV, 414 *f.;* 486–498).

351. The state of disorganization and helplessness which was gradually evolving is revealed to us in a chapter from the government of the Theban necropolis, preserved in certain legal archives of Ramses IX's reign. Thebes, forsaken as a royal residence by the Pharaohs two hundred years before, was now rapidly

declining, but it continued to be the burial place of all the royal dead. In the lonely valley behind the western plain, deep in the heart of the cliffs, slept the great emperors, decked in all the magnificence which the wealth of Asia had brought them. In the sixteenth year of Ramses IX's reign the royal tombs of the plain before the western cliffs were found to have been attacked by tomb robbers. Within a generation, as the work of plunder continued, all the bodies of Egypt's kings and emperors buried at Thebes were despoiled, and of the whole line of Pharaohs from the beginning of the Eighteenth to the end of the Twentieth Dynasty, only one body, that of Amenhotep II, has been found still lying in its sarcophagus; although it had by no means escaped spoliation. Thus, while the tombs of the Egyptian emperors at Thebes were being ransacked and their bodies rifled and dishonoured, the empire which they conquered was crumbling to final ruin (BAR, IV, 499–556).

352. At the accession of Ramses XII (1118 B.C.) we are able to discern the culmination of the tendencies which we have been endeavouring to trace. Before he had been reigning five years a local noble at Tanis named Nesubenebded, the Smendes of the Greeks, had absorbed the entire Delta and made himself king of the North. There was now nothing for the impotent Pharaoh to do but retire to Thebes,—if this transfer had not indeed already occurred before this,—where he still maintained his precarious throne. Thebes was thus cut off from the sea and the commerce of Asia and Europe by a hostile kingdom in the Delta, and its wealth and power still more rapidly declined. The High Priest of Amon was now virtually at the head of a Theban principality, which we shall see becoming

gradually more and more a distinct political unit. Together with this powerful priestly rival, the Pharaoh continued to hold Nubia (BAR, IV, 557; 581).

353. The swift decline of the Ramessids was quickly noticed and understood in Syria long before the revolution which resulted in the independence of the Delta. The Thekel and Peleset (Philistines), whose invasion Ramses III had for a time halted, as we have before stated, had continued to arrive in Syria. They had moved gradually southward, pushing before them the Amorites and scattered remnants of the Hittites, who were thus forced southward into Palestine, where they were found later by the Hebrews. By 1115 B.C. the Thekel were already established as an independent kingdom at Dor, just south of the seaward end of Carmel. As we do not find them mentioned in the surviving records of the Hebrews, they must have merged into the larger mass of the Philistines, whose cities gradually extended probably from Beth-Shean in the Jordan valley westward and southward, through the plain of Esdrælon or Megiddo to the southern sea-plain, cutting off the northern tribes of Israel from their kinsmen in the south. Continually replenished with new arrivals by sea, they threatened to crush Israel, as they had done the kingdom of Amor, before the Hebrew tribal leaders should have welded the Palestinian Semites into a nation. With their extreme southern frontier at the very gates of Egypt, these hardy and warlike wanderers from Crete and the far north could not have paid tribute to the Pharaoh very long after the death of Ramses III (1167 B.C.). In the reign of Ramses IX (1142–1123 B.C.), or about that time, a body of Egyptian envoys were detained at Byblos by the local dynast for seventeen years, and, unable to return, they at last

died there. The Syrian princes, among whom Ramses III had won his victories, were thus indifferent to the power of Egypt within twenty or twenty-five years of his death (BAR, IV, 558; 585; Jer. XLVII, 4; Amos, IX, 7).

354. A few years later, under Ramses XII, these same conditions in Syria are vividly portrayed in the report of an Egyptian envoy thither. In response to an oracle, Wenamon, the envoy in question, was dispatched to Byblos, at the foot of Lebanon, to procure cedar for the sacred barge of Amon. Hrihor, the High Priest of Amon, was able to give him only a pitiful sum in gold and silver, and therefore sent with him an image of Amon, called "Amon-of-the-Way," who was able to bestow "life and health," hoping thus to impress the prince of Byblos and compensate for the lack of liberal payment. Nothing more eloquently portrays the decadent condition of Egypt than the humiliating state of this unhappy envoy, dispatched without ships, with no credentials, with but a beggarly pittance to offer for the timber desired, and only the memory of Egypt's former greatness with which to impress the prince of Byblos. Stopping at Dor on the voyage out, Wenamon was robbed of the little money he had, and was unable to secure any satisfaction from the Thekel prince of that city. After waiting in despair for nine days, he departed for Byblos by way of Tyre, having on the way somehow succeeded in seizing from certain Thekel people a bag of silver as security for his loss at Dor. He finally arrived in safety at Byblos, where Zakar-Baal, the prince of the city, would not even receive him, but ordered him to leave. Such was the state of an Egyptian envoy in Phœnicia, within fifty or sixty years of the death of Ramses III. Finally, as the despairing

Wenamon was about to take passage back to Egypt, one of the noble youths in attendance upon Zakar-Baal was seized with a divine frenzy, and in prophetic ecstasy demanded that Wenamon be summoned, honourably treated and dismissed. This earliest known example of Old Testament prophecy in its earliest form thus secured for Wenamon an interview with Zakar-Baal.

355. While the Phœnician prince quite readily admits the debt of culture which his land owes Egypt as a source of civilization, he emphatically repudiates all political responsibility to the ruler of Egypt, whom he never calls Pharaoh, except in referring to a former sovereign. The situation is clear. A burst of military enthusiasm and a line of able rulers had enabled Egypt to assume for several centuries an imperial position, which her unwarlike people were not by nature adapted to occupy; and their impotent descendants, no longer equal to their imperial rôle, were now appealing to the days of splendour with an almost pathetic futility. It is characteristic of the time that this appeal should assume a religious or even theological form, as Wenamon boldly proclaims Amon's dominion over Lebanon, where the Phœnician princes had, only two generations before, worshipped and paid tribute at the temple of Amon, erected by Ramses III. With oracles and an image of the god that conferred "life and health" the Egyptian envoy sought to make his bargain with the contemptuous Phœnician for timber which a Thutmose III or a Seti I had demanded with his legions behind him. The image of "Amon-of-the-Way" failed to impress Zakar-Baal, as the Pharaoh's armies had impressed his ancestors; and it was only when Wenamon's messenger to Egypt returned with a few vessels of silver and gold, some fine linen, papyrus rolls, ox-hides, coils

of cordage, and the like, that the Phœnician ruler ordered his men to cut the desired logs; although he had sent some of the heavier timbers for the hull of the barge in advance, as an evidence of his good faith. Having escaped from a fleet of eleven Thekel ships which pursued him, the barque of the unhappy Wenamon was driven by a tempest from the homeward course upon the coast of Cyprus, where the populace was about to slay him at the palace of Hatiba, the queen. Her he fortunately intercepted as she was passing from one palace to another. Among her following, Wenamon, by inquiry, found a Cyprian who spoke Egyptian, and by skillful intercession he gained her protection. At this point his report breaks off, and the conclusion is lost; but here again, in Cyprus, whose king, as practically his vassal, the Pharaoh had been wont to call to account for piracy in the old days of splendour, we find the representative of Egypt barely able to save his life only two generations after a great war-fleet of Ramses III had destroyed the powerful united navy of his northern enemies in these very waters. This unique and instructive report of Wenamon (BAR, IV, 557 *ff.*), therefore, reveals to us the complete collapse of Egyptian prestige abroad and shows with what appalling swiftness the dominant state in the Mediterranean basin had declined under the weak successors of Ramses III. When an Assyrian king, presumably Tiglath-pileser I, appeared in the West about 1100 B.C., a Pharaoh, who was probably Nesubenebded, feeling his exposed position in the Delta, deemed it wise to propitiate the Assyrian with a gift. Thus Egyptian influence in Syria had utterly vanished, while in Palestine a fiction of traditional sovereignty, totally without practical political significance, was maintained at the Pharaoh's court,

In resumption of that sovereignty we shall see future kings making sporadic campaigns thither after the establishment of the Hebrew monarchy.

356. Meanwhile there was but one possible issue for the conditions at Thebes. The messenger who procured the timber for the sacred barge of Amon was no longer dispatched by the Pharaoh, but as we have seen, by the High Priest of Amon, Hrihor. He has now become head of the Pharaoh's military forces, with the title "commander in chief of the armies of the South and North." On the temples there are now two dedications: the usual one by the Pharaoh and another by the High Priest; while in the temple reliefs, in the place for thousands of years occupied by the Pharaoh, stands the High Priest Hrihor. Like the shadowy caliph, whom the Egyptian sultans brought from Bagdad to Cairo, and maintained for a time there, so the unfortunate Ramses XII had been brought from his Delta residence to Thebes, that the conventionalities of the old Pharaonic tradition might still be continued for a brief time. A letter written to his Nubian viceroy in his seventeenth year shows that he still retained some voice in Nubia; but he is soon deprived of his authority there also, and Hrihor appears as "viceroy of Kush." Already at the beginning of the Nineteenth Dynasty we recall that Amon had gained possession of the Nubian gold-country; the High Priest has now gone a step further and seized the whole of the great province of the Upper Nile. The same inscription calls him also "overseer of the double granary," the most important fiscal officer in the state, next the chief treasurer himself. There is now nothing left in the way of authority and power for the High Priest to absorb; he is commander of all the armies, viceroy of Kush, holds the treasury in his hands, and

executes the buildings of the gods. When the fiction of the last Ramessid's official existence had been maintained for at least twenty-seven years the High Priest's supreme position seems to have been confirmed by an oracle of Khonsu, followed by the approval of Amon. The shadowy Pharaoh vanishes, and on the royal buildings the High Priest's name, preceded by the Pharaonic titles and enclosed in the royal cartouche at last appears alone (BAR, IV, 592–594; 602; 609; 611; 595–600; 640; 614–626).

XXV

PRIESTS AND MERCENARIES: THE SUPREMACY OF THE LIBYANS

357. THE result of the development of Thebes into an independent sacerdotal principality was not only the downfall of the empire, but of course also the end of the unity of the kingdom. This disunion and division continued in more or less pronounced form from the rise of Hrihor and Nesubenebded, in the latter part of the eleventh century, for four hundred and fifty years or more. The complacent Hrihor maintained the fiction of a united "Two Lands," of which he called himself the lord, as if he really ruled them both. With amazing mendacity he filled his titulary with references to his universal power, and affirmed that the Syrian princes bowed down every day to his might. We recall, however, the adventures of the luckless Wenamon among them (pp. 352 *ff.*). The state which Hrihor maintained was a theocracy, pure and simple. As far back as the days of Thutmose III there are remarkable examples of Amon's intervention in the affairs of government. Thutmose III himself was crowned by an oracle of the gods. But this and other examples of the god's intervention occurred on extraordinary occasions. Under Hrihor's theocracy such oracles became part of the ordinary machinery of government. Whatever the High Priest wished legally to effect could be sanctioned

by special oracle of the god at any time, and by prearrangement the cultus image before which the High Priest made known his desires invariably responded favourably by violent nodding of the head, or even by speech. All wills and property conveyances of members of the High Priest's family were oracles of Amon, and civil documents thus became divine decrees. Banished political exiles were recalled by oracle of the god, criminal cases were tried before him, and by his decision the convicted were put to death. Priestly jugglery, ruling if necessary in utter disregard of law and justice, thus enabled the High Priest to cloak with the divine sanction all that he wished to effect (BAR, IV, 620; 623; 795; 670-674).

358. Hrihor must have been an old man at his accession (1090 B. C.). He did not long survive Ramses XII, and at his death his son, Payonekh, also advanced in years, was unable to maintain the independence of Thebes against Nesubenebded at Tanis, who extended his authority over the whole country for a brief time. He is, therefore, called the first king of the Twenty-first Dynasty by Manetho, who knows nothing of the independence of Thebes. Payonekh's son, Paynozem I, quickly succeeded him, and while he was ruling at Thebes in more or less independence, but without royal titles, Nesubenebded was followed at Tanis by Pesibkhenno I, probably his son. Paynozem I now achieved a master-stroke of diplomacy and gained in marriage the daughter of the Tanite, Pesibkhenno I. Thus on the death of the latter (1067 B. C.), he obtained through his wife the Tanite crown and the sovereignty over a united Egypt, which he maintained for some forty years. Three of his sons became high priests at Thebes, but not without disturbance. These Tanite kings were not

great builders, although Pesibkhenno I raised a massive enclosure wall eighty feet thick around his temple at Tanis. As they show little initiative in other directions, the century and a half during which they maintained themselves was one of steady industrial and economic decline (BAR, IV, 627; 631; 633–635; 642; 650–658; 661; PT, I, 19).

359. The Tanites as a whole did nothing for the once great capital of the empire, and its decline was steady and rapid. They respected the memory of their royal ancestors and vied with the high priests at Thebes in protecting the bodies of the emperors, which they hurried from place to place to conceal them from the persistent tomb-robbers. Finally, under Pesibkhenno II, the last king of the Tanite Dynasty, they were hurriedly removed to their final hiding place, an old and probably unused tomb of Amenhotep I, near the temple of Der el-Bahri. Here the greatest kings of Egypt slept unmolested for nearly three thousand years, until about 1871 or 1872, when the Theban descendants of those same tomb-robbers whose prosecution under Ramses IX we can still read, discovered the place and the plundering of the royal bodies was begun again. In 1881, by methods not greatly differing from those employed under Ramses IX, the modern authorities forced the thieves to disclose the place. Thus nearly twenty-nine centuries after they had been sealed in their hiding place by the ancient scribes, and some three thousand five hundred years after the first interment of the earliest among them, the faces of Egypt's kings and emperors were disclosed to the modern world (BAR, IV, 681; 627 *ff.*; 664–667; 691 *f.*; 499–556).

360. Abroad, the Twenty-first Dynasty was as feeble as its predecessors at the close of the Twentieth had

been. They probably maintained Egyptian power in Nubia, but as for Asia, there was only the court fiction of a nominal suzerainty over Palestine in continuance of century-long tradition. During this period of Egypt's total eclipse the tribes of Israel were given opportunity to consolidate their national organization and under Saul and David they gradually gained the upper hand against the Philistines. Egypt's exact relation to these events it is as yet impossible to determine, as we have no contemporary monuments. The sea-peoples no longer appear upon the monuments, and from the west, the Delta was now the peaceful conquest of the Libyans, who accomplished by gradual immigration what they had failed to gain by hostile invasion. Libyan mercenaries still filled the ranks of the Egyptian army, and the commanders of the Meswesh in control of the fortresses and garrisons of the important Delta towns soon gained positions of power. A titleless Tehen-Libyan named Buyuwawa settled at Heracleopolis early in the Twenty-first Dynasty, and the family slowly rose till Sheshonk the seventh descendant of the line was a powerful mercenary prince at Heracleopolis, in control of a principality reaching probably as far as Memphis on the north and on the south as far as Siut. The other Libyan commanders in the Delta were evidently enjoying similar prosperity. Whether the Tanite line died out or its last representative was too feeble to maintain himself we cannot now discern, but such was the power of Sheshonk at Heracleopolis that he now transferred his residence to Bubastis in the eastern Delta, where he seized the royal authority and proclaimed himself Pharaoh about 945 B. C. His line was known to Manetho as the Twenty-second Dynasty. Thus, in a little over two centuries

THE SUPREMACY OF THE LIBYANS 361

after the death of Ramses III, who had smitten them so sorely, the Libyans gained the crown of Egypt without so much as drawing the sword. The forces which thus placed a soldier and a foreigner upon the venerable throne of the Pharaohs had developed hand in hand with those which had delivered the country to the priests; but the power of the priest had culminated a little more rapidly than that of the mercenary, although both were equally rooted in the imperial system of the Eighteenth Dynasty (BAR, IV, 785–793; 669–687; 785 ff.).

361. Sheshonk immediately gave to the succession of his line a legitimacy which he could not himself possess, by marrying his son to the daughter of Pesibkhenno II, the last of the Tanite kings of the Twenty-first Dynasty. A difficult situation confronted the new ruler. It was essentially a feudal organization which was now effected by Sheshonk I, and the princes who owed him fealty were largely the turbulent Meshwesh chiefs like himself, who would naturally not forget his origin nor fail to see that a successful coup might accomplish for any one of them what he had achieved for himself. It is evident that they ruled the Delta cities, rendering to the Pharaoh their quota of troops, as did the Mamlukes under the Sultans of Moslem Egypt. Upper Egypt was organized into two principalities; that of Heracleopolis embracing, as we have seen, northern Upper Egypt as far south as Siut, where the Theban principality began, which in its turn included all the country southward to the cataract and perhaps Nubia also. The country thus already fell into three divisions roughly corresponding to those of Ptolemaic and Roman times. Sheshonk by his origin controlled Heracleopolis, and he and his family after him maintained close relations with the High Priests of Ptah at

Memphis. He likewise attempted to hold the support of Thebes to his house by appointing his own son as High Priest of Amon there; but it still remained a distinct principality, capable of offering serious opposition to the ruling family in the Delta. The city itself at least was not taxable by the Pharaoh, and was never visited by his fiscal officials. Under these circumstances an outbreak among the Libyan lords of the Delta or in the two powerful principalities of the South might be expected as soon as there was no longer over them a strong hand like that of Sheshonk I (BAR, IV, 738; 745–747; 699 *f.*; 750).

362. Under the energetic Sheshonk Egypt's foreign policy took on a more aggressive character, and her long merely formal claims upon Palestine were practically pressed. Solomon was evidently an Egyptian vassal who possibly received in marriage a daughter of the Pharaoh and whose territory his Egyptian suzerain extended by the gift of the important city of Gezer, a Canaanite stronghold unsubdued by the Israelites, which the Pharaoh now captured, burned, and presented to Solomon, who rebuilt it. The Pharaoh with whom Solomon had to deal cannot have been one of the degenerate kings at the close of the Twenty-first Dynasty, but an aggressive ruler who resumed Egypt's control in Palestine; and we know of no other king at this time who answers this description save Sheshonk I. After the division of the kingdom of the Hebrews under Solomon's son, Rehoboam, Sheshonk I, who had already harboured the fugitive Jeroboam, Rehoboam's northern enemy, thought it a good opportunity to make his claims in Palestine unquestionable, and in the fifth year of Rehoboam, probably about 926 B. C., he invaded Palestine. His campaign penetrated no further north

than the Sea of Galilee and extended eastward probably as far as Mahanaim on the east of Jordan. According to the Hebrew records, the Egyptians also entered Jerusalem and despoiled it of the wealth gathered there in Solomon's day; but it is clear that Sheshonk's campaign was directed impartially against the two kingdoms and did not affect Judah alone. Among other Palestinian towns which Sheshonk records as taken by him is a place called "Field of Abram," in which we find the earliest occurrence of the name of Israel's patriarchal hero. Sheshonk was able to return with great plunder to replenish the long depleted Pharaonic coffers. He placed a record of the tribute of Palestine and of Nubia, of which he had now gained control, beside those of the great conquerors of the Empire on the walls of the Karnak temple at Thebes. Thus for a time at least the glories of the Empire of the Nineteenth Dynasty were restored with tribute flowing into the treasury from a domain extending from northern Palestine to the upper Nile, and from the oases to the Red Sea (BAR, IV, 750; 709-722; 723-724 A; 782-784; I Kings IX, 15-17; Ibid., XIV, 25; AJSL, XXI, 22-36).

363. With his treasury thus replenished Sheshonk was able to revive the customary building enterprises of the Pharaohs which had been discontinued for over two hundred years. He beautified Bubastis, his Delta residence, and at Thebes undertook a vast court before the Karnak temple. By its south gate, now known as the "Bubastite Portal," the Pharaoh had executed a huge relief in the old style, depicting himself smiting the Asiatics before Amon, who leads and presents to Sheshonk one hundred and fifty-six Palestinian prisoners, each symbolizing a town or locality captured by

Sheshonk and bearing its name. A number of Biblical names may here be recognized (BAR, IV, 709-722).

364. The Libyan rulers who succeeded Sheshonk I were completely Egyptianized, though they retained their Libyan names. When Osorkon I, Sheshonk I's son and heir, followed him, probably about 920 B. C., he succeeded by right of inheritance through his wife, the daughter of Pesibkhenno II. He inherited a prosperous kingdom and enormous wealth, but Thebes, as in the Twenty-first Dynasty, caused great friction, and the problem was not solved by the appointment of the Pharaoh's son as High Priest there. The declining fortunes of the Twenty-second Dynasty can only be dimly discerned in the career of the Theban principality, which, however, clearly exhibits the turbulent and restless character of the feudal princes who now make up the state. We see the High Priest driven from Thebes in a civil war lasting many years, and these events are such as filled the reigns of the last three Bubastites, who continued to hold Thebes and ruled for a hundred years; although their city of Bubastis has perished so completely that little or no record of their careers has survived. To revolt must be added hostilities between the two principalities of Thebes and Heracleopolis, of which there are plain traces, and feuds among the mercenary lords of the Delta. The situation will have closely resembled that under the Mamlukes, when the people, groaning under every oppression and especially exorbitant taxation, often successively taxed by two different lords, rose in revolt after revolt, only to be put down by the mercenaries with slaughter and rapine. Under such circumstances the Pharaoh's influence in Palestine must have totally vanished; but, alarmed at the growing power of Nineveh in Syria, one

THE SUPREMACY OF THE LIBYANS 365

of the Bubastites, probably Takelot II, contributed a quota of a thousand men to the western coalition against the Assyrians, which was defeated by Shalmaneser II at Qarqar on the Orontes in 854 B.C. (BAR, IV, 729–792).

365. It is impossible to determine with certainty the family connection of the last three Bubastites. They held Memphis and Thebes, and their names occasionally appear here and there on minor monuments. It is evident that during their rule the local lords and dynasts of the Delta were gradually gaining their independence, and probably many of them had thrown off their allegiance to the Bubastite house long before the death of Sheshonk IV (745 B.C.), with whom the Twenty-second Dynasty certainly reached its end.

366. One of these Delta lords, named Pedibast, gained the dominant position among his rivals at the death of Sheshonk IV, and founded a new house known to Manetho as the Twenty-third Dynasty. Manetho places this dynasty at Tanis, but Pedibast was of Bubastite origin, like the family which he unseated. A late Demotic papyrus in Vienna contains a folk-tale of long feudal strife, which significantly reveals the unsettled conditions of the time among the turbulent dynasts, whom Pedibast was unable to control. Under his successor, Osorkon III, conditions were no better, until there was at last an independent lord or petty king in every city of the Delta and up the river as far as Hermopolis. We are acquainted with the names of eighteen of these dynasts, whose struggles among themselves now led to the total dissolution of the Egyptian state. Its power was completely paralyzed and the political sagacity of such statesmen as the Hebrew prophets was quite sufficient to perceive how utterly

366 THE DECADENCE OF ANCIENT EGYPT

futile was the policy of the Egyptian party in Israel, which would have depended upon the support of Egypt against the oppression of Assyria. When the troops of Tiglath-pileser III devastated the West down to the frontier of Egypt in 734–732 B.C., the kinglets of the Delta were too involved in their own complicated and petty wars to render the wretched Hebrews any assistance; nor did they foresee that the day must soon come when the great power on the Tigris would cross the desert that separated Egypt from Palestine and for a brief time absorb the ancient kingdom of the Nile. But before this inevitable catastrophe should occur, another foreign power was to possess the throne of the Pharaohs (BAR, IV, 794; 878; 796 *ff*.; 830, No. 2; WZKM, XVII; MSPER, VI, 19 *ff*.).

XXVI

THE ETHIOPIAN SUPREMACY AND THE TRIUMPH OF ASSYRIA.

367. LOWER NUBIA had now been dominated by the Egyptians for over eighteen hundred years, while the country above the second cataract to the region of the fourth cataract had for the most part been under Egyptian control for something like a thousand years. The fertile and productive lands below the fourth cataract, the rich gold mines in the mountains east of Lower Nubia, which compensated in some measure for its agricultural poverty, and the active trade from the Sudan which was constantly passing through the country, made it a land of resources and possibilities, which the Egyptianized Nubians, slowly awakening to their birthright, were now beginning to realize.

368. Shehonk I had still held Nubia, and it is probable that the cataract country was still a dependency of Egypt until the middle of the Twenty-second Dynasty, about 850 B.C. It will be recalled that Nubia had for five centuries been very closely connected with Thebes and the temple of Amon. The control of the Theban High Priest had finally strengthened into full possession of Nubia for two hundred and fifty years. It must have been the Theban priesthood, perhaps as political exiles, who founded the Amonite theocracy which now, as a fully developed Nubian kingdom emerges upon our

view, with its seat of government at Napata, just below the fourth cataract. Napata had been an Egyptian frontier station from the days of Amenhotep II, seven hundred years earlier. It was, moreover, the remotest point in Egyptian Nubia, and hence safest from attack from the North (BAR, IV, 796; 614 *f.*; III, 640).

369. The state which arose here was, in accordance with our explanation of its origin, a reproduction of the Amonite theocracy at Thebes. The state god was Amon, and he continually intervened directly in the affairs of government by specific oracles. The king bore all the Pharaonic titles, calling himself Lord of the Two Lands as if he governed all Egypt. He built temples of Egyptian architecture, decorated with Egyptian reliefs and bearing hieroglyphic inscriptions and dedications of the traditional Egyptian form.

370. By 721 B.C. we suddenly find the Nubian king Piankhi, then over twenty years upon the throne, in possession of Upper Egypt as far north as Heracleopolis, just south of the Fayum, with Nubian garrisons in the more important towns. At this time the Twenty-third Dynasty, represented by Osorkon III at Bubastis, no longer actually ruling more than the district of Bubastis and surrounded by rivals in every important town of the Delta, was confronted by an aggressive and powerful opponent in Tefnakhte, the dynast of Sais, in the western Delta. This Saite had subdued all his neighbours in the western Delta, and beginning the absorption of upper Egypt had already captured Hermopolis. Piankhi sent an army against him, which drove him back into the Delta and began the siege of Hermopolis. Several months later Piankhi himself reached Hermopolis with reinforcements and vigorously pushed the siege, soon forcing the surrender of the place.

THE ETHIOPIAN SUPREMACY

371. The advance to the Delta, sailing down the Bahr Yusuf, was then begun, and the chief towns of the west side surrendered one after another on seeing Piankhi's force. The Nubian king offered sacrifice to the gods in all the cities which he passed, and took possession of all the available property for his own treasury and the estate of Amon. On reaching Memphis it was found to have been very strongly fortified by Tefnakhte, who exhorted the garrison to rely on their strong walls, their plentiful supplies and the high water, which protected the east side from attack, while he rode away northward for reinforcements. Having landed on the north of the city, Piankhi, surprised at the strength of the place, devised a shrewd plan of assault, which speaks highly for his skill as a strategist. The high walls on the west of the city had been recently raised still higher, and it was evident that the east side, protected by waters perhaps artificially raised, was being neglected. Here was the harbour, where the ships now floated so high that their bow ropes were fastened among the houses of the city. Piankhi sent his fleet against the harbour and quickly captured all the shipping. Then, taking command in person, he rapidly ranged the captured craft together with his own fleet along the eastern walls, thus furnishing footing for his assaulting lines, which he immediately sent over the ramparts and captured the city before its eastern defenses could be strengthened against him.

372. The entire region of Memphis then submitted, whereupon the Delta dynasts also appeared in numbers with gifts for Piankhi and signified their submission. Piankhi now crossed the river and followed the old sacred road to Heliopolis, where he camped by the harbour. His annals narrate at length how he entered

the holy of holies of the sun-god here, that he might be recognized as his son and heir to the throne of Egypt, according to custom since the remote days of the Fifth Dynasty. Here king Osorkon III of the Twenty-third Dynasty at Bubastis, now but a petty dynast like the rest, visited Piankhi and recognized the Nubian's suzerainty. Having then moved his camp to a point just east of Athribis, Piankhi there received the submission of the principal Delta lords, fifteen in number.

373. Meantime the desperate Tefnakhte, having been driven from his last fortress, had taken refuge on one of the remote islands in the western mouths of the Nile. Many miles of vast Delta morass and a network of irrigation canals separated Piankhi from the fugitive. It would have been a hazardous undertaking to dispatch an army into such a region. When, therefore, Tefnakhte sent gifts and an humble message of submission requesting that Piankhi send to him a messenger with whom he might go to a neighbouring temple and take the oath of allegiance to his Nubian suzerain, Piankhi was very glad to accept the proposal. This done, a Nubian Pharaoh had obtained complete recognition, had supplanted the Libyans and was lord of all Egypt.

374. When his Delta vassals had paid Piankhi a last visit he loaded his ships with the wealth of the North and sailed away for his southern capital amid the acclamations of the people. Arrived at Napata, Piankhi erected in the temple of Amon a magnificent granite stela, inscribed on all four sides, recording in detail the entire campaign. It is the clearest and most rational account of a military expedition which has survived from ancient Egypt. It is this document of course which has enabled us to follow Piankhi in his conquest of the North (BAR, IV, 796–883).

375. Tefnakhte, while he had nominally submitted to Piankhi, only awaited the withdrawal of the Ethiopian to resume his designs. He eventually succeeded in establishing a kingdom of Lower Egypt, assumed the Pharaonic titles and ruled at least eight years over a feudal state like that of the Twenty-second Dynasty. His reign is parallel with the last years of the Twenty-third Dynasty, which seems to have struggled on at Bubastis as vassal princes under him. In Upper Egypt, Piankhi controlled Thebes long enough to do some slight building in the temple of Mut. In order to gain control of the fortune of Amon with an appearance of legitimacy, Piankhi had caused his sister-wife, Amenardis, to be adopted by Shepnupet, the daughter of Osorkon III, who was sacerdotal princess of Thebes. The device was probably not new. But as Piankhi withdrew, the decadent Twenty-third Dynasty put forth its last expiring effort and established an ephemeral authority in Thebes. Piankhi's invasion of Egypt and entire reign there seem therefore to have fallen within the reign of Osorkon III. But the rising power of Sais soon overwhelmed the failing Bubastites, and Bocchoris, son of Tefnakhte of Sais, gained the throne of Lower Egypt probably about 718 B.C., to be later known as the founder, and in so far as we know, the sole king of the Twenty-fourth Dynasty. The monuments of his brief reign have perished. A doubtless reliable tradition of Greek times makes him a wise lawgiver, and a remarkable Demotic papyrus dated, in the thirty-fourth year of the Roman Emperor Augustus, narrates the prophecies of a lamb uttered in the sixth year of Bocchoris, in which the imminent invasion of Egypt and its conquest by the Assyrians are foretold, seemingly with the assurance that the misfortunes of the unhappy

country should continue nine hundred years. It is the last example of that school of prophetic literature of which Ipuwer of the Middle Kingdom (p. 168) was the earliest representative known to us. Manetho characteristically narrates this marvellous tale as an important occurrence of Bocchoris's reign (BAR, IV, 811; 940; KFB).

376. Egypt had now been under the divided authority of numerous local dynasts for probably over a century and a half. With its vast works of irrigation slowly going to ruin, its roads unprotected, intercourse between cities unsafe and the larger communities suffering from constant turmoil and agitation, the productive capacity of the country was steadily waning, while foreign commerce disappeared. The hopeless state of the country was clearly understood by the sagacious Isaiah, who declared to his people: "Behold the Lord rideth upon a swift cloud and cometh unto Egypt; and the idols of Egypt shall be moved at his presence, and the heart of Egypt shall melt in the midst of it. And I will stir up the Egyptians against the Egyptians; and they shall fight every one against his brother, and every one against his neighbour; city against city and kingdom against kingdom. . . . And I will give over the Egyptians into the hand of a cruel lord; and a fierce king shall rule over them, saith the Lord, the Lord of Hosts. . . . The princes of Zoan [Tanis] are utterly foolish; the counsel of the wisest counsellors of Pharaoh is become brutish. . . . The princes of Zoan are become fools, the princes of Noph [Napata?] are deceived; they have caused Egypt to go astray that are the corner stone of her tribes. The Lord hath mingled a spirit of perverseness in the midst of her; they have caused Egypt to go astray in every work thereof, as a drunken man staggering in

his vomit. Neither shall there be for Egypt any work which head or tail, palm-branch or rush, may do" (Is. XIX). No truer picture could possibly be portrayed.

377. Meantime profound political changes, fraught with the greatest danger to Egypt, were taking place in Asia. Twice already had the westward march of Assyria disquieted the Pharaoh (pp. 354, 366,). Rousing Assyria from a period of temporary decadence, Tiglath-pileser III had brought her full power to bear upon the West, and in 734 to 732 B.C. had ravaged Syria-Palestine to the very borders of Egypt. The Aramæan kingdom of Damascus fell and the whole west was organized as dependencies of Assyria. In the short reign of Shalmaneser IV, who followed Tiglath-pileser III, Israel with others was encouraged to revolt by Sewe or So, probably an otherwise unknown Delta dynast. Before the Assyrian invasion which resulted, Samaria held out for some years; but under Shalmaneser IV's great successor, Sargon II, it fell in 722 B.C. The chief families of Israel were deported and the nation, as such, was annihilated. Unable to oppose the formidable armies of Assyria, the petty kinglets of Egypt, constantly fomented discontent and revolt among the Syro-Palestinian states in order if possible to create a fringe of buffer states between them and the Assyrian. In 720 B.C. Sargon again appeared in the west to suppress a revolt in which Egypt doubtless had a hand. Completely victorious in the north, he marched southward to Raphia, where he totally defeated the allies of the south, among whom Egypt had a levy of troops under a commander named Sib'i. The Assyrian hosts had now twice swept down to the very borders of Egypt, and the dynasts must by this time have been fully

aware of their danger. In 715 B.C. Sargon's records report the reception of gifts from Pir'u (Pharaoh) of Egypt, who will probably have been Bocchoris (II Kings, XVII, 4; WUAG, 93 *f.*).

378. Such was the threatening situation of Egypt when, probably about 711 B.C., after an interval of some ten years since the retirement of Piankhi, the Nubian kings again appeared in the North. Piankhi had now been succeeded by his brother, Shabaka, with whom the uninterrupted series of pure Ethiopian royal names begins. We possess no native records of his conquest of the country, but Manetho states that he burned Bocchoris alive. Lower Egypt was completely subdued, Ethiopian supremacy acknowledged and Shabaka entrenched himself so firmly that he became the founder of the Twenty-fifth or Ethiopian Dynasty, as reported by Manetho. Appreciating the serious danger of Assyria's presence on his very borders, Shabaka immediately sent his agents among the Syro-Palestinian states to excite them to revolt. In Philistia, Judah, Moab and Edom he promised the vassals of Assyria support in rebellion against their Ninevite suzerain. Remembering the ancient supremacy of Egypt, failing to understand the state of decadent impotence into which she had fallen, and anxious to shake off the oppressive Assyrian yoke, they lent a ready ear to the emissaries of Shabaka. Only in Judah did the prophet-statesman, Isaiah, foresee the futility of depending upon Egypt, and the final catastrophe which should overtake her at the hands of Assyria. The vigilant Assyrian, however, hearing of the projected alliance, acted so quickly that the conspirators were glad to drop their designs and protest fidelity. In spite of difficulties in Babylon and rebel-

lions in the north, the able and aggressive Sargon pushed the consolidation of his power with brilliant success and left to his son Sennacherib in 705 B.C. the first stable and firmly compacted empire ever founded by a Semitic power (Is., XX; WUAG; BAR, IV, 920).

379. Sennacherib was embarrassed in his earlier years with the usual complications in Babylon. Mardukbaliddin (Merodach-baladan), an able and active claimant of the Babylonian throne, who had already caused Sennacherib's father much trouble, now sent his emissaries to stir up defection and create a diversion in his favour in the west. As a result Luli, the energetic king of Tyre, Hezekiah of Judah, the dynasts of Edom, Moab and Ammon, with the chiefs of their Beduin neighbours, in fact, all the southern half of the Assyrian conquests in the west besides Egypt were finally organized in a great alliance against Nineveh. Before the allies could act in concert, Sennacherib suddenly appeared in the west, marched down the Phœnician coast, capturing all its strongholds save Tyre; and pressed on southward to the revolting Philistine cities. Here, having punished Askalon, he advanced to Altaqu, where he came upon the motley army gathered by the tardy Shabaka among his northern vassals, whom Sennacherib calls "the Kings of Muçri" (Egypt). We know nothing of the strength of this force, although Sennacherib claims that they were "without number;" but it is safe to conclude that it was not a formidable army. A loose aggregation of levies from the domains of the local Delta princes was little fitted to meet the compact and finely organized armies which the Assyrian kings had gradually developed, till they had become the dread and terror of the west. Although small Egyptian

contingents had before served as auxiliaries against the Assyrians, the armies of the two empires on the Nile and the Tigris had never before faced each other. Sennacherib led his own power in person while the Egyptian army was entrusted by Shabaka to his nephew, a son of Piankhi, named Taharka, who some thirteen or fourteen years afterward became king of Ethiopia, a fact which led the Hebrew annalist to give him that title already at the time of this campaign. There was but one possible issue for the battle; Sennacherib disposed of Taharka's army without difficulty, having meanwhile beleaguered Jerusalem and devastated Judah far and wide. He had effectually stamped out the disaffection in the west and completely discomfited the allies, but before he could take Jerusalem the plague-infected winds from the malarial shores east of the Delta had scattered death among his troops. This overwhelming catastrophe, together with disquieting news from Babylon, forced him hastily to retire to Nineveh, thus bringing to Jerusalem the deliverance promised by Isaiah, an event in which pious tradition afterward saw the destroying angel of the Lord. This deliverance was perhaps as fortunate for Egypt as for Jerusalem. For the third time the invincible Assyrian army had stood on the very threshold of Egypt, and still the decrepit nation on the Nile for a little time was spared the inevitable humiliation which was now so near. The Syro-Palestinian princes, however, were so thoroughly cowed that Egypt was thenceforth unable to seduce them to rebellion. Like the Hebrews, they at last recognized the truth, as mockingly stated by the officers of Sennacherib to the unhappy ambassadors of Jerusalem: "Now behold, thou trustest upon the staff of this bruised reed, even upon Egypt; whereon if a man lean it will go into his hand and pierce it; so is Pharaoh king of Egypt unto all that trust on him" (Note VIII; BAR, IV, 892; 2 Kings, XIX, 9; XVIII, 21).

380. Shabaka apparently ruled his vassal Egyptian states for the remainder of his reign in peace. The fragments of a clay tablet bearing the seal of Shabaka and a king of Assyria, found at Kuyunjik, may indicate some agreement between the two nations. At Thebes Shabaka reinstated Amenardis, his sister, who must have been temporarily expelled by Osorkon III. Together with her, he built a chapel at Karnak, and his building operations necessitated an expedition to the distant quarries of Hammamat. We also find records of his temple restorations at Thebes, and it is evident that he governed Egypt at least in his relations with the temples, precisely as a native Pharaoh would have done. It was probably Shabaka who now broke the power of the High Priest of Amon, of whose impotence we shall see further evidence as we proceed.

381. About 700 B.C., Shabaka was succeeded by Shabataka, another Ethiopian, whose connection with the reigning Ethiopian or Nubian family is a little uncertain, although Manetho, who calls him Sebichos, makes him a son of Shabaka. As the western vassals remained quiet and Sennacherib was now absorbed in his operations at the other extremity of his empire, Shabataka was unmolested by the Assyrian. His name is rare in Egypt, but it is evident from the conditions which survived him that he was entirely unable to exterminate the local dynasts and consolidate the power of Egypt for the supreme struggle which was before her. It was indeed now patent that the Ethiopians were quite unfitted for the imperial task before them. The southern strain with which their blood was tinct-

ured began to appear as the reign of Shabataka drew to a close about 688 B.C.

382. It is at this juncture that we can trace the rising fortunes of a son of Piankhi, prince Taharka, whose features, as preserved in contemporary sculptures, show unmistakable negroid characteristics. He had been entrusted with the command of the army in the campaign against Sennacherib. While we know nothing of the circumstances which brought about his advent to the throne, Manetho states, that leading an army from Ethiopia he slew Sebichos, who must be Shabataka, and seized the crown. The contemporary monuments, without intimation of these events, abruptly picture him in Tanis as king, summoning his mother, whom he has not seen for many years, from Napata to Tanis, that she may assume her proper station as queen-mother there. In view of this fact and the trouble to be anticipated from Assyria, it is not improbable that the Ethiopians at this time maintained Tanis as their Egyptian residence (BAR, IV, 892–896).

383. For some thirteen years Taharka ruled his kingdom without molestation from Asia. The west had for twenty years seen nothing of Sennacherib, who was now assassinated by his sons, in 681 B.C. As soon as his son, Esarhaddon, could arrange the affairs of the great empire to which he had succeeded, he determined to resort to the only possible remedy for the constant interference of Egypt with the authority of Assyria in Palestine, viz., the conquest of the Nile country and humiliation of the Pharaoh. With farseeing thoroughness, he laid his plans for the execution of this purpose, and his army was knocking at the frontier fortresses of the eastern Delta in 674 B.C. But Taharka, who was a man of far greater ability than his two Ethiopian pred-

ecessors, must have made a supreme effort to meet the crisis. The outcome of the battle (673 B. C.) was unfavourable for the Assyrian if indeed, as the documents perhaps indicate, he did not suffer positive defeat. But Esarhaddon nevertheless quietly continued his preparations for the conquest of Egypt. Baal, king of Tyre, perhaps encouraged by the undecisive result of the first Assyrian invasion, then rebelled, making common cause with Taharka. In 670 B. C. Esarhaddon was again in the West at the head of his forces. Having invested Tyre, he defeated and scattered the Egyptian army. As the Ethiopian fell back upon Memphis, Esarhaddon pressed him closely, and besieged and captured the city, which fell a rich prey to the cruel and rapacious Ninevite army. Fleeing southward Taharka abandoned Lower Egypt, which was immediately organized by Esarhaddon into dependencies of Assyria. He records the names of twenty lords of the Delta, formerly Ethiopian vassals, who now took the oath of fealty to him. Among these names, written in cuneiform, a number may be recognized as those of the same men with eighteen of whom Piankhi had to deal in the same region. Necho, doubtless a descendant of Tefnakhte, occupies the most prominent place among them as prince of Sais and Memphis. The list also includes a prince of Thebes, but Esarhaddon certainly possessed no more than a merely nominal authority in Upper Egypt at this time. As he returned to Nineveh, northward along the coast road, he hewed in the rocks at the Dog River, beside the triumphant stelæ of Ramses II (p. 303), a record of his great achievement; while in Samal (Senjirli), in north Syria, he erected a similar monument representing himself of heroic stature, leading two captives, of whom one is probably Baal of Tyre, and the other, as his negroid features indicate, is the unfortunate Taharka (WUAG, 97 *ff.*).

384. After the domination of Libyan and Nubian in turn, Egypt was now a prey to a third foreign conqueror, who, however, differed essentially from the others, in that he resided abroad, and evinced not the slightest sympathy with Egyptian institutions or customs. The result was that the Delta kinglets, who had sworn allegiance to the Ninevite, immediately plotted with Taharka for the resumption of his rule in Lower Egypt, which he thereupon assumed without much delay on the withdrawal of the Assyrian army. Esarhaddon was thus forced to begin his work over again; but in 668 B. C., while on the march to resume operations in Egypt, he died. With but slight delay the campaign was continued by his son, Ashurbanipal, who placed one of his commanders in charge of the expedition. Between Memphis and the frontier of the eastern Delta, Taharka was again routed. He fled to Thebes, this time pursued by the Assyrians who made the forty days' march thither, determined to expel him from Egypt. Whether the enemy actually captured Thebes at this time is somewhat doubtful. In any case, Ashurbanipal was still unable to extend his authority to Upper Egypt. He had hardly restored his supremacy in the Delta when his vassals there again began communicating with Taharka, purposing his restoration as before. But their correspondence with Taharka was discovered by the Assyrian officials in Egypt, and they were sent to Nineveh in chains. There the wily Necho, whom Esarhaddon had made king of Sais, was able to win the confidence of Ashurbanipal, who pardoned him, loaded him with honours and restored him to his kingdom in Sais, while his son was appointed to rule Athribis. At the same

time Ashurbanipal accompanied him with Assyrian officials, intended of course to be a check upon his conduct. Taharka was now unable to gain any further foothold among the Assyrian vassals in the Delta. He probably held Thebes, where he controlled the fortune of Amon by causing his sister, Shepnupet, to be adopted by Amenardis the "Divine Votress," or sacerdotal princess of Thebes, who had been appointed by Piankhi in the same way. At Napata Taharka either built or enlarged two considerable temples, and the Ethiopian capital evidently became a worthy royal residence in his time (BAR, IV, 901–916; 940; 897 *ff.*).

385. Taharka survived but a few months his appointment of Tanutamon, a son of Shabaka as coregent, who then succeeded to the crown in 663 B. C. Encouraged by a favourable dream, Tanutamon undertook the recovery of Lower Egypt, defeated the Assyrian commanders, retook Memphis, and demanded the submission of the Delta dynasts. He had hardly settled in Memphis, when Ashurbanipal's army appeared and drove the Ethiopian for the last time from Lower Egypt. The Assyrians pursued him to Thebes, and as he ingloriously withdrew southward, they sacked and plundered the magnificent capital of Egypt's age of splendour. The story of the ruin of Thebes spread to all the peoples around, and when the prophet Nahum was denouncing the coming destruction of Nineveh, fifty years later, the desolation of Thebes was still fresh in his mind. From this time the fortunes of the venerable city steadily declined and its splendours, such as no city of the early orient had ever displayed, gradually faded. It entered upon the long centuries of lingering decay which have left it at the present day still the

mightiest ruin surviving from the ancient world (BAR, IV, 919–934; Nahum, III, 8–10; WUAG).

386. As the Assyrians withdrew from Thebes, Tanutamon again entered the desolated city, where he maintained himself for at least six years more (till 655 B. C.). By 654 B. C. he had disappeared from Thebes, whether by death or retirement, and his disappearance was the termination of Ethiopian supremacy in Egypt (see Note IX). At a time when Assyria was dominating the East, without a worthy rival elsewhere to stay her hand, it was to be expected that the historic people of the Nile should confront her and dispute her progress on even terms. To this great task the Ethiopians were appointed; but in fact Assyria was never dealing with a first-class power in her conquest of Egypt. The Nubians were not the men to reorganize a long decadent and disorganized nation, and the unhappy Nile-dwellers, in hopeless impotence, looked in vain for a strong ruler, throughout the supremacy of the inglorious Ethiopians.

387. Withdrawing to Napata, the Ethiopians never made another attempt to subdue the kingdom of the lower river, but gave their attention to the development of Nubia. As the Egyptians resident in the country died out and were not replaced by others, the Egyptian gloss which the people had received began rapidly to disappear, and the land relapsed into a semi-barbaric condition. The theocratic character of the government became more and more pronounced until the king was but a puppet in the hands of the priests, at whose behest he was obliged even to take his own life and make way for another weakling whom the priests might choose. The nation soon turned its face southward. By 560 B. C. the Nubian kings were occupying their new capital,

far above the fifth cataract, known to the Greeks as Meroe. Apart from other considerations, the wisdom of thus placing the difficult cataract region between the capital and invaders from the north was shown by the discomfiture of Cambyses' expedition against Nubia at the hands of its king Nastesen in 525 B. C. As the nation shifted southward it was completely withdrawn from contact with the northern world; and Ethiopia, gradually lost behind a mist of legend, became the wonderland celebrated in Greek story as the source of civilization. The Egyptian language and hieroglyphics, which the kings had hitherto used for their records, now slowly disappeared, and by the beginning of our era the native language was finally written in a script which as yet is undeciphered. When a century or two after the Roman conquests, the Ethiopian kingdom slowly collapsed and fell to pieces, its northern districts were absorbed by wild hordes of the Blemmyes who pushed in from the east; while in the south it was succeeded by the Christian kingdom of Abyssinia, which rose at the sources of the Blue Nile in the fourth century A. D. and finally acquired the name of its ancient Ethiopian predecessor.

PART VIII

THE RESTORATION AND THE END

XXVII

THE RESTORATION

388. On the death of Necho of Sais, probably at the hands of Tanutamon, Psamtik his son had fled to the Assyrians. Having thus shown his fidelity, he was installed over his father's kingdom of Sais and Memphis by Ashurbanipal. The Delta continued under the mercenary lords in control there with some interruptions since the Twenty-first Dynasty, while in Upper Egypt, as we have seen, Tanutamon at first maintained himself at Thebes. Outwardly there was little indication of the brilliant day which was now dawning upon the long afflicted nation. Psamtik, scion of a line of men of marked power and political sagacity, soon shook off the restraint and supervision of the resident Assyrian officials. He can hardly have been unaware that Ashurbanipal was ere long to be engaged in a deadly struggle with his brother, the king of Babylon, involving dangerous complications with Elam. As this war came on (652 B. C.) an attempt of the Arabian tribes to send aid to Babylon demanded an Assyrian expedition thither; while disturbances among the peoples on the northern borders of the Ninevite empire and the necessity of meeting the Cimmerians in Cilicia required liberal assignments of Ashurbanipal's available military forces to these regions. It was over twelve years before these difficulties were all adjusted, and when in 640 B. C.

peace at last settled upon the Assyrian empire, Psamtik's movement had gone too far and Ashurbanipal evidently did not care to risk opposing it.

389. With Psamtik, the Greek traditions regarding Egypt begin to be fairly trustworthy, if the folk-tales which the Greeks so readily credited be properly sifted. In these, as transmitted by Herodotus, we can follow the rise of Psamtik, as he employs the Ionian and Carian mercenaries dispatched from Asia Minor by Gyges, king of Lydia, who at this juncture, after courting the Assyrians to save himself from the Cimmerian hordes, is anxious to combine with Egypt in common opposition to Ninevite aggression. The Assyrian annals state that he sent assistance to Egypt. It is not to be doubted that Psamtik took advantage of these favouring circumstances in the creation of which he had of course had a hand, and by such means gained permanent ascendency over the local dynasts.

390. His progress was rapid. By 654 B. C., while Ashurbanipal was attacking Babylon, he had gained Thebes, where Tanutamon had by that time either died or retired to Napata (See Note IX). In order to obtain legitimate control of the fortune of Amon, now of course much depleted, Psamtik decreed that his daughter Nitocris should be adopted by the Divine Votress at Thebes, Shepnupet, the sister of the deceased Taharka. The collapse of the high priesthood of Amon was now so complete that within sixty years the once powerful office was actually held by these sacerdotal princesses. The High Priest of Amon was a woman! In the suppression of the mercenary lords and local dynasts by Psamtik, the nation was at last rescued from the unstable rule of a body of feudal lords and their turbulent military adherents, under whose irresponsible

tyranny it had suffered, with but brief respites, for some four hundred years. This remarkable achievement of Psamtik I places him among the ablest rulers who ever sat on the throne of the Pharaohs. He was not, however, able completely to exterminate the dynasts, as is commonly stated. Some of them would of course espouse his cause and thus gain immunity, like Mentemhet, prince of Thebes, or Prince Hor of Heracleopolis (BAR, IV, 937; 949; 935-958; 988 D; 967-973; 902 end).

391. A not less troublesome problem was the organization of the military class. The now completely Egyptianized Libyans who had lived in Egypt for centuries had finally developed into a warrior-class of no great effectiveness, whose numbers at this time absurdly exaggerated by Herodotus, we cannot determine. Besides that of the feudal lords, it was also the opposition of this class which Psamtik had been obliged to face; and he had no recourse but to pit against them his northern mercenaries, the Greeks and Carians. Thus Egypt, having suffered the inevitable fate of a military kingdom in the ancient world, was passing into the control of one foreign warrior-class after another. The army which Psamtik I now put together was made up of Greeks, Carians and Syrians on the one hand, and on the other of Libyans and their Egyptianized kindred. The Ionians and Carians were stationed on the northeastern frontier near Daphnæ, with a branch of the Nile running through their camp; while the border of the western Delta was secured by a body of the warrior-class in a stronghold at Marea, not far from the site of later Alexandria. At Elephantine a similar garrison was maintained against any invasion from the south. Herodotus relates that two hundred and forty thousand

of the warrior-class, having been kept at one station for three years without being relieved, thereupon deserted and departed in a body southward to offer their services to the king of Ethiopia at Meroe. While his numbers are incredibly exaggerated, as usual, the story must contain a germ of fact as it accords with all that we know of the conditions in Psamtik's time. As a concession to this class his body-guard contained a thousand men from each of the two classes, the Hermotybies and Calasyries; but he will have had many more of his hardy Greeks and Carians at his hand on all occasions.

392. The prosperous and powerful Egypt which was now emerging from the long Decadence was totally different from the Egypt of any earlier renascence. It was impossible again to rouse the nation to arms as in the days when the Hyksos were expelled; it was therefore inevitably the deliberate policy of Psamtik I, while expending every effort to put the nation on a sound economic basis, at the same time to depend upon foreign soldiery for the military power indispensable to an oriental ruler. His necessarily constant care was to transmute the economic prosperity of the land into military power. In a word, the wealth of the land must nourish and maintain a formidable army, even though the effective portion of this army might be aliens. A revival under such conditions as these is due almost solely to the personal initiative of the sovereign who manipulates the available forces: those of power and those of industry; so employing them all in harmonious interaction that prosperity and effective power result. Psamtik was himself the motive and creative power, while the people were but given the opportunity to fulfil their proper functions and to move freely in their wonted channels. There was no longer any great

relative vitality in the nation, and the return of ordered government and consequent prosperity enabled them to indulge the tendency to retrospect already observable in the Twenty-third Dynasty. The nation fell back upon the past and consciously endeavoured to restore and rehabilitate the vanished state of the old days before the changes and innovations introduced by the Empire. Seen through the mist of over a thousand years, what was to *them* ancient Egypt was endowed with the ideal perfection of the divine régime which had preceded it. The worship of the kings who had ruled at Memphis in those remote days was revived and the ritual of their mortuary service maintained and endowed. Their pyramids were even extensively restored and repaired. The archaic titles and the long array of dignities worn by the lords at the court and in the government of the pyramid-builders were again brought into requisition, and in the externals of government everything possible was done to clothe it with the appearance of remote antiquity. The writing of the time was also given an archaic colour on formal and official monuments, and its antique forms must have cost the Saite scribes long and weary study. In religion every effort was made to purify the pantheon of all modern interlopers and to rid the ritual of every innovation. Everything foreign in religion was banished, and Set, the god of the waste and the desert, was everywhere exterminated. An inexorable exclusiveness, like that which was soon to take possession of the new-born Jewish community, was also now universally enforced. The ancient mortuary texts of the pyramids were revived, and although frequently not understood were engraved upon the massive stone sarcophagi. The Book of the Dead, which now received its last redaction, becoming a roll sixty feet long, shows plain traces of the revival of this ancient mortuary literature. In the tomb-chapels we find again the fresh and pleasing pictures from the life of the people in marsh and meadow, in workshop and shipyard. They are perfect reproductions of the relief scenes in the mastabas of the Old Kingdom, so perfect indeed that at the first glance one is not infrequently in doubt as to the age of the monument. Indeed, a man named Aba at Thebes sent his artists to an Old Kingdom tomb near Siut to copy the reliefs thence for use in his own Theban tomb, because the owner of the ancient tomb was also named Aba.

393. In this endeavour to reconstitute modern religion, society and government upon ancient lines, the archaizers must consciously or unconsciously have been constantly thwarted by the inevitable mutability of the social, political and economic conditions of a race. The two thousand years which had elapsed since the Old Kingdom could not be annihilated. Through the deceptive mantle of antiquity with which they cloaked contemporary conditions, the inexorable realities of the present were discernible. The solution of this difficulty, when perceived, was the same as that attempted by the Hebrews in a similar dilemma: it was but to attribute to the modern elements also a hoary antiquity, as the whole body of Hebrew legislation was attributed to Moses. The theoretical revival was thus rescued. This was especially easy for the Egyptian of the Saitic restoration; for, long before his time it had been customary to attribute to the Old Kingdom especially sacred mortuary texts, favourite medical prescriptions and collections of proverbial wisdom. While in some cases such attribution may have been correct in the

days of the Empire, this was no longer generally true in the Twenty-sixth Dynasty. In one particular especially, it was impossible to force the present into the ancient mould; I refer to the artistic capacity of the people. This always fruitful element of their culture was now a marked exception to the lifeless lack of initiative displayed in all other functions of life. Here their creative vitality, already revived in the Ethiopian period, was still unblighted, and their artistic sense was keenly alive to the new possibilities open to them under the new order. We have seen that the Restoration in religion demanded the revival of the old subjects in the tomb-chapel reliefs, and in spite of the likeness of these copies to their ancient models, more than a superficial examination invariably discloses a distinct character and manner peculiarly their own. There is just that touch of freedom which the art of the Old Kingdom lacked, and a soft beauty in their sinuous and sweeping lines which adds an indescribable grace to the reliefs of the Saitic school. While the old canons and conventionalities still prevailed in general, there was now and then an artist who could shake them off and place the human body in relief with the shoulders drawn in proper relations and freed from the distortion of the Old Kingdom. It was this freedom and ability to see things as they are which led to a school of portraiture surpassing the best work of the Old Kingdom. These portrait heads both in relief and in the round, display a study of the bony conformation of the skull, the folds and wrinkles of the skin, in fine a mastery of the entire anatomical development and a grasp of individual character such as no early art had yet achieved. Such works can only be compared with the portraits of the Greek sculptors at the height of their skill, and they do not suffer by the comparison. The artist in bronze was now supreme, *hollow* casts of considerable size were made and animal forms are especially fine. Superb bronze statues elaborately inlaid with rich designs in gold, silver and electrum display surprising refinements in technique. Works in bronze are now very numerous and most of those which fill the modern museums were produced in this age. Industrial art flourished as never before and the Egyptian craftsman was rarely rivalled. In fayence the manufactories of the time were especially successful and prolific, and the museum collections are filled with works of this period. The architecture of the time has, alas, perished, and if we may judge from the achievements of the Saitic sculptor, we have in this respect suffered irreparable loss; for it is probable that we owe the origin of the rich and beautiful columns of Ptolemaic temples to the Saite architect.

394. While the material products of art offered visual evidence of marked divergence from the ancient prototype which it was supposed to follow, such incongruities in the organization of the government, while not less real, were probably not so evident. From the few surviving monuments of the period the real character of the state is not clearly determinable. Geographically the Delta had forever become the dominant region. The development of commerce with the northern world and related political reasons had made this northward shift inevitable and permanent. Psamtik and his descendants lived in their native Sais, which now became a great and splendid city, adorned with temples and palaces. Thebes no longer possessed either political or religious significance. The valley of the Nile was but an appendage upon the Delta. We have already referred to the survival of certain of the feudal lords. They

may have retained their lands, but, judging from the case of Mentemhet of Thebes, they could not bequeath them to their sons. With these exceptions all the land belonged to the crown and was worked by the peasant serfs, who rendered twenty per cent. of the yield to the Pharaoh. Priests and soldiers were exempt from taxation. The administration must have been conducted as under the Empire by local officials of the central government, who collected the taxes and possessed judicial powers. The archaic titles which they bear, as far as I have been able to trace them, usually correspond to no real functions in government. In education and training these men are fundamentally different from the scribal officials of the Empire, in that they are not of necessity possessed of a knowledge of the old hieroglyphic. Since the Ethiopian Dynasty there has grown up a very cursive form of hieratic, the ancient running hand. This new and more rapid form, an unconscious development, is better suited to the needs of practical business and administration, and being in common and everyday use was therefore known to the Greeks as "demotic" writing, a term now usually applied to it at the present day. It represented the language then spoken, while the hieroglyphic of the time, which continued to lead an artificial existence, employed the archaic form of the language which had prevailed centuries before. That this fundamental change was but one among many modifications and alterations in the government, must of necessity have resulted from the changed conditions. Socially, the influence of revived industry had divided the people into more or less sharply defined classes or guilds, determined by their occupations; but "caste" in the proper significance of the term, was as unknown as at any time in Egyptian history.

395. The priests succeeded little better than the officials in their revival of the good old times. It is, indeed, to the priesthoods in general that the attempted restoration must be largely attributed. The religious, like the political, centre, had completely shifted; Thebes, as we have stated, no longer possessed any religious significance. In the Delta cities of Sais, Athribis and Buto were the wealthiest temples. Quite in contrast with conditions in the Old Kingdom, the priests now constituted a more exclusive and distinct class than ever before, and the office had become inalienably hereditary. Venerated by the people, it was a political necessity that their maintenance should be provided for by liberal revenues. While they no longer possessed any political influence to be compared with that which they exercised under the Empire, yet we find the old count of Thinis deprived of his ancient revenues from the oases and the local ferry, that they may be transferred to Osiris. The reverse was, however, the rule, as we shall see. The old gods could not be resuscitated; among them only Osiris still maintained himself. His consort, Isis, contrary to the ancient customs, acquired an elaborate cultus, and the wide celebrity which afterward brought her such general favour in the classic world. Imhotep, the wise man of Zoser's court twenty-five hundred years earlier, now gained a place among the gods, as son of Ptah, an innovation of which the priests were unconscious. The religion which the priests represented was the inevitable result of the tendencies observable at the close of the Empire. It consisted as far as daily life and conduct were concerned, like the Rabbinical faith born under very similar conditions, in innumerable external usages, and the most painful observance of the laws of ceremonial purity. It was an age of unhealthy

and excessive religiousness. We find nobles and officials everywhere erecting sanctuaries to the gods. While formerly only one of a class of animals was sacred, now in many cases every representative of that class was inviolable. The increased reverence for these manifestations of the gods is especially illustrated in the elaborate worship of the Apis-bull, a form of Ptah, and the vast sepulchre, where they now received their gorgeous burial, the Serapeum of Memphis became famous among the Greeks. While a slight inclination toward this tendency was observable already in the Old Kingdom, it now took on the crass form, which finally led to the fanatical excesses of the Alexandrians in Roman times. It is probable that the priests read into all these outward manifestations, as into their mythological tales, a higher meaning, which they never originally possessed; but we are unable to determine whether they actually taught all that the Greeks attribute to them of this character. While their education in the Empire had kept them in contact with the living times, they were now obliged to learn a language and a method of writing, and to acquaint themselves with a mass of inherited literature, with which the busy world around them had long parted company. It was by this process that the ancient writing, already early regarded as of divine origin, became a sacred accomplishment, the especial characteristic of sacred learning, and was therefore called by the Greeks "hieroglyphs" or sacred glyphs. Such an education necessarily projected the priests far back into a long forgotten world, whose inherited wisdom, as among the Chinese or the Mohammedans, was the final word. The writings and sacred rolls of the past were now eagerly sought out, and with the dust of ages upon them, they were collected, sorted and arranged. Thus the past was supreme; the priest who cherished it lived in a realm of shadows, and for the contemporary world he had no vital meaning. Likewise in Babylon the same retrospective spirit was now the dominant characteristic of the reviving empire of Nebuchadrezzar. The world was already growing old, and everywhere men were fondly dwelling on her faraway youth (BAR, IV, 956; 1024; 967 *ff.*; 989 *ff.*; 1015 *ff.*).

396. While the internal aspects of the Saitic period are so largely retrospective that it has been well called the Restoration, yet its foreign policy shows little consideration for the past. In sharp contrast with the attempted restoration and especially with the national exclusiveness, now more intense than ever, was the foreign policy of Psamtik I. The reorganization of ordered and centralized government, and the restoration of the elaborate irrigation system, were quite sufficient to ensure the internal prosperity of the country along traditional lines. But Psamtik's early life and training led him to do more than this. He comprehended the great economic value of foreign traffic to the nation he was building up; nor did he fail to perceive that such traffic might be variously taxed and made to yield large revenues for his own treasury. He therefore revived the old connections with Syria; Phœnician galleys filled the Nile mouths, and Semitic merchants, forerunners of the Aramæans so numerous in Persian times, thronged the Delta. If Psamtik was able to employ the Greeks in his army he found them not less useful in the furtherance of his commercial projects. From the eighth century B.C. those southern movements of the northerners, of which the incursions of the "sea-peoples" over five hundred years earlier (pp. 333 *ff.*) were

the premonitory symptom, had now become daily occurrences. The Greeks, pushing in from the far North, and emerging clearly for the first time into history, had long since gained possession of the Greek peninsula and its adjacent archipelago, with their centres of Mycænean civilization, and they now appeared as prosperous communities and rapidly growing maritime states, whose fleets, penetrating throughout the Mediterranean, offered the Phœnicians sharp and incessant competition. Their colonies and industrial settlements, with active manufactories, rapidly fringed the Mediterranean and penetrated the Black Sea. Psamtik was probably the first of the Egyptian rulers who favoured such colonies in Egypt. Ere long the country was filled with Greek merchants and their manufacturing settlements were permitted, especially in the western Delta, near the royal residence at Sais. There was a Greek and also a Carian quarter in Memphis, and not unlikely other large cities were similarly apportioned to accommodate foreigners, especially Greeks.

397. Lines of communication between the Greek states and Egypt soon established direct, continuous and in some respects intimate relations between them. Greek recruits for the army of course followed constantly upon those whom Psamtik had employed in his conquest, and these, with the active intercourse of the indefatigable Greek merchants, carried back to the mother-country an ever increasing fund of folk-tales, telling of the wondrous Egyptian world, which was so new and strange to them. The marvels of Thebes were celebrated in the Homeric songs, now assuming their final form, and Egyptian gods appeared in their myths.

398. Ultimately the Greeks became very familiar with the externals of Egyptian civilization, but they never learned to read its curious writing sufficiently well to understand its surviving records, or to learn the truth as to its ancient history. As time passed a body of interpreters arose, who became so numerous as to form a recognized class. By these such questioners as Herodotus were often grossly imposed upon. The impenetrable reserve of the Egyptians, and again their unlimited claims, profoundly impressed the imaginative Greek. This impression could only be deepened by the marvels with which the land was filled: the enormous buildings and temples, whose construction was often a mystery to him; the mystic writing which covered their walls; the strange river, unlike any he had ever seen; the remarkable religion, whose mysterious ritual seemed to him the cloak for the most profound truths; the unquestionably vast antiquity of countless impressive monuments all about him; all this, where an unprejudiced, objective study of the people and their history was impossible, inevitably blinded even the Greek of the highest intelligence and culture, who now visited the country. Thus the real character of the Egyptian and his civilization was never correctly understood by the Greeks, and their writings regarding the Nile country, even though often ridiculing its strange customs, have transmitted to us a false impression as to the value especially of its intellectual achievements. The Greek, with his insatiable thirst for the truth, and his constant attitude of healthy inquiry, was vastly superior, I need hardly say, to the Egyptian, whose reputed wisdom he so venerated. Under these circumstances it was only the later political history of the country, the course of which came under their own

immediate observation, with which the Greeks were familiar. From the time of Psamtik I we possess a fund of popular Greek tradition regarding the Twenty-sixth Dynasty, which, if properly used, throws an invaluable light upon a time when native records and monuments, located as they were in the exposed Delta, have almost entirely perished.

399. Before the impact of the foreign life, which thus flowed in upon Egypt, the Egyptian showed himself entirely unmoved, and held himself aloof, fortified behind his ceremonial purity and his inviolable reserve. If he could have had his way he would have banished the foreigners one and all from his shores; under the circumstances, like the modern Chinese, he trafficked with them and was reconciled to their presence by the gain they brought him. Thus, while the Saitic Pharaohs, as we shall further see, were profoundly influenced by the character of the Greeks, the mass of the Egyptians were unscathed by it. On the other hand, the Greeks must have profited much by the intercourse with Nile valley civilization although it will have been chiefly material profit which they gained. They found there, perfected and ready at hand, the technical processes, which their unique genius was so singularly able to apply to the realization of higher ends than those governing the older civilizations. They certainly borrowed artistic forms in plenty, and the artistic influences from the Nile, which had been felt in the Mycenæan centres of civilizations as far back at least as the Twelfth Dynasty (2000 B.C.), were still a power in the same regions of the North. It can be no accident, in spite of the widespread "law of frontality," that the archaic Apollos (so-called), first produced by the Ionian Greeks, reproduce the standing posture prevalent in

Egypt in every detail, including the characteristic thrusting forward of the left foot. Of the Saitic portrait sculptor, the Greeks might have learned much, even far down toward the days of their highest artistic achievements. Evidence of intellectual influence is more elusive, but there is a grain of truth in the Greek tradition that they received their philosophy from Egypt. The philosophizing theology of the Egyptian priests contained suggestive germs, which may easily have found their way into the early Ionian systems. The notion of the primeval intelligence and the creative "word," already conceived as far back as the Eighteenth Dynasty (p. 266), could hardly fail to influence the educated Greeks who very early visited Egypt, long before such a conception had arisen in Greece. The insistent belief of the Egyptian in the life hereafter and his elaborate mortuary usages, unquestionably exerted a strong influence upon Greek and Roman alike; and the wide dissemination of Egyptian religion in the classic world, demonstrates the deep impression which it now made. To this day its symbols are turned up by the spade throughout the Mediterranean basin. It was under Psamtik I that these influences from Egypt begin to be traceable in the states, which were then laying the foundations of later European civilization; and it is significant as an indication of the great restorer's personal prestige in the Greek world that the powerful Periander of Corinth named his nephew and successor Psammetichos.

400. By 640 B. C. Psamtik felt himself strong enough to resume the old projects of conquest in Asia, to revive Egypt's traditional claims upon Syria-Palestine, and to dispute their possession with Assyria. He invaded Philistia and for many years besieged Ashdod; but his

THE RESTORATION

ambitions there were rudely dashed by the influx of Scythian peoples from the far north, who overran Assyria and penetrated southward to the frontier of Egypt. According to Herodotus they were bought off by Psamtik, who by liberal gifts succeeded thus in ransoming his kingdom. It was more probably his own strong arm that delivered his land. He had already saved it from centuries of weakness and decay, and when he died after a reign of fifty-four years, he left Egypt enjoying such peaceable prosperity as had not been hers since the death of Ramses III, five hundred years before.

XXVIII

THE FINAL STRUGGLES: BABYLON AND PERSIA

401. When Necho succeeded his father Psamtik I on the throne of Egypt in 609 B. C., there seemed to be nothing to prevent his re-establishment of the Egyptian Empire in Asia. As Psamtik's kingdom had prospered, that of the once powerful Ninevites had rapidly declined. From the fearful visitation of the Scythian hordes in the reign of Psamtik I, it never recovered, and when Babylon made common cause with Cyaxares, king of the rising Median states, Nineveh was unable to withstand their united assaults. Its inevitable fall was anticipated by the western peoples, and being clearly foreseen by the Hebrew Nahum, he exultingly predicted its destruction. At the accession of Necho it was in such a state of collapse that he immediately began the realization of his father's imperial designs in Asia. He built a war-fleet both in the Mediterranean and the Red Sea, and in his first year invaded Philistia. Gaza and Askalon, which offered resistance, were taken and punished, and with a great army Necho then pushed northward. In Judah, now freed from the Assyrians, the prophetic party was in the ascendancy. As they had been delivered from Sennacherib nearly a century before, so they fondly believed they might now face Egypt with the same assurance of deliverance. On the historic plain of Megiddo, where Egypt had

first won the supremacy of Asia nearly nine hundred years before, the young Josiah recklessly threw himself upon Necho's great army. His pitiful force was quickly routed and he himself, fatally wounded, retired to die at Jerusalem. Expecting to meet at least some attempt on the part of Assyria to save her western dominions, Necho pressed on to the Euphrates without delay. But Assyria was now too near her end to make even the feeblest effort to stay his progress; he found no army there to meet him, and not feeling himself strong enough to advance against Nineveh, he returned southward, having gained all Syria, and at one stroke recovered the whole of the old Egyptian conquests of the Empire. Arriving at Ribleh on the Orontes, three months after the battle of Megiddo, he sent for Josiah's son, Jehoahaz, whom the Judeans had placed upon his father's throne, and threw him into chains. He then installed Eliakim, another son of Josiah, as king of Judah under the name Jehoiakim, and imposed upon him a tribute of one hundred talents of silver and one of gold. The unfortunate Jehoahaz was carried to Egypt by the Pharaoh and died there. It is characteristic of the altered spirit of the times that Necho dedicated to the Milesian Branchidæ the corselet which he had worn on this victorious campaign,—of course in recognition of the Greek mercenaries, to whom he owed his successes. How different all this from the days of Amon's supremacy, when victory came from him alone ! Fragments of a stela dating from Necho's supremacy in Syria and bearing his name in hieroglyphic, have been found at Sidon (Jer., XLVII, 1–5; PSBA, XVI (1894), pp. 91 *f.*).

402. Necho's new Asiatic empire was not of long duration. In less than two years the combined forces

of Nabupaluçur, the king of Babylon, and of the Medes
under Cyaxares, had accomplished the overthrow of
Nineveh. The city was destroyed and the nation
utterly annihilated as a political force. The two conquerors divided the territory made available by their
conquest, the Mede taking the north and northeast and
the Babylonian the south and southwest. Thus Syria
fell by inheritance to Nabupaluçur. He was now old
and unable to undertake its recovery; but he quickly
dispatched his son, Nebuchadrezzar, to oppose Necho.
Hearing of his coming, Necho was wise enough to collect
his forces and hasten to meet him at the northern
frontier on the Euphrates in 605 B. C. At Carchemish
the motley army of the Pharaoh was completely routed
by the Babylonians. The victory was so decisive that
Necho did not attempt to make another stand or to
save Palestine, but retreated in haste to the Delta
followed by Nebuchadrezzar. The ignominious retreat
of Necho's proud army, as it hurried through Palestine,
created a profound impression among the Hebrews of
Judah, and Jeremiah, who was interpreting to his people
in Jerusalem the movements of the nations, hurled
after the discomfited Egyptians his burden of sarcasm
and derision. Had not the young Kaldean prince now
been summoned to Babylon by the death of his father,
the conquest of Egypt, or at least its further humiliation,
must inevitably have followed. Unwilling to prolong
his absence from the capital under these circumstances,
Nebuchadrezzar came to an understanding with Necho,
and returned home to assume the crown of Babylon.
Thus Syria-Palestine became Babylonian dominion
(Jer., XLVI, 1–12).

403. Necho's agreement with Babylon involved the
relinquishment of his ambitious designs in Asia. He

THE FINAL STRUGGLES

held to the compact, and made no further attempt to maintain Egyptian sovereignty there, as the Hebrew annals record: "And the king of Egypt came not again any more out of his land: for the king of Babylon had taken from the brook of Egypt unto the river Euphrates, all that pertained to the king of Egypt" (II Kings, xxiv, 7). He even made no effort to intervene when Nebuchadrezzar besieged and captured Jerusalem and deported the chief families of Judah in 596 B.C. The Pharaoh's energies were now employed in the furtherance of his father's commercial enterprises. He attempted to re-excavate the ancient canal from the Delta, connecting the eastern arm of the Nile with the Red Sea, but did not succeed. Necho's interest in maritime progress is further evidenced by his famous exploring expedition. He dispatched a crew of Phœnician mariners with instructions to sail around Africa, or as Herodotus calls it, Libya. As the Egyptians had from the earliest time supposed their land to be surrounded by sea, the Okeanos of the Greeks, with which the Nile had connection in the south, the feat of the Phœnicians, which they actually accomplished in three years, excited no surprise.

404. Psamtik II, who followed his father Necho about 593 B.C., either regarded Egypt's prospects in Asia as hopeless or continued the compact of his father with Babylon. Unable to accomplish anything in the North, he turned his attention southward and attempted the recovery of Nubia, lost to Egypt since the foundation of the Ethiopian kingdom. He invaded lower Nubia, and an advanced body of his troops pushed up almost to the second cataract, where they left a record of their visit at Abu Simbel, in a Greek inscription on one of the colossi of Ramses II, before his great temple there.

Although, as we have before remarked, this invasion doubtless furnished the Ethiopians a further reason for transferring their capital above the cataracts to Meroe, yet the results of the expedition were probably not lasting, and Lower Nubia never became an integral part of the Saite kingdom (Note XII; BAR, IV, 988 A-988 J).

405. Meanwhile the Saites were still casting longing eyes upon the ancient dominions of Egypt in Asia, and when Apries (the Ha'abre' of the Egyptians, or Hophra' of the Hebrews) succeeded his father Psamtik II early in 588 B. C., he immediately resumed the old designs of his house to recover them. Already under Necho, in 597 B. C., as we have seen, Nebuchadrezzar had been obliged to advance on Jerusalem in consequence of the rebellion of Jehoiachin, an event in which Necho may have secretly had a hand. The next year the unhappy city capitulated, and some nine or ten thousand of the better class were deported to Babylonia, leaving only "the poorest sort of the people of the land." Jehoiachin's uncle, Zedekiah, was appointed by Nebuchadrezzar as king over the afflicted land. When he had been ruling nine years we find him in revolt against Babylon. The reasons for this foolish policy are quite evident. The date of his rebellion coincides with the accession of Apries. Tyre and Sidon, Moab and Ammon had also sent their emissaries to the Judean king, and when the weighty influence of Apries also fell into the scales the vacillating Zedekiah was no longer able to withstand, and he half-heartedly joined the rest in casting off the sovereignty of Babylon. The events formerly following similar revolts from Assyrian authority were now re-enacted under the Babylonians; the allies were unable to act quickly in concert. Indeed Apries made it im-

THE FINAL STRUGGLES

possible that they should do so by attacking Tyre and Sidon. He dispatched an expedition to attempt the conquest of the north by sea, perhaps hoping to meet Nebuchadrezzar on the Euphrates as his grandfather Necho had done. He fought a victorious naval engagement with the Tyrians and Cyprians and landed enough troops to take Sidon, whereupon the other Phœnician cities yielded. It is possible also that he hoped thus to divert Nebuchadrezzar from the south where a portion of his army had appeared early in 587, or to cut off this southern army now operating against Jerusalem; and if so, the movement was brilliantly conceived. But it was never pushed far enough to accomplish anything inland; and Nebuchadrezzar wisely fixed his base of operations well northward, at Ribleh on the Orontes, where he was able to contemplate the Egyptian operations without concern. His enemies were exhausting themselves against each other, and had Apries advanced inland Nebuchadrezzar could have quickly confronted him with a force from Ribleh. It is perhaps during this brief supremacy of the Pharaoh in Phœnicia that we should place the fragmentary Egyptian monuments, pieces of stone statues, altars and bits of inscribed stone from the Saite age, found by Renan at Arvad, Tyre and Sidon. Now also the Pharaoh apparently controlled for a time a domain in Lebanon (II Kings, xxiv, 15; Diodorus, I, 68; Rev. arch, n. s., VII, 1863[1]; pp. 194–198; BAR, IV, 970).

406. When in the spring of 586 B.C. the troops of Apries at last appeared in the south to threaten the Babylonian besiegers of Jerusalem, they brought the beleaguered city a brief moment's respite only; for the Egyptian forces again showed themselves unable to cope with the armies of Asia. Indeed, it is possible that

Apries relinquished his claims in Palestine without a blow. Thus the predictions of Jeremiah, who had constantly proclaimed the folly of depending upon assistance from Egypt, were brilliantly confirmed. In the summer of 586 B.C. Jerusalem fell; it was razed to the ground and the inglorious Zedekiah, having been taken to Nebuchadrezzar's camp at Ribleh, was blinded, after witnessing the slaughter of his sons. The Judean nation was annihilated, but no decisive blow had been struck which might cripple the power of Egypt, the instigator of the trouble. It was not for many years that Nebuchadrezzar was able to attempt anything in this direction; his first obligation being the punishment of Tyre, which maintained itself for thirteen years, finally yielding in 573 B.C.

407. In spite of ill success in Asia, Apries enjoyed unbounded prosperity in the internal administration of his realm, and the kingdom flourished as only under his great grandfather, its founder. From the west also he received the revenues of the Oasis region and in the Northern Oasis his official Wahibrenofer built a temple. But in the full enjoyment of his wealth and splendour a tragic end was awaiting him from an unexpected quarter. He found great difficulty in bridling his troops, of whatever nationality. On one occasion the Libyans, Greeks and Syrians attempted to desert and migrate to Nubia, as in the days of Psamtik I a body of the warrior-class had done. How many were involved in this revolt under Apries it is impossible to establish, but they were sufficiently numerous to render the king very apprehensive, and the record of the event distinctly states that "his majesty feared." Another misunderstanding with the *native* warrior-class did not end so happily. The new Greek settlement at Cyrene

was growing into a flourishing state and encroaching upon the Libyans who lay between Cyrene and Egypt. Apries deemed it wise to check the development of the Greek colony and sent to the aid of the Libyans a body of Egyptian troops naturally not including among them any of his Greek mercenaries. Despising their adversaries, the Egyptians advanced in careless confidence, but were totally defeated and almost annihilated by the Cyrenian Greeks. Smarting under their discomfiture they were so filled with resentment toward Apries that they concluded he had dispatched them against Cyrene with the purpose of ridding himself of them. A revolt of the warrior-class followed, which swelled to dangerous proportions. Apries thereupon commissioned one of his nobles, Ahmose, or Amasis, as Herodotus calls him, a relative of the royal house, to conciliate the revolters. So skilfully did Amasis manipulate the situation that the disaffected soldiery soon proclaimed him king, and a messenger of Apries, sent to recall the traitor, was dismissed with insult and contumely. Herodotus narrates that a battle now ensued in which the Greek mercenaries of Apries, heavily outnumbered by the native troops of Amasis, were beaten and Apries taken prisoner. It is possible that he is here confusing the situation with the later battle which, as we know from a contemporary document, occurred between the forces of the two rivals. However this may be, Amasis, while treating Apries with kindness and not yet dethroning him, laid a vigourous hand upon the sceptre. A coregency ensued in which Apries doubtless played but a feeble part; and a monument or two showing the two rulers together has survived. Alongside the cartouche, which he now assumed, Amasis continued to bear the old titles belonging to his former less exalted offices. In the third year of the coregency, however, a struggle between the two regents arose. Apries, as Herodotus knew, gained the adherence of the Greeks, and with an army of these mercenaries, supported by a fleet, advanced upon Sais from the North. Some time after the resulting battle, which went against Apries, he was slain by his pursuers. Amasis gave him honourable burial, befitting a king, among his ancestors in Sais, and established for him mortuary offerings endowed with a liberal revenue (BAR, IV, 989; 999 *f.;* 996 *f.;* KSGW, 1900, p. 226).

408. It might have been supposed that Amasis, who owed his crown to an ebullition of national feeling, as opposed to the partiality shown the Greeks, would now have evinced his appreciation of this indebtedness in a marked reaction against foreign influence; but for this he was too sagacious a statesman. While seeming to curtail the privileges of the Greeks, he really gave to them all they wanted. The Greek merchants, who had hitherto enjoyed unlimited latitude in their selection of a field for their merchandizing, were now not allowed to land anywhere in the Delta, save at a city appointed for them by Amasis. On the Canopic mouth of the Nile in the western Delta, at a place where there was probably an older settlement of but slight importance, Amasis founded the new city of Naucratis as a home and market for the Greeks, which they speedily made the most important commercial centre of Egypt, if not of the whole Mediterranean. It was in all essentials a Greek city, and the wares which were manufactured within its walls were, with but slight exceptions, in no sense Egyptian. The busy life which throbbed in its thronging markets and factories, the constitution of the city and its daily administration were just such as pre-

vailed in any industrial and commercial Greek community of the mother country. All the Greeks were concerned more or less in its success and prosperity. Hence when the chief temple of Naucratis was to be erected, the Ionian cities of Chios, Teos, Phocæa and Clazomenæ, with Rhodes, Cnidus, Halicarnassus and Phaselis of the Dorians, and the Æolian Mitylene, together contributed a common fund to erect the Hellenium, a large and stately sanctuary, with a spacious enclosure, protected by a massive wall. The powerful states of Ægina, Miletus and Samos, however, were able to possess each a temple of their own. Thus while apparently restricted, the Greeks were still enjoying the greatest privileges in Egypt, nor did the regulations of Amasis ever impress them as hostile to their welfare in his land. When an embassy of the Delphians approached him for a contribution toward the erection of their temple, which had been burned (548 B.C.), he responded liberally. He sent gifts likewise to the temples of Lindos, Samos and Cyrene, and presented a magnificent corselet to the Spartans. He thus maintained close relations with the Greek world in Europe and Asia, and with the wealthy and powerful Polycrates of Samos he sustained a friendship which amounted to an alliance. He was always very popular with the Greeks, both at home and abroad, and many tales of his career and personal character circulated among them.

409. Unfortunately it is almost solely in his dealings with the Greeks that we know anything of the achievements of Amasis. He did not neglect his interests among the Egyptians, as in view of the catastrophe which had overtaken Apries, he was not likely to do. He built splendid additions to the temples of Sais and

Memphis, and a vast monolithic chapel from the quarries of the first cataract, which he set up in Sais, excited the admiration of Herodotus. The people enjoyed the greatest prosperity and Herodotus avers that the land "contained at that time twenty thousand cities." He again revised the system of laws, one of which, demanding that every inhabitant "should annually declare to the governor of his district by what means he maintained himself," was adopted by Solon on his visit to Egypt, and enforced at Athens. But eventually his evident liking for the Greeks could not escape the notice of the Egyptian party. He had two frontier forts in the northeastern Delta, and from Daphnæ, one of these two, he was obliged to transfer the Greek garrison stationed there to Memphis, and thus ensure the safety of the latter strong and populous city, so near his residence at Sais. He was finally compelled to throw off the mask, and for the support of his mercenary army and fleet to draw upon the fortunes and revenues of the temples. It was no longer compatible with modern statesmanship that the priesthoods should be permitted to absorb so large a proportion of the resources of the land. A navy such as Egypt now possessed, and the large body of mercenaries in his army, drew heavily upon the treasury of Amasis; and his curtailment of the temple incomes was inevitable. It was the beginning of still more serious inroads upon the temple-estates in the Persian period, resulting under the Ptolemies in great reduction of the priestly revenues and the taxation of the temple-property. Politically impotent, the priesthoods could only swallow their discontent, which, however, gradually permeated all the upper classes. But Amasis, with a cleverness which became proverbial, was always able so to manipulate the forces at his command that the Egyptian party found itself helpless and obliged to accede to his wishes (BAR, IV, 1014; Rev. égypt., I, 59 *ff*.; III, 105).

410. The good understanding which Amasis constantly maintained with the Greeks made him secure upon the Mediterranean. In the west he controlled the oases and erected a temple in the Northern Oasis; but he was not so fortunate in his relations with the east. His usurpation of the crown had furnished Nebuchadrezzar with the coveted opportunity of humiliating Egypt, which the Kaldean naturally supposed would have been weakened by the internal dissensions incident to such a revolution. Already before the death of Apries in 568 B. C., the army of the Kaldeans appeared on the Delta frontier, but the course of the subsequent operations is unknown. It is not probable that Nebuchadrezzar purposed the conquest of Egypt, which was now in a condition very different from the state of impotent anarchy in which the Assyrians had found it under the Ethiopians. In any case, he did not achieve the conquest of the country; and Jeremiah and Ezekiel, who were awaiting with feverish longing the complete overthrow of the hated Pharaoh's kingdom, must have been sorely disappointed that the catastrophe which they had confidently predicted to their countrymen failed to occur. As a result of the campaign, however, Amasis was obliged to renounce any ambitions which he may have cherished for the conquest of Syria-Palestine. His strong navy, nevertheless, enabled him completely to subdue Cyprus, which he organized as an Egyptian dependency, paying tribute to him. His naval strength, which now became formidable, was the foundation of the sea-power, which under the Ptolemies, made Egypt the dominant state

on the Mediterranean (KSGW, 1900, p. 226; Jer., xliii., 8–13; Ezek., xl, 10–18).

411. Meanwhile Nebuchadrezzar had died (562 B.C.), and the disappearance of his powerful personality distinctly diminished the prestige of the Babylonian Empire. As internal dissensions arose, the alliance with the Medes was no longer possible, and when finally Cyrus of Anshan, a Persian, succeeded in supplanting the Median dynasty by the overthrow of the Median king, Astyages (550 B.C.), the position of Babylon was critical in the extreme. The extraordinary career of Cyrus was now a spectacle upon which all eyes in the west were fastened with wonder and alarm. Amasis was fully alive to the new danger which threatened his kingdom in common with all the other powers of the West. He therefore in 547 B.C. made common cause with them, forming a league with Crœsus of Lydia, and the Spartans in the west; and in the east with Nabuna'id of Babylon. Before the allies could move together, Crœsus was defeated and dethroned (546–545 B.C.); and the overflowing energies of the new conqueror and his people, fresh and unspent for centuries among their native hills, were then directed upon Babylon, which fell in 539 B.C. Amasis was powerless to check their progress, while the vast Persian Empire was being raised upon the ruins of the valley of the two rivers and the kingdoms of Asia Minor. It was inevitable that the new world power should now look toward Egypt, and the last years of Amasis must have been darkened with anxious forebodings as he contemplated the undisputed supremacy of Cyrus. But he was spared the fate of Crœsus for, when he died, late in 526 or early in 525 B.C., the impending catastrophe had not yet overtaken his kingdom.

412. Amasis had ample opportunity during his long reign of forty-four years to display his qualities as a statesman. With his fertility of resource and never-failing cleverness, be belonged to, and was largely the product of, the Greek world. His nature was fundamentally opposed to the conventional and sacerdotal conception of the Pharaoh, which so dominated the ancient kingship that its monuments, largely of priestly origin, force all the Pharaohs into the same mould, and depict them as rigid and colourless forms, each like all the others, with the same monotonous catalogue of divine attributes. These formal and priestly traditions of what constituted a Pharaoh were treated with scant consideration by Amasis. When he had devoted the morning hours to the transaction of public business, he loved to throw aside the pomp and formalities of state, and, gathering at his table a few choice friends, he gave himself without reserve to the enjoyment of conviviality, in which wine played no small part. A thorough man of the world of his day, not too refined, open to every influence and to every pleasure which did not endanger his position, he showed himself nevertheless a statesman of the first rank. Of his wit and humour the Greeks told many a tale, while the light and skilful touch with which he manipulated men and affairs won their constant admiration. But the character and policies of Amasis clearly disclose the fact that the old Egyptian world, whose career we have been following, has already ceased to be. Its vitality, which flickered again into a flame, in the art of the Saitic age, is now quenched forever. The Saitic state is but an artificial structure, skilfully built up and sustained by sagacious rulers, but the national career, the characteristics of which were determined by the initiative

and vital force of the nation itself had long ago ended. The fall of Egypt and the close of her characteristic history, were already an irrevocable fact long before the relentless Cambyses knocked at the doors of Pelusium. The Saitic state was a creation of rulers who looked into the future, who belonged to it, and had little or no connection with the past. They were as essentially non-Egyptian as the Ptolemies who followed the Persians. The Persian conquest in 525 B.C., which deprived Psamtik III, the son of Amasis of his throne and kingdom, was but a change of rulers, a purely external fact. And if a feeble burst of national feeling enabled this or that Egyptian to thrust off the Persian yoke for a brief period, the movement may be likened to the convulsive contractions which sometimes lend momentary motion to limbs from which conscious life has long departed. With the fall of Psamtik III, Egypt belonged to a new world, toward the development of which she had contributed much, but in which she could no longer play an active part. Her great work was done, and unable, like Nineveh and Babylon, to disappear from the scene, she lived on her artificial life for a time under the Persians and the Ptolemies, ever sinking, till she became merely the granary of Rome, to be visited as a land of ancient marvels by wealthy Greeks and Romans, who have left their names scratched here and there upon her hoary monuments, just as the modern tourists, admiring the same marvels, still continue to do. But her unwarlike people, still making Egypt a garden of the world, have verified the words of the Hebrew seer, "There shall be no more a prince out of the land of Egypt" (Ezek., XXX, 13).

CHRONOLOGICAL SUMMARY

(N. B.—All dates with asterisks are astronomically fixed.)

Predynastic kingdoms already flourishing........... 4500 B. C.
Introduction of calendar and earliest fixed date in
  history..*4241 "
Kingdoms of Upper and Lower Egypt probably flourishing by..................................... 4000 "
Accession of Menes and beginning of dynasties....... 3400 "

FIRST AND SECOND DYNASTIES—3400–2980 B. C

Eighteen Kings, 420 years, ruling at Thinis. Tombs in Abydos and vicinity. Wars with Libyans, with Beduin of East, with Delta. Mining in Sinai. Stone masonry and arch introduced.

OLD KINGDOM—2980–2475 B. C.

THIRD DYNASTY—2980–2900 B. C.

Zoser to Snefru, 80 years, ruling at Memphis. Zoser builds terraced pyramid of Sakkara, the oldest existing large stone building; continues mining in Sinai; wise man Imhotep. Snefru builds first real pyramids: one at Medûm, another at Dahshur; sends fleet to Lebanon (*earliest known sea-voyage and expedition into Syria in history*); continues mining in Sinai.

420 CHRONOLOGICAL SUMMARY

Egypt	B. C.	Asiatic Countries (See Note XIII)
FOURTH DYNASTY (Memphis?), 150 years. Pyramids at Gizeh and Abu Roash.	2900–2750	
1. Khufu, 23 years. Great Pyramid of Gizeh. Highest prosperity of Old Kingdom.	2900–2877	
2. Dedefre, 8 years.	2877–2869	
3. Khafre X years. Second Pyramid of Gizeh.	2869–2774	
4. Menkure X years. Third Pyramid of Gizeh.		
5. ....X years.	2774–2756	Babylonian City Kingdoms and small local States.
6. ....18 years.	2756–2752	
7. Shepseskaf 4 years.	2752–2750	
8. ....2 years.	2750	
Triumph of Heliopolis and Solar Theology.	2750–2625	
FIFTH DYNASTY (Memphis), 125 years. Offices become hereditary. Pyramids at Abusir and Sakkara.		
1. Userkaf, 7 years First Pharaoh recorded at First Cataract.	about 2750–2743	
2. Sahure, 12 years. Mining in Sinai. First expedition to Punt (Ophir). Naval expedition to Phoenicia. Earliest colonnades.	about 2743–2731	

3. Neferirkere, X years.	2731–2721
4. Shepseskere, 7 years.	
5. Khaneferre, X years.	2721–2691
6. Nuserre, 30 years.	2691–2683
7. Menkuhor, 8 years.	2683–2655
8. Dedkere-Isesi, 28 years.	
First Pharaoh recorded at Hammamât.	
Second Expedition to Punt.	
9. Unis, 30 (+ X) years.	2655–2625
Earliest Pyramid Texts.	
SIXTH DYNASTY, (Memphis), 150 years.	2625–2475
Pyramids at Sakkara.	
Appearance of landed nobles detached from court.	
1. Teti II. X years.	2625–2590
2. Userkere. X years.	
3. Pepi I. 20 years.	2590–2570
Residence now first called Memphis.	
Five primitive expeditions into Sinai.	
Earliest Expedition into Palestine in history.	
Control of Northern Nubia. Nubian mercenaries common in Egyptian army.	
4. Mernere I. 4 years.	2570–2566
Canal in first cataract.	
Pharaoh receives homage of Nubian chiefs at first cataract.	

Babylonian City Kingdoms and small local States.

Egypt	B.C.	Asiatic Countries
Harkhuf's trading expeditions to far south, Yam and the Sudan,—earliest expeditions into inner Africa.		
5. Pepi II. 90 (+X) years (longest reign in history). Harkuf's trading expeditions in Sudan continue. Mekhu and Sebni's expeditions in Sudan. Campaigns in northern Nubia. Loose sovereignty in northern Nubia. Expeditions to Punt (Ophir) common. Commerce with Lebanon and Ægean. Decline of Memphis.	2566–2476	*Babylon* Sargon and son Naram Sin of Agadé temporarily rule to the Mediterranean. *some records.*
6. Mermere II. 1 year. Fall of Old Kingdom.	2476–2475	
SEVENTH AND EIGHTH DYNASTIES. Known total 30 years. Collapse of Memphis.	2475–2445	⎱ Kings of Sumer and Akkad.
NINTH AND TENTH DYNASTIES. Heracleopolis. Estimated 285 years. Eighteen feeble kings residing at Heracleopolis. Rise of Thebes under Intefs.	2445–2160	⎰

CHRONOLOGICAL SUMMARY

Struggle with Thebes; Tombs at Siut; Fall of Heracleopolis; Triumph of Thebes. **MIDDLE KINGDOM, 2160–1788 B. C.** **ELEVENTH DYNASTY**, Thebes, 160 years. (See Note I.) Pyramids at Thebes.	2160–*2000	} Kings of Sumer and Akkad.
1. Horus Wahenekh-Intef, 50 + X years. Tomb at Thebes.		
2. Horus Nakhtneb-Tepnefer-Intef, X years.		
3. Horus Senekhibtowe-Mentuhotep, X years.		
4. Nibhapetre-Mentuhotep, X years. Tomb at Thebes.		
5. Nibtowere-Mentuhotep, 2 + X years. Expedition to Hammamat.		Rise of Assyria, 2100–2000 B.C. Ilu-shūma king of Assyria wars against Su-abu king of Babylon.
6. Nibhepetre-Mentuhotep, 46 + X years. Expedition against Nubia. Earliest Temple at Thebes.		Babylon gains supremacy in Lower Mesopotamia. First Dyn. of Babylon, begins (ab. 2050).
7. Senekhkere-Mentuhotep, 8 + X years. Expedition to Hammamat and Punt.		
TWELFTH DYNASTY, Thebans, 213 years. Residence at Lisht and in Fayum.	*2000–*1788	
1. Amenemhet I. 30 years. Feudal organization perfected; great prosperity. Sesostris I 10 years coregent (1980–1970). Expedition into Wawat (1971). Canal connecting Nile and Red Sea; frequent intercourse with Syria; Egyptians in Syria. Pyramid at Lisht.	*2000–*1970	Byblos, already important port of Phœnicia.

Egypt	B.C.	Asiatic Countries
2. Sesostris I. 45 years. 10 years coregent with Amenemhet I. Nubian conquest carried into Kush,—first foreign campaign led by a Pharaoh personally. Amenemhet II, 3 years coregent. Pyramid at Lisht.	*1980–*1935	Khammurabi, king of Babylon (1900).
3. Amenemhet II. 35 years. 3 years coregent with Sesostris I; expeditions to Sinai, Nubian mines, Punt. 3 years coregent with Sesostris II; Pyramid at Dahshur.	*1938–*1903	
4. Sesostris II. 19 years. 3 years coregent with Amenemhet II. Traffic with Punt. Pyramid at Illahûn.	*1906–*1887	Second Dynasty in Babylonia rules the "Country of the Sea", (parallel with First Dynasty at Babylon).
5. Sesostris III. 38 years. New canal through first cataract. Subjugation of Lower Nubia to second cataract complete. Expeditions thither in years 8, 12, 16, 19. Southern frontier established at Semneh in year 8 (1879 B.C.). First campaign of M. K. in Syria. Semitic traders in Egypt. Monuments of Egyptian officials in Gezer (Palestine). Commerce with Ægean. Nomarchs decline. Oldest known drama; Strophic poetry; tales, "Messianic" prophecy, Earliest Book of the	*1887–*1849	

CHRONOLOGICAL SUMMARY

Dead. Coregency with son. Pyramid at Dahshur.		
6. Amenemhet III. 48 years. Coregency with father. Great development of resources; Nomarchs suppressed; activity in Sinai; regulation of Nile and irrigation; Lake Moeris; Fayum exploited; Labyrinth; Pyramid at Dahshur, possibly also at Hawara (see p. 72).	*1849–*1801	
7. Amenemhet IV. 9 years. Decline of Middle Kingdom.	*1801–*1792	
8. Sebeknefrure (queen). 4 years. Fall of Middle Kingdom.	*1792–*1788	
Thirteenth to Seventeenth Dynasties, 208 years. Great confusion, usurpation, civil war. Hyksos rule about 100 years (1675–1575 B. C.?). Horse introduced. Sekenenre king at Thebes, mummy in Cairo.	*1788–1580	Hittites war against Samsu-ditana, king of Babylon, and invade Babylonia. First Dynasty falls (about 1750). Hyksos consolidate Syrian power, probably at Kadesh, and absorb Egypt. Third (Kassite) Dynasty of Babylon (about 1750 to 1150). Ulam-Buriash, king of Babylon supplants Second Dynasty in the "Country of the Sea", (17th century).
EMPIRE, FIRST PERIOD. 1580–1350 B. C.		
Eighteenth Dynasty, Thebes, 230 years.	1580–1350	Assyrian and Babylonian power in decline.

CHRONOLOGICAL SUMMARY

Egypt	B. C.	Asiatic Countries
1. Ahmose I. 22 (+ X) years. Expulsion of Hyksos by 1580. Extermination of landed nobles. Lands revert to crown. First standing army; military state organized. Campaign in Syria. Tomb at Thebes. Mummy at Cairo.	1580–*1557	Hyksos driven from Egypt retire slowly to Syria. Syria-Palestine tributary to Egypt.
2. Amenhotep I. 10 (+ X) years............ Campaign in Syria; against Libyans. Tomb at Thebes; mummy at Cairo............ 3. Thutmose I. 30 (+ X) years............ Conquest of Kush to above third cataract. Conquest of Syria, tablet of victory on upper Euphrates.	*1557–*1501	
4 & 5. Thutmose III, including Thutmose II and Hatshepsut. 54 years. Accession of Thutmose III and Hatshepsut, May 3, 1501. Feuds in royal family. Coregents supplanted about 1496 by	*1501–*1447	All Syria-Palestine tributary to Egypt.
6. Thutmose II. About 3 years. Expedition against Nubia. Accepts coregency of Thutmose III. Mummy at Cairo. Succeeded by	about 1496–1493	

4 & 5. Thutmose III and Hatshepsut. Splendid buildings and expedition to Punt by queen. She dies 1481–1479. Tomb at Thebes.	1493–1480	
4. Thutmose III alone. 33 years. Seventeen campaigns in Asia (1479–1459 B. C.). Asiatic empire consolidated, frontier established on Upper Euphrates. Egyptian fleet developed. Empire organized from Euphrates to fourth cataract. First great empire in history. Great buildings; vast wealth. Son coregent (1448). King dies, March 17th, 1447. Tomb at Thebes. Mummy at Cairo.	*1479–*1447	Consolidation of Hittite power at Boghaz-köi (Khatti) as "Great Kheta." "Great Kheta," Assyria and Babylon semi-tributary to Thutmose III. Phœnician maritime city-states already flourishing. All states of Syria-Palestine Egyptian vassals. Power of Kadesh, leading Syrian state, centre of Hyksos power, now broken.
7. Amenhotep II. 26 (+ X) years. Coregent with father. Campaign to Euphrates, to Napata. Empire maintained. Mummy still in tomb at Thebes.	*1448–1420	
8. Thutmose IV. 8 (+ X) years. Campaign in Asia; in Nubia. Asks and secures Mitannian princess in marriage. Tomb at Thebes, mummy at Cairo.	1420–1411	Hittite dynasty already flourishing in Mitanni. Artatama, king of Mitanni.

Egypt	B.C.	Asiatic and Other Countries
9. Amenhotep III. 36 years. Greatest splendour of the Empire. Imperial Thebes. Vast temples. Clear-story architecture evolved. Campaign in Nubia. Amarna Letters. Pharaoh marries Mitannian princess Gilukhipa. Cyprus, vassal-kingdom. Hittites seize Pharaoh's north Syrian dependencies; Khabiri Semites begin migration into Syria and Palestine. Decline of Empire. Commerce with Babylonia, Syria, Ægean; Egyptian monuments in Crete and Mycenæ. Tomb at Thebes, mummy at Cairo.	1411–1375	Shuttarna, king of Mitanni, seeks Egyptian alliance. Kadashmanbel, king of Babylon, seeks Egyptian alliance. Dushratta, king of Mitanni, seeks Egyptian alliance, is successful against Assyria. Kheta (Hittites) begin absorption of Syria (by 1385). Cyprus, vassal of Egypt. Seplel (cuneiform Subbiluliuma), king of Hittites in correspondence with Egypt.
10. Ikhnaton (Amenhotep IV). 17 (+ X) years. Introduction of earliest monotheism. Religious revolution. Thebes forsaken, Amarna, and Amarna letters. Hittites seize Syria to Amor. Khabiri Semites invade Palestine, Hebrews with them. Complete dissolution of Egyptian Empire in Asia. Tomb at Amarna. Fall of Eighteenth Dynasty. Disorganization.	1375–1358	Burraburyash, king of Babylon, seeks Egyptian alliance. Establishment of Amorite kingdom on Upper Orontes. Hebrew tribesmen begin to enter Palestine in Khabiri invasion. General anarchy in Palestine. Hittites in possession of Syria as far as Amor.

CHRONOLOGICAL SUMMARY

11. Sakere. X years.		
12. Tutenkhamon. X years. Return to Thebes, Amon partially restored.	1358–1350	Former Asiatic vassal-kingdoms of Egypt all gain independence or are absorbed by Hittites.
13. Eye. 3 + X years. End of Empire, First Period.	1350	
EMPIRE, SECOND PERIOD 1350–about 1150 B.C.		
NINETEENTH DYNASTY. City of Ramses, 145 years.	1350–1205	
1. Harmhab. 34 (+ X) years. Restoration of traditional religion, triumph of Amon, reorganization of government, Thebes restored. Campaign in Nubia.	about 1350–1315	Merasar (cuneiform Mursili), king of the Hittites, in possession of Syria.
2. Ramses I. 2 years. Great hall of Karnak begun.	about 1315–1314	
3. Seti I. 21 (+ X) years. Palestine recovered; first conflict with Hittites. Campaign against Libyans. Great Karnak Hall continued. Nubian gold mines exploited. Tomb at Thebes. Mummy at Cairo.	about 1313–1292	Hebrew tribesmen still pushing into Palestine. Hittites hold Syria as far as Amor against attacks of Seti I. Metella (Cuneiform Muttallu), king of Hittites.
4. Ramses II. 67 years. Nubian gold mines exploited. Asiatic war, chiefly with Hittites (1288–1271). Penetrates	about 1292–1225	Hittites hold Syria against 16 years war (1288–1271) by Ramses II. Khetasar (cuneiform Hattusil), king of

CHRONOLOGICAL SUMMARY

Egypt	B. C.	Asiatic Countries
to North Syria, but Syria not recovered. Treaty with Hittites (1271). Great Karnak Hall completed. Immense buildings everywhere. Decay of art and architecture begin. Hebrew oppression (?). Semitic influences. Libyan aggression. Tomb at Thebes. Mummy at Cairo.		Hittites (from about 1172), concludes peace with Ramses II, Hittites retaining bulk of Syria. Jacob tribes now probably oppressed in Egypt.
5. Merneptah. 10 (+ X) years. Asiatic campaign, "Israel," among defeated, year 3. Libyans and northern allies defeated in Delta, year 5. Tomb at Thebes. Mummy at Cairo.	about 1225–1215	Tukulti-Ninib, king of Assyria, conquers Babylon (about 1250). Slow consolidation among Libyans; they push into the western Delta, in combination with peoples of northern Mediterranean. "Israel" first mentioned on the monuments (BAR III, 603–605; 617). First occurrence of European peoples in written documents (1220). Libyans and northern Mediterranean peoples driven from western Delta (1220) by Merneptah.
6. Amenmeses. X years. Tomb at Thebes.	about 1215	
7. Siptah. 6 (+ X) years. Tomb at Thebes.	about 1215–1209	
8. Seti II. 2 (+ X) years. Exodus of Jacob tribesmen (?). Tomb at Thebes. Mummy at Cairo.	about 1209–1205	

CHRONOLOGICAL SUMMARY

Complete anarchy and Syrian usurper.	about 1205–1200	
TWENTIETH DYNASTY. City of Ramses, 140 years.	1200–1190	
1. Setnakht. 1 (+ X) years. Order restored. Tomb at Thebes. Mummy at Cairo.	ab. 1200–1198	
2. Ramses III. 31 years. 1st War. Defeat of Libyans and northern "sea-peoples" in western Delta, year 5. 2nd War. Defeat of northern "sea-peoples" in Syria, year 8.	about 1198–1167 about 1193 about 1190	Continuation of southern movement of northern "sea-peoples," of Crete, Asia Minor, and Ægean, including Philistines (from Crete) and probably Sicilians. They overrun Hittite Possessions in Syria and reach Amor.
3rd War. Second defeat of Libyans and "sea-peoples" in western Delta, year 11. 4th War. Campaign in Amor. Increase of mercenaries in army. Increasing power of Amon. General decline. Tomb at Thebes. Mummy at Cairo.	about 1187 about 1185	Consolidation of Libyan power; rise of Meshwesh (Maxyes). Libyans and northern allies twice attempt absorption of Egypt. Disappearance of Hittites in Syria.
3. Ramses IV. 6 years. Tomb at Thebes. Mummy at Cairo.	about 1167–1161	Jacob tribes enter Palestine.
4. Ramses V. 4 (+ X) years. Tomb at Thebes. Mummy at Cairo.	ab. 1161–1157	Philistines push into Palestine and settle; constant conflict with Hebrews.
5. Ramses VI. X years. Tomb at Thebes. Mummy at Cairo.	about 1157–1150	

432 CHRONOLOGICAL SUMMARY

Egypt	B.C.	Asiatic and Other Countries
DECADENCE 1150–663		
6–7. Ramses VII and VIII. X years.	ab. 1150–1142	
8. Ramses IX. 19 years. Decay of Thebes begins. Royal tombs robbed. Tomb at Thebes. Power of High Priest of Amon rapidly increasing.	ab. 1142–1123	Fourth Dynasty of Babylon. Revival under Nebuchadrezzar I (1140–1123); he reaches Mediterranean (?).
9. Ramses X. 1 (+ X) years. Tomb at Thebes.	ab. 1123–1121	
10. Ramses XI. X years. Tomb at Thebes.	ab. 1121–1118	
11. Ramses XII. 27 (+ X) years. Pharaoh reduced to a mere puppet. Delta kingdom founded at Tanis by Nesubenebded (Smendes). Sends gift to Tiglath-pileser I (?). High Priest of Amon, Hrihor seizes throne at Thebes. Pharaoh's tomb at Thebes.	ab. 1118–1090	Expansion of Assyria under Tiglath-pileser I. His advance to Syria (?). Heavy influx of Aramæans into Syria and Upper Mesopotamia.
TANITE-AMONITE PERIOD. 1090–945		
TWENTY-FIRST DYNASTY. Tanis, 145 years Libyans migrate steadily into Delta and fill army as mercenaries.	about 1090–945	Steady eastward drift of Libyans.

CHRONOLOGICAL SUMMARY

1. Nesubenebded. Tanite......... ⎫ X years 2. Hrihor. High Priest at Thebes...⎬ Egyptian power in Asia gone. ⎭ 3. Pesibkhenno I. 17 (+ X) years.	about 1090–1085 about 1085–1067	Fifth Dynasty of Babylon.
4. Paynozem I. 40 (+ X) years. 5. Amenemopet. 49 (+ X) years.	about 1067–1026 about 1026–976	Decline in Assyria. Sixth Dynasty of Babylon. Rise of Hebrew monarchy; Saul and David.
6. Siamon. 16 (+ X) years. 7. Pesibkhenno II (Psusennes). 12 (+ X) years. Libyans seize throne. (End of Tanite-Amonite Period.) LIBYAN PERIOD. 945–712 B.C. TWENTY-SECOND DYNASTY. Bubastis, 200 years.	about 976–958 about 958–945 about 945–745 about 945–924	Seventh (Elamite) Dynasty of Babylon. Eighth Dynasty of Babylon (about 1000?). Aramæans push successful war on Babylon. Solomon vassal of Egypt. Disruption of Hebrew monarchy.
1. Sheshonk I. 21 (+ X) years. Campaign in Palestine, Jerusalem captured. Gezer presented to Solomon. Campaign in Nubia. 2. Osorkon I. 36 (+ X) years.	about 924–895	Rise of Damascus; development of Syrian and Palestinian powers.

CHRONOLOGICAL SUMMARY

[handwritten marginalia at top: Philistines came originally from Crete. Highly civilized and greatly settled on S.E. corner of Mediterranean]

Egypt	B. C.	Asiatic and Other Countries
	ab. 895–874	Ashurnaçirpal III, king of Assyria (885–860), pushes westward to Mediterranean (876?). General Assyrian supremacy.
3. Takelot I. 23 (+ X) years.	ab. 874–853	
4. Osorkon II. 30 (+ X) years.		
5. Sheshonk II. 00 years. Died about 877 B. C. during coregency with Osorkon II.	about 860–834	Shalmaneser II, king of Assyria (860–825). Revival. Conquest of Syria. Great expansion of Assyria. *[marginalia: 854 a Hebrew king ——— appeared in document.]*
6. Takelot II. 25 (+ X) years. Probably contributed 1000 men against Shalmaneser II at Qarqar, 854. (7 years coregent with Osorkon II.)	about 834–784	Assyria loses Syria.
7. Sheshonk III. 52 years.	about 784–782	Adadnirari III, king of Assyria (812–783), regains Syria. *[marginalia: and Salmanesar II. Then decline in this, rough by follows a bridliant father and son.]*
8. Pemou. 6 (+ X) years.	about 782–745	
9. Sheshonk IV. 37 (+ X) years. Rise of independent kingdom in Nubia.	about 745–718	Tiglath-Pileser III, king of Assyria (745–727). Assyria again expands to Mediterranean. Syria and Palestine Assyrian Provinces.
TWENTY-THIRD DYNASTY. Bubastis, 27 years.		

CHRONOLOGICAL SUMMARY

1. Pedibast. 23 (+ X) years.	about 745–721	Tiglath-Pileser III reaches Philistia (734–732). Shalmaneser IV, king of Assyria (727–722); campaigns in Syria-Palestine; siege of Samaria (724–722). Ahaz of Judah (735–715). Sargon king of Assyria (722–705). Samaria captured. Kingdom of Israel destroyed (722).
NUBIAN PERIOD, 722–661 B. C.		
2. Osorkon III. 14 (+ X) years. Conquest of Piankhi. Tefnakhte of Sais.	about 720 to 718	Sargon captures Hamath (720).
3. Takelot III. X years. TWENTY-FOURTH DYNASTY. Sais, 6 years. Bekneranef (Bocchoris) 6 (+ X) years. Slain by Shabaka.	about 718–712	Sargon captures Ashdod (711).
TWENTY-FIFTH DYNASTY. Napata, 50 years.	712–663	
1. Shabaka. 12 years. Gains all Egypt. Incites revolt in Syria and Palestine against Sargon. Ægypto-Nubians under Taharka defeated by Sennacherib at Altaqu (701).	712–700	Mardukbaliddin king of Babylon. Sennacherib king of Assyria (705–681).
2. Shabataka. 12 years.	700–688	Destruction of Sennacherib's army in Palestine by pestilence (701). Aramæans plunder Babylonia.

CHRONOLOGICAL SUMMARY

Egypt	B. C.	Asiatic and Other Countries
3. Taharka (Tirhaka). 26 years. Defeats Esarhaddon (673). ASSYRIAN SUPREMACY, 670–660 B.C. Taharka defeated by Esarhaddon, Memphis taken by Assyrians, Delta becomes Assyrian province (670); Delta rebels, Ashurbanipal retakes Memphis (668–666). Taharka retires to Napata.	688–663	Scythians and Cimmerians emerge. Esarhaddon, king of Assyria (681–668). Rapid expansion of Assyria. Baal of Tyre having revolted submits to Assyria (670–669). Ashurbanipal, king of Assyria (668–626).
4. Tanutamon. Nubians resume control of Delta (663); rise of Psamtik of Sais; beginning of Twenty-sixth Dynasty (663); Nubians expelled by Ashurbanipal, Thebes plundered (661). Nubians return to Thebes and hold upper Egypt (661–655); Nubian rule at Thebes ended by 654.	663–655 (see Note IX)	Greatest power of Assyria.
TWENTY-SIXTH DYNASTY. Sais, 138 years.	663–525	
1. Psamtik I (Psammeticus). 54 years. Several years under Assyrians.	663–609	Nabupaluçur, king of Babylon (626–605).

CHRONOLOGICAL SUMMARY

RESTORATION, 660-525 B. C.

Alliance with Gyges of Lydia. Gained Thebes (by 654). Renaissance in art, religion, literature and government. Archaizing, retrospective age. Great prosperity.

2. Necho. 16 years. 609–593
Invades Palestine; defeats Josiah; advances to Euphrates. Defeated at Carchemish by Nebuchadrezzar (605). Egypt again loses Syria. Palestine. Circumnavigation of Africa.

Fall of Assyria (608–606?). Babylon independent (606?).
Influx of Scythians.
Nebuchadrezzar II king of Babylon (605–562).
Jehoiakim of Judah, vassal of Egypt (607–605), of Babylon (605–597).
Palestine and Syria become Babylonian dependencies (605).
Jehoiachin of Judah (597).
Zedekiah of Judah (597–586).

3. Psamtik II. 5 years. 593–588
Campaign in Nubia.

Destruction of Jerusalem; Judah disappears (586).
Astyages of Media.

Egypt	B.C.	Asiatic and Other Countries
4. Apries (Hophra). 19 years. Egyptian fleet developed. Phoenician coast taken. Unsuccessful invasion of Palestine against Nebuchadrezzar (586).	588–569	
5. Amasis (Ahmose II). 44 years. Nebuchadrezzar attempts invasion of Egypt (568). Death of Apries (567 or 566). Alliance with Polycrates of Samos. Greeks numerous in Egypt. Naucratis built. Great prosperity. Egyptian navy greatly increased; Cyprus tributary. Alliance with Babylonia, Lydia (Croesus) and Sparta against Cyrus (547).	569–525	Death of Nebuchadrezzar II (562).
	550	Rise of Cyrus of Anshan. Nabuna'id of Babylon (555–539). Medo-Persian Empire founded by Cyrus.
6. Psamtik III. A few months. Conquest of Egypt by Cambyses, the Persian. Egypt becomes a Persian province.	525	Nubian Kingdom of Meroe developes.

NOTES ON RECENT DISCOVERIES

NOTE I.—Since my attempt to reconstruct the Eleventh Dynasty (Abhandlungen der Berl. Akad., 1904, pp. 156–161; and AJSL, XXI, 163 *ff.*; later and better BAR, I, 415–419), important new documents have turned up, which show that my reconstruction was in several places premature and based on too little evidence. According to a new stela now in Cairo (see Maspero, Rev. critique, Nov., 1905; Sethe, AZ, 42, 132–134), an important official named Henu served under the following kings in succession:

1. Horus Wahenekh-Intef ("many years").
2. Long lacuna.
3. His predecessor's son Horus Senekh ———, son of Re, Mentuhotep.

A second stela in the British Museum (Naville & Hall, The XIth Dynasty Temple at Deir el-Bahari, part I, 1907, p. 1), gives the same succession completely as follows:

1. Horus Wahenekh-Intef.
2. Horus Nakhtneb-Tepnefer-Intef.
3. Horus Senekhibtowe-Mentuhotep.

This gives us a new Mentuhotep. Furthermore, the continuation of the excavations behind Nibhepetre-Mentuhotep's temple at Der el-Bahri, shows that Nibhotep-Mentuhotep (of Lepsius) was a misreading of Nibhapetre-Mentuhotep, another new Mentuhotep (replacing Nibhotep), whose tomb lies behind Nibhepetre-Mentuhotep's temple, showing that he was a predecessor of Nibhepetre. The Turin Papyrus and the development of the titularies of these five Mentuhoteps give us their probable order as below. They were preceded by the two Intefs, 1 and 2 above. Thus we have seven kings who may possibly have been preceded by a Mentuhotep, and one or two (?) Intefs who follow (?) the nomarch in the erratic Karnak list. Sethe has, however, now shown (AZ, 42, 132 *f.*) that the Turin Papyrus contained but *six* kings in this dynasty. I have drawn some of this matter from a full reëxamination of the materials by Eduard Meyer (Abh. der Berl. Akad., Jan., 1908). The dynasty thus reconstructed is as follows:

ELEVENTH DYNASTY, 2160–2000 B. C.

(Preceded by Nomarch Intef and possibly a Mentuhotep and another Intef.)

1. Horus Wahenekh-Intef, $50 + X$ years.
2. Horus Nakhtneb-Tepnefer-Intef, X years.
3. Horus Senekhibtowe-Mentuhotep, X years.
4. Nibhapetre-Mentuhotep, X years.
5. Nibtowere-Mentuhotep, $2 + X$ years.
6. Nibhepetre-Mentuhotep, $46 + X$ years.
7. Senekhkere-Mentuhotep, $8 + X$ years.

Known length, 160 years.

NOTE II.—The two huge colossi on the Island of Argo, above the third cataract, do not belong to a Sebekhotep, as all the histories state, so far as I know (including my own, p. 212 and Fig. 99). These colossi are late Nubian, dating centuries after the separation of Nubia and Egypt. The only statue of Sebekhotep on the island is a small life-size sitting figure of the king in granite, which I had the privilege of inspecting this year (1907). It weighs *far less* than the Soleb lions of Amenhotep III (now in the British Museum), which were transported by a late Nubian king from Soleb to Napata at the foot of the fourth cataract (BAR, II, 896, note d). In view of the total collapse of the kingdom after the fall of the Twelfth Dynasty, there cannot be the slightest doubt, that this easily transportable statue of Sebekhotep was carried by some late Nubian king from some lower Nubian temple to Argo, just above the third cataract, a feat involving far less distance and much less weight than the transport of the Soleb lions. It is thus evident that this Sebekhotep did not erect the monument on Argo, and we are relieved of the long current, but anomalous, conclusion, that a king of the dark age, after the fall of the Twelfth Dynasty, accomplished a great extension of the kingdom southward.

NOTE III.—The siege of Sharuhen which I supposed from the worn Berlin squeeze to have lasted *six* years (BAR, II, 13; BH, p. 227), has been shown by Sethe's examination of the original to have lasted *three* years.

NOTE IV.—The inscription recording an Asiatic war, formerly attributed to Thutmose II, has been shown by Sethe's examination of the original at Der el-Bahri to belong to Thutmose I.

NOTE V.—The appearance of the Kheta under Thutmose III has hitherto always been the earliest occurrence of the Hittites. Mr. King of the British Museum has now found evidence in Babylonian records of an invasion of Babylonia in 1750 B. C. by a people, the reading of whose name coincides with that of the Kheta (KSEH, II, 72, 148).

NOTE VI.—The Nubian city of Ikhnaton was found by the author in 1907 at Sesebi, at the foot of the third cataract, where the columns of Seti I were observed to bear palimpsest reliefs. Through the reliefs of Seti I, the older records of Ikhnaton can still with some difficulty be discerned (See the author's essay in the Independent, Jan. 16, 1908), proving the present temple of Sesebi to have been built as a temple of Aton by Ikhnaton.

NOTE VII.—The inscription in the rear of the first hall at Abu Simbel, published as belonging to Ramses II's first year, I have found by examination of the original, does not belong to Ramses II. Hence the Abu Simbel temple was not begun by Seti I, as this inscription led me to think (BAR, III, 495; BH, 415).

NOTE VIII.—A scarab of Shabaka, recently offered to the Berlin Museum for sale, has now been published by Maspero (Annales du Service des Antiquités, VII, 22). It contains an evident reference to the Asiatic war, in the inscription which it bears. This inscription reads:
"Shabaka, given life, beloved of Amon more than any king who has been since the foundation of the earth, he has slain those rebelling against him in South and North, in all countries; the Sand-Dwellers (Beduin) revolting against him have fallen by his blade. They come of themselves as living captives, each one of them urging his brother, because he has done excellent things for his (?) father, because he so much loved him."
The mention of the Beduin is of course a reminiscence of Shabaka's Asiatic war. The scarab is said to have been found in Asia.

NOTE IX.—Quite unexpectedly an inscription of Tanutamon's eighth year has just turned up at Thebes (Legrain, Annales du Service des Antiquités, VII, 226). As he of course numbered his years from the beginning of his coregency (663 B. C.), he therefore held Thebes until 655 B. C. This is the year before Psamtik I established his daughter as sacerdotal princess of Thebes.

Evidently this establishment of his daughter by Psamtik I followed directly upon Tanutamon's death or retirement, in the same year. The fact that the Nubians returned to Thebes after its sack by the Assyrians in 661 B. C., and held it for at least six, and perhaps seven, years longer, places the close of the Nubian supremacy, and their final retirement from Egypt (655–654 B. C.), in a less ignominious light.

NOTE X.—The excavations of Winckler at Boghaz-köi in Asia Minor, east of the Kisil-irmak (Halys), five days' journey east of Angora, in 1906 and 1907, have shown that this place was the seat of Hittite power. In the numerous cuneiform tablets which he found there, some in Babylonian and some in Hittite, this place is called "Khatti." Here Winckler found the cuneiform original of the treaty of peace between Ramses II and the Hittite king Khetasar (cuneiform Hattušil). (See Winckler's report, OLZ, 15th Dec., 1906; MDOG, No. 35.) The recent evidence of a Hittite invasion of Babylonia about 1750 B. C. (King, KSEH, II, 148) shows that there was a great expansion of Hittite power at just the time when the Hyksos were entering Egypt. The Hyksos empire was thus thrown back upon Egypt. Or was the Hyksos invasion of Egypt itself Hittite?

NOTE XI.—Recently two reliefs now in the Cairo Museum have been put forward by W. Max Müller (Publ. No. 53, Carnegie Inst., Washington, Pl. I–II, pp. 5–11) as showing intercourse between Egypt and the Ægean, as well as Mesopotamia in the Sixth Dynasty or "about (and 'before') 2500 B. C." The first relief depicts a row of men bearing blocks of tin (*dhty*) and is dated by Müller on grounds of style in the Sixth Dynasty. The accompanying inscription, however, writes the *y* in *dhty* with the two oblique strokes, a palæographic peculiarity *which never occurs so early as the Sixth Dynasty*. The sculpture cannot be older than the Twelfth Dynasty (2000–1788 B. C.) The other relief (Pl. II) shows two fragmentary human figures wearing Syrian or Semitic costumes, supposed by Müller to be "Mesopotamians," and dated by him "before 2500 B. C.," perhaps "Dynasty 5." The relief is a characteristic Empire work not older than the sixteenth century B. C.

NOTE XII.—Recently the Nubian expedition of Psamtik II has been attributed to Psamtik I, and the famous Greek inscription left by mercenaries at Abu Simbel has been made the oldest of Greek inscriptions, furnishing a "firm basis" for "Greek epigraphics" (W. Max Müller, Publ. No. 53, Carnegie Inst., Washington, pp. 22–23, Pl. 12–13). This conclusion of Müller is based upon an inscription at Karnak stated by him to record an expedition of *Psamtik I* against Nubia. In this inscription, however, as published by Müller himself, the name of the royal author thereof (occurring twice) is *Psamtik II!* (*Nfr-yb-Rˤ* and *Mnḫ-yb*). No expedition of Psamtik I against Nubia is known.

NOTE XIII.—Readers who notice the discrepancy between the Babylonian dates given above in the Chronological Summary and those heretofore current, should note that recent researches have disclosed the fact that the First Dynasty of Babylon was immediately followed by the Third, the Second being a parallel dynasty of kings ruling at the mouth of the Euphrates. It is thus no longer possible to maintain the early date of Sargon I and Naramsin, a fact long ago accepted by Eduard Meyer and Lehmann-Haupt. Even so ardent an advocate of extremely early Babylonian dates as Hilprecht, has relinquished the early date of Sargon I and Naramsin. Indeed, as Eduard Meyer recently remarked to the author, it is highly improbable that we possess a single Babylonian document older than 3000 B.C. A highly organized, centralized, stable and enduring state in Egypt (the Old Kingdom) is over a thousand years older than in Babylonia (First Dynasty), for the consolidation of the smaller kingdoms into one nation, under the first of successive dynasties, took place twelve to thirteen hundred years earlier in Egypt than in Babylonia (See Ranke., Univ. of Penn. Publ., Series A, Vol. I, part I, p. 8, note 1, and for the final results on the parallel character of the Second Dynasty, see KSEH, II).

A SELECTED BIBLIOGRAPHY

I. GENERAL HISTORIES OF ANTIQUITY

See list in GHBA (G. S. Goodspeed, A History of the Babylonians and Assyrians, New York, 1906, second edition). It may be added that a new edition of Meyer's Geschichte des Altertums is in preparation and the first volume containing the early Orient is now in press. A new edition of Maspero's smaller history of antiquity (Histoire ancienne des Peuples de l'Orient) appeared in 1904.

II. EGYPTIAN HISTORY

Maspero's three volumes already cited among General Histories of Antiquity (GHBA), especially full on Egypt (Steindorff, see p. 450).

MG..... Eduard Meyer—Geschichte des Alten Aegyptens. Berlin, 1887.

Wiedemann—Aegyptische Geschichte. Gotha, 1884–1885.

W. M. F. Petrie—History of Egypt. Vol. I–III. London.

Budge—History of Egypt. Vol. I–VIII. London.

Brugsch—A History of Egypt under the Pharaohs. London.

Bissing—Geschichte Aegyptens. Berlin, 1904.

BH ..... Breasted—A History of Egypt. New York, 1905.

NGH ... Newberry and Garstang—A Short History of Ancient Egypt. London, 1904.

On the later periods:

Mahaffy—History of Egypt under the Ptolemaic Dynasty. London 1899.

Milne—History of Egypt under Roman Rule. London, 1898.

Stanley Lane-Poole—History of Egypt in the Middle Ages. London, 1901. (These three forming volumes IV–VI in Petrie's series.)

III. TEXTS AND TRANSLATIONS

A. TEXTS

It would be impossible in the limits here imposed to give even a selected list of the great number of Egyptian texts already published. The science is now engaged upon the great task of replacing the old and inaccurate, but once standard, editions of the Egyptian monuments, by new and final standard publications, meeting all the modern requirements of accuracy and detail. The largest of the old publications still in use are the following three large folios of plates:

LD.....Lepsius—Denkmaeler aus Aegypten und Aethiopien. Abth., I–XII. Berlin, 1849–1858.
CM.....Champollion—Monuments de l'Egypte et de la Nubie. Vol. I–IV. Paris, 1835–1845.
RM.....Rosellini—Monumenti dell' Egitto e della Nubia. Vol. I–III. Pisa, 1834.

The most important monuments are now being placed at the disposal of students in a convenient and handy form combining accuracy, perspicuity and cheapness in Urkunden des aegyptischen Altertums, ed. Steindorff. Leipzig, 1903 *ff*.

B. TRANSLATIONS

Many monuments have been translated in special publications or in the current journals of the science. The translations of religious texts are noted below (V. Religion), and those in literature (belles lettres) in VI. A limited selection of translated texts will be found in Records of the Past. The historical documents in English, complete from the earliest times to the Persian conquest, will be found in:

BAR....Breasted—Ancient Records of Egypt. Vol. I–V. Chicago, 1906–1907.

The references to BAR in this history refer to the paragraphs, *not* to the pages. Full information on the bibliography of each monument will be found therein, so that further references herein can be dispensed with.

IV. GEOGRAPHY, TRAVEL, EXPLORATION, ETC.

Contemporary descriptions of ancient Egypt are chiefly Herodotus and Strabo. The condition of the monuments in the Middle

Ages is scantily indicated in the Arab geographers and historians, particularly:

>Abd el-Latîf—Relation de l'Egypte par Abd al-Latîf ... traduit ... par Silvestre de Sacy. Paris, 1810.
>El-Idrisi—Description de l'Afrique. ed. Dozy et De Goeje. Leyden, 1866.
>—Géographie d'Idrisi. Traduite ... par P. Amadée Jaubert. Paris, 1836–1840.
>Ibn Dukmak—Description of Egypt (in Arabic) Bulaḳ Press, A. H. 1309.
>Makrizi—Description Historique et Topographique de l'Egypte traduit par P. Casanova (in Mémoires ... de l'Institut français ... du Caire. III. Cairo, 1906).

The monuments of the Nile valley were first disclosed to Europe in published form in the great "Description de l'Egypte," published by the members of Napoleon's Egyptian expedition (Plates Vol. I–XI; Texte, Vol. I–XXVI. Paris, 1820–1830). The gradual exploration of the country, and the discoveries among the monuments in modern times, may be traced in the following works:

>J. Lobo—A Short Relation of the River Nile. London, 1669.
>Wansleben—The Present State of Egypt or a New Relation of a Late Voyage into that Kingdom, performed in the years 1672 and 1673. London, 1678.
>Leach—Travels on the Nile. London, 1742.
>Pococke—World Displayed, or a Curious Collection of Voyages and Travels. Vol. XII. London, 1774.
>—Voyages de Richard Pococke. Vol. I–VI. Neufchâtel, 1772.
>—A Description of the East. London, 1743.
>Norden—Travels in Egypt and Nubia (1737–1738), translated and enlarged by Dr. Peter Templeman. Vol. I–II. London, 1757.
>Bruce—Travels to Discover the Source of the Nile in the Years 1768–1773. Vol. I–VII. London and Edinburgh, 1813.
>W. G. Browne—Travels in Africa, Egypt and Syria, 1792–1798. London, 1806.
>Denon—Travels in Africa. London, 1803.
>Legh—Narrative of a Journey in Egypt and the Country Beyond the Cataracts. London, 1816.
>Burckhardt—Travels in Nubia. London, 1819.

A SELECTED BIBLIOGRAPHY

Belzoni—Narrative of Operations and Discoveries . . . in Egypt and Nubia. London, 1820.

Cailliaud—Voyage à Meroe . . . 1819–1822. Paris, 1826–1828.

Drovetti—Voyage a l'Oasis de Dakel. Paris, 1821.

Waddington and Hanbury—Journal of a Visit to Some Parts of Ethiopia. London, 1822.

Champollion—Lettre à M. Dacier, relative à l'alphabet des hiéroglyphes. Paris, 1822. (Contains an account of the decipherment of the hieroglyphic by him.)
Lettres écrites d'Egypte et de Nubie. Paris, 1833.
Notices descriptives (Text of Monuments de l' Egypt). Vol. I–II. Paris, 1844.

Hartleben—Champollion, sein Leben und sein Werk. Vol. I–II. Berlin, 1906.

Prudhoe—Extracts from Private Memoranda kept by Lord Prudhoe on a Journey from Cairo to Sennaar in 1829. Journal Royal Geogr. Soc., V., 1835.

Wilkinson—Topography of Thebes and General View of Egypt. London, 1835.

Wilkinson—Modern Egypt and Thebes. Vol. I–II. London, 1843.

Hoskins—Travels in Ethiopia. London, 1835.

D'Athanasi—Researches and Discoveries in Upper Egypt. London, 1836.

Russegger—Reisen in Europa, Asien und Afrika, 1835 bis 1841. Vol. I–III. Stuttgart, 1841, (Vol. II is on the Nile valley).

Ferlini—Cenno sugli Scavi Operati nella Nubia e Catalogo degli Oggetti Ritrovati. Bologna, 1837.

Ferlini—Relation Historique des Fouilles Opéreés dans la Nubie. Rome, 1838.

Holroyd—Notes on a Journey to Kordofan in 1836–1837. London, 1839.

L'Hôte—Lettres écrites d'Egypte en 1838–1839. Paris, 1840.

Lepsius—Discoveries in Egypt, Ethiopia and the Peninsula of Sinai in the Years 1842–1845. London, 1852. Second ed., 1853.

Lepsius—Letters from Egypt, Ethiopia and Sinai. Translated by J. B. Horner. London, 1853. Text (Vol. I–VI), accompanying the Denkmaeler aus Aegypten und Nubien.

Brugsch—Die Géographie des alten Aegypten. Leipzig, 1857.

A SELECTED BIBLIOGRAPHY

Brugsch—Reiseberichte aus Aegypten. Leipzig, 1855.

Brugsch—Reise nach der grossen Oase el-Khargeh. Leipzig, 1878.

Brugsch—Dictionnaire géographique. Leipzig, 1879.

Mariette—Description des fouilles éxécutées en Egypte, en Nubie, et au Soudan, 1850–1854. Paris, 1863–1867.

Speke—Journal of the Discovery of the Source of the Nile. London and Edinburgh, 1864.

> With this compare the discovery of higher sources behind the equatorial lakes by

Baumann—Durch Massailand zur Nilquelle, 1891–1893. Berlin, 1894.

Baker, Sir S.—Albert N'yanza and the Great Basin of the Nile. Vol. I–II. London, 1866, 1872.

Baker, Sir S.—The Nile Tributaries of Abysinia. London, 1867.

Dillmann—Ueber die Anfaenge des Axumitischen Reichs. Berlin, 1879.

Duemichen—Geographical Introduction in Meyer, Geschichte des Alten Aegyptens. Berlin, 1887.

Ebers—Egypt, Descriptive, Historical, Picturesque. London, 1881.

Hilmy, Prince Ibrahim—Bibliography of Egypt and the Soudan. Vol. I–II. London, 1886.

Brown, Maj. R. H.—The Fayum and Lake Moeris. London, 1892.

Steindorff—Durch die Libysche Wueste zur Amonsoase. Leipzig, 1904.

Gleichen—The Anglo-Egyptian Sudan. Vol. I–II. London, 1905.

Borchardt—Nilhoehe und Nilstandsmarken. Abhandlungen der Kgl. Preuss. Akad., 1905.

Lyons—The Physiography of the River Nile and its Basin. London, 1906.

Petrie—Ten Years Digging in Egypt. London, 1893.

Petrie—Methods and Aims in Archæology. London, 1901.

Budge—The Egyptian Sudan, Vol. I–II. London, 1907. Egypt Exploration Fund—Memoirs, 28 vols.—Archæological Survey, 16 vols.—Græco-Roman Branch, 8 vols.—Special Publications, 5 vols. N. B. A survey of all discoveries in Egypt each year, beginning 1892, is furnished by the Annual Archæological Reports, edited by F. Ll. Griffith.

See also the series of volumes by
Petrie, and his Egyptian Research Account; also those of the
Deutsche Orientgesellschaft, and those of
Reisner—University of California Expedition, now about to appear; and
Breasted—The Temples of Lower Nubia. Chicago, 1906. University of Chicago Expedition.
The Monuments of Upper Nubia and the Sudan. Chicago, 1908. University of Chicago Expedition.
Mémoires publiés par les Membres de la Mission archéologique française au Caire. From 1881 on. Continued as Mémoires publiés pas les Membres de l'Institut Français d'Archéologie orientale du Caire. Cairo.

A visit to all the chief monuments of Egypt with maps, plans of all great temples, and one hundred stereographic views accompanied by popular explanations and discussions:
Breasted—Egypt Through the Stereoscope. A Journey Through the Land of the Pharaohs. New York, 1905.

V. RELIGION

The principal texts are:
Maspero—Les Inscriptions des Pyramides de Saqqarah. Paris, 1894 (Reprint from Recueil de Travaux. Vols. III–V, VII–XII, XIV.
Naville—Das aegyptische Totenbuch der 18–20 Dynastie. Berlin, 1886.
Budge—The Book of the Dead. Vol. I–III. London, 1898.
Budge—The Hieratic Papyrus of Nesiamsu. Westminster, 1891.
Lepsius—Ælteste Texte des Totenbuches. Berlin, 1867.
Lepsius—Das Totenbuch der Aegypter nach dem hieroglyphischen Papyrus in Turin . . . Leipzig, 1842.
Lefebure—Hypogées royaux (Mém. de la Mission archéolog. française, II–III, 1–2).
Schack—Das Zweiwegebuch.
von Bergmann—Das Buch vom Durchwandeln der Ewigkeit. Vienna, 1877.
Jéquier—Livre de ce qu'il y à dans l'Hadès. Paris, 1894.

There are many more mortuary and magical texts not included above.

The treatises are:

Erman—A Handbook of Egyptian Religion. Translated by A. S. Griffith. London, 1907.

Steindorff—The Religion of the Ancient Egyptians. New York and London, 1905.

Wiedemann—Die Religion der alten Aegypter. Muenster, 1890 (also to be had in English).

Maspero—Etudes de Mythologie et d'Archéologie égyptiennes. Vol. I–III. Paris, 1893–98.

Lange—Contribution on Egyptian religion in Saussaye's Lehrbuch der Religionsgeschichte.

Budge—Gods of the Egyptians. Vol. I–II. London, 1902.

The chief translations are:

Maspero—Translation of the Pyramid Texts in above edition of same.

Renouf—Book of the Dead in Life Work of the Late Sir Peter Le Page Renouf, Vol. IV. Paris, 1907. Conclusion by Naville.

Budge—The Book of the Dead. Vol. I–III. London, 1898.

VI. MANNERS AND CUSTOMS; ART AND LITERATURE

Erman—Life in Ancient Egypt. Translated by H. M. Tirard. London, 1895.

Wilkinson—Manners and Customs of the Ancient Egyptians. Vol. I–III. London, 1885. Now out of date, but an invaluable treasury of materials.

Steindorff—Die Bluetezeit des Pharaonenreichs. Bielefeld, 1900.

Perrot & Chipiez—History of Ancient Art. I. Egypt.

Maspero—Egyptian Archæology.

Spiegelberg—Geschichte der Aegyptischen Kunst. Leipzig, 1903.

Borchardt—Die Aegyptische Pflanzensaule. Berlin, 1897.

von Bissing—Denkmaeler aegyptischer Sculptur. München, 1905–1907 (not yet complete).

Erman—General Sketch of Egyptian literature proper. ELAE. Chapter XV.

Griffith—Best series of translations in English in

Library of the World's Best Literature, edited by C. D. Warner.

Maspero—Les Contes populaires de L'Egypte ancienne, 3rd ed. Paris, 1905.

Petrie—Egyptian Tales. London. (After Griffith and Maspero.)

Erman & Krebs—Aus den Papyrus der Königlichen Museen. Berlin, 1899.

Müller—Die Liebespoesie der alten Aegypter. Leipzig, 1899.

Demotic tales:

Griffith—Stories of the High Priests of Memphis. London, 1900.

Krall—in KFB and WZKM, XVII.

VII. EGYPTIAN MONUMENTS AND THE BIBLE

Eduard Meyer—Der Moses-Sage und die Leviten. Sitzungsber. Berlin. Akad., 1905, 640.

Eduard Meyer—Die Israeliten und Ihre Nachbarstaemme.

Steindorff—In Recent Research in Bible Lands, ed. Hilprecht. Philadelphia, 1906.

Griffith—In Authority and Archæology, ed. Hogarth. New York, 1899.

Müller—Asien und Europa nach altaegyptischen Denkmaelern. Leipzig, 1893.

Spiegelberg—Aegyptische Randglossen zum Alten Testament. Strassburg, 1904.

Spiegelberg—Aufenthalt Israels in Aegypten. Strassburg, 1904.

VIII. COLLECTIONS OF ESSAYS, SERIES, JOURNALS, ETC.

Zeitschrift für Aegyptische Sprache und Altertumskunde, ed. by Erman & Steindorff. Leipzig.

Untersuchungen zur Geschichte und Altertumskunde Aegyptens, ed. by Sethe. Leipzig.

Recueil de Travaux relatifs à la Philologie et à l'Archéologie égyptiennes et assyriennes, ed. Maspero. Paris. Vol. I, 1870; Vols. II ff., 1880 ff.

Revue égyptologique, ed. by Revillout. Paris, 1880 ff.

Sphinx, ed. Ernst Andersson, Upsala (formerly K. Piehl). From 1897 on.

Mélanges d'archéologie égyptienne et assyrienne. Paris, 1872–1878.

Mélanges égyptologiques, ed. Chabas. Chalon-sur-Saône, 1862–1873.

L'Egyptologie, ed. Chabas. Paris, 1876–1878.

Bulletin de l'institut français d'archéologie orientale au Caire.

Annales du Service des Antiquités de l'Egypte. Cairo, 1900 *ff*.

Bibliothèque égyptologique, ed. Maspero. Vol. I–XII. Paris, 1893 *ff*.

Maspero—Etudes égyptiennes. Paris, 1886 *ff*.

Proceedings of the Society of Biblical Archæology. London. From 1879 on.

Transactions of the Society of Biblical Archæology. Ten vols. only. 1872 on.

American Journal of Semitic Languages, ed. Harper. Chicago. (Continuing Hebraica.)

IX. CHRONOLOGY

Eduard Meyer—Aegyptische Chronologie. Abhandl. der Berl. Akad., 1904.

Ginzel—Handbuch der Mathematischen und Technischen Chronologie. Vol. I. Zeitrechnung der Babylonier, Aegypter, Mohammedaner, Perser, etc. Leipzig, 1906.

Lehmann—Zwei Hauptprobleme der altorientalischen Chronologie. Berlin, 1898.

King—Studies in Eastern History: Chronicles Concerning early Babylonian Kings. Vol. I–II. London, 1907.

Niebuhr—Die Chronologie der Geschichte Israels, Aegyptens, Babyloniens und Assyriens. Leipzig, 1896.

Breasted—BAR, I, 38–75.

X. ABBREVIATIONS

AS......Annales du Service.
AJSL....American Journal of Semitic Languages.
AL......Winckler, Amarna Letters.
BAR.....Breasted, Ancient Records of Egypt.
BFLM...Brown, Fayum and Lake Moeris.
BH......Breasted, A History of Egypt.

A SELECTED BIBLIOGRAPHY

BIHC... Birch, Inscriptions in the Hieratic Character.
BI ...... Bulletin de l'Institut.
BK ...... Breasted, Battle of Kadesh.
BT ...... Brugsch, Thesaurus.
BTLN .. Breasted, Temples of Lower Nubia.
CC ...... Catalogue of Cairo Museum.
DG .... Duemichen, Grabpalast.
EA ...... Erman, Aegypten u. aegypt. Leben.
EG ...... " Gespräch eines Lebensmüden.
ELAE ... " Life in Ancient Egypt.
EHEL .. " Handbook of Egyptian Religion.
FE ...... Festschrift für Ebers.
GHBA .. Goodspeed, History of the Babylonians and Assyrians.
GIM .... Gardiner, Inscription of Mes (ŠU, IV).
GJL .... Gautier-Jéquier, Fouilles de Licht.
GKP .... Griffith, Kahun Papyri.
GLWBL " Library of World's Best Literature.
GMBK .. Garstang, Mahasna and Bet Khallaf.
GTD .... " Tombs of the Third Dynasty.
KFB .... Krall, Festgaben für Budinger, Innsbruck, 1898.
KSEH ... King, Studies in Eastern History, I–II.
KSGW .. Berichte der Phil.-hist. Classe der Königl. Sächs. Gesell. der Wissenschaften zu Leipzig.
LD ...... Lepsius, Denkmäeler aus Aegypten und Aethiopien.
MA ..... Mariette, Adydos.
MAAG .. Meyer, Das erste Auftreten der Arier in der Gesch. Sitzungsber. der Berl. Akad., 1908 (9. Jan.).
MC ..... Meyer, Aegyptische Chronologie.
MCd'AB Mariette, Cat. gén. d'Abydos.
MCM ... de Morgan, Catalogue des Monuments.
MCP .... Maspero, Contes populaires.
MD ..... de Morgan, Fouilles à Dahchour.
MDOG .. Mitteilungen der Deutschen Orientgesellschaft.
MG ..... Meyer, Gesch. des alten Aegyptens.
ML ..... Müller, Liebespoesie.
MM ..... Mariette, Les Mastabas.
MMD ... " Monuments diverse.
MMR ... Maspero, Momies royales.
MNC ... Meyer, Nachtrag zur aeg. chron. Abh. der Berl. Akad., 1908.
MSPER . Mitth. aus d. Samml. d. Pap. Erzherzog Rainer.
NA ...... Naville, Ahnas el-Medineh.
NGH ... Newberry-Garstang, History of Egypt.
OLZ .... Orientalistische Literaturzeitung.
PA ...... Papyrus Anastasi (Brit. Mus. Select Papyri).

A SELECTED BIBLIOGRAPHY

PB......Papyrus de Boulaq.
PCH....Perrot-Chipiez, History of Art.
PEFQS..Palestine Expl. Fund, Quart. Statement.
PG......Petrie, Pyramids and Temples of Gizeh.
PHE.... " History of Egypt.
PI....... " Illahun.
PKGH.. " Kahun, Gurob & Hawara.
PKM ...Erman-Krebs, Papyrus des Königl. Museums.
PP......Papyrus Prisse.
PPS.....Petrie, Cat. of Egyptian Antiquities found in the Peninsula of Sinai.
PS......Petrie, Season in Egypt.
PSall....Papyrus Sallier.
PScar...Petrie, Scarabs.
PSBA...Proceedings of the Soc. of Bib. Arch.
PT......Petrie, Tanis.
PET.... " Egyptian Tales.
PW.....Papyrus Westcar, ed. Erman.
QH.....Quibell, Hieraconpolis.
RIH....de Rouge, Inscr. hierogl.
Rec......Recueil de Travaux, ed. Maspero.
SBA.....Sitzungsberichte d. Berlin. Akad.
SEI.....Sharpe, Egyptian Inscriptions.
SS......Spiegelberg, Studien und Materialien.
TP......Turin Papyrus of Kings.
WAL....Winckler, Amarna Letters.
WRS....Weill, Recueil des Inscr. Egypt. du Sinai.
WUAG..Winckler, Untersuchungen zur altorientalischen Geschichte.
WZKM..Wiener Zeitschr. f. d. Kunde d. Morgenl.

INDEX OF NAMES AND SUBJECTS

NOTE. For a full statement of the system of transliteration adopted, the reader is referred to the preface of BAR, I., pp. xiv. ff. Hieroglyphic writing does not indicate vowels. They must be supplied by the modern scholar more or less arbitrarily in most cases, even the *place* of the vowel among the consonants being often uncertain. The vowels thus supplied are commonly given the continental or Italian sounds and no vowels are silent. "Kh" indicates a single sound, a deep guttural ch as in the Scotch *loch* or German *nach*. W and Y are always consonantal, and are pronounced as in English. The latter statement is for practical purposes also true of all the remaining consonants. The primary accent is indicated by '; the secondary, if any, by '. The letter after a name indicates its character: *e.g.*, c = city; d, district; g, god or goddess; k, king; n, noble; o, officer; p, people; q, queen; r, river; t, town. M. K. = Middle Kingdom; O. K. = Old Kingdom; Emp. = Empire; Rest. = Restoration.

A'-BA, 392
A-bab'-deh, p, 7
Ab-sha', 158
Abd-a-shir'-ta, n, 282, 298
Abd-khi'-ba, n, 285, 297
Abram, 363
Abu Sim'-bel, 312, 319, 407; Greek inscription at, 407
A-bu-sir', 115
Abydos, 43, 46, 50, 148, 300, 301, 302
Abyssinia, 4, 8, 383
Achae'ans, 329
Aegean, earliest commerce with, 50; in M. K., 159; in Emp., 211, 234, 235, 253, 325
Ae-gi'-na, 413
Aeolians, 413
Africa, 3, 4, 7, 29; earliest exploration of, 124 ff.; circumnavigation of, 407

Agriculture, 9-10, 88; earliest, 32
Ah-mo'-se I., k, 186-193, 205 f.
Ahmose II. = A-ma'-sis, q. v.
Ahmose, q, 208, 214
Ahmose (son of Ebana), n, 187, 188
A-khet-a'-ton, c (see also Amarna), 270-272, 285, 286, 287, 288
Akh-tho'-es, k, 134
Alabastron'polis, c, 293
A'-la-sa, or Alasia, see Cyprus.
A-lep'-po, 232, 239, 303, 305
Al-ta'-qu, c, 375
A'-ma-da, 247
A-mar'-na, t (see also Akhetaton), 270
Amarna Letters, 250, 288
A-ma'-sis, k, 411-18
A-men-ar'-dis, q, 371, 377, 381

455

456 INDEX OF NAMES AND SUBJECTS

A'-men-em-hab', n, 233, 237
A'-men-em-het' I., k, 137 f., 139 f., 152 f., 164, 167
Amenemhet II., k, 154, 155
Amenemhet III., k, 160–163, 169, 170
Amenemhet IV., k, 170
A-men-ho'-tep I., k, 205, 207 f., 258, 359
Amenhotep II., k, 241, 245–7, 253
Amenhotep III., 248–263, 280, 331
Amenhotep IV., see Ikhnaton.
Amenhotep, son of Ha'pu, 255
Amenhotep (High Priest of Amon), 349
A-me-ni', n, 154
A-men-me-ses', k, 332
Ammon, 375, 408
Amon and Amon-Re, g, 203, 228, 267, 268 f., 286 f., 288, 304, 322 f., 337, 341–3, 352 f.; in Syria, 230, 337, 352 f.; in Nubia, 367 ff.
Amon, High Priest of, 202 f., 268, 322 f., 342, 348 ff., 352, 362, 364, 377, 388; as King, 350 ff., 355 f., 357–361
Amor and Amorites, 282, 298, 317, 327, 335, 337, 351
A'-nath, g, 318, 324
Animal worship, 61 f., 324, 397
Annals (see also Palermo Stone), 47, 238
An'-shan, 416
A-nu'-bis, g, 48
A'-pis, g, 48, 397
A-po'phis, k, 176, 179, 183, 184, 185
Ap'-ri-es, k, 408–412
Arabia, 29, 210, 387
Arabian Desert, 7
A-rai'-na, c, 239

Aramaeans, 210, 284; in Egypt, 398
Arch, 94
Architecture, earliest, 44–45; in O. K., 99–100; in M. K., 165; in Emp., 218 f., 255–9, 339; in Rest. 394
Armenians, 281
Army, 82, 144 f., 193–5, 200, 202, 224, 252, 318 f., 389 f., 410 f., 414
Ar'-ra-pa-khi'-tis, c, 239
Ar-si'noe, 160, 162
Art, earliest, 30–32; proto-dynastic, 42–43; in O. K., 88–100; in M. K., 165 f.; in hither Asia, 211 f.; in Emp., 255–261, 278 f., 300, 301, 319 f., 338; in Rest., 393 f.
Ar-ta'-ta-ma, k, 247, 251
Ar'-vad, c, 211, 230, 231, 303, 310, 335, 409
Aryans, in Mitanni, 212.
Ash'-dod, 402
A-shur-ban'-i-pal, k, 380–382, 387 f.
Asia, 3, 29
Asia Minor, 4, 89, 159, 211, 212, 280 f., 233, 235, 304, 334, 343, 388
As'-ka-lon, c, 285, 328, 331, 375, 404
Asklep'ias, 105
Assuan', c, 7, 125
Assyria and Assyrians, 177, 229, 249, 250, 251, 368 f., 402 f.; Western empire of, 373 ff., 375–388, 402; fall of, 404, 406
As-tar'-te, g, 318, 324
Astronomy, 93
As-ty'-a-ges, 416
At-ba'-ra, r, 4
Athens, 414
A-thrib'-is, c, 380, 396

INDEX OF NAMES AND SUBJECTS

Atlantic, 3
A'-ton, g, 267 ff., 299; cities of, 269 f.
A-tum', 58, 59
Ava'ris, c, 176, 177, 178, 179, 180, 185, 186, 187
A'-yan, d, 88
A-zi'-ru, 282, 283, 284, 298

BAAL, g, 210; in Egypt, 318, 324
Baal, k, 379
Babylonia, Old, 33, 46, 149, 159, 212, 229, 248, 249, 250, 262, 280, 281, 317, 375, 376, 387, 398, 404; gifts from, 233
Babylonia, New, 404, 406–416
Ba'-hr Yu'-suf, r, 5, 6
Bast, g, 60
Beduin, 50, 121, 159, 182, 213, 283, 284, 297, 316, 337, 375
Be'-ga, p, 29
Bek, o, 270, 278
Bek-et-a'-ton, 270
Ben-A'nath, 318
Ben-'O'zen, n, 318
Berber, 329
Berût', c, 284, 303
Beth-She'an, c, 351
Bet Khallâf', d, 105
Bi-khu'-ru, n, 283
Bint-A'nath, 318
Blemm'-yes, p, 383
Blue Nile, 4, 8, 9
Boats, see ships
Boc'-cho-ris, k, 371 f., 374
Bo-ghaz-Kö'-i, t, 281
Book of the Dead, 150, 203 f., 391
Brick, 89–90; earliest, 31
Bronze, 394
Bu-bast'-is, c, 60, 110, 165, 177, 184, 363, 364; kings at, 360–366, 370
Bur-ra-bur'-yash, k, 280

Bu-sir'-is, 61
Bu'-to, g, 36, 41
Buto, c, 34, 36, 46, 396
Bu-yu-wa'-wa, 360
Byb'los, c, 158, 211, 245, 263, 282, 283 f., 351, 352

CA-LA-SYR'-I-ES, 390
Calendar, 15, 25, 35–36, 46
Cam-by'-ses, 247, 383, 418
Canaanites, 210, 331, 362
Canal, 5, 9, 11; through first cataract, 122, 155 f., 209; from Nile to Red Sea, 159, 218, 407
Cappado'cia, 159
Car'-che-mish, c, 232, 303, 335; battle of, 406
Carians, 388, 389, 399
Carmel, m, 224
Cataract, 4–5, 8–9, 122
Cedar, 90, 247, 338, 352
Chariot, 195
Chi'-os, 413
Chronology, 24–26, 46
Cilicia, 89, 304
Cim-mer'-i-ans, p, 387, 388
City-state, 33, 210
Cla-zo-me'-nae, 413
Climate, 8, 10–11
Cni'-dus, 413
Cnos'-sos, 179, 253
Column & Colonnade, 99–100, 257, 394
Commerce and Trade, 91–92; earliest, 33; in O. K., 83, 106, 114, 122, 127; in M. K., 159; in Emp., 210 f., 253 f.; in Rest., 398 f., 407
Copper, 31, 32, 42, 89, 92, 106, 246, 251, 338; as money, 163
Cop'-tos, 31, 127, 154 f., 237
Court, royal, 74 f.
Costume, 86–87; earliest, 30 f.

INDEX OF NAMES AND SUBJECTS

Courts of justice, 79 f., 143, 195, 198 f., 344
Crete, 179, 235, 253, 254, 333
Crocodilo′polis, c, 162
Croesus, k, 416
Crown, 34, 36, 41
Cy-ax′-a-res, k, 404, 406
Cyprus, 211, 234, 235, 239, 250, 251, 253, 298, 317, 335, 354, 409, 415
Cy-re′-ne, c, 411, 413
Cyrus, 416 f.

Dah-shur′, t, 106, 107
Damascus, 227, 263
Da-mi-ette′, c, 6
Dan-a′-oi, p, 334
Daph′-nae, c, 389, 414
Darda′nians, 304
David, 360
Dead, beliefs regarding, 36, 65–73, 149–51, 203 f.
Decadence, 347–388; sketch of, 21–22; sources, 27–28
De′du, c, 61
Delphians, 413
Delta, 5–6, 7, 8, 11, 12, 15, 33, 34, 35, 38, 121, 236, 237, 311, 314, 329 f., 333, 336, 350, 360 ff., 365, 379 ff., 394, 398, 407
De-mot′-ic, 395
Den′-de-reh, c, 37, 60, 110
Den′-yen, p, 334
Der el-Bah′ri, d, 216, 217
Desert, 3, 4, 6–7, 11–12
De-suk′, t, 110
Dog River, 303, 379
Don′-go-la Province, 208 f.
Dor, c, 351, 352
Dorians, 413
Drama, earliest, 148, 169
Drawing, 97–98, 261
Dush-rat′-ta, k, 251, 280 f.
Dynasties, 15

Ed′-fu, 5, 40, 60, 152
E′-dom, 374, 375
Edomite, 316
Education, 92–94, 395
Egypt, limits of, 4–8, 11; soil of, 5–6, 8–9; shape of, 8 climate, 8; wealth of, 9–10; ruins of, 12; population, 83
Egypt, Lower (see also Delta), 34, 35, 49, 379, 381
Egypt, Upper, 36–39, 41, 49, 78–79, 379, 380
Egyptians, race of, 29 f.; earliest, 29–34
Egyptian Language, origin, 29
Eighteenth Dynasty, 186–9, 205 f., 207–289; date of, 24–25
Eighth Dynasty, 133–4
E-ke′-reth, c, 303
Ek′-wesh, p, 329
E′-lam, 387
E-le-phan-ti′-ne, c, 5, 33, 92, 121, 124, 125, 126, 197, 389
Eleventh Dynasty, 135–7; date of, 25
E-leu′-the-ros, r, 231
E-li′-a-kim, k, 405
El Kab′, c, 36, 41, 46, 157, 186 f., 187, 189
Empire, 186–344; sketch of, 19–21, 24; sources for, 27
E′-nekh-nes-Me-ri-re′, q, 125
En-en′-khet, n, 127
En′-khu, n, 182
E′-reth, c, 337
E-sar-had′-don, k, 378–380
Es-dra-e′-lon, d, 224, 225, 226, 298, 351, 404
Es′-neh, 189
Ethiopia, 383, 390
Ethiopian period, sketch of, 22, 24
E-trus′-cans, p, 329

INDEX OF NAMES AND SUBJECTS

Euphrates, r, 3, 208, 209, 232, 248; northern frontier of Egypt, 213, 233, 234, 405 f.
Europe, 4, 7
European civilization, rise of, 3 f., 7, 12, 13, 14, 50, 159, 253, 329 f., 337 f., 339
Eusebius, 15
Extradition, 251
E'-ye, n, and k, 264, 289
Ezekiel, 415

FAMILY, 83–84
Fayum', d, 6, 161 f., 170
Fifth dynasty, 112–116, 117
First dynasty, 40–51, 300; length and date of, 25
Flax, 91
Flint, 32
Fo-a-khir', Wady, 89
Fourth dynasty, 107–112
Fourteenth dynasty, 182
Furniture, 42–44, 85, 86, 259; earliest, 31
Future life, 36, 65–73, 149–51, 203 f.

GALILEE, 283, 298, 363
Gal'-la, p, 29
Ga'-za, c, 404
Ge-be-len', 182
Gebel Ze-bâ'-ra, 300
Gem-A'-ton, 268, 270, 288
Ge'-zer, t, 158, 285, 331, 362
Gi-lu-khi'-pa, q, 251
Gi'zeh, t, 108, 110, 111
Glass, 90, 259; earliest, 31, 42
God, 265 ff.; local, 33
Gold, 42, 89, 92, 122, 142, 154, 155, 157, 197, 235, 245, 250, 251, 254, 301, 340, 405
Governor of the South, 118–19, 120, 121, 124, 142
Greece, 211, 253

Greeks, 399; influence of Egypt on, 399–402; in Egypt, 389, 398, 399, 400, 410 f., 412–415
Gy'-ges, k, 388

HAL-I-CAR-NAS'-SUS, 413
Ha'-math, c, 280
Ham-ma-mat', 88, 136 f., 142, 153, 348, 377; opening of, 115
Har-khuf', n, 124, 125, 126
Harmhab', k, 287, 289, 293–7
Ha-ti'-ba, q, 354
Hat-sho', c, 336
Hattusil', k, 311
Hauran', 298
Hathor, g, 48, 60, 64
Hatnub', 88, 110, 120
Hat-shep'-sut, q, 214 f., 216–222
Hatshepsut-Mer-et-re', q, 241
Hebrews (see also Israel), 182, 284, 351, 366
Hebrew language in Egypt, 318
Heliopolis, 46, 57, 59, 60, 64, 110, 112, 196, 203, 267, 268, 300
Hel-le'-ni-um, 413
He'-nu, n, 136
Heracleopolitans, 17, 23, 134–136; duration of, 25
Heracleo'polis, 46, 360; late principality of, 360, 361, 364
Herds, 88
Her-mon'-this, 135
Hermo'polis, 60, 368
Her-mo-ty'-bi-es, 390
Hezeki'ah, 375
Hieracon'polis, 36, 43, 45, 46, 48, 49
Hierat'ic, writing, 92–93, 395
Hieroglyphic (see also Writing), 397

INDEX OF NAMES AND SUBJECTS

Hittites, in M. K., 159; in Emp., 212, 233, 239, 240, 262 f., 280, 283, 298, 299, 303–312, 317, 327 f., 331, 335, 337, 351
Hoph-ra'', k, 408
Hor, n, 389
Horse, 184, 195, 229, 317
Horus, g, 36, 48, 49, 59, 60
Horus (title), 40–41, 112
House, 85, 87; earliest, 31
Hri-hor', k, 352, 355, 357
Hunting, earliest, 32, 42; royal, 262
Hyk'-sos, 18–19, 23, 175–188, 240

Ian'nas, k, 183
I-ka'-thi, c, 246
I'-kher-nof'-ret, n, 157
Ikh-na'ton, k, 250, 264–288, 293; meaning of, 269
Im-ho'tep, n, 81, 100, 104, 396
I-mou'-thes, see Imhotep.
Indian Ocean, 127
Indo-Germanic people first enter Asia Minor, 28 p, 334
Industries, 88–92, 166, 205; earliest, 30–33
I-nen'-i, n, 213
In'tef (nomarch), 135
Intefs, k, 136, 184
Inundation, 8–10
Ionians, 388, 389
Ipuwer', 168
Iran, 212
I'rem, 238
Iron, 89, 122
Irrigation, 8–9, 11, 49, 161 f.
Ir'thet, 123, 126
Isaiah, 372 f., 374, 376 f.
I-se'-si, k, 115
Ish'-tar, g, 263
I'-sis, g, 58, 60
Isis, q, 214, 396

Israel, 149, 181 f., 328 f., 331, 351, 360, 365, 373
I-ta'-ka-ma, k, 282
Ith-to'-we, c, 139, 143

Jacob-her (or Jacob-el), 181, 183
Je-ho'-a-haz, k, 405
Je-hoi'-a-chin, k, 408
Je-hoi'-a-kim, k, 405
Jeremi'ah, 406, 410, 415
Jerobo'am, 362
Jerusalem, 285, 363, 406, 407, 408; destruction of, 410
Jewelry, 42–43, 51, 89, 166, 206; earliest, 31
Joppa, c, 238
Jordan, 298, 363
Joseph, 189, 197, 200, 316, 321
Josiah, k, 405
Judah, 362 f., 374, 375 ff., 404 f., 406
Judge, 79–80, 198
Judgment, hereafter, 67, 149 f.
Julius Africanus, 15
Josephus, 15

Ka, 65, 70
Ka-by'-les, p, 30
Ka-dash-man-Bel', k, 250
Ka'-desh, 181 f., 210, 223, 224, 226, 227, 228, 229 f., 231, 239 f., 282, 299, 303, 304, 337; battle of, 304 ff.
Kadesh (in Galilee), c, 298
Ka-ka'i, k, 112
Kaldeans, 415
Kar'-nak, 229, 257 f., 315, 319, 339, 363
Ka'-roy, 246
Kassites, 212
Keb, g, 57
Ke'desh, g, 324
Keft'-yew, p, 211, 254
Ke-gem'-ne, n, 81, 100, 168

INDEX OF NAMES AND SUBJECTS

Ke-mo'-se, k, 186
Ke'-per, k, 336
Ket'-ne, c, 212, 310
Kez-we'-den, 304
Kha-bi'-ri, 263, 284, 285
Khartum', 4
Khaf-re', k, 110–11
Khamwe'-se, 325
Kha-se'-khem, k, 43, 49
Kha'-se-khem-u'-i, k, 45, 103
Kha'-yu, k, 38
Khen'-zer, k, 182, 183
Khep'-ri, g, 59
Khe'-ta, see Hittites
Khe-ta'-sar, k, 311, 312
Khi'-an, k, 178, 179, 183
Khnum-ho'-tep, n, 138, 158
Khon'-su, g, 312
Khu'-fu, k, 107–110
King, 115, 117–119, 355 f.; earliest, 38 f., 40–50; as priest, 63–64; as mortuary benefactor, 71; in O. K., 74–78; titles of, 112–13; in M. K., 139 ff.; in Emp., 195 f., 266 f.; in Rest., 417
Ko'-de, 303, 312
Ko-ros'-ko, t, 153
Koser', 127
Ku-mi'-di, n, 283
Kum'-meh, t, 156, 247
Kush, 123, 126, 154, 156, 341, 355

LABYRINTH, 162 f.
La'-chish, c, 285
Land, ownership of, 45–46, 141, 188, 189, 196, 341, 395
Law, 80, 143, 199 f., 414
Lebanon, in O. K., 106, 114, 127; in Emp., 209 f., 223, 224, 227, 231, 233, 238, 239, 245, 298, 338; in Decadence, 352; in Rest., 409
Leucos Limen', 127

Libyans, 7, 29, 50; in Delta, 34, 325, 327 ff., 333 ff., 336, 360 ff., 389; Egyptian affinity, 30; in M. K., 153; in Emp., 207 f., 298, 318, 325, 327 ff., 336 f., 343; in Egyptian army, 318, 360, 389, 410 f.; in Decadence, 360–387; in Rest., 389, 410 f.
Libyan period, 360–387; sketch of, 21–22, 24
Lin'-dos, 414
Lisht, t, 139
Li-ta'-ny, r, 299
Literature, in O. K., 100 f.; in M. K., 153, 159, 166–170; in Emp., 261, 320–322
Lu'-li, k, 375
Lux'-or, 257, 315, 320
Lycia, 254, 304, 325, 329
Lydia, 388, 416

MA-GHÂ'-RA, Wady, d, 50, 120
Magic, mortuary, 150, 203 f.
Ma-ha-na'-im, c, 363
Mai, n, 271
Ma-ket-a'-ton, 287
Manetho, 15, 26, 27, 321
Mar'-duk-bal-id'-din, k, 375
Mare'a, c, 389
Mastaba, 69, 105, 107
Mathematics, 93–94
Maxyes=Meshwesh, q. v.
Mazoi', p, 123, 153
Mechanics, 94
Medes and Media, 404, 406, 416–18
Medicine, 94–95
Medi'net-Ha'-bu, 338, 339
Mediterranean, 3, 10, 12, 253, 317, 338; peoples of northern, 327 ff., 329, 333 ff.
Me-gid'-do, c, 224, 225, 285; battle of, 225 ff.
Me'khu, n, 126

INDEX OF NAMES AND SUBJECTS

Memphis, 39–40, 46, 61, 64, 103, 119, 199, 203, 265 f., 268, 300, 314 f., 317, 381, 387, 391, 414; captured by Piankhi, 369; captured by Assyrians, 379
Menat-Khu'-fu, t, 108, 158
Menes, 16; date of, 25; reign of, 39–40
Men-ku-re', k, 111
Ment-em-het', n, 389, 395
Men'-tu-ho'-teps, k, 136 ff.
Mentuho'tep, n, 154
Me'-ra-sar, k, 299
Me-rit-a'-ton, q, 287
Mer-ne-ptah', k, 312, 316, 318, 319, 327–332
Mer-ne-re', k, 121–125; campaign in Nubia, 124
Merodach-bal'adan, k, 375
Me'-ro-e, c, 383, 390, 408
Mer-yey', k, 329 f.
Me-she'-sher, k, 336
Mesh'-wesh, p, 329, 336, 360, 361
Me-tel'-la, k, 299, 303, 304, 305, 306, 307–311
Middle Class, 83, 146, 194, 201 f.
Middle kingdom, 137 f., 139–170; sketch of, 17–18, 23, 27
Miebis', k, 49, 50
Mi-le'-tus, 413
Min, 31, 48, 203
Mis-phrag-mou'-tho-sis, k, 181
Mi-tan'-ni, 212, 223, 230, 231, 232, 233, 245, 247, 248, 249, 250, 251, 262, 280
Mi-ty-le'-ne, 413
Moab, 374, 375, 408
Moeris, lake, 162
Money, 92, 161
Monotheism, 147
Monuments, 26–27
Morality, 84 f.
Muc-ri, 375

Mummy (see Future Life and Tomb), discovery of royal, 359
Mur'sili, k, see Merasar
Music and Song, 101, 321 f.
Mut-em-u'-ya, q, 248
Mut-nof'-ret, q, 214
Muttal'lu, see Metella
Mycenaeans, 159, 211 f., 253, 254
Mysians, 304

NA-BU-NA'-'ID, k, 416
Na-bu-pal-u'-cur, k, 406
Na-ha-rin', 213, 230, 231, 232, 233, 234, 239, 240, 245, 246, 263, 264, 303, 310, 317
Nahum, 381 f., 404
Na'-pa-ta, c, 208, 246, 319, 368, 370, 381
Narmer, k, 49
Nas'-te-sen, k, 383
Nau'cratis, c, 412–413
Navy (see Ships), 414, 415
Ne'-bu-cha-drez'-zar, k, 406, 407, 408–410, 415, 416
Ne'-cho, k, 404–407
Ne'-cho, n, 379, 380, 387
Ne-fer-ho'-tep, k, 173, 182
Ne'-fer-khe-re', k, 173
Nef-ret-i'-ri, q, 316
Ne-ga'-deh, c, 40
Negroes, 7, 8, 157
Ne'hi, n, 241
Neit, 33, 34, 48, 60, 64
Ne'kheb (see also El Kab), 36
Nekh'-bet, g, 36, 41
Ne'-khen, c, 36, 45, 46, 80, 207
Ne-ku-re', n, 71
Nemathap', 103
Neph'-thys, g, 58
Ne'-su-be-neb'-ded, k, 350, 354, 358
Neterimu', k, 49
Nib-a'-mon, o, 230

INDEX OF NAMES AND SUBJECTS

Nib'-hep-et-re', k, 136, 218
Nile, 4–5, 8–10, 57; months of, 5–6
Nile Valley, 3, 4, 5, 6, 7, 11–12
Nineteenth dynasty, 293–333
Nin'eveh (see also Assyria), c, 263, 375
Ninth dynasty, 134
Ni-to'-cris, q, 128
Ni-to'-cris, 388
Niy, c, 233, 246, 282
Nobles, 45–46, 83, 107, 117–118, 128, 135, 137 f., 139–142, 188 f., 196, 202
Nof'-et-e'-te, q, 264
Nomarch (see also Noble), 139–146
Nome, earliest, 33; in O. K., 79, 81–82, 128; in M. K., 137 f.; in Emp., 188 f.
Nubia and Nubians, in army, 82, 120 f., 252, 304, 318; in earliest times, 40; in O. K., 104, 106, 120 f., 121–127; in M. K., 142, 152, 154, 155–157; in Emp., 188, 207, 208 f., 216, 232, 235 f.; 238, 241, 246, 248, 249, 296, 301, 316, 331; in Decadence, 351, 355, 360, 363; independent, 367–383, 407
Nub'-khep-ru-re'-In'-tef, k, 184
Nu'-ges, c, 303
Nut, g, 57, 60

Oases, 6, 106, 234, 329, 410, 415
Obelisk, 47, 220 f., 234, 256, 315; in New York, 234; in Constantinople, 234; in London, 234; of Thutmose III., 234, 248; in Rome, 234, 248, 315; in London, 234; in Paris, 315
Official Class, 115, 119 f., 143, 201 f.

Okapi, 32
Oke'anos, 57, 407
Old Kingdom, 74–129; sketch of, 16–17, 23, 27; length and date of, 25; revived in Restoration, 391 ff.
On (see Heliopolis)
Orcho'menos, c, 253
Oron'tes, r, 209, 230, 231, 232, 239, 240, 262 f., 282, 298, 299, 303, 304, 310, 327
Oryx-nome, 154
Osir'is, g, 48, 49, 51, 57, 60, 61, 67, 148–150, 286, 396
O-sor'-kon I., 364
Osorkon III., 365, 368, 370, 371, 377
O'-thu, c, 298

Painting, 98, 165 f., 261
Palace, earliest, 42; in O. K., 78; in Emp., 259, 261
Palermo Stone, 25, 27, 47, 100
Palestine, 121, 351; in M. K., 158 f., 176; under Hyksos, 179 f., 181 f.; in Emp., 209–212, 223–227, 228, 235, 239, 244, 245, 250, 263, 283, 284 f., 297 f., 299, 303–311, 316 ff., 318 f., 328–331, 337; in Decadence, 354, 360, 361, 362 ff., 373 f., 375 ff., 378; in Rest., 402 f., 406 f., 408–410, 415· Hebrews entering, 284 f.
Papyrus, 34, 91, 338
Papyrus Harris, 340, 347 f.
Pay-no'-zem I., k, 358
Pay-o'-nekh, 358
Pe, c, 36, 45, 46
Pe'-des, 304
Pe-di-bast', k, 365
Pentaur', 320
Pen-te-we'-re, 320
Pe'-pi I., k, 37, 119–121
Pepi II., k, 125–128

INDEX OF NAMES AND SUBJECTS

Pe-pi-nakht', n, 126, 127
Perian'der, k, 402
Peri're, 330
Per-Ramses, c, 314
Pe-sib'-khen-no' I., k, 358 f.
Pesibkhenno II., 359, 361
Pe'-yes, 344
Peles'et, p (see also Philistines), 333, 351
Persia, 416–418
Pharaoh (see King)
Pha-se'-lis, 413
Philistines, 333, 351, 360, 374, 375, 402, 404 f.
Pho-cae'-a, 413
Phoenicia and Phoenicians, in O. K., 106, 114, 121; in Emp., 210–212, 230, 233, 235, 237, 253, 282, 297 f., 299, 334 ff.; in Egypt, 317; in Decadence, 352, 375; in Rest., 398 f., 404 f., 408 f.
Phrygians, enter Asia Minor, 281, 334
Pi-an'-khi, 368–371
Pir'u, 374
Pithom, c, 314, 316
Poetry, oldest, 101; in M. K., 168 f.; in Emp., 273–277, 312, 320, 321 f.
Polycra'tes, k, 413
Population, 83
Portraiture, see Sculpture
Pottery, 42, 92, earliest, 31
Prammares', g, 170
Predynastic civilisation, 16, 30–39
Priest, 48, 63–65, 70–71, 72, 148, 199, 202 f., 265 ff., 322 ff., 340–343, 355 f., 357–361, 367 ff., 395, 396
Prophecy, 353
Psam'-tik I., k., 387, 398, 401, 402–404
Psamtik II., 407 f.

Psamtik III., 418
Ptah, g, 48, 61, 265 f., 304, 325, 338, 397
Ptah-ho'-tep, n, 81, 100, 114; wisdom of, 116, 168
Punt, 30; earliest voyage to, 114; in O. K., 114, 115, 127; in M. K., 137, 142, 155; in Emp., 218 f., 234, 238, 296, 338
Pyramid, 72, 78, 106, 107, 391; the great, 108–110; of Khafre, 110; of Menkure, 111; of Gizeh, 108–111; of Shepseskaf, 111; of Fifth Dynasty, 115; of Eleventh Dynasty, 137; of Twelfth Dynasty, 164 f.; of Thirteenth, 173; Seventeenth, 184; last, 205, 219
Pyramid texts, 37, 68, 101, 116, 391

Qarqar, c, 365
Queen, 75, 76

Raamses, see Ramses, c
Rain, 8, 10–11
Ramesse'um, 319
Ramessids, 324
Ram'ses I., 297
Ramses II., 164, 301 f., 304–310, 340
Ramses III., 333–344, 347
Ramses IV., 347–348
Ramses V., 348
Ramses VI to VIII., 348
Ramses IX, 348, 349 f., 351
Ramses X and XI., 350
Ramses XII., 350, 352, 355 f.
Ramses, c, 314, 316
Ramses-nakht, 349
Raphia, battle of, 373
Re, 58, 66, 110, 112, 147 f., 203, 267 ff., 304, 338, 342; temples of, 113

INDEX OF NAMES AND SUBJECTS

Rehobo'am, 362
Red House, 35
Red Sea, 3, 7, 90, 114, 115, 124, 127, 137, 142, 218 f., 338; canal from Nile to, 159, 407
Religion, 30, 47; earliest, 37; in O. K., 55–73, 111–113; in M. K., 147–151; in Emp., 265–288, 322–324, 340–343; in Rest., 391 f., 396 f.; in Europe, 402
Re'shep, g, 324
Residence, royal, 77 f., 119, 139, 394
Restoration, 387–418; sketch of, 22–23, 24; sources, 27–28
Ret'-e-nu, 158, 310
Rhodes, 211, 253, 413
Rib-ad'-di, n, 263, 283 f., 288
Rib'leh, c, 405, 409, 410
Rome, 418
Rosetta, c, 6

Sahara, 4, 5, 6
Sa-hu-re', k, 112, 114–115
Sais, c, 33, 34, 46, 60, 368, 379, 380, 387, 394, 396, 413 f.
Sa-ke-re', k, 287, 288
Sak-ka'-ra, t, 115
Sa'latis, k, 177
Samal', 379
Sa'-mos, 413
Sandstone, 4, 5
Sarbut el-Kha'dem, d, 160
Sardinians, 252, 304, 325
Sargon, k, 373 f., 375
Saul, 360
Scarabae'us, 204, 248
Scorpion, k, 38
Sculpture (see also art), earliest, 30, 31, 32; protodynastic, 43; in O. K., 96–99; in M. K., 165; in Emp., 259 ff., 278 f., 300, 309, 320, 339; in Rest., 393 f.

Scythians, p, 403, 404
Sebek-em-saf', k, 173
Sebek-ho'-tep, k, 173, 182
Se-bek-khu', n, 158
Se'bek-nefru-Re', q, 163, 170
Seben'nytos, 15
Seb'-ni, n, 126
Second Dynasty, 40–51, 103, 300; length and date of, 25
Sed, feast of, 42
Seir, 338
Seka, k, 38
Se-ken-en-re', k, 176, 185, 186
Se-khem-re' Khu-to'-we, k, 173
Sek'-mem, d, 158
Semerkhet', k, 49
Semites, 210–212, 263; earliest, 7, 29, 114; invading Egypt, 29–30, 180; in Egypt, 158, 236, 254, 317 f., 398
Semitic language, in Egypt, 29–30, 253
Sem'-neh, t, 156, 157, 161
Se'-nekh-ke-re', k, 134
Sen-jir-li', c, 379
Sennach'erib, k, 375
Sen'-zar, c, 232
Sep'-lel, k, 281, 299
Se'-ra-pe'-um, 397
Sesostris, legendary, 159 f.
Se-sos'-tris I., 152, 154 f., 349
Sesostris II., 155, 163
Sesostris III., 155–160
Set, 32, 41, 48, 58, 113
Sethroite nome, 177
Se'-thut, 123
Se'-ti I., 297–301, 302, 303, 317
Seti II., k, 332
Set-nakht', k, 333
Seventh dynasty, 133, 186
Samaria, 373
Se'-we, k, 373
Sha'baka, k, 374–377, 381
Sha-ba-ta'-ka, k, 377–378

466   INDEX OF NAMES AND SUBJECTS

Shab-tu'-na, t, 306
Shalmane'ser II., 365
Shalmaneser IV., 373
Sha'-ru-hen', c, 187, 188
Sheke'lesh, p, 329, 334
She'mesh-E'dom, 245
Shep-nu'-pet (daughter of Osorkon III.), 371
Shepnupet (sister of Taharka), 381, 388
Shep-ses-kaf', k, 111
Sher'den, 252, 283, 304, 318, 329 f., 334, 335, 338
She'shonk I., 360-364
Sheshonk IV., 365
Sheshonk, n, 360
Ships (including boats), 90, 106, 122, 137, 200, 218, 230, 240, 253 f., 317, 334 f., 338, 339, 341, 354, 398, 404, 414, 415; earliest, 31, 32, 33; earliest sea-going, 106, 114
Shmûn, c, 60
Shu, g, 57
Shubbiluliu'ma, see Seplel
Shut-tar'-na, k, 251
Sib'i, 373
Sicily, 329, 334
Sidon, 211, 252, 263, 408, 409
Si-ha'-thor, k, 173
Si'keli, p, 329, 334
Sil'sileh, d, 88
Silver, 89, 92, 197, 235, 254, 340, 405
Si'-my-ra, c, 211, 231, 282, 283, 298
Sinai, 7, 50, 91, 104, 106, 110, 115, 120, 121, 142, 155, 160 f., 221, 338, 348
Sind'bad, 167
Si-nou'-he, n, 158, 166 f.
Sirius, 24-25, 35-36
Siut', c, 5, 196, 197; nomarchs, 134-136
Sixth dynasty, 117-129

Ske-mi-o'-phris, q, 170
Slaves and serfs, 46, 82-83, 85, 196, 202, 236, 254, 317, 341, 343, 395
Smen'-des, 350
Snef'-ru, k, 106-107
So, k, 373
Sobk, g, 162 f.
Society, 82-86, 145-147, 201 f., 395
Soil of Egypt, 5-6, 8-9
So'-kar, g, 48
Solomon, 362, 363
So'lon, 414
Soma'li, p, 29, 30
Soul, 65
Sources, character of, 26-28
Spartans, 413, 416
Sphinx, Great, 110-111, 247
State, earliest, 45; in O. K., 74-83, 113-114; in M. K., 139-147; in Emp., 193-202, 322; in Rest., 394 f.
Stone, 42, 88-89, 92; earliest work in, 31 f., 44 f., 105
Suan', c, 7
Sudan, 7, 156
Suez, 29, 106, 253, 316, 317; canal, 159, 218, 407
Su'-tekh, g, 176, 179, 183, 304, 324, 339
Syria and Syrians, in O. K., 90, 106, 114; in M. K., 158 f.; under Hyksos, 180, 181; in Emp., 208, 209-212, 223-227, 228, 235, 237, 239, 240, 244, 247, 250, 251 f., 263 f., 282-284, 285, 297 f., 299, 303-311, 316 ff., 319, 327, 333-336, 337, 341, 343; in Decadence, 351 f., 375 ff., 379 f.; in Rest., 389, 398, 402 f., 405 f., 406 f., 408-410, 415; in Egypt, 158, 236, 254, 317 f., 398, 410

INDEX OF NAMES AND SUBJECTS 467

Ta-du-khi′-pa, q, 251
Ta-har′-ka, k, 376, 378–381
Takelot′ II., 365
Tale, 112, 166 f., 176, 185, 237 f., 247, 312, 320 ff., 365
Ta′-nis, c, 165, 314, 315, 350; kings at, 350–361
Tanite-Amonite period, 350–361; sketch of, 21–22, 24
Ta-nut-a′-mon, k, 381–382, 387, 388
Tapestry, 259
Taxation, 79, 141–143, 197, 295 f., 395
Tef-nakh′-te, k, 368–371, 379
Tef′-nut, g, 57
Te′henu, p, 328 ff.
Tell el-Amarna, see Amarna, and Akhetaton
Tell el-Yehudi′yeh, 314
Temple, 147 f., 203, 229, 236, 255–259, 299 f., 314 f., 316, 338 f.; earliest, 33, 37, 45, 47 f., 62–63; of sun, 113; terraced, 217–219; endowments, 300, 341 ff.
Tenth dynasty, 134–6
Te′-os, 413
Te′resh, p, 329
Te′-ti II., k, 119
Tha′-ru, c, 224, 295, 297, 304, 316, 317
Thebes, rise of, 135, 174, 182, 196, 199, 204 f.; in Emp., 257 ff., 314, 315; in Decadence, 350, 355 f., 357 ff., 362, 364, 371, 380; captured by Assyrians, 380, 381 f.; in Rest., 394
The′-kel, 333, 351, 352, 354
The′-mer, k, 334
Thesh, k, 38
Thi′-nis, c, 16, 39, 40, 46, 120, 125, 396
Third dynasty, 48, 103–7

Thirteenth dynasty, 173–5, 182
Thoth, g, 48, 59, 60, 113
Thu′-re, n, 209
Thu′-tiy, n, 238
Thut-mo′-se I., k, 208 f., 213–216, 217
Thutmose II., 214, 215, 216
Thutmose III., 214 f., 216–243, 282; 1st campaign, 223–228; 2nd campaign, 228 f.; 3rd campaign, 229; 4th campaign, 229; 5th campaign, 230; 6th campaign, 231; 7th campaign, 231; 8th campaign, 232–234; 9th campaign, 238 f.; 11th and 12th campaigns, 239; 13th campaign, 239; 14th campaign, 239; 15th and 16th campaigns, 239; 17th campaign, 239 f.; 295
Thutmose IV., 247 f., 251, 261, 289
Tig-lath-pi-le′-ser I., k, 354
Tiglath-pileser III., 366
Tigro-Euphrates Valley, 3, 212
Tikh′-si, c, 246
Timai′os, k, 177
Timsah′, lake, 317
Tiy, q, 248, 253, 264, 270
Tiy, q (wife of Tutenkhaton), 289
Tomb, 36–37, 43–44, 51, 68–73, 105, 106–107, 149, 150 f., 164, 202, 204 f., 219 f., 272 f., 301, 349 f.; endowment of, 44, 45, 70–72
Tom′-bos, 208
Tosor′thros, k, 105
Trade, see Commerce
Treasury and Treasurer, 45, 46, 79, 118, 141–143, 195, 197 f., 200
Treaty, 299, 303, 311, 377
Troglodytes, 50, 207

INDEX OF NAMES AND SUBJECTS

Troia, d, 88
Tu'-nip, c, 230, 240, 282, 305, 310
Tut-enkh-a'-ton, k, 288, 289
Tut-enkh-a'-mon, k, 288
Tu'-ya, q, 301
Twelfth dynasty, 152–170; date of, 27
Twentieth dynasty, 333–356
Twenty-first dynasty, 357–361, 362
Twenty-second dynasty, 360–366
Twenty-third dynasty, 365 f., 368
Twenty-fourth dynasty, 371
Twenty-fifth dynasty, 374–383
Twenty-sixth dynasty, 387–418
Two Lands, 15
Tyre, 211, 235, 298, 299, 316, 375, 379, 408, 409, 410

U'-bi, d, 263
Uga'rit, 304
Ul'-la-za, c, 298
Une'shek, 249
U'-ni, n, 120, 121, 122, 124, 125
U'-nis, k, 115
Usephais', k, 45, 49, 50
U-ser-kaf', k, 112, 114
U'-ser-ke-re', k, 119

VALLEY OF THE KINGS' TOMBS, 219 f., 241, 247, 263, 301, 348, 350

Vizier, 80–81, 113–114, 119, 144, 182, 195, 196, 197, 198, 199, 200 f.

WADY A-LÂ'-KI, 301, 302
Wady-Halfa, 154
Wady Tu-mi-lât', 153, 314, 316, 317
Wa-wat', p, 123, 126, 153, 155, 241
Wen-a'-mon, 352–4
We'shesh, p, 334
White House, 36, 197
White Nile, 4
White Wall, c, 46, 103, 119
World, 57
Worshippers of Horus, 38–39, 48

Writing, 91, 92–93, 281, 337 f., 395; earliest, 37 f., 46 f.

Xois, c, 175

YAM, d, 123, 126
Ya'-ru, 66, 203
Year, 35, 46
Ye-no'-am, c, 331

ZA'-HI, 223, 238
Zakar-Ba'-al, 352–4
Zau, n, 125
Zed-e-ki'-ah, k, 408, 410
Zer, k, 51, 148
Zo'-ser, k, 103–106

INDEX TO OLD TESTAMENT REFERENCES

Genesis, xlvii. 19-20, 189
" xlvii. 21, 202
" xlvii. 23-27, 197
Exodus i. 11, 314
Joshua xix. 6, 187
II Samuel x. 10, 159
I Kings ix. 15-17, 362 f.
" xiv. 25, 362 f.
" xvii. 4, 373
II Kings xviii, 21, 376
" xix. 9, 376
" xxiv. 7, 407
" xxiv. 15, 408 f.

Psalm civ. 273 ff.
Isaiah xix. 376 f.
" xx. 374
Jeremiah xliii, 8-13, 415
" xlvi. 1-12, 406
" xlvii. 4, 351
" xlvii. 1-5, 405
Ezekiel xxx. 13, 418
" xl. 10-18, 415 f.
Amos ix. 7, 351
Nahum ii.-iii. 404
" iii. 8-10, 381

1.P.M.
To go to Jail – Cook County

Take cottage G. to 22
                and walk
Then 22 – to State walk 3 blocks
  Electric   ave.
       Blue Island car – to jail
Meet at 2. On California Ave –
    Old fashioned prison for men
   New
   John Worthy School " women
            Reform School

   Mr. Whitman in charge

Blue island car. St. and 22 –

Walk from Ind ave to State on 22